THE INTERWEAVIN

THE INTERWEAVING OF RITUALS

FUNERALS IN THE CULTURAL EXCHANGE BETWEEN CHINA AND EUROPE

NICOLAS STANDAERT

A CHINA PROGRAM BOOK

UNIVERSITY OF WASHINGTON PRESS

Seattle & London

This publication was supported in part by the China Studies Program, a division of the Henry M. Jackson School of International Studies at the University of Washington.

© 2008 by the University of Washington Press
Printed in the United States of America
12 11 10 09 08   5 4 3 2 1

University of Washington Press
P.O. Box 50096, Seattle, WA 98145 U.S.A.
www.washington.edu/uwpress

Library of Congress Cataloging-in-Publication Data

Standaert, N.
    The interweaving of rituals : funerals in the cultural exchange between China and Europe / Nicolas Standaert.
        p.   cm. — (A China program book)
    Includes bibliographical references and index.
    ISBN 978-0-295-98810-8 (hardback : alk. paper)
    ISBN 978-0-295-98823-8 (pbk. : alk. paper)
    1. Funeral rites and ceremonies—China.   2. Funeral rites and ceremonies—Europe.
3. Death—Religious aspects—Christianity.   4. Social exchange—Religious aspects—
Christianity.   5. China—Social life and customs.   6. China—Religious life and customs.
I. Title.
GT3283.A2S83   2008
393—dc22   2007052235

The paper used in this publication is acid-free and 90 percent recycled from at least 50 percent post-consumer waste. It meets the minimum requirements of American National Standard for Information Sciences—Permanence of Paper for Printed Library Materials, ANSI Z39.48–1984.♾♻

Cover illustration: "Funerale gentile," drawing attached to a letter of Anselmo da Santa Margarita OSA, Beijing, 30 September 1791. Courtesy of Archivio Storico, Congregazione de Propaganda Fide: *Scritture Originali della Congregazione Particolare delle Indie Orientali e China,* vol. 68, f. 199r.

Contents

Acknowledgments

One of the theses of this book is that many texts emerge from multiple inter-actions and are ultimately the result of coauthorship, even if they carry the name of a sole author. *The Interweaving of Rituals* is likewise the outcome of many dialogues, and consequently it contains the voices of many people. In the first place, I thank my close colleagues at Leuven University who have provided an enthusiastic intellectual environment over the past decade. I express my gratitude in particular to Carine Defoort, with whom I have had many stim-ulating conversations and who supported the project in many other regards, and to Ad Dudink, who as a long-term collaborator continuously encouraged me to go deeper into the matter. Both have critically and thoroughly read the whole manuscript. So too did Adam Chau, Dorothee Schaab-Hanke, and two anonymous readers; Eugenio Menegon read part of an earlier version during his stay in Leuven. I am grateful for their many suggestions, which have greatly improved the text. I also thank Noël Golvers, Pablo Alonso, and Hugo Roef-faers, who were always willing to help me with language problems. Timothy Brook, Susan Naquin, and Michael Nylan deserve special mention because of their encouragement and help to get this research published.

Some sections of this book were delivered as lectures and conference talks at Beijing University, Centre National de Recherche Scientifique, Harvard University, Princeton University, Renmin University, Xiamen University, Fujen University, The Chinese University of Hong Kong, and at a ritual work-shop at Leuven in June of 2004. I thank among others Pierre-Antoine Fabre, Michael Puett, Antonella Romano, Sun Shangyang, Yang Nianqun, and Zhang Xianqing for creating these moments of dialogue. I am very grateful to the many scholars whose comments on those occasions have been helpful to the devel-opment of the ideas in this book.

I express my gratitude to colleagues who were so kind to share fruits of their research and to provide me with primary and secondary sources: Liam Brockey, Claudia von Collani, Hilde De Weerdt, Michele Fatica, Ge Zhaoguang, Han Qi, Henrietta Harrison, Huang Xiaojuan, Wilt Idema, Catherine Jami, Roman Malek, and Erik Zürcher. I am also grateful to Benedicte Vaerman,

Hanno Lechner, and Martin Heijdra for the help they provided to me as librarians. For finalizing the manuscript, I thank Els Ameloot, Marleen De Meyer, and the editors at the University of Washington Press, Lorri Hagman, Lenore Hietkamp, and Marilyn Trueblood. Support for this research was generously provided by Onderzoeksraad K.U. Leuven, FWO-Vlaanderen and the Institute for Advanced Study, Princeton.

Finally, I express my deep appreciation to everyone whose friendship has been so important to me throughout this period. I think especially of my family members and companions, colleagues, and friends who encouraged me by smiling at the idea that someone could take pleasure in doing research on funerals in seventeenth-century China.

THE INTERWEAVING OF RITUALS

Introduction

In spring of the year 1681, the Kangxi Emperor ordered the entombment of Empresses Xiaocheng and Xiaozhao, both of whom had died several years earlier. Their bodies had been kept seven and three years, respectively, in a village close to Beijing, awaiting the completion of the emperor's mausoleum. His wives were the first people the Kangxi Emperor mourned as an adult. For their entombment, he arranged a cortege of great pomp. The Jesuit missionary Ferdinand Verbiest briefly wrote about this event in a letter to Europe:

> When they were transferred to the place of sepulture, the whole Court of Beijing spread out, that is countless officials followed the funeral procession in a great and noisy escort. The two coffins in which the bodies were put were most splendid and looked like great houses made out of pure gold. One thousand eight hundred bearers carried them on their shoulders, alternating at determined distances. Six hundred officials had been appointed who only took care of the bearers. I also was in the midst of the funeral procession (Ego quoque pompae funebri interfui).[1]

The image of a foreign missionary being present in the midst of a Chinese funeral procession represents what this book will explore: the role of ritual in the exchange between cultures, and more particularly funerary rites in China and Europe in the seventeenth century.

The quest for such a focus in the exchange between cultures arises from the emergence of new ritual studies in recent years. One generation ago, research on Chinese religions focused almost exclusively on doctrinal questions and analyzed religious texts rather than practices. The study of the ritual aspects of religion has been gaining importance, however, particularly because of developments in the study of Daoism. As a result, *orthopraxy*, or right practice, rather than *orthodoxy*, or right belief, is viewed as one of the major keys for the understanding of Chinese religions. In the scholarship of the Christianity of medieval and early modern Europe, ritual has also recently become a major topic of analysis. In an important historiographical study of Christianity, the historian John

Van Engen points out that "the real measure of Christian religious culture on a broad scale must be the degree to which time, space, and ritual observances came to be defined and grasped essentially in terms of the Christian liturgical year."[2] Little investigation has been undertaken of the extent to which observance of ritual persists when Christianity moves to another culture in which a different "ritual time" prevails. There is, of course, the "Chinese Rites Controversy"—a major dispute about whether Christians could be allowed to participate in certain Chinese rituals—that shaped Sino-European relations at the end of the seventeenth century and the beginning of the eighteenth. Surprisingly, however, the ritual aspect of this controversy has been overlooked as well. Most studies on the Rites Controversy have stressed doctrinal discussions among the Western missionaries. In a stimulating article titled "Some Naive Questions about the Rites Controversy: A Project for Future Research," scholar of Daoism Kristofer Schipper calls attention to the potential significance the ritual aspect of the Chinese Rites Controversy may have for a comparison of European and Chinese ritual systems. Through such a comparison, scholars may gain some insight into the mutual perception and interaction of the two entirely different ritual traditions. Schipper encourages an investigation into the extent of their respective adaptability and permeability, since that might contribute to our understanding of Chinese and Christian ritual culture.[3] A final reason for choosing the ritual perspective is that the study of the contact between China and Europe, and especially of Christianity in seventeenth-century China, has usually focused on religious doctrine and the sciences. Yet, the study of the equally important topic of ritual has so far been neglected.

Research contributing to this book has benefited from substantial transformations in the field of the study of Christianity in China during recent decades.[4] There has been a paradigm shift from a mainly missiological and Eurocentric viewpoint to a sinological and Sinocentric approach, characterized by, among other things, the use of Chinese texts as primary sources for research and thus taking the Chinese actors as primary subjects. A result of this paradigm shift is that Christianity is taken as a broad cultural phenomenon, not limited to typically religious phenomena—such as theology, liturgy, and catechetics—but also embracing a wide variety of cultural elements that came along with Christian faith and practice, such as mathematics, astronomy, botany, philosophy, and the arts. Because of the intercultural and interdisciplinary character of this field of research, there is, moreover, a growing interest in questioning the basic notions—for example, of religion, Christianity, China, mathematics, and ritual—that are the very foundation of such research.

A focus on ritual advances these shifts, prodding us to surpass European-centered and China-centered discussions by using the paradigm of interaction. This phenomenological, descriptive, and differentiated approach contrasts with essentialist views holding that Chinese and European cultures are incompatible and that cultural transfer is thus impossible. This approach focussing on interaction is also reflected in the complementarity and confrontation found among the various Chinese and European primary sources. Taking historical anthropology rather than intellectual history as a focal point, this approach also encourages a shift downward from the converts belonging to the Chinese elite or the missionaries working at the court, to the common, often anonymous, Christians in the provinces and to the itinerant missionaries doing pastoral work. In addition, not individuals, but communities become the focus of attention.

The concept of ritual, just like the Chinese term *li* that is often taken as its equivalent, is a topic of research in itself. Rather than providing a new definition, one may refer to recent studies. A useful reference work in this regard is Catherine Bell's *Ritual: Perspectives and Dimensions*.[5] Bell, who is trained in Chinese studies, offers a general and comparative approach to the theme of ritual, while also taking into account the fact that the term is a cultural and historical construction. Her book gives a good overview of the various ways in which rituals have been studied (psychoanalytic, evolutionary, functionalist, structuralist, etc.) and of the characteristics of ritual-like activities in general (formalism, traditionalism, invariance, rule-governance, sacral symbolism, performance). Moreover, it offers a catalogue of the types of (mainly religious) rituals, as studied by scholars over the last century: *rites of passage* (birth, coming of age, marriage, death); *calendrical rites* (such as major feasts recorded in liturgical calendars); *rites of exchange and communion* (offerings and sacrifices to gods); *rites of affliction* (rites involving healing and appeasement of spirits and gods); and *feasting, fasting, and festivals* (public display of religious sentiments). These general categories can be supplemented by a theological typology that focuses more directly on Catholicism, and distinguishes *sacraments* (baptism, confirmation, Eucharist, confession, marriage, ordination to priesthood, extreme unction) from *non-sacramental rites* (fasting, recitative prayers, exorcism, blessings, funerals).

The Interweaving of Rituals focuses on one type of ritual: the rites related to death, and more specifically, funerals, because these are often considered to be at the core of Chinese culture. The central question is: What happened to the funerary ritual after the European and Chinese ritual traditions came into contact with each other? Though ancestral rites are relevant, they are not at the center of this research, since, according to the classical Chinese classification of *li,* they are considered to be a kind of sacrifice (*ji*) and not a funeral (*sang*). Sacrifices for the ancestors are certainly also part of the funerary rituals, but they continue to be conducted after the burial (*zang*), which is the final act of the funerary rites. Moreover, the present study is limited to the seventeenth century, primarily because of the rich variety of extant sources concerning funeral rites of that time. For instance, there exist both European and Chinese descriptive texts of Chinese funerals and of Christian funerals in China, Chinese and European descriptions of imperial sponsorship of funerals of missionaries, Chinese prescriptive documents that are translated from European prescriptive texts, and new Chinese Christian guidelines based on experience. Another major reason for limiting the time frame is that this study does not concern the Chinese Rites Controversy as such—a topic that has been studied extensively by other authors—because rituals such as funerals are worthwhile studying on their own without necessarily reading them through the lens of the Rites Controversy and its results. Yet, documents related to funerals in China dating from the 1690s onwards are increasingly affected by this controversy. While the topic of the Rites Controversy is touched upon only marginally in this study, ritual tensions are considered in the context of ritual controversies that took place in China at that time and that illuminate characteristics of Chinese and European ritual behavior. A final reason for this restriction to the seventeenth century is that this period is characterized by several features that render it particularly apt for the observation of cultural contact, especially when compared with other intercultural contacts at that time.

First, the size of the observation sample in this period is sufficiently representative without being too broad. The number of foreign actors involved was very small. When one of the most famous missionaries, Matteo Ricci, SJ (1552–1610), died in Beijing in 1610 after spending thirty years in China, there were in total sixteen Jesuits in China—eight foreigners and eight Chinese. In 1690, the approximate closing year of this book, there were in total sixty-seven foreign and ten Chinese clerics. The number of other Chinese affected by these Europeans was also limited. The number of Christians, for instance, reached a maximum of two hundred thousand around the year 1700, which was small compared to the overall population (well over 250 million inhabitants).[6] Thus the interaction was clearly between groups of markedly divergent size, but the overall restricted size of this nonetheless significant segment of the population facilitates observation.

Second, while many studies on cultural transmission involve cultures of unequal complexity, both Europe and China were relatively similar in their means of cultural reproduction, such as printing and education. In China, unlike in other countries, it was not the missionaries who introduced the printing press; a printing system was already widely available. In addition, missionary orders such as the Jesuits, known for having established schools in many countries, were met in China with a well-established educational system of very high quality, which made it nearly impossible for them to establish new schools. Due to these similarities, Europeans and Chinese were able to engage in communication at a level that, at least from the European perspective, was very different from that of contemporary encounters in other countries.

Third, the role of external power within China was relatively small. Though the missionaries themselves remained exponents of European culture and continued to depend on material support from ecclesiastical institutions and the colonial administration, it was the Ming and Qing administrations that distinguished the missionary from the trader and the colonist and that ultimately decided whether they could enter and stay. Several anti-Christian movements resulted in the expulsion of missionaries, but the Chinese administration remained relatively open during the whole period, at least open enough to allow a constant influx and renewal of the missions. To a large extent, it was the Chinese who occupied the dominant position, since they were hosting the foreigners on Chinese territory, obliging them through the Chinese strategy of "cultural imperative" to adapt to the native culture.[7] The clearest example of this was the predominance of the Chinese language throughout the exchange. In contrast to the interaction between Jesuits and local people in Japan, where Japanese learned Portuguese or Latin, or to Chinese participation in cultural exchange today that requires learning a foreign language, in the seventeenth century, no Chinese involved in the interaction learned a foreign language, with the exception of a very small number of Chinese educated for the priesthood. This aspect is important because, as the China historian Paul Cohen explains, "before these [foreign] ideas could evoke response, they had to be communicated, and they could be communicated only by being filtered through Chinese language and thought patterns."[8]

These three characteristics of the seventeenth century are not unique to the Christian experience in China, as one can find similar situations in the cultural exchanges of China with the outside world that took place with the arrival of Judaism, Islam, and especially Buddhism. The seventeenth century thus merely offers a framework that facilitates the study of intercultural contacts and the investigation into the place of the funeral ritual within this Sino-European exchange.[9]

The book is divided into eight chapters. The first one provides necessary background on funeral rites in China and Europe before their encounter at the end of the sixteenth century. In particular it presents the essential characteristics and elementary structure of Chinese and European funeral rites, and outlines the changes they underwent between the tenth and the sixteenth centuries.

The second chapter looks at Chinese funeral rites as depicted by European proto-ethnographic descriptions dating from the seventeenth century. These European primary sources deepen the knowledge not only of what Chinese funerals in the seventeenth century looked like, but also of how contemporary Europeans interpreted them and experienced them in comparison with European funerals.

The third and fourth chapters discuss the changes in funeral rites that occurred between the 1580s and 1680s. By confronting European and Chinese sources, the third chapter traces the gradual embedding of Christian funerals. It sketches the evolution of the attitude of missionaries and Chinese Christians towards the funerals in which they were directly involved, from an initial purist and exclusivist approach stressing the necessity of sober and essentially Christian funerals, to a time of experimentation by Chinese Christians that resulted in an interweaving of rituals and a reframing of Christian prescriptive texts, to the embedding, in the 1660s, of funerary rituals within the activities of lay associations. The fourth chapter explores the period after 1671 when funerals turned into an explicit and conscious Christian "policy" promoted by the missionaries as a reaction against the accusation that Christians did not fulfil the devotion of filial piety. The Chinese cultural imperative moved Christianity in a direction that its proponents had not initially planned.

The next chapters are case studies, for which most of the material dates from the 1680s. In the fifth chapter the attention shifts to the creation of a Chinese Christian funeral ritual, whose framework was the common Chinese funeral, onto which Christian ritual was grafted. The analysis is based on a guideline, in thirty-two articles, for funerals that was drafted in Canton in 1685. The tensions connected with this ritual exchange, and more particularly the shifts that took place in Chinese rituals arising from the missionaries' imperative decisions around correct practice, is the subject of the sixth chapter. On the basis of European prescriptive sources and European descriptions of Chinese rituals practised by Chinese Christians, the chapter looks at which rituals could be tolerated because they were considered merely civil, political, or non-superstitious. It also focuses on rituals considered superstitious, such as the inscription of the ancestral tablet, the usage of food offerings, and the burning of paper money. With a contextual analysis of a set of documents in which missionaries and the Kangxi Emperor discuss the burning of paper money, this part ends in a paradox about rituals: the Christian tradition, often considered orthodoxy-oriented, began to stress correct praxis, while Kangxi himself moved away from orthopraxy.

The seventh chapter continues this paradoxical line. The imperial sponsorship of the funerals of some missionaries who had served at the court imparted to those foreigners the honors given by the state to a deceased member of the nobility or official. These imperial decisions not only encouraged missionaries and Christians to pay more attention to funerals, but missionaries were also overtaken by these initiatives: they were buried according to rites in which the Chinese traditional customs, even in their own reports about it, took the lead.

The final and concluding chapter draws lessons from the analysis of the funeral rituals. For intercultural studies, the metaphor of textile weaving helps to elucidate the complexity of changes funerals underwent as a result of intercultural contact. In addition, analyzing communities that are perceived as "communities of effective rituals" illuminates characteristics of both European and Chinese forms of religiosity. Finally, ritual plays an essential role in the construction of a new identity; not only did the newly created Chinese Christian funeral ritual identify and consolidate the identity of participants as Christians but it also allowed them to remain integrated within the wider Chinese community.

1 / Chinese and European Funerals

Prescriptive texts influenced, but not necessarily fully controlled, the actual performance of both Chinese and European funerals before their encounter in the early seventeenth century. Such texts are a good starting point for understanding what anthropologist James Watson calls the "elementary structure" of funeral rites—the coherent package of actions, routines, and performances that constitutes the structure of these rites.[1] Much can be inferred from the contents of these texts, not only about the rules that came to be accepted as orthoprax, but also about the various ways these rules diverged from contemporary customs at various social levels.[2] This variation can also be illustrated by the historical evolutions funeral traditions underwent. They demonstrate, in the Chinese case, how the prescriptive text was used to bring unity into the varieties of ritual and, in the European case, how the text that standardized the practices represents the culmination of quite radical changes in views on death and funeral liturgy that took place in the period between the tenth and the sixteenth centuries.[3]

CHINESE FUNERAL RITUALS

The Chinese funeral rituals that are the starting point of this book are those of the Confucian tradition as practised in the Ming dynasty (1368–1644).[4] The origin of this tradition goes back to early texts, such as the *Book of Rites* (*Liji*) and the *Book of Ceremonies* (*Yili*), both probably compiled in their present form in the first century B.C.E.[5] These classical writings contain detailed instructions about how to conduct a funeral, from the initial stages, such as the ritual washing of the corpse, to the final burial. In the Song dynasty (960–1279) these texts were revisited by scholars of the Neo-Confucian movement (the Daoxue or the learning of the Way), who aimed at reviving the orthodox Confucian tradition. An important contribution of Song thinkers such as Zhu Xi (1130–1200) was to have sought to replace errant ritual practices among commoners with approved classical rites.[6] When the first emperor of the Ming dynasty and his successors chose interpretations of the Confucian teaching contained within the Four

Books and Five Classics as orthodox curriculum, they continued this reorientation toward the propagation of standards that would cover both commoner and gentleman-official. Because of the unique combination of a central examination system and the early development of printing, Neo-Confucianism reached a wide radius of scholars and commoners, even if it never became a fully single-minded orthodoxy.[7] This spread of Neo-Confucianism also affected the normative texts for funerals, composed by the same Song scholars.

The Major Chinese Prescriptive Text

The most important Chinese prescriptive text concerning funerals in the Ming dynasty was *Family Rituals (Jiali)*, compiled by the Song scholar Zhu Xi. It is a manual for the private performance of the standard Chinese family rituals—capping, wedding, funeral, and ancestral sacrifice—with one chapter devoted to each rite. Judging by chapter length, funerals are by far the most important of the rites of passage in China.[8] Funerals were indeed the quintessential expressions of "filial piety" or "reverence toward parents" (*xiao*), a value that by late imperial times was embedded in the core of the orthodoxy and orthopraxy accepted by most Chinese.[9] Through funerary rites, filial sons could fulfil their duty to repay the kindnesses they had received from their parents, a duty that did not end with death.[10]

The elementary structure of these funeral rites comprises the two principal moments of encoffining and burial, which are separated by the condolence rites. *Family Rituals* stipulates a precise sequence.[11] Once the dying person has expired, the mourners wail and perform the calling-back ceremony. The presiding male mourner, the presiding female mourner, the funeral director, the letter recorder, and the gift recorder are all identified. The family alters their clothing and stops eating. The coffin, usually bought well in advance, is prepared, and announcements of the death are sent to relatives, colleagues, and friends. Attendants immediately prepare the corpse for eventual encoffining, the first major event in the funeral sequence. They wash and dress the body and then move the bier on which it rests to the central hall of the house, where an oblation is then set out. The soul seat (tablet), soul cloth, and inscribed banner are made. The next morning the attendants arrange the clothes and shrouds for the preliminary laying out (*xiaolian*, or "dressing the corpse"). The family makes an oblation for the dressing of the body and afterward the presiding male and female mourners embrace the body, wail, and beat their chests. The final laying out (*dalian*, or "encoffining") is performed the following morning. Attendants raise the coffin and bring it into the hall, placing it a little to the west of the center, where the encoffining is then performed. At this point

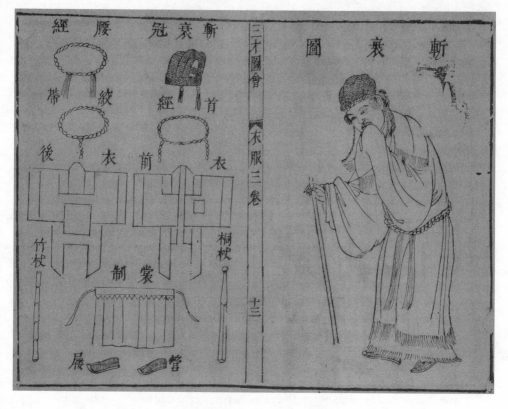

1.1. Dress in the first grade of mourning: robe and apron of untrimmed sackcloth, with walking stick, belts, slippers, and hat.
From *Sancai tuhui* (1607), *yifu, juan* 3, 13a–13b. Courtesy of Princeton University, Gest Library, Rare Books T9299/1142.

the wailing by turns is ended. The next morning those belonging to the five mourning grades put on mourning garments. The donning of white clothing, shoes, and hoods (made of sackcloth or hemp) by mourners is coded and reflects the degree of kinship between the deceased and the mourner. In the system for mourning garments, the first grade, called "untrimmed sackcloth" (*zhan-cui*), involves obligations into the third year (fig. 1.1). The second grade, "even sackcloth" (*zicui*), is worn for three years, for a year with the staff, a year without the staff, five months, or three months. The third is called "greater processed cloth" (*dagong*) and is worn for nine months; the fourth, "lesser processed cloth" (*xiaogong*), for five months; and the fifth, "fine hemp" (*sima*), for three months.[12] In the next period, an oblation is made every morning and evening and food is offered at meals (fig. 1.2). During that time close relatives

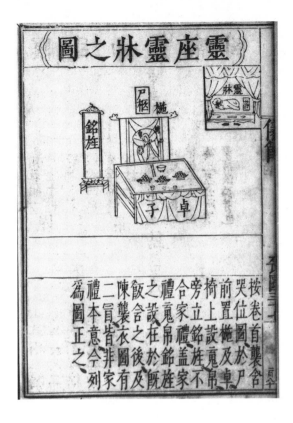

《靈座祔林之圖》

銘旌

尸柩櫬

卓子

祔靈

1.2. Layout of coffin and
soul seat with offerings
on the front table.
From *Jiali yijie* (1608), comp.
Qiu Jun, ed. Yang Tingyun,
juan 4, 37b. Courtesy of
Naikaku bunko, Tokyo.

and friends come to pay their condolences wearing plain clothes. They bring incense, tea, candles, wine, or fruit as presents, and contribute money or silk. They also prepare a calling card to inform the mourners of the condoler's name. After entering the hall, visitors wail and offer an oblation, then condole with the family and leave.

After three months, and the selection of a suitable site and day for the burial has occurred, the body is buried—the second important moment in the funeral sequence. After the grave is opened, the family members worship the god of the earth and prepare the inscription stone, funerary objects, catafalque, and tablet. The day before the departure, they lift the coffin and present it to their ancestors, after which they move it to the reception hall. The next morning at dawn the coffin is moved to the catafalque. At that point, the family sets out the sending-away oblation. A procession accompanies the coffin to the grave, with male and female mourners, from the presiding ones on down, walking behind and wailing, followed first by seniors, then relatives without mourning obligations, and finally the guests. When the coffin arrives at the grave, the principal mourners take up their stations to wail. The coffin is lowered into the grave, followed by the funerary objects and inscription stone. The grave is then covered with soil, pounded until hard. To the left of the grave, the liturgist guides a worship of the god of the earth. After the inscribing of the spirit tablet, the liturgist takes it onto the carriage and the procession returns home. Arriving at the house, the liturgist brings the tablet inside and puts it on the soul seat so the mourners can wail in front of it. A sacrifice of repose is performed and from this point on, the morning and evening oblations are no longer conducted. A few days later, a rite of cessation of wailing occurs, followed by a sacrifice for associating the tablet. The family offers a good fortune sacrifice after one year has passed, and a second one after two years, along with a peace sacrifice.

Variation in Chinese Funerals

The sequence as represented by *Family Rituals* reflects the elementary structure adopted by the orthoprax tradition. In a wider context of diversity of funerary practices, however, at least three factors interacted with this orthoprax sequence and caused variation: regional differences; relationships with other funerary traditions; and the historical implementation of *Family Rituals*.

Differences in regional influence do not denote dissimilarities between Han and non-Han cultures but rather the regional variation that existed *within* Han culture. Sources documenting these differences are not easy to obtain, since local practices were not always recorded.[13] The Chinese preference for describing the ideal ritual gives the strong but false impression that funeral rituals were similar from county to county and unchanging over time. Much information about this regional variation is based on nineteenth- and twentieth-century ethnographical descriptions and is not immediately applicable to the seventeenth century.[14] Nevertheless, distinctions, in general terms, can be made between practices in the north and the south, as shown by Susan Naquin. A number of the most significant differences between the regions of China were, for instance, associated with the corpse and the grave. In the Canton delta, where the contrast with north China seems most dramatic, very different ideas about the corpse seemed to exist. This appears most obviously in the practice of secondary burial: after the body is buried in a coffin, it is later unearthed and the bones scraped and temporarily stored in an urn, to be later reburied in a geomantically suitable setting. Another striking difference between these regions is that in the north the preferred location of burial for an individual was with his family, whereas in the Canton area family and lineage graves were dispersed and each person was sited separately.[15] These and many other practices, such as contrasting grave shapes, the rites of reporting to the temple, or calling back the soul, appear to have been structurally different and the differences widespread. Moreover, these geographical disparities interacted with variations according to family status, class, and religion that were deliberately encouraged by society to mark what people saw as significant social distinctions.[16]

The second and most obvious source of variation is the relationship of the orthoprax tradition with other funerary traditions. As the *Family Rituals* sequence shows, the focus of funerary ritual in China was the family: the family members themselves and, since the late Ming, the members of the lineage were the principal liturgical officiants. Yet various other actors, such as corpse handlers and musicians, participated in specific actions during the funeral.[17] The family could also engage religious specialists. These specialists were monks and priests with accumulated spiritual merit and authority on matters related to the salvation of the soul. They were hired to relieve the soul's sufferings and guide it through the underworld.[18]

The participation of specialists was a significant aspect of the widespread Buddhist funerary ritual, as it existed in the sixteenth and seventeenth centuries. As Timothy Brook and Stephen Teiser explain, the Buddhist ritual is organized around the conviction that the dead are not altogether lost, and that the living can do something to ease their passage beyond this life.[19] In the eyes of Chinese Buddhists, after death the deceased lives in a liminal stage lasting forty-nine days and possesses a body that is not fully human. The stay in "purgatory" ends in accordance with the dead person's own karma and the solicitude of the family in sponsoring mortuary rituals.[20]

Buddhist funerary rites have their own sequence. They start on the first day after death, between dressing the corpse and enclosing it in the coffin, when monks perform a ceremony to facilitate the transfer of the soul from the body to the soul tablet. This done, the monks conduct the main funeral service for the soul's repose, which consists mainly of chanting the Amitabha Sutra, dedicated to the Pure Land deity who oversees the Western Paradise in which the pious hope to be reborn. The length of the funeral, and the number and frequency of subsequent funeral services, varies according to the desires and means of the descendants. Services are usually held throughout the night of the first day after death, or for the first three nights, and then again on the seventh. Thereafter they can be held every seventh day for a total of seven weeks (following the Indian septenary cycle), although three sevens or five sevens (twenty-one or thirty-five days) is sometimes deemed quite sufficient. This is called "doing the sevens" (*zuoqi*) and the ceremony on the forty-ninth day is known as "the feast of ending the sevens" (*duanqizhai*). The chanting performed at these occasions is intended to see the soul of the deceased through the underworld to its next rebirth. If the family has sufficient financial means, services can be held twice a day, morning and evening, for a hundred days (following the Chinese decimal cycle), the hundredth day marked by a ceremony known as "cessation of weeping" (*zuku*). Subsequent memorial services can be held on the first three anniversaries of death, the last of which is known as the "termination of mourning" (*chusang*). At that point, the obligations of the survivors to the deceased are complete; from that moment on, the deceased is to be treated as an ancestor rather than simply as a person who has died.[21]

The Daoist tradition places postmortem services on a similar footing, as Teiser also explains. To the Daoist, gods oversee all aspects of life and death, and each person is endowed with multiple deities residing in different parts of the body. Those internal guests, together with the ranks of gods in the external world, are organized in a bureaucratic structure and cooperate in recoding each act that an individual performs. The balance of good and evil is affected not only by one's deeds but also by acts of offering. Therefore sacrifices to the gods both before and after death are beneficial. Daoist funeral rituals consisted of ten memorial rites, organized according to the same time rhythm as the Buddhist ones, with services of deliverance and offerings to the various gods.[22]

These descriptions of specific aspects of the Buddhist and Daoist rituals help to explain the status of *Family Rituals*. Like other of Zhu Xi's works, *Family Rituals* is the culmination and synthesis of the Confucian revival movement of the eleventh and twelfth centuries. Scholars participating in this movement were troubled by the discrepancy between what people commonly practiced as rituals and what was specified in such classical writings as the *Book of Rites* or the *Book of Ceremonies*. With regard to the common funeral and burial practices, scholars saw much to condemn. Over the centuries, mortuary practices had drawn elements from divergent traditions, including the Buddhist teachings about death, karma, transmigration, heaven, and hell, much of which had, by Song times, also been adopted by Daoists. The practices also drew from indigenous ideas about yin and yang, auspiciousness and inauspiciousness of times, places, and activities that were vaguely associated with shamans and geomancers, as well as indigenous ideas about ghosts of ancient origins that had been modified over time by Buddhist and Daoist conceptions of the fate of the dead.[23] To loosen the hold of Buddhism on the general public, local officials needed to promote the practice of Confucian rituals, including funerals. It was only because of the decay of these rituals, some scholars argued, that Buddhism had managed to penetrate the daily lives of the common people. Therefore, Zhu Xi was of the opinion that one "should not perform Buddhist services" (*buzuo foshi*).[24]

The historical development and implementation of the rites described in Zhu Xi's *Family Rituals* is the third factor in the variation of funeral rites. In Song and Yuan times the scholarly community, especially Zhu Xi's personal disciples, did much to promote knowledge of the text. This movement received strong political support in the early Ming, when the first emperor wanted to dispense with the foreign rituals of the Yuan and return to the ancient Chinese rituals. Ming Taizu (r. 1368–1398) looked on ritual as a means of social control, a way of reinstituting hierarchical order to society, and the court relied heavily on *Family Rituals* in establishing ritual regulations. For instance, the funeral rules for officials and commoners in the *Collected Rituals of the Great Ming Dynasty* (*(Da)Ming jili*, 1370; 1530) often conform closely to it and sometimes directly cite it.[25] The *Record of Filial Piety and Parental Tenderness* (*Xiaocilu*), written in 1374 after an emperor's consort died without children, gives detailed mourning rules. Since the emperor felt that mourning one's mother for only a year was at odds with human feelings, in the new rules the mourning for mothers, including mothers who were concubines, was extended to three years.[26] *Family Rituals* is also included in full in the officially sponsored and widely circulated compilation of Neo-Confucian writings, the *Great Compendium on Nature and Principle* (*Xingli daquan*), issued in 1415.[27] Confucian scholars did not simply advocate that the state promote the use of *Family Rituals*; many also tried to use it themselves as a guide for their families' ceremonies. Demand for this sort of liturgy, much simpler than the classics or government manuals, was apparently strong enough for it to be printed many times, in a variety of places, and reshaped to suit the audience. There was also a scholarly interest in the work which crystallized with the publication of the authoritative annotated and revised version, the *Etiquette of the "Family Rituals"* (*Jiali yijie*, 1474), by the eminent statecraft scholar Qiu Jun (1420–1495). By the late fifteenth century, the text was common fare among the educated.[28]

Developments in the Sixteenth and Seventeenth Centuries

Developments in the sixteenth and seventeenth centuries deserve special attention. By the middle of the Ming Dynasty, Zhu Xi's *Family Rituals* came to be looked upon as orthoprax by the state, by the Confucian scholarly community, and, more generally, by the educated elite.[29] Despite this reception, Neo-Confucian funerary rituals did not replace Buddhist ones, and Buddhism remained strongly associated with the passage from life to death. But from the sixteenth century onwards, a minority within the gentry again challenged Buddhism's monopoly on death, advocating instead the exclusive use of Neo-Confucian rites. References linking an adherence to *Family Rituals* with gentry status appear in gazetteers from the beginning of the sixteenth century. Members of the late-Ming gentry were increasingly conscious that they had to make a choice between Buddhist and Neo-Confucian rites when deciding how to mourn and bury a member of their family, with the educated generally choosing to abstain from Buddhist services and other funerary practices not considered orthoprax.[30] A major factor in this development was the commercialization of the economy, perhaps the most striking change of the sixteenth century, as pointed out by Cynthia Brokaw. Expanding economic opportunities had a profound impact on China's social structure, both upsetting conventional definitions of hierarchy and intensifying tensions between classes. Just as some wealthy merchants overstepped the status boundaries prescribed for them in Confucian orthodoxy and imperial law, so too some bondservants commanded a wealth and a social authority incommensurate with their low legal status. These changes also profoundly affected the economic and social security of the elite. On the one hand, both gentry and literati could profitably participate in the commercial boom of the late Ming. But as a consequence of these expanded opportunities, they also faced much more intense competition for elite status.[31] These challenges deeply influenced the discourse and practice of funeral rituals.

Major Criticism

Recent studies by Ho Shu-yi, Zhang Shouan, and Norman Kutcher have shown that at the level of rhetoric, members of the gentry voiced three criticisms of funeral practices in local gazetteers, jottings (*biji*), or privately edited ritual handbooks. The late Ming scholar Xie Zhaozhe (1567–1627), who also knew about Christianity and was sympathetic toward it because of "its similarity with Confucianism,"[32] summarizes the criticisms in his *Five Random Jottings* (*Wuzazu*): "[The common people] holding a funeral but not grieving, only paying attention to appearances, is the first error; not following the *Rites* but performing Buddhist services is the second error; not burying the dead swiftly but waiting to choose an auspicious site is the third error."[33]

These critiques voiced in the late Ming were not entirely new, but they gained more importance through the growth of commercialization in Chinese society. The first criticism was directed against the growing extravagance of funerals.[34] With the development of a commercial economy, the popular funeral customs became more excessive in their deployment of wealth, with luxurious paraphernalia, performances (plays and dances) to amuse the guests, and extensive banquets. Extravagant funerary rituals became a social means to demonstrate one's level of filial piety, and an occasion to extend one's social network so as to enhance one's status. Critical literati were of the opinion that with such practices funerals lost their primary meaning of expressing sentiments of sorrow. Moreover, the literati were less critical of the waste of money and more concerned that commoners adopting these practices were over-stepping their authority and failing to mark the established class differences and social hierarchies.[35]

The second criticism was specifically directed against the Buddhist and Daoist funeral rites that were increasingly being practiced by the elite, who considered services officiated by a large group of monks or priests as an external manifestation of filial piety. In addition to traditional reasons—for example, the intermingling of men and women during Buddhist and Daoist ceremonies that was clearly at odds with traditional elite practices—orthodox literati criticized the basic concepts underlying these services, such as heaven, hell, and rebirth. These, they argued, introduced a utilitarian angle to funerals: the rituals were necessary in order to obtain a good afterlife. In contrast, they themselves valued Confucian morality based on good behavior itself and not on a system of compensation in heaven or punishment in hell.[36] Thus the demonstration of Confucian morality by means of funeral eulogies and the strict application of Confucian rituals were perceived as a way to resist Buddhist and Daoist thought and practice. The orthodox scholars' criticism was also directed against the growing practice of cremation, an old custom originally introduced by Buddhism. Its popularity, especially among commoners, was not based on arguments of belief, but on economic concerns. With larger crowds living in smaller areas, poor people often could not afford to buy burial space, and were consequently forced to cremate their dead.[37]

The third criticism concerned the social problems caused by the burial masters who selected a burial place on the basis of *fengshui* (geomancy or siting). Orthodox literati were concerned about the role of these burial masters, who, because of their professional status, became increasingly interested in economic gain. Literati argued that fortune-telling undermined the real practice of *fengshui*, which in principle should help the cultivation of a prudent and cautious attitude toward death and the careful selection of a burial place as a peaceful place for the souls of one's relatives. Their arguments were very much linked to practice and to the threat that these funerary customs could pose to the social order. They pointed out that the practices of burial masters led to all kinds of social conflicts: people competing for a fortuitous burial place, which increased prices; lawsuits concerning the acquisition of burial ground and disputes arising from people trying to take farmland away from peasants; and, in some extreme cases, burial masters obliging people to rebury a coffin because a new, more fortuitous burial place had been determined by *fengshui*. Critics were particularly concerned because burials were being deferred for longer periods, as people adhered rigidly to the words of funeral masters advising them to wait for an appropriate time and place. Thus, a coffin could easily be kept unburied for several years, and as long as relatives were not buried, the mourning period was not considered finished. The Confucian system of the mourning grades, however, imposed limits on these mourning periods that were dependent on class and position: usually members of the elite were to be buried within three months, ordinary people within the month. Confucian scholars denounced the postponement of burial by commoners as disrupting the traditional ritual system.[38]

Reaction by the Gentry

Facing the challenges raised by the funeral and other rituals, members of the gentry reacted in various ways. The growing concern to implement *Family Rituals* also led to a surge in its publication at the end of the Ming, when the text was often edited through private initiatives with scholars rearranging, simplifying, elaborating, or otherwise altering it.[39] Some versions were essentially revisions of Qiu Jun's *Etiquette of the "Family Rituals"* of 1474, such as the re-edition of 1608 that was a joint production by important officials in the Jiangnan area. Among these officials was Yang Tingyun (1562–1627), who, a few years later would be baptized as a Christian.[40] There were also short versions of *Family Rituals*. For instance, Lü Kun (1536–1618), a scholar deeply impressed by the need to bring the basic Confucian message to ordinary people, including women, wrote his *Supplement to the Four Rituals* (*Sili yi*, preface dated 1573) and *Doubts about the Four Rituals* (*Sili yi*, preface dated 1614), publicizing his thoughts about funeral rituals.[41] His follower, Lü Weiqi (1587–1641), manifests a particularly thorough knowledge of local customs in his *Brief Sayings on the Four Rituals* (*Sili yueyan*, preface dated 1624).[42] These and other ritual books addressed not just the elite, but were intended to spread Confucian rituals among the common people. Rather than merely explaining the ritual orthopraxis, they dealt with and criticized the problem of popular customs directly. As a result, there was a certain accommodation of Confucian rituals to popular customs. Though these authors were tolerant of popular customs such as burning mock money, they maintained a firm line against Buddhist practices. They held to the principle that family rituals were to be Confucian, not Buddho-Confucian.[43] This was also the case in the transition period from Ming to Qing, when writings on rituals often took the form of treatises, essays, and notes on specific rituals. The format of short writings arose from the need to clarify ritual practice. For example, Chen Que (1604–1677) wrote notes on miscellaneous rituals used in obsequies and ancestor worship.[44] Known in particular for his attack on Buddhist rites, Chen Que, who was familiar with European culture in China and even acquired a pair of Western spectacles, was in fact opposed to all barbarian teachings. He argued that "Rote-learning the works of the duke of Zhou and Confucius is what makes China China. Worshipping according to Buddhist, Muslim, or Catholic teachings is what makes barbarians barbarians."[45] In his eyes, of those heresies that harm the empire, the practices of funeral masters are the most extreme, while those of Buddhism and Daoism are secondary. To express his objection to the prevailing practices of cremation and delays in burial, Chen wrote a *Book on Burials* (*Zangshu*, 1650), which treats the proper ways to construct a burial vault and to inter the dead. Chen favored a burial method according to six essentials: timeliness, within three months (*shi*); proximity, close to the village (*jin*); unity, tied to the lineage (*he*); depth, sufficiently deep within the ground (*shen*); solidity, with sand between the inner and outer coffins (*shi*); and frugality, without useless ceremony (*jian*).[46]

Another sign of the implementation of orthoprax funeral rites is shown by "family instructions" (*jiaxun*), practical precepts originally compiled as instruction for family members, which were sometimes printed as a booklet. In the Ming dynasty, these instructions often included ritual guidelines for funerals. By late Ming times, family instructions were frequently included in the lineage rules and served for members of the lineage as a whole.[47] *Family Rituals* in general, and its funeral rites in particular, also played a role in the formation of organized lineages, as shown by Timothy Brook. By adapting pre-Ming kinship arrangements, perhaps under the pressure of a growing polarization between the gentry and the common people, the gentry created kinship organizations that could enhance their position of dominance and provide them with a range of strategies to mobilize their socially subordinate kin.[48] Although *Family Rituals* was not written as a handbook to guide the ritual needs of the lineage, through gradual emendation it became exactly that.[49] As the gentry came to assert their formal leadership with the creation of lineages, every funeral presented them with the opportunity to assemble all their subordinate kinsmen at a group ceremony. Through such a ceremony, the gentry could reaffirm the corporate identity of the lineage, and funerals of the Neo-Confucian type thus came to be recognized as useful for lineage building.[50] This willingness of some gentry members to opt for Neo-Confucian over Buddhist funerary rites was regarded in local elite circles as a sign of commitment to the highest ideals of gentry culture.[51]

In addition to the publication of ritual manuals and the implementation of orthoprax funerary rites in their own families and lineages, the gentry also took some concrete actions aimed at changing the practice of commoners. Since in the early seventeenth century, scholar officials and local elites could not really rely on the government to restore order, local elites acted on their convictions within their own communities. They established, for instance, a "community compact" (*xiangyue*) for the moral instruction and political regulation of the people. During the Ming, this lecture program was no longer a voluntary association as it had been at its origin, but one that its planners expected all the common people of the community to join. The compact also included funeral regulations that were not just instructions for correct behavior, but were an efficacious way to spread Confucian concepts of funerary ritual among the commoners.[52] Other measures included the benevolent societies, "societies for sharing goodness" (*tongshanhui*) for the provision of aid to the local poor. Using monthly dues, these groups sponsored initiatives for the benefit of the local community, such as road repair or the construction of granaries. They also provided financial assistance for the burial of the poor. With the commercialization of the economy and the increasing expenses of popular funerals themselves, a number of people could not afford decent funerals or had to delay funerals for a long time. In the transition period between Ming and Qing, some associations specialized in burials. In addition to practical support in providing coffins, these associations urged commoners to conduct funerals according to the Confucian rituals and insisted on burial instead of cremation. Since the associations had access to the inner family sphere, they became an important forum for spreading Confucian ideas.[53]

By the end of the seventeenth century a new trend appears, as scholars became more critical of Zhu Xi's *Family Rituals*. Chow Kai-wing has demonstrated that more and more scholars realized that Zhu Xi had adapted elements of ancient ritual to meet the circumstances of his time, so they decided that his solutions were not necessarily the best for their own circumstances, some five hundred years later. The search for external and objective sources of authority that could establish how people should act led to new interpretations of Song orthodoxy with a focus on ritual.[54]

A well-known scholar in this regard is Xu Qianxue (1631–1694), Gu Yanwu's (1613–1682) nephew, who wrote the voluminous compendium, the *Comprehensive Study of Rituals* (*Duli tongkao*; 120 *juan*). Xu began studying rituals in 1677, while in mourning for his mother. With the help of famous scholars of his time, such as Wan Sitong (1638–1702), Yan Ruoju (1636–1704), Gu Yanwu, Zhu Yizun (1629–1709), and others, he was able to accumulate a formidable collection of information on mourning ceremonies and obsequies. He died before the completion of his manuscript, which was printed posthumously in 1696. Encyclopaedic in conception, it was undertaken largely in response to practical needs and cumulative inquiries into the theory and practice of rituals.[55] There were also studies on specific rituals. Mao Qiling (1623–1716), for example, known for his textual purism, produced several treatises on rituals that often challenge the prescriptions of *Family Rituals* by purging them of textual impurities. To meet the growing concern about proper rites, he wrote two manuals on funerary and ancestral rites: *My Exposition of Funeral Rites* (*Sangli wushuo*) and *Study of Three-Year Mourning Dress* (*Sannian fuzhi kao*). Along with these practical writings, he wrote extensively on classical rituals.[56]

Manchu Funerals

A new event on the ritual stage in the seventeenth century was the arrival of the Manchus. In 1644, the Manchu rulers of the Qing took control of a state that had traditionally been involved in the regulation of its people's mourning system. The Manchus had their own death rituals, some distinctly Manchu, others identical to Han practices.[57] Differences in Manchu and Han practices are found in both major rituals and minor details. The most important practices of the Manchus that differed from those of the Han Chinese were the cremation of corpses and frequent widow suicide. In addition, the Han requirement of a three-year mourning period was largely foreign to the Manchus. Male Manchus were instead required to mourn by cutting their queues, the length corresponding to the degree of relationship to the deceased, and removing their hats. Women were required to remove their jewelry, and to cut their hair in some circumstances, and in others to merely let it down.

The Manchu and Han practices also differed in smaller details. For instance, the Han laid out the corpse in the main hall and later removed it via the doorway, but the Manchus laid the body in the western room and removed it via the window. While Han practice generally prescribed burial to occur three months after encoffining, in Manchu practice the period between encoffining and burial depended on social or economic status: for the poorest it was on the same day as their death, for the elite, because of Buddhist influence, after a maximum of forty-nine days. Manchus hung up a red banner, rather than white, the mourning color of the Han, putting it up at sunrise every day and taking it down at sunset, and placed it next to the coffin, which had a raised ridge, unlike the flat lid of the Han coffin. All the things that were to be offered as sacrifices, including food, were completely burned, whereas the Han mainly burned paper objects. Manchus did not organize large banquets at funerals.[58]

Just as there were among the Han, there were differences among the Manchus themselves. For instance, Manchu customs for disposal of the corpse were very diverse. Cremation was most often practiced, but some groups practiced in-ground burial, others tree burial.[59]

After the Manchus entered China, their funeral rituals underwent changes. There were, for instance, adaptations, some actually encouraged by the Qing rulers themselves. For the new rulers, the major change in Manchu funerary customs was the abandonment of cremation during the late seventeenth century. The Manchu rulers before the conquest of China, Nurhaci (1559–1626) and Huangtaiji (1592–1643), and the first Qing emperor, Shunzhi (1638–1661), had all been cremated, as had their consorts, but thereafter, rulers and most of their consorts were buried. As for the Manchu garrison bannermen, they were not allowed to establish cemeteries in the provinces, but had to bury their dead in Beijing. This practice, in fact, at first consolidated the habit of cremation, since ashes were easier to store and transport than corpses. Yet later Qing rulers, such as the Kangxi Emperor (1654–1722), considered cremation a practice opposed to filial piety. They issued imperial orders forbidding cremation, and as a result ordinary Manchus also opted primarily for in-ground burial as they moved south. The custom of putting valley grass in the bottom of the coffin, along with branches of the chestnut tree, is a legacy of cremation. The Kangxi Emperor also forbade widow suicide.[60]

Manchus did not, however, drop all the distinctive elements of their funeral practices and in several cases Manchu and Han practices were interwoven. While Han Chinese males, after the Manchu conquest, kept their own tradition of leaving the head unshaven for a period of one hundred days, and did not cut the queue, by the eighteenth century, Manchus had appropriated the Han practice of not shaving for a hundred days during the mourning period, but continued their tradition of cutting the queue. Manchus also gradually adopted the custom of removing the coffin via the door, while keeping the windows open—a legacy of their own tradition.[61] On the whole, Manchu funerals became more complex and elaborate. As a result, Manchu rulers focused on the wastefulness of Han rituals as pitfalls to avoid, insisting that mourning rituals should not waste precious resources. In imperial funerals, actual clothing and furniture continued to be burned in awesome quantities, but among the bannermen, paper objects (of furniture, people, and animals) gradually replaced this tradition.[62]

Interwoven Chinese Funerary Rituals

The instant collapse of the Ming regime had an enormous impact on the thinking of the Chinese gentry. Chow Kai-wing has demonstrated that, in the wake of the Manchu conquest, a powerful current of demonstrating Chinese culture among ethnic Han further fuelled the growth of ritualism and purism, especially during the Kangxi reign (1662–1722). Ritual became more than the practical means to resist Buddhism that it had been in the late Ming. It instead became a powerful symbol of Chinese identity. To practice it was to show defiance of Manchu authority.[63] However, though vigorously condemned in elite writings, Buddhist and Daoist funeral services persisted throughout the imperial period. In practice they were often juxtaposed to Zhu Xi's *Family Rituals*. This was because in many cases commitments to Neo-Confucian and Buddhist ritual systems were neither total nor mutually exclusive. Rather, not only were religious practices interwoven, but the gentry often sided with popular custom against the normative preference of high culture.[64] For the bereaved, the belief that they could help their dead relatives avoid suffering was strong motivation for holding Buddhist services. Interwoven rites, which drew on both Buddhist and Confucian cosmologies, allowed people to express the principles that were most compelling to them. For the large majority of the population who took these Buddhist conceptions for granted, purely Confucian rites could only serve to express allegiance to Confucianism as an ideology. Confucian rituals were detached from the general population's conceptions of death and afterlife and thus were emotionally unsatisfactory.[65] Members of the elite who would search for all possible means to give their deceased relatives a peaceful repose found satisfaction in those Buddhist conceptions.[66] The interaction of elite and popular cultures was not only true for Buddhist or Daoist practices, but also for those promoted by funeral masters. Although the funeral masters' practices were often criticized by the elite, some scholars became deeply interested in the study of *fengshui* and could not avoid practicing siting when it really mattered.[67]

Only a small segment of the gentry regarded Buddhist and Neo-Confucian rites as conflicting. For almost everyone, funerals involved ceremonies whose origins were indistinct and unimportant. Families chose from among various practices, largely on the basis of local custom and financial means, not according to any intellectual allegiance or commitment to larger social goals.[68]

EUROPEAN FUNERAL RITUALS

Just as in China, funeral rites in Europe were characterized by their many variations. Yet, before the sixteenth century, Europe did not possess an equivalent to China's rather well-structured and unified bureaucratic organization that could circulate throughout its territory prescriptive texts defending orthoprax rituals. The only organization that might be comparable to the Chinese bureaucratic system was the Catholic Church, though the latter never attained the same level of unified selection as the Chinese examination system. Moreover, the later introduction of printing in Europe also explains why attempts to standardize rituals by means of printed handbooks occurred later than in China. Well into the sixteenth century manuscript handbooks for rituals in Europe were mainly locally oriented, not transnational, and various religious orders and dioceses had introduced their own prayers and gestures adapted to their own needs and settings.[69] The structural and ritual decisions of the Council of Trent (1545–1563) changed all this. In 1588, Pope Sixtus V (r. 1585–1590) founded the "Congregation of Rites," to see to it that everywhere in the Latin Church the prescribed manner of celebrating Mass and performing other functions of the liturgy was carefully followed.[70] It took at least one century before the decisions became effective on a local level.

European Prescriptive Texts

Several official prescriptive texts formed the background of the funeral practices of the missionaries brought to China in the seventeenth century.[71] One was the most important prescriptive text concerning funerary rites emanating from the Council of Trent, the *Roman Ritual* (*Rituale Romanum Pauli V. Pont. Max. iussu editum*). It was published in 1614 and recommended for adoption by all Roman Catholic dioceses. This liturgical book contains texts for several non-eucharistic liturgies intended generally for presbyteral use: sacramental celebrations, such as baptism, matrimony, confession, and anointing of the sick; and other services, including visitation of the sick, processions, and benedictions. The fourth and fifth chapters relate to death and dying. The fourth contains instructions for the sacrament of extreme unction (*De sacramento extremae unctionis*), for the visitation of the sick (*De visitatione et cura infirmorum*) and for the provision of assistance to the dying (*Modus iuvandi morientes, Ordo commendationis animae, De exspiratione*). The fifth includes the order of the exequies, or funeral rites (*Exsequiarum ordo*), describing the different steps to be followed and prayers to be said from the transfer of the corpse from its home to the church until the return of the priest from the cemetery. In general, the funeral rite as prescribed by the *Roman Ritual* consists of five parts: the bringing of the body to the church, the Office of the Dead, the funeral Mass, the absolution, and the burial.[72]

The funeral ritual begins when the priest, wearing surplice and black stole and accompanied by servers and clergy, goes to the house where the coffin waits. On the arrival at the house, he first sprinkles the coffin with holy water three times and then recites "From the depths" (*De profundis*; Psalm 129) with whoever is present. The funeral procession is then formed, and the body is carried to the church, while the participants intone "Be merciful" (*Miserere*; Psalm 50), with the antiphon "The humiliated bones will rejoice in the Lord" (*Exultabunt Domino ossa humiliata*), concluding with "Grant them eternal rest" (*Requiem aeternam dona ei*). In the procession, servers bear the cross in front of the lay members of the confraternities and the clergy who wear the cassock and surplice. Regular clergy proceed before the secular clergy, all walking two and two, holding lighted candles. The priest walks immediately in front of the coffin; the lay mourners behind the coffin pray for the dead person silently. On arrival at the church, the bier is carried inside to the responsory "Come to his aid, saints of God" (*Subvenite, Sancti Dei*) and is placed before the altar, surrounded with candles. The body of a layperson is set with the feet toward the altar; that of a priest with the head toward the altar. A black pall is usually laid over the coffin. Then begins the Office of the Dead, including matins (with three nocturns) and lauds. The traditional lessons from the book of Job are also read during matins. At the end of the Office, the Lord's Prayer and the prayer "Forgive" (*Absolve*) are said. Then the funeral Mass is celebrated according to the rules for a Requiem Mass. After Mass follows the absolution. Those officiating proceed to the bier and say the prayer "Do not put me on trial" (*Non intres in iudicium*), then the responsory "Free me Lord from eternal death" (*Libera me Domine de morte aeterna*), the kyries ("Lord have mercy"), and the Lord's Prayer. The principal celebrant, accompanied by the deacon, goes around the coffin twice, first sprinkling it with holy water and then incensing it. He concludes with the prayer "O God, whose property is always to have mercy" (*Deus, cui proprium est misereri*). The procession forms again, and as the coffin is carried to the cemetery, the clergy sings the antiphon "May angels lead you into paradise" (*In paradisum deducant te angeli*). On arrival at the grave, should the tomb not have been blessed already, the priest blesses it and the corpse with holy water and incense, saying the prayer "God through whose mercy" (*Deus cuius miseratione*). The body is then placed in the grave. The benediction (*Benedictus*; Luke 1:68–79) is said, with "I am the resurrection and the life" (*Ego sum resurrectio et vita*) as the antiphon, followed by the kyries and the Lord's Prayer. While this is said, the priest sprinkles the corpse, not going around it. Then, after the prayer "Make us, we beseech Thee" (*Fac quaesumus*), the priest makes the sign of the cross over the grave, saying the response "Eternal rest" (*Requiem aeternam*) followed by "Rest in peace" (*Requiescat in pace*). On the return from the place of burial to the church, "From the depths" (*De profundis*; Psalm 129) is again recited with the antiphon "If you took note" (*Si iniquitates*).

The two most significant rituals in this sequence that constitute the elementary structure of the Catholic funeral rite at the end of the sixteenth century are the Office of the Dead and the funeral Mass. The texts for the Office of the Dead (*Officium defunctorum*) are included in the same chapter of the *Roman Ritual*. They consist of a series of psalms and scripture readings arranged according to the evening, night, and morning prayers of the monastic tradition. The Office was recited, originally in monasteries, on the occasion

ilexi quoniam
exaudiet domi
nus: uorem ora
tionis mee

of a death or a commemorative day for the dead.[73] Miniatures in the beautifully illustrated manuscript versions from Catholic monasteries of the late Middle Ages and Renaissance offer lively depictions of the different stages of the funeral (fig. 1.3).[74] The *Office of the Dead* was often published separately or in other liturgical books.[75] It was, for instance, also included at the back of the *Roman Breviary* (*Breviarium Romanum ex decreto Sacrosancti Concilii Tridentini restitutum*, 1568; revised in 1602 and 1632), the daily prayer book for the clergy.[76]

Texts and prayers for the funeral Mass are included in the *Roman Missal* (*Missale Romanum ex decreto Sacrosancti Concilii Tridentini restitutum*, 1570; revised in 1604 and 1634), the text used in celebrating the Eucharist. In the *Missal* the section "Masses for the dead" (*Missae defunctorum*) includes the funeral Mass, the masses celebrated at the third, seventh and thirtieth day after the funeral, the anniversary Mass and the commemorative Mass of all the deceased, and the section "Various prayers for the dead" (*Orationes diversae pro defunctis*) to be said at ordinary masses during which one can also have a commemoration of a dead person.[77]

Thus, at the beginning of the seventeenth century, a Catholic priest had three major written sources for the organization of a funeral: the *Roman Ritual*, the *Office of the Dead* (included in the *Ritual* but also published separately) and the *Roman Missal*. Roman authorities promulgated them all after long deliberations and historical investigations by liturgical specialists. Publication of the *Roman Ritual* took the longest time of the three; begun in 1575, it was not finished until 1614. During that period, several local *ritualia* were compiled. One was the *Manual for the Celebration of the Sacraments of the Church* (*Manuale ad sacramenta Ecclesiae ministranda*), compiled for the Japanese mission by the Jesuit bishop Luís Cerqueira (1552–1614) and published in Nagasaki in 1605.[78]

These different prescriptive texts were also the ritual handbooks used by missionaries going to China. These missionaries came from different countries—especially from present-day Italy and Portugal, but also from Spain, Germany, Belgium, France, and Poland—and different regions in these countries. Given the many differences in the concrete performance of funeral rites among these regions, the missionaries differed in ritual experience among themselves. The actual printing of ritual handbooks, however, and the fact that they could be

1.3. The Catholic funeral Mass, as depicted in a fifteenth-century illuminated manuscript. The souls are being released from purgatory, as a result of prayers and charitable deeds. Text at bottom is from Psalm 114, which is recited at the beginning of the Office of the Dead, preceding the funeral Mass.
From *Book of Hours: Office of the Dead*, by the Coëtivy Master (Henri de Vulcop?), Angers (?), France, 1460s, fol. 118. See also Wieck (1988), 146. Courtesy of Walters Art Museum, Baltimore: Walters 274; cat. no. 42.

carried easily, made it possible, at least in principle, for missionaries in China to have common reference works for ritual practice.

Shifts in European Funeral Rituals

The European prescriptive texts are important in several respects. They reflect the renovation of liturgy that went along with a concern for the better formation of the clergy, both of which emerged from the decisions of the Council of Trent. The uniformity these decisions aimed at was facilitated by the printing press that enabled a wider and quicker dissemination of books and thus a more universal regulation of Catholic rituals. But these texts also represent the culmination of changing attitudes towards death and the funerary ritual that had been developing in Europe between the eleventh and fifteenth centuries, as discussed in detail by Philippe Ariès.[79] Four major shifts in attitude during that period laid the groundwork for what would happen when these European rituals came into contact with Chinese funeral rituals and were transformed into rituals adapted to Chinese funerary traditions.

First, an optimistic conception of death shifted to a pessimistic one, as reflected in the prayers for the dead that appear in the ritual prescriptive texts discussed earlier. Before the tenth century these prayers took the form of a commemoration (*memento*) revealing a predominantly optimistic conception of life after death. The dead were considered to be already saved, only waiting in the bosom of Abraham (also called the *refrigerium*) for the resurrection at the end of the world. In the funerary liturgy, the living recognized their helplessness, but affirmed their faith, gave thanks to God, and celebrated the entrance of the deceased into the repose or sleep of blissful expectation.[80] Moreover, in an ordinary Mass, at the moment of commemoration (after the consecration) the names of the dead were usually read in a long list together with the names of the living, reflecting the spontaneous solidarity of the living with the dead. In the following centuries important changes occurred in the liturgical exposition of death, changes that express a new conception of human destiny. They emerged from divergent theological opinions (such as the more pessimistically oriented Augustinianism), the development of the monasteries, and an increase in the number of clergy. The age-old confidence in immediate salvation was shaken. The people of God became less assured of divine mercy, and there was a growing fear of being abandoned forever to the power of Satan. As a result, a prayer of intercession replaced the prayer of commemoration. Christians now believed that their prayers and good works—the indulgences they earned—might intervene in favor of those who languished in purgatory, which now replaced the *refrigerium*.[81] The issue of judgment and the terror of death came to replace the earlier vision. This is apparent in several prayers and responses of the *Roman Ritual* asking God to absolve sinners from their offences, thus bringing to the fore the medieval fear and pessimism in the face of death.[82] During Mass the names of the dead became separated from the names of the living, and no longer appear as part of the same genealogy. This isolation of the commemoration of the dead expressed a new and different attitude: the spontaneous solidarity of the living and the dead had been replaced by solicitude on behalf of individual souls in danger (fig. 1.4).[83]

The second important shift that took place after the thirteenth century and that is reflected in the prescriptive texts was that death became "clericalized."[84] The family and friends of the departed ceased to be the main actors at the funerals. The leading roles were henceforth reserved for priests, especially mendicant friars, or certain individuals with religious duties, members of the Third (or lay) orders or confraternities. They became new specialists in death. From the moment of their last breath, dead persons belonged no longer to their friends or family but to the Church. One example of the growing role of the clergy is the importance given to the *Office of the Dead*. The psalms had constituted since early times the fundamental prayers of Christian funerals, but the *Office of the Dead* itself had developed in a monastic context, and the reading of it now replaced the traditional lamentations. The vigil had become an ecclesiastical ceremony that began at home and sometimes continued in the church, where the clergy took up the recitation of the prayers for the dead—the prayers commending the soul to God.[85] Another example of clericalization is that the funeral procession came to play an important role in the symbolism of the funeral, as also reflected in the *Roman Ritual*. In the late Middle Ages, particularly after the founding of the mendicant orders, the character of this ceremony had begun to change. The small group of escorts became a solemn ecclesiastical procession. Relatives and friends were certainly not excluded, but the priests and monks, on the one hand, and poor people and children from foundling homes on the other, were the new officiants, occupying all the space. The solemn procession of mourners, rather than the entombment, became the symbolic image of death and funerals.[86]

A third shift, closely related to the previous one, was the new relationship of the Mass to death and funerals. In earlier times the religious ceremony, properly speaking, was limited to "absolution" (*absoute*)—the benediction of the dead, once over the dying body, once over the dead body at the place of death, and once again at the grave. No masses were said, or if they were, they went unnoticed.[87] The emergence of a service in the church, accompanied by a Mass, as the focal point of monastic funeral liturgy was the most important consequence of ritual development during the five-hundred-year period following the tenth century.[88] With the growing importance of masses in the monasteries,

1.4. The Catholic graveside burial service, as depicted in a fifteenth-century illuminated manuscript. A body wrapped in cloth is being lowered into the grave. Border vignettes show the preparation of the body prior to its burial.

From *Book of Hours: Office of the Dead*, Troyes (?), France, ca. 1470, fol. 119. See also Wieck (1988), 130. Courtesy of Walters Art Museum, Baltimore: Walters 249; cat. no. 49.

every time a life came to its end, a regular series of Low Masses began, either at the onset of the agony or immediately following death, and lasted for days, weeks, months, or even a year. These masses succeeded one another without any relation to the funeral rites. Common practice required no ceremony at the church before the absolution at the grave. After the thirteenth century this situation changed. On the day of burial, which was almost always the day after death, it became customary to hold a service in the local church that ended with a final absolution at the grave. Until the sixteenth century this service in the church did not require the presence of the body, which did not arrive until the time for burial. However, it became more usual for testators to ask that the body be carried to the church on the day of burial. By the seventeenth century the presence of the body during the ceremony had become the rule.[89] By that time, whatever the number of masses, commendations, or psalms, priority was given to the Requiem Mass above all others, to be said in the presence of the body and immediately preceding burial. There was a relative decline in the importance of absolution and the ceremony of entombment; the main part of the funeral service took place in church.[90]

A final shift, which is less reflected in the prescriptive texts, was the growing importance paid to the concealment of the corpse. Around the thirteenth century, at the same time that the vigil, mourning, and the funeral procession were becoming ceremonies of the Church, organized and directed by clergymen, the dead body, formerly a familiar object and an image of repose, came to possess such power that the sight of it became unbearable. The corpse was removed from view, hidden in a coffin, where it was no longer visible.[91] The development of the coffin for use in the pre-burial procession was first restricted principally to northern Europe; in the south, where change in attitudes to the corpse were less apparent, the old habit of exposing the body at the funeral survived. Made-to-measure coffin construction took place in the house of the wealthy deceased, whereas the ready-to-wear variety, for paupers, was rented.[92] The adoption of concealment was a gradual process; when *Roman Ritual* was composed, no liturgical prescriptions for the encoffining of the body existed.[93] Moreover, later, the bare coffin inspired the same aversion as the uncovered body and had, in its turn, to be covered and concealed by a piece of cloth—the *pallium* or pall—and later on even by a catafalque. The naked face of death was hidden beneath the coffin lid, with a shroud over the coffin and the whole beneath the canopy of the catafalque.[94]

These four changes to European funerary ritual do not reflect all the variations that appeared. The growth in commercial wealth, for example, also led to increasingly complex funerals, especially over the course of the sixteenth century. Testators demanded more people file in the ranks of funeral processions, and the number of burial masses to be said at different moments in different churches rose.[95] Yet these shifts became characteristics representing the elementary structure of Catholic funerals as missionaries probably experienced them before going to China.

CONCLUSION

From this overview, it is obvious that Chinese and European funerary traditions corresponded in many ways, despite the historical transformations those traditions underwent. Many of those parallels are not only characteristic of these two cultures, but, as anthropologists have indicated, they are shared by funeral practices in other cultures.[96]

The differences are significant, however. The comparison between the prescriptive texts helps to highlight some essential characteristics of the elementary structure of funerary rituals. A first major difference between Chinese and European funerals in the seventeenth century concerns the main actors. In China these are primarily the family members who are non-specialists and non-professionals, while in Europe the main actor is the priest, a specialist and professional. In practice Chinese funerals also avail themselves of various specialists, including Buddhist and Daoist professionals, but these are marginalized by the text of the *Family Rituals*. Conversely, non-specialists are also involved in European funerals, but the prescriptive texts do not address them. This aspect points at a difference in elementary structure in terms of personnel. Catholic priests can be called professionals because the performance of ritual is one of their major occupations. Moreover, they are specialists because the ritual acts they perform are learned both through apprenticeship and theological training. Some of the gestures they carry out, especially during Mass, are prescribed in great detail, such as the position of the fingers in holding the host. In contrast, Chinese family members are neither professionals nor specialists. All key ritual actions—prostrations, offering of incense, libations—do not require a specific apprenticeship with a ritual master, as they are actions that have been performed by all Chinese in family rituals since their youth. In short, Chinese funerals were family rituals, as the name *jiali* indicates; the European were ecclesiastical rituals.

What these actors do also differs between the two cultures. *Family Rituals* mainly prescribes which actions to perform; *Roman Ritual* which texts to read. *Family Rituals* also contains some texts about what to write or to say: model letters for sending gifts and acknowledgment; texts to be written on the inscription stone or tablet; the ritual expressions to be used at the moment of condoling; and the words of the prayers to be said at the moment of the different offerings.[97] But they occupy a very limited space in the overall sequence.

Mostly the main actors remain silent and their most important oral expression is ritual wailing. The contrast with the European prescriptive text is striking. While the *Roman Ritual*, like *Family Rituals*, contains instructions about how to organize space (for processions and arrangements in the church), what to do (sprinkling and incensing), and what to wear (liturgical dress), it primarily provides the full text of the words to be pronounced by the priest and other participants. These include biblical texts, such as scripture readings and psalms, and a large number of prayers. In this regard the Christian funeral service resembles Buddhist and Daoist rituals in which the recitation of scriptures also occupies an important place.

The prayers reveal a further difference between Chinese and Christian funerals. In Chinese funerals, prayers are addressed to the deceased themselves. They are asked to enjoy the offerings presented to them. In the Christian ritual, not one prayer is addressed to the deceased; all are addressed to God, who is asked to bring salvation to the deceased's soul. In other words, in China there is a direct relationship between the family members and the deceased; in Europe, the priest and other people who pray mediate on behalf of the deceased.

These differences reflect divergences in ideology. James Watson argues that the most essential notion regarding the relationship between life and death in China was a strong belief in the continuity between this world (life) and the next (death). With both worlds governed by bureaucratic principles that mirrored the imperial bureaucracy, one's social status remained largely unaffected by death. No radical dualism in Chinese thought separated body from soul, unlike the central concern that governed European notions of life and death. The "moment of death," whereby body and soul were forever parted, did not have the same meaning among Chinese as it had among Europeans. One of the primary goals of Chinese funeral rites, in fact, was to keep corpse and spirit together during the initial stages of death; separation prior to the ritualized expulsion from the community was thought to bring disaster. Much of the ritual at Chinese funerals was aimed specifically at settling the volatile and disoriented spirit of the recently dead. Without proper attention to ritual details one would create a hungry ghost who would return to plague the living.[98] In the Catholic tradition, upon the death of the body, the soul went to heaven or hell, or in most cases to purgatory, and the aim of the ritual was to help the salvation of the soul.[99]

The notion of a continued exchange between living and dead, according to Watson, is the foundation of the ideological domain in late imperial China. This exchange is concretely expressed in the transfer of food, money, and goods to the deceased. In return, the living expect to receive certain material benefits, including luck, wealth, and progeny. In the Confucian tradition, this exchange was not based on any elaborated idea of an underworld. In Christianity, meanwhile, there is no exchange between the living and the dead; the latter are not believed to be able to receive anything from the living. There is, rather, a relationship between the living and God and the dead and God. This is very much linked to specific notions about heaven and the underworld. In the Catholic tradition, the living could mediate in the expiation of the sins of the deceased, and the salvation of their souls, through meritorious deeds, such as prayers and works of charity. These were addressed to God on behalf of the deceased. Some of these aspects can be compared to Buddhism with its notions of a punitive underworld, salvation, and merit-making. Buddhist death rituals repaid parents, especially mothers, for their sacrifices in their children's upbringing and required the intervention of the Buddhist clergy to aid in this effort.[100] But it is with the Confucian tradition that the Christian tradition contrasted most.

Watson also points out that in China all rituals associated with death are performed *as if* there were a continued relationship between living and dead. It is irrelevant whether or not participants actually believe that the spirit survives or that the presentation of offerings has an effect on the deceased. What matters is that the rites are performed according to the accepted procedure.[101] In Europe rituals were founded on the belief that no earthly relationship continued after death; the salvation of the soul was in the hands of God. And while in China the standardization of ritual practice almost always took precedence over efforts to legislate or control beliefs, in Europe the maintenance of a centralized belief system seems to have been given priority to the standardization of funeral rites. Compared to China this standardization took place relatively late.

Important analytic terms in this regard are those of orthopraxy—correct practice, with its corresponding neologistic adjective "orthoprax"—and orthodoxy—correct belief.[102] The differences demonstrated above seem to indicate that, in China proper, procedure was more important than proper belief, while in Christian Europe, correct articulation of faith and doctrine were more important than correct ritual practice. The prescriptive liturgical codes, such as *Family Rituals* and *Roman Ritual*, seem to confirm this difference in emphasis. Identifying Chinese tradition with only orthopraxy and Christianity with only orthodoxy, however, would lead to reductionism. Correct doctrine was also important in Neo-Confucian China, and in Catholic Europe many efforts were made to introduce a correct ritual practice. Still, these notions can be used as helpful tools in gaining deeper insights into the complexity of ritual practices in both Confucian China and Christian Europe and to discover some differences in accent, if not in essence, between them.

2 / Missionaries' Knowledge
of Chinese Funerals

W hat European missionaries knew about Chinese funeral practices can be discovered from the texts they sent to Europe. These texts included private letters often used for correspondence internal to their religious order, but also reports and historical narratives that were published and destined for a larger public.[1] The latter were widely spread, and often translated into different European languages. Moreover, contemporary European scholars who never traveled outside Europe adopted the missionaries' information in their own publications about China.

EUROPEAN SOURCES

One of the most comprehensive descriptions of China is contained in the *Remarkable Enterprise of the Dutch East-Indian Company on the Coast and in the Empire of DaQing or China (Gedenkwaerdig bedryf der Nederlandsche Oost-Indische Maetschappye op de Kuste en in het Keizerrijk van Tasing of Sina)*, compiled by the Amsterdam physician Olfert Dapper (1639–1689) and published in the Netherlands in 1670. This beautifully printed and lavishly illustrated book contains the reports of the Dutch admiral Balthasar Bort's expeditions along the Fujian coast in 1663 and 1664 and of Pieter van Hoorn's embassy to Beijing (1666–1668).[2] Dapper himself never visited China; his book is a conglomeration of reports from members of Bort's expeditions and van Hoorn's embassy together with descriptions of China gleaned from other sources. Dapper was a compiler rather than an author, and his compilation efforts were very extensive.[3] He often reproduced parallel passages from several writers on a single topic without any comment of his own. Probably because of his complete dependence on others, he acknowledged his sources of information more freely than his contemporaries. In addition to the original Dutch edition of 1670, the publisher, Jacob van Meurs, produced four German editions each year from 1673 to 1676. John Ogilby's English translation, published in London in 1671, is entitled *Atlas Chinensis* (Atlas of China) and has been erroneously attributed to Arnoldus Montanus (1625?–1683). Dapper's book is virtually an encyclopaedia of things Chinese for the Dutch, German, and English readers of the latter part of the seventeenth century.[4]

The second volume of Dapper's work, *Description of the Empire of China or DaQing*, contains a long chapter called "Funerals and Mourning for the Dead" comprising material gathered from almost every important seventeenth-century account of China.[5] The first is *The Christian Expedition into China, Undertaken by the Society of Jesus, From the Notes of P. Matteo Ricci from the Same Society* (*De Christiana expeditione apud Sinas. Suscepta ab Societate Iesu. Ex P. Matthaei Ricij eiusdem Societatis commentarijs*, 1615), the Latin translation of Matteo Ricci's story of the introduction of Christianity into China.[6] It was edited by Nicolas Trigault, SJ (1577–1628) who, after having spent about three years in China, was sent back to Europe as procurator of the Jesuits' China mission. Within ten years of its publication, the work was not only reprinted several times, but was also translated into French, German, Spanish, Italian, and partially into English.[7] The second source used by Dapper is by Adriano de Las Cortes, SJ (1578–1629), "Account of the Voyage, Shipwreck, and Imprisonment Which He and Others Experienced in Chaozhou, Kingdom of Great China, and Also What He Saw Along the Way" ("Relación del viage, naufragio y captiverio que, con otras personas, padeció en Chaucao, reino de la gran China, con lo demás que vió en lo que della anduvó," 1625).[8] This Spanish Jesuit spent eleven months in captivity on the mainland, after his ship had wrecked on the Chinese coast east of Canton while heading towards Macao. After his liberation, Las Cortes wrote an extensive account of his experiences, some parts of which may be based on Chinese written sources. This manuscript is unique because of its extensive description of the realities of daily Chinese life, including vestments of the Chinese, ritual objects in the temples, and methods of corporal punishment. It is still not known how Dapper gained access to Las Cortes' text, since it has only been published in the late twentieth century.[9] Some of Dapper's illustrations are based on Las Cortes' drawings.

Another important account of China was written by Álvaro Semedo, SJ (1586–1658), who first worked as a missionary in China from 1613 to 1637. Like Trigault before him, he was eventually sent back to Europe as procurator in Rome for the China mission. In Goa in 1638, during his return voyage, he completed his *Account of the Propaganda of the Faith in the Kingdom of China and Neighbouring Areas* (*Relação da propagação da fé no reyno da China e outros adjacentes*). A Spanish translation was printed as *Imperio de la China* (The Empire of China) in 1642, and the Italian version, printed in 1643, was translated into French in 1645, and into English, in 1655, as *The History of that Great and Renowned Monarchy of China.*[10] Semedo devotes an entire chapter to funerals and burials, and another chapter to the funeral in 1614 of the Empress Dowager, the natural mother of the Wanli Emperor. Fresh news on China was brought to Europe in the 1650s by Martino Martini, SJ (1614–1661). He had returned to Europe aboard a Dutch ship that was forced off course by channel storms and finally landed in Norway. Martini made his way south through Germany to Amsterdam. There he had his *New Atlas of China* (*Novus atlas sinensis*, 1655) printed by the famous Dutch publisher Johan Blaeu (1598–1673). It was later translated into Dutch, French, and German. This book contains individual maps of Ming China's fifteen provinces, each accompanied by detailed descriptions, from which Dapper selected passages on funeral customs.[11]

Dapper also quotes from another work by Martini, *The First Ten Books on Chinese History* (*Sinicae historiae decas prima*, 1658), which was the first serious attempt by a European to write the history of China.[12] Dapper's last important source was Johann Adam Schall von Bell's (1592–1666) *Historical Narration of the Start and Progress of the Mission of the Society of Jesus to the Chinese, Especially in the Court of Beijing* (*Historica Narratio de Initio et Progressu Missionis Societatis Jesu apud Chinenses, Praesertim in Regia Pequinensi*, 1665). This work, edited by the Austrian Jesuit Johan Foresi (1624–1682), was mainly based on a report that Schall had written in 1658, partly as a response to the discussions among the missionaries concerning the legitimacy of Schall's supervision of the Chinese imperial Astronomical Bureau. The report contains many details about Christianity in the transition period from Ming to Qing. Three of the final chapters—from a different source and of a later date—are devoted to the death and funeral of the Shunzhi Emperor, who died on the night of 5–6 February 1661, and contain a long explanation of funerals in general.[13]

PROTO-ETHNOGRAPHIC DESCRIPTIONS OF CHINESE FUNERALS

In general the information contained in these sources gives a fairly good idea of the practice of funerals in China in the seventeenth century.[14] They can be called "proto-ethnographic" descriptions of China.[15] They are ethnographic because they primarily describe such practices of another culture as rituals, education systems, language, and modes of production. They are "proto"-ethnographic because their objectives, methodology, and standards do not yet correspond to those of ethnography as it developed as an academic discipline in the nineteenth and twentieth centuries. This does not mean that seventeenth-century ethnographical writings did not reflect on their own method and aims. One of the first writings Dapper uses, Trigault and Ricci's *The Christian*

Expedition into China, is a good example of methodological positioning. Several modern authors have discussed how this account fit into a larger propaganda project and how Trigault made several changes and additions to Ricci's original Italian text in order to adapt it to his propaganda.[16] Yet as editor, Trigault was, in his own words, "more interested in offering the truth of facts than the pleasure of literary style."[17] In doing so, he wanted to offer an alternative to the two kinds of authors who had written about China until then—"those who have imagined much, and those who have heard much and have published the same without due consideration."[18] From this latter class Trigault can hardly make exceptions for certain Jesuits. Then Trigault gives the clue to his own empirical approach:

> No one, as is evident, could be expected to acquire a thorough understanding of European life without long years of contact. So too in China, in order to obtain a complete knowledge of this country and its people, one must consume years in travelling through the different provinces, learning to speak the native language and to read their books. All this we have done, and so it is only reasonable to believe that this most recent account of ours should supersede those that appeared before it, and that what it records should be taken for the truth, with due allowance, of course, for human errors, which if brought to our attention will be gratefully corrected and replaced in favour of more recent observation.[19]

Present-day approaches are less inclined to follow Trigault's opinion about the possibility of capturing truth, but his reflection makes clear that the descriptions in his work were based on an attempt to live among and communicate with the Chinese. This is particularly important for the specific ethnographic section of the work. Like many other Jesuit writings, *The Christian Expedition into China* is composed of two parts. Most of the work (books two to five) is devoted to the history of the "Christian expedition"—the introduction of Christianity into China. This is the general frame of the text. Yet in book one, the work is introduced by an ethnographical description of the geographical, cultural, religious, and political situation of China, part of which had been published earlier in Europe by the Jesuit missionary Diego de Pantoja (1571–1618).[20] The descriptions of mourning and funerals appear in this first book in the chapter on Chinese customs, titled "De Sinarum ritibus nonnullis" in Trigault's edition and "Delle cortesie et alcuni riti della Cina" in Ricci's original manuscript. It refers more specifically to courtesy and rites, which form a direct reference to *li*, one of the five cardinal virtues, rendered in the English translation by Purchas as "civilitie." To Ricci and Trigault, the Chinese surpass not only other "uncivilized and barbarian" kingdoms but also the Europeans.[21] It is noteworthy that funerals are not included in the chapters on superstitions or religious sects.[22] As such, the discussion of funerals contains the two fundamental characteristics of Renaissance ethnology that Joan-Pau Rubiés has discerned. The first is that, by disconnecting it from the chapters on religious sects and practices, the description of funerals tends to be independent from any serious analysis of beliefs. The second is that, by linking funerals to practices of civility, it shares in the gradual clarification and separation between the language of faith and the language of reason—the language of Christianity and the language of civilization.[23] These characteristics apply to most of the works that are discussed here.

Funerals occupy a limited space in *The Christian Expedition into China*. They appear in the context of the external display of filial piety, for which "there is no people in the whole world who can compare with the Chinese."[24] In Dapper's book the whole section from Trigault and Ricci is quoted at the beginning of his chapter on funerals, presenting the general characteristics of mourning:

> All the Chinese Books which Treat of their Customs, endeavor nothing more than to incite Children to shew Obedience to their Parents, and Respect to their Ancestors; which they shew in nothing more than in their Funerals and Obsequies: for they not onely Habit themselves in Mourning, but bestow great Cost on a Coffin.
>
> In the preparing for their Funerals, which may rather be call'd a glorious Show, they strive to exceed one another according to their State and Quality; nay, often go beyond their Capacity. They Mourn not in black, but White. The Sons at their Parents Death wear a course Flaxen Coat, or rather Frock, which reaches down to their Feet, their Hats and Shoes are also very pitiful to behold; and they tie a Cord about their Wastes like the Franciscan Monks. This Mourning, according to an inviolable Law, for Father or Mother is strictly observ'd by the Children three whole years, for this reason (as they say in their Books,) that they should requite their Parents, and as a testimony of thankfulness that they have carry'd them three years in their Arms, and brought them up with great trouble during their Infancy. But the time which they Mourn for other Relations is much shorter; for some leave off Mourning within the Year, others in three Moneths, as in Europe.
>
> The lawful time to Mourn for the Emperor or Empress, is also three years, which all the Subjects observe through the whole Empire: But now upon the Emperor's permission, made known by Proclamation, Days are reckon'd for Moneths, and so the whole Realm in a Moneths time express their Sorrow for the Emperor's Death in Mourning.[25]

This passage shows that the text is clearly written for a European audience, with comparisons that the contemporary European reader could understand ("they tie a Cord about their Wastes like the Franciscan Monks") and with explicit reference to Europe.[26] These comparisons reflect the inevitable understanding of another culture based upon the observer's own. That the audience is an implied "European" one, as is characteristic for seventeenth-century sources, rather than one specific to any country, indicates that a consciousness of Europe as a cultural entity prevailed among Europeans themselves.

Trigault's words appear to have been based not only on eyewitness observations but also on written Chinese sources. In his description of funerary rites, as described in the next section, Trigault seems to make an explicit reference to Zhu Xi's *Family Rituals* or one of its popularized editions:

> The Funeral Ceremonies and Customs of the Chineses observ'd at Burials, are written in a large Book, wherefore upon any ones Decease, those that are to take care to Interr the Body repair to that, wherein their Mourning Clothes, Shoes, Caps, Girdles, and the like, are not onely describ'd in it, but also represented in Pictures.
>
> When a Person of Quality happens to die, the Son of the Deceased, or nearest Kinsman, acquaints all the other Relations and Friends with it by a Book written in a mournful Style. Mean while the Coffin is made, and the Body put into it, and likewise the Hall or Chamber in which the Corps stands, hung, and cover'd with white Cloth; in the middle of the Chamber is an Altar, on which stands the Coffin, and the Effigies of the Deceased.
>
> Into this Chamber on certain Days come all the Kindred of the Deceased clad in Mourning; whither they bring Rice, and setting two Wax-Candles on the Altar, burn Perfumes [i.e., incense] to the Honor of the Deceased. When the Candles are lighted, then they shew Reverence to the Dead by bowing their Bodies and Kneeling four times; but they first put Frankincense into a Perfuming Pot with Fire, which is plac'd against the Coffin and the fore-mention'd Image. Whilst these Ceremonies are performing, one or more Sons of the Deceased stand on each side of the Chest crying and lamenting; behind the Coffin all the Women of his Alliance, standing behind a Curtain, cry without ceasing. The Priests have ordain'd a Custom to burn Papers, cut after a peculiar fashion, as also white Silk-Stuffs; which is done (they say) that thereby the Deceased may be provided of Clothes in the other World.
>
> The Children oftentimes keep their dead Fathers and Mothers in a Coffin in the House three or four years together, without the least nauseating smell coming through the Crannies, being colour'd all over with the Gum which they call *Cie*. All which time they set before them every day Meat and Drink as if they were alive.
>
> The Sons during this time of Mourning do not sit on their usual Stools, but on low Benches cover'd with white Cloth; neither do they sleep on Beds, but on Mats

of Straw, spread over the Floor near the Coffin. They eat no Flesh, nor drink, but upon pure necessity, not being suffer'd to be at any Feasts, nor for some Moneths to go abroad publickly, but are carry'd in Sedans cover'd with Mourning Cloth.[27]

Trigault succinctly provides the essential characteristics of the funeral procedure, admitting that there are "Many other things they observe, which would be too tedious to relate." He makes an exception for the detail of a funeral procession that Dapper ends up using:

At the Day when the Corps is to be carry'd out, the Friends and Relations are invited by another Book, and meet all in white Apparel to attend the Funeral; which is perform'd like the Romans Processioning; several Shapes of Men, Women, Elephants, Tygers, and Lyons, made of Paper, but curiously Gilt and Painted, being carry'd before, and afterwards burnt at the Grave. The Priests mumbling their Heathen Prayers, follow the Corps also in a long Train, and use several Ceremonies by the Way, beating on Drums, playing on Pipes, Cymbals, Bells, and the like. Before go likewise several Men, carrying of great Copper Perfuming-Pots on their Shoulders.

Lastly, the Bier on which the Corps lieth, is brought in great State under an Arch'd Canopy, made very artificially of Wood, and hung with Flannel, which is carry'd by forty, and sometimes by fifty Men.

Behind the Bier follow the Sons on Foot, every one leaning on a Crutch, as if fainting with sorrow. Next follow the Women Kindred in Sedans hung with white Curtains, so that none can see them. The other Women which are not so nearly Ally'd to the Deceased, are also carry'd in Mourning Sedans.

All their C[h]urch-Yards and Tombs are near the City.[28]

In his conclusion on funerals Trigault describes various other rules and characteristics, such as in the case of being absent at the parents' death or of dying outside of one's native province. Though this whole section is rather short, it gives a fairly well-developed idea of Chinese funeral customs.

In Dapper, the excerpt taken from Trigault is followed by ones taken from Semedo, Las Cortes, and finally Schall von Bell, which is interrupted by short quotations from Martini. Dapper accumulates his information without avoiding repetition. The result is that the reader gets a reasonably wide and detailed overview of the different actions involved in the funerary rituals. Naturally, however, any one description varies slightly from another.

The various descriptions of condolence rites, for example, demonstrate such differences.[29] These rites certainly caught the attention of the missionaries. In European practice, the time between death and burial was rather short, so

Europeans were not accustomed to ceremonies taking place over the course of several days. Semedo describes the condolence rites in the following way:

> After [laying out the body], they advise all their friends and kindred thereof, sending them a *Thie* [*tie*, invitation card] of Mourning, wherein, with words of much affliction and humilitie, they give them notice of their sorrow.
>
> Then presently begin their Visits of Condoling, which are done in this manner: When the Visitant is come into the first Court, presently he putteth on his Mourning-garment, which he bringeth with him for that purpose. The drummer beateth his drumme to give notice of his arrivall, and while he passeth through the Court, the Trumpets sound; as soone as he cometh into the Hall, the women behind the Curtains begin to weep and lament. When he cometh up to the Table he layeth thereon a purse of paper; with money in it to the value of twelve pence, or eighteen pence; (which serveth for an Aide of the cost,) and some little perfumes. Then upon the Carpet he maketh foure reverences, part kneeling, and part standing on his feet. When they are ended, presently the Sonnes rise up from the place where they are, and go and place themselves on the left hand of the Visitant, and make him as many reverences, partly kneeling, and partly on their feet, at which time they are to weep, or at least to make as if they wept. When this is done, without speaking a word, they return to their place againe. In the meane time the Visitant goeth forward, and presently one of the remotest of the kindred, in slighter mourning, cometh to receive him, and leadeth him into another roome; where as soone as they are sate, presently there is brought in some of their drink, called *Chia* [*cha,* tea], and dried fruits, or else dried sweet meats; of which for the most part they do not eat, but taking a little, put it into their sleeve, and so take their leave.
>
> This courtesie is esteemed so due, that those friends, who are at hand, may by no means omit it; and they who are farther off, if they dwell in neighbouring Cities, come in their own person. But if they live very farre off, they send one from home to do it in their name. This ceremonie commonly lasteth eight or ten daies. But they who live farre off, may come, or send to do it, at what time they please.[30]

In Schall's version, written twenty years later, the same ceremonies read as follows:

> When any one dies, whoe're he be, all the Friends and Relations come about the Corps, crying and Mourning over it.
>
> Persons of Quality send a piece of very thin white Linnen, with a Letter to their Friends, to acquaint them of the dead Corps, who at an appointed day come

thither, bringing with them Perfumes, Wax-Candles, and Money; coming into the House they go to a Table, plac'd opposite to the Coffin in the midst of the Hall; having set fire on the Perfumes that stand upon the Table, they step a little backward and shew Reverence to the Effigies of the Deceased, Painted at the Head of the Coffin, by kneeling four times, and bowing their Heads to the Ground, whilst they make a mournful Cry.

These Ceremonies being perform'd, the nearest Relations appear also on one side of the Coffin between the Curtains; and coming forth shew the same Reverence, also kneeling, and bowing their Heads four times to the Ground. The time of Visiting ended, the nearest Kindred come the next day into the House of Mourning, from whence they convey the Corps to the Grave, or at least to the City Gates; for which Kindness the Children go from House to House in Sack-Cloth, and with their Faces looking down on the Ground, return Thanks, by shewing Reverence to their Visitants, who on purpose stand at their Doors.[31]

It is difficult to know where the missionaries got their information. The descriptions of condolence visits may be partially based on textual sources and partially on their own experience. However, in the case of the description of the initial rites—the initial laying out and ritual bathing of the corpse and the final laying out with encoffining[32]—one wonders whether they were recording actual personal observations. The information may very well have come from informants, the answers of whom may well have been ones they believed the inquirers sought. There are certainly other limitations to the participant approach of these early texts. For example, the nature of gender relations in both seventeenth-century China and Europe may explain why these texts contain little information about the role of women in the funeral rituals. Moreover, these proto-ethnographic descriptions do not aim at completeness; virtually absent is such information as how children, childless adults, or parents with only daughters were mourned. But on the whole, these sections contain much detailed and precise information about the culture the missionaries observed, which not only corroborates the information from Chinese contemporary sources and from modern studies, but also supplements it.

RITUAL VARIATION

As a whole, the description of Chinese funerals in Dapper's chapter provides the "elementary structure" James Watson outlines as characteristic of Chinese funerary rites. Through the accumulation of documents, however, Dapper's chapter presents not only a wide but also a complex view on funerary rituals in China. For instance, funerals are linked to social positions in society. The excerpts from Trigault's account indicate how funerals are differentiated according to social class, mentioning funerals for persons of high status and imperial funerals. These are practices that, as Semedo describes, differ for the less wealthy: "if they are so poor, that they cannot make them a Coffin, they burne them, and bury their ashes" and, "For the poorer sort of people, that cannot have a peculiar place of Sepulture, there is ordinarily, in every City, a common place of Buriall."[33] Jesuit accounts also show an awareness of regional differences within China. Dapper presents a carefully chosen selection, from Semedo: "In the Province of Sucheú [possibly Sichuan] they burn the bodie, and put the ashes in earthern Iarres, close stopped; and then cast them into the rivers,"[34] and also from Martini: "Most of the Inhabitants in the Province of Junnan [Yunnan], by reason of their Neighborhood with the Indians, lay the dead Corpse on Heaps of Wood, and burn it; . . . The Inhabitants of the City Sintien [Xintiansi], in the Province of Queicheu [Guizhou], express great sorrow for either Father or Mothers Death, by cutting off the Hair of their Heads."[35] Even more significant is that the early Qing sources, such as Martini's and Schall von Bell's accounts, clearly distinguish between Chinese and Manchu ("Tartar") funerary customs, supplementing modern sources that pay less attention to such Manchu practices. One example is the construction of the coffins:

> The upper Planks (said *Scall*) of the Tartars Coffins are sloaping like a Roof, and Painted on the out-side, not regarding the thickness of the Planks, because they put their Coffins to no other use, than to hold the Body for a short time, and carry them out in; for coming to their Funeral Piles, they burn the Coffins with the Corps. But those of the Chineses are narrower at the Feet, and broader and higher at the Head, the upper Plank smooth, and reaching over the sides, that the thickness thereof may be seen, which is chiefly observ'd and taken notice of.[36]

Another example concerns the burial customs: "But the Tartars observe quite another way of Interring their Dead, viz. on the same day that any one dies, the Corps being put in a Coffin, and the Friends having Wept over it in the House, they carry it away, except the Deceas'd was a Vice-Roy or Governor."[37] Schall's account also contains the description of recent imperial decisions concerning the abolishment of widow suicide and the reduction of wasteful funerals:

> Moreover, if the Deceas'd had a more than ordinary belov'd Concubine, or Prime Favorite, they murther themselves; for the Concubine, whether willing or unwilling, is forc'd to Hang her self, to comfort, delight, and accompany (as these ignorant People say) the Deceas'd in the other World: Yet the more understanding Persons, being somewhat better instructed, have of late, dreading such horrid

Murthers, Petition'd the Emperor, by his Proclamation, to forbid such Cruelties; and likewise the wasting and burning of Houshold-stuff, and other Materials, which his Imperial Majesty hath accordingly Order'd, so that in stead of rich Cloth of Tissue, they only burn Gilded Paper, and have in a manner left off the Barbarous Custom of killing themselves at the Grave.[38]

Some aspects receive relatively little attention. For example, given the importance the funerary tablet had for later debates linked to the Rites Controversy, these earlier texts seem to underestimate the topic. One exception is the ritual of "completing the tablet" (*chengzhu*) as described in Schall's account. The wooden tablet that would become the home for the soul of the deceased after burial was prepared in advance, leaving only the single dot in the character *zhu* (host, owner) to be filled in. The most distinguished literary acquaintance of the family would be invited to mark with a brush the finishing dot that gave life to the tablet:[39]

Lastly, They step aside and make room for him who is to write on a Board made before, being three Fingers broad, and an Ell long, the Name and Quality of the Deceas'd, first they set down this Mark 王, which signifies *Emperor*; and for this cause they that are to do this, must be clad in such Apparel, as any of Quality might appear in before the Emperor. This Person with the Pencil in his Hand, craves pardon of all the Spectators, for his bold attempt, excusing his unworthiness of that Office; then he writes over the first Mark, on the upper end of the Board with black Ink, another in this manner 主 for then that which signifi'd *Emperor* is chang'd, and is as much as *Lord*; so that in this manner, with the first under written Name of the Deceas'd, a full Sentence is made, viz. *The Lord N.N.* This Board the Deceased's Friends carry with his Image to his House, that it may be yearly Worship'd and remember'd by his Predecessors.[40]

By portraying the funeral rituals in China in their variation and in their details, these proto-ethnographic descriptions not only contributed to an understanding of China as another culture but also to the awareness of human diversity, which would later put the European classificatory schemes with their universalistic claims into question.[41] This diversity not only pointed to an opposition between China and Europe, but also to diversity within China itself.

DIFFERENCES WITH EUROPE

To what extent did the missionaries experience the Chinese funeral customs as different from their own? One way of answering this question is to look at the importance certain topics receive in these descriptions. By depicting extensively one or another aspect of the Chinese otherness, they may also refer in a subtle way to differences with Europe. Yet an additional type of source, in which missionaries present Europe to the Chinese, helps identify the missionaries' perspective. Indeed, missionaries not only tried to explain China to Europe, they also interpreted Europe to China. A telling example of this type is Giulio Aleni's (1582–1649) *Questions and Answers Regarding the West* (*Xifang dawen*, 1637).[42] Aleni, who had settled in Fujian in 1625, was often questioned by Chinese scholars about the West, and this book was written to satisfy their curiosity. In this endeavor he was assisted by Chinese scholars such as Jiang Dejing (d. 1646), who revised (*yue*) Aleni's text; Jiang had passed the metropolitan examination in 1622 and had been president of the Chinese government's Board of Rites. The text is written in the form of a dialogue between the author and his Chinese friends in which a Chinese scholar takes China as his template and questions European customs. Yet as the following examples relating to questions concerning funerals show, the interplay is more subtle. While selecting certain questions, and answering them in a specific way, Aleni not only explains the Western customs, but also highlights the differences between these and the Chinese ones.

The introduction to the answer of the first question in Aleni's section on funerals states that the European burial rites are both similar to and different from those in China. Accommodating himself to a Chinese audience, Aleni is of the opinion that "funerals are considered important ceremonies in both Europe and China."[43] This answer contrasts with the Jesuit texts quoted in Dapper, which claim that, in general, funerals in China are much more important than in Europe. Semedo, for instance, expresses the following opinion:

> Although the Chineses, in many things, especially those which concerne the government of their life, have been of the same opinion with the Europæan Philosophers, yet they are very different from them in that which belongeth to Death. For the others [the Europeans] have taken little or no care about the Sepulture of the body, whereas these [the Chinese] esteem nothing more; using in their life time all possible diligence to leave every thing ready and in order for it; and their sonnes do in nothing more shew their pietie and obedience, than by putting it in execution after their Fathers death.[44]

Schall von Bell makes his opinion clear in a nutshell: "Both Tartars and Chineses take a peculiar care for the burying of their Dead; for they imagine that all the happiness of their Successors depends upon it."[45] Depending on the audience, what was explained as something quite similar appears to be quite different. Aleni's other questions related to funerals insist on differences rather than similarities, showing that there were at least four aspects of Chinese funerary customs that the missionaries experienced as very different from their own: the graves and tombs, the coffin, the mourning clothes, and the funerary procession. Aleni's answer about seventeenth-century funerary customs in Europe can be supplemented by the descriptions of contemporary Chinese funerals in Dapper.

Graves and Tombs

Question: What are the burial rites in your country?

Answer: They are both similar to, and different from, the burial customs of China. Funerals are considered important ceremonies in both Europe and China. However, in Europe the coffins with the dead are not allowed to stand for any length of time. Instead, the dead are buried on the day following their demise. Furthermore, the graves are not on hills or uninhabited places, but within the towns near a church. Every town has many churches, and behind each of them there is a vacant piece of land for a graveyard. All members of the church hope for God's protection in this life and after death; hence they do not want to be far away from a church. Besides, it is more convenient for the descendants of the dead to pray for them and to make offerings at their graves; both the living and the dead are then at peace, thus honouring their religion. While ordinary people just dig a pit in the ground for a grave, rich people build vaults underground which are no different from dwelling houses and large enough to hold husband and wife, brothers, a whole family, or even an entire clan. For great dignitaries, noblemen, princes and the like, imposing tombs of marble are built with inscribed tombstones.[46]

Characteristic of this passage are the negative definitions by which Aleni first describes those aspects the European funerals do *not* contain, before giving a positive definition. Such negative definitions clearly highlight the differences between European and Chinese traditions. In Europe the coffins with the dead are *not* allowed to stand for any length of time, whereas in China, as Trigault pointed out, they could remain in the house of the deceased for three to four years. Most often, however, as prescribed by the *Family Rituals*, people are buried after three months, and in the case of poor people, after a much shorter period. Moreover, in Europe the graves are located *not* on hills or uninhabited

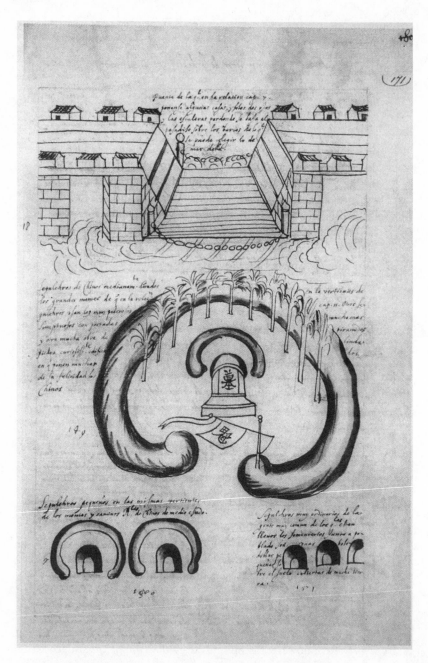

2.1. The "half-moon" structure of the Chinese tombs.

From Adriano de Las Cortes, "Relación del viage, naufragio y captiverio . . ." (1625), 171r. See also Las Cortes (2001), 463. Courtesy of British Library, mss. Sloane 1005.

places, as they frequently are in China, but within the towns near a church, and in fact very often inside a church building.[47] This is a clear difference between traditions, one that both Semedo and Pantoja make note of briefly but specifically: "The place of Sepulture, which every one provideth for himself and his posterity, [is] without the wals, for within, it is not permitted," says Semedo,[48] and as Pantoja notes, "They hold it very unluckie to borie a dead man in the Citie."[49] Semedo goes on to describe how expensive these places can be:

> There are many times little worth, in respect of the quantitie of ground they contain, but do cost them a great deal of mony, if their Astrologer do judge them lucky places, and fortunate for the Familie, for none do make choice of them, without his opinion. . . . The great men, especially the Eunuches use another way of more vast expence. For they build in such places, Sumptuous Palaces, with Halls underneath them like Cemeteries, where there are Niches fitted to receive the Coffins of the deceased.[50]

Schall von Bell gives a more detailed description of the shape of the graves:

> They are very careful to chuse a Burying-place; for if they have not Land of their own, then they purchase it at a great Rate. Those Places are principally made choice of in a dry Soyl, where no Rivers nor High-ways are near, nor any Temples or Towers, but must be on a Plain, which neither rises before nor behind. Such a Place being chosen, they surround it with a Bank of Earth lik a Half-Moon, which rises in the Middle, and runs sloaping down on both sides, yet not smooth but scollope-like; at the upper end of which they bury the eldest, and below him on each side the Sons and Nephews, not in one Grave, but every one apart under a little Hillock, and the chief of the Family under the highest Hill: In the middle on a Stone Table are plac'd variety of Provisions, Perfumes, and other things, in honor of the Deceased.[51]

The description of this tomb, with its "half-moon" shape, corresponds closely to the illustrations that are added to the manuscript version of Las Cortes' account (fig. 2.1).[52] Present-day anthropologists compare this configuration of the grave to a capital omega, while they compare the grave mound to a pregnant womb.[53] The crucial element of the tomb's architecture is the tombstone, located in the opening of the omega.

Schall gives a good description of the difference between, first, an epitaph on a tombstone (*mubei*)[54] and second, a tomb epitaph (*muzhi*)[55]:

2.2. Ordinary tombs of Han Chinese.
From the eighteenth century text *Recüeil de Tombeaux Chinois*, no. 1. Courtesy of Bibliothèque nationale de France, Cabinet des estampes, Oe 27.

The Chineses also erect a Tomb-stone, on which is Engraven the Age of the Deceased, his Office, and the Emperor's Favors to him: and to prevent the Characters from being defaced, and the remembrance of the Deceased's Exploits from being worn out, besides the Tomb-stone they bury another square Stone in the Ground with the same Inscription, that when the first is worn out, that may appear perfect, and serve as a Memorial of all his Achievements.[56]

2.3. Burial place for Manchus.
From the eighteenth-century text *Recüeil de Tombeaux Chinois*, no. 19. Courtesy of Bibliothèque nationale de France, Cabinet des estampes, Oe 27.

An eighteenth-century illustrated compilation shows that Jesuits continued to have a genuine interest in Chinese tombs. It contains the representation of twenty-two different types of tombs, for ordinary Han or Manchu people, for eunuchs, for members of the imperial family, for Buddhist monks and Daoist priests, and even for Muslims and Catholic missionaries (figs. 2.2–2.5).[57]

2.4. Burial place of an imperial prince.
From the eighteenth-century text *Recüeil de Tombeaux Chinois*, no. 21. Courtesy of Bibliothèque nationale de France, Cabinet des estampes, Oe 27.

Coffins

Since the use of coffins was rather recent in Europe, it is not surprising that the description of Christian coffins in Aleni's text is rather short:

> Coffins are made of wood, stone, or lead. Lead is used because it is not destroyed or affected by water. For the bodies of saints, coffins are made of fragrant wood

2.5. Tomb of a missionary in Beijing.
From the eighteenth-century text *Recüeil de Tombeaux Chinois*, no. 22. Courtesy of Bibliothèque nationale de France, Cabinet des estampes, Oe 27.

with outer coffins of fine stone inlaid with gold and jewels. Churches are built for them and altars erected to preserve their memory.[58]

Aleni's description of coffins for saints in Europe does not correspond to the burial practices of commoners in Europe, who were carried in a rented coffin from their home to the church and then to the graveyard, but were usually not buried with a coffin. The missionaries' familiarity with the more common and less costly European practice underlies the negative attitude toward Chinese burial practices conveyed by Semedo, who is also astonished by the money Chinese spend on a coffin:

> It is a generall custome of the whole Kingdome, not to bury any one barely in the earth, although it be a child of two daies old. Every one is to have his Chest, or Coffin according to his qualitie, and abilitie. Wherefore the rich men, (although the Chinesses are very thrifty, and parcimonious) do in this exceed all extreames, seeking out wood for that purpose, of the greatest price and esteem, that they possibly can.
>
> The Eunuches are the most excessive this way, because they have no children to inherit their wealth, giving many times five hundred or one thousand Crowns for Bords to make a Coffin, though in realitie, these are not so much worth. . . .
>
> When the Chest is made with all sort of exquisite ornament on the outside, as of gold, Charan, and other gallantries, they keep it in their house, and many time in the same chamber where they lie, with much satisfaction and contentment. As contrariwise, if, being in yeares, they have not already made it, they are alwayes ill satisfied and discontented; and truly it is a great trouble and charge to the Sons, if they have ancient Fathers, and their Funerall Chest be not yet prepared.[59]

The sealing of the corpse in an airtight coffin is one of the actions of the elementary structure of the Chinese funeral rites and was considered by many Chinese to be the most important feature. Settling the corpse in the coffin, usually constructed of wood, and packing it so that no movement was possible, were tasks assigned to paid specialists. The ceremonial hammering of nails to seal the coffin was a centerpiece of the ritual sequence, usually performed by the chief mourner or an invited guest.[60]

Missionaries clearly saw coffins as a point of significant difference from European practice:

> The place whither the Corps goeth is adorned with many figures: the Corps is put into a very great Coffin. This Nation holdeth a great part of their felicitie, for them and their Successours to consist in these things of their Funerals, especially in two, the Coffin or Chist wherein the Corps is to be layed, and the place of their buriall. The stuffe to make the Coffin of, wherein themselves are to bee buried, and the making of the Coffin, they leave not to others to doe after their

deathes, neither then may the body looke for much cost to make one of these Coffins, neither in this (as a thing of great importance) will they trust, no not their owne Sons; but they themselves at leisure seeke some kind of Wood that is least corruptible, and Plankes which are commonly foure, sixe, or eight fingers thicke: which because they bee so thicke, and the Chists or Coffins very closely shut they can keepe their Corps in their Houses without any evill smell. Some spend in making their Coffin seventy, eighty, and an hundred Duckets. They hold it for a felicity to be able to get one of these that is good; on the contrary for a great disgrace, not to have a Coffin to burie himselfe in, and they are very few which faile in that one point.[61]

Mourning Clothes

Clothes to express mourning differed considerably between European and Chinese customs. Color was the most visible difference, one which Aleni addresses in *Questions and Answers Regarding the West*:

Question: Is the color of your mourning clothes the same as in China?

Answer: In my country white garments are used for auspicious occasions; they are esteemed because they are pure and have not been dyed. For mourning rites, therefore, white is avoided and black is used instead because it suggests the idea of the darkness of the after-life. In mourning for parents, black clothes of coarse wool are worn during the first year; in the following year the black cloth used is somewhat less coarse; in the third year, the mourning clothes are discarded. There are definite periods of mourning for brothers, wives, and children. On the day of the funeral not only are the clothes worn black, but the walls of the dwelling house are also hung with black cloth.[62]

Aleni's explanation for why the Chinese take white as the color of mourning is very similar to Martini's:

The reasons why they make White to be Mourning, and not Black, is, as themselves say, because White is Natural, when as all other things are Dy'd, or Artificial; by which, as they say, is signifi'd, that in Sorrow, neither Art nor Pride must be shewn, for where a true Sorrow is, Nature sufficiently expresses it.[63]

Schall describes differences between Manchu and Chinese customs around funeral clothes. The way he described the progressive changes to mourning expressions over a three-year period in Chinese practice resembles Aleni's description of European practices:

> The Chineses and Tartars use one Colour, but not one Fashion for their Mourning.
>
> All the Tartars, both Friends and Relations, wear a long Coat of Sack Cloth, reaching down to their Feet, and gird it about their Middle with a Hempen Cord; they put on their oldest Buskins, and worst Hats, without the red Silk Fringe, which at other times they wear for an Ornament.
>
> The Hair of their Head or Beard is not shaven in all that time.
>
> After the expiration of a Moneth, every one throws in a fire of Paper, and other such Materials, their Mourning Girdle, with which they judge their Mourning to be ended, and Habit themselves again in their usual Apparel.
>
> Neighbors and acquaintance shew that they Mourn by pulling their Silk Fringe from their Hats.
>
> The Tartar Women, in the time of Mourning, change their Apparel, being usually Black, into White; their Coifs, which else are cover'd with their Hair, resemble a White Cap, with Taffels that hang over their Shoulders.
>
> The Chineses Mourning alters yearly, their first year, both Men and Women wear all over their Bodies a Sute of Sack-Cloth full of holes, with Shooes of White Cloth, and a Rope about their Wastes, seeming thus by the carelesness of their Garb, to express their sorrow for the Death of their Parents. The second year their Habit is made of sleight Cloth, their Hat of the usual Fashion, but of another Colour, their Shooes handsomer, and their Girdles of Hemp left off. The third year they may wear Silk Clothes, and their Hats of the same Stuff, but White, or else of the usual Colour, which is generally Black.[64]

China at this time had a much more elaborate system of mourning garments than did Europe. Another detailed account of Chinese mourning clothes in Dapper is based on Las Cortes' account that contains illustrations of the different mourning garments (figs. 2.6, 2.7).[65] Dapper's book gives the legend to these illustrations, but the prints themselves have been left out for some unknown reason.[66] The illustrations in Las Cortes are probably based on one or another illustrated version of *Family Rituals* or of an encyclopaedia.[67] Similar illustrations can be found, for instance, in Wang Qi's (who had passed the metropolitan examination in 1565) *Illustrated Encyclopaedia of the Three Realms* (*Sancai tuhui*, 1607).[68] (See fig. 1.1.)

There is reason to believe, however, that Las Cortes' source represented traditions from the south of China. Another picture that Dapper copied from Las Cortes shows a person whose dress corresponds very well to his description

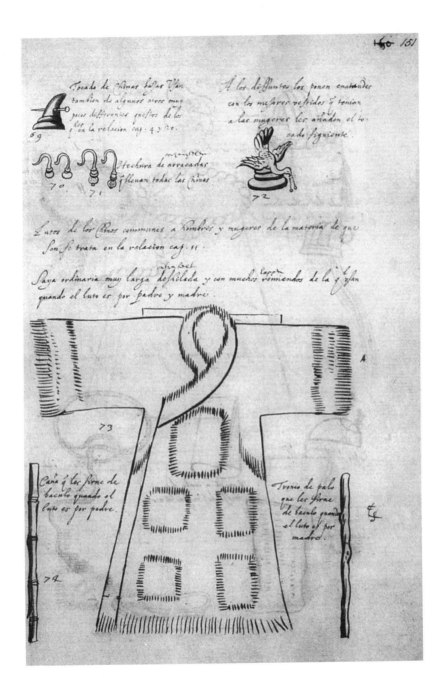

2.6. Chinese mourning clothes.
From Adriano de Las Cortes, "Relación del viage, naufragio y captiverio . . ." (1625), 151r. See also Las Cortes (2001), 395. Courtesy of British Library, mss. Sloane 1005.

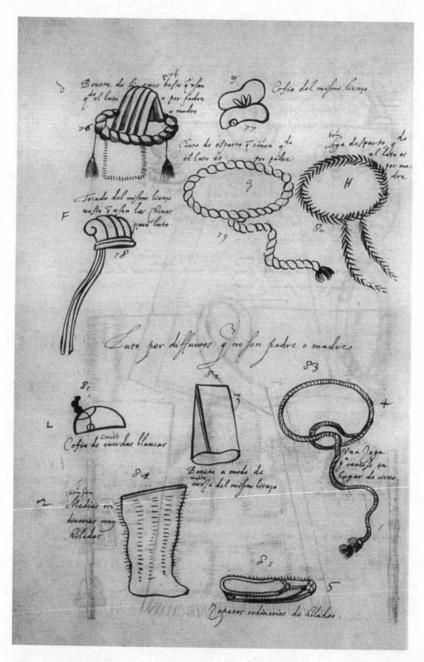

2.7. Accessories for Chinese mourning clothes, including a hempen helmet. From Adriano de Las Cortes, "Relación del viage, naufragio y captiverio . . ." (1625), 151v. See also Las Cortes (2001), 396. Courtesy of British Library, mss. Sloane 1005.

2.8. Chinese mourning clothes with hempen helmet partly covering the face.
From Adriano de Las Cortes, "Relación del viage, naufragio y captiverio . . ." (1625), 153 v. See also Las Cortes (2001), 404. Courtesy of British Library, mss. Sloane 1005.

(figs. 2.8, 2.9): "The ordinary Mourning Coat, which both Men and Women wear, is very wide, made of course white Hemp, ravel'd and full of Patches. The Sons carry a Cane in their Hands, on which they lean when their Fathers die; but when their Mothers die, a Stick or Truncheon of Wood. On their Heads the Men wear a Bonnet of course Linnen; from whence a great ravel'd Cloth hangs down over their Faces."[69] This description corresponds to the observations made by de Groot at the end of the nineteenth century in Amoy (Xiamen), close to the region where Las Cortes suffered his shipwreck. De Groot observes that male mourners wear a so-called "hempen helmet" (makui): "From the rope which goes around the head there hangs down over each ear, and also in front and at the back, a square, unhemmed piece of sackcloth, measuring only a couple of inches. These four pieces obviously represent much larger sheets which were intended to hide the entire face and the ears of the mourner, so as to render him inaccessible to any kind of impression from without; for it beseems not the mourner to have eyes or ears for anything but the loss he has sustained" (figs. 2.10, 2.11).[70]

2.9. Chinese mourning clothes with hempen helmet, adapted by Dapper from Las Cortes' drawings; a funeral procession has been added in the background.
From Olfert Dapper, *Gedenkwaerdig bedryf* . . . (1670), 414 / (1671), 378. Courtesy of Maurits Sabbe Library, Faculty of Theology, K. U. Leuven.

2.10. Hempen helmet from the Amoy area.
From Jan J. M. De Groot, *The Religious System of China* (1892–1897), vol. 2, 587, pl. xiv. Courtesy of East-Asian Library, K. U. Leuven.

2.11. Hempen helmet worn by man from the Amoy area.
From Jan J. M. De Groot, *The Religious System of China* (1892–1897), vol. 2, 588; fig. 26. Courtesy of East-Asian Library, K. U. Leuven.

Funeral Processions

The last question raised by Aleni's interlocutor concerns the funeral procession:[71]

Question: On the day of the funeral, do the relatives escort the deceased and employ music?

Answer: In my country there is a tower by the side of every church, with large bells suspended from its top. During every Mass or sermon, and for every funeral, the bells are rung to let everybody know. Funerals are attended, in addition to the relatives, by religious associations at people's request. Their members pray for the soul of the deceased to God. The chief mourner gives each person a candle to be lit and carried in the procession, so that it is illuminated brilliantly. Whether these candles be large or small, many or few, everybody strives to procure them according to his means; they are made of beeswax. At the funeral of a lay or ecclesiastical dignitary or a man of great virtue, whose merits are superior to the average, a scaffold is erected in the church (the more revered the deceased, the higher the scaffold), which may reach tens of stories. The coffin is placed on top of it, and thousands of candles are lit. After a solemn funeral Mass the coffin is taken down and buried. Also on the day of the funeral food, drink, and money are distributed among the poor to atone for the sins of the deceased and acquire merit. This is an important ceremony for which people dare not save expense. In the case of a great dignitary this may amount to thousands of ounces of silver.[72]

This description focuses more on what happens in the church than in the procession, corroborating the assumption that the church was the main liturgical place for the funeral ritual in Europe and that the prayers and acts of charity were destined to the salvation of the soul. From this single, short description of the procession, however, one may not conclude that processions were unimportant in Europe. In fact, especially in the second part of the sixteenth century, corteges became increasingly complex and crowded.[73] Yet compared to Chinese funeral corteges, they seem to have been much simpler, for several reasons. First, there was the question of distance. For city dwellers, a church was usually never very far away, with its graveyard, often called a churchyard, close by, as mentioned in the previous discussion of tombs. As a result, the mainly ecclesiastical procession had to cover only a limited distance, and with limited ecclesiastical paraphernalia. The clergy marched first, holding a cross aloft at the head of the procession and singing psalms. Behind came the confraternities—lay associations devoted to acts of charity and intercessory gestures—followed by the people carrying the coffin. Behind the corpse trailed the mourners

2.12. Catholic funeral procession in which the clergy conducts the coffin to the burial place located besides the church.
From *Book of Hours: Office of the Dead*. Rouen(?), France, early 16th century, fol. 62v. See also Wieck (1988), 128. Courtesy of Walters Art Museum, Baltimore: Walters 424; cat. no. 74.

in silence: the family, friends, and acquaintances of the deceased, along with poor people and orphans who had been paid to join the cortege. Many participants held candles; as Aleni's text highlights, the most important way to express solemnity was as much in the number of candles and torches as in their use. (See fig. 2.12.)

Extensive descriptions by missionaries of the elaborate Chinese processions show that they experienced these as quite different from their European counterparts:

> After [the period of condolence], they begin to think of the buriall, which (if they are able) is performed with a great deale of expence; if not, they leave the Chest standing at home, till they are better able; which is some times whole years first. They give notice of the funerall to their friends, by sending a Thiè to each, as at the first. Who being assembled, come presently to the place above mentioned. First of all, are carried the Pageants, which are severall great statues of men, Horses, Elephants, Lyons, Tigers, etc. They are all made of painted paper, and adorned with gilding. Besides these, are carried severall other machines, as Triumphant Chariots, Pyramids, and such like things; every thing being set out with various works, in silke, and flowres, and roses of the same materialls; all which is to be burnt, if the Person be of great qualitie. For otherwise all these are but hired, and none of them is burnt.
>
> After these Pageants, followeth the multitude of people which come to looke on; then come all their friends cloathed in mourning. After these, the Bonzi, singing out their prayers, and sounding their Cymballs. After them, come another sort of Bonzi, who weare beards, and long haire, and leading a single life, live in communitie: These go playing upon severall musicall Instruments. After these, follow another race of Bonzi, of a different sect. These are shaved, and go along also saying their prayers. After these, come the more intimate friends; after them, follow all the kinsmen; after these, come the sonnes and grand-sonnes of the deceased Person, cloathed in a very austere mourning, bare footed, with certaine staves in their hand, fashioned like those which pilgrimes carry; so short, that they are little above two palmes long; and so they go along hanging their heads downe.
>
> Immediately after these cometh the Coffin, which if it be made of precious wood, is uncovered, that it might be seen; else it is varnished over, and richly adorned with gold and Charan. It is placed on a very large Machine, carried sometimes by thirty, forty or fifty men, which is still the greater state, the more they are. Above it is fastened a Baldacchino or cloath of state, which covereth it all over head, having his rich Taffels and strings hanging downe by the sides. Neere to this on both hands, are carried many lights in great wooden frames, made like lanthorns; behind the Coffin, are carried the women, crying and lamenting in sedans fast locked, and covered all over with mourning, accompanied in the same manner by their female-friends and kindred. When they are come to the place of Sepulture, they performe severall ceremonies both before and after the Coffin is buried. And a sumptuous banquet, (which they make for all those that accompanyed the hearse) is none of the worst ceremonies among them. And this is one of the occasions, wherein they make use of those faire houses they build in those places.[74]

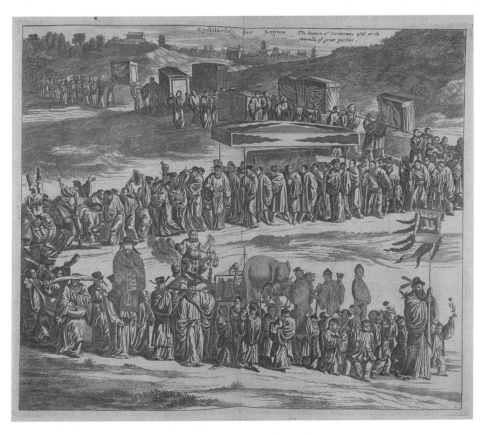

2.13. Chinese funeral procession for a "great person," conducting the coffin to the burial place out of the town.
From Olfert Dapper, *Gedenkwaerdig bedryf . . .* (1670), opposite 422–423 / (1671), opposite 388–389.
Courtesy of Maurits Sabbe Library, Faculty of Theology, K. U. Leuven.

In addition to the length and complexity of the procession with its elaborate paraphernalia, this description indicates that European and Chinese processions also contrasted in their use of music. In the European funerary procession, normally no musical instruments were used, with only the chanting of psalms interrupting the silence of the cortege.[75]

Another difference in processions is structure. At first sight, the Chinese procession resembles the three-cluster configuration of European processions, with the corpse as the most important element at the center, and two distinct and hierarchically ranked groups arranged in front and behind.[76] However, on the basis of these descriptions, it is difficult to call the coffin the physical "center" of the procession. It instead interrupts the processional sequence that is defined

Obseques des Chinois

2.14. Chinese funeral procession in an eighteenth-century European source. Different types of tombs appear in the background.

From Jean-Baptiste Du Halde, *Description . . . de la Chine* (1735), vol. 2, between 126–127 / (1736), vol. 2, between 148–149 / (1738–1741) vol. 1, between 306–307. Courtesy of Maurits Sabbe Library, Faculty of Theology, K. U. Leuven.

in terms of gender or in terms of family relationship; in the above-mentioned description by Trigault the sons follow behind the bier. Yet as a symbolic center it draws its charisma from the fact that the corpse is concealed, and it gains its symbolic significance not only from the people but also from the insignia, ritual objects, music, and lamentation that precede and succeed it.

The importance of the processions and the impression they made on the missionaries is also evident from the partly imaginative illustrations included in such European writings as Dapper's[77] and later European sources (figs. 2.13, 2.14).[78] Illustrated versions of *Family Rituals* and encyclopaedia also include images showing the order and major components of a funerary procession (fig. 2.15).[79]

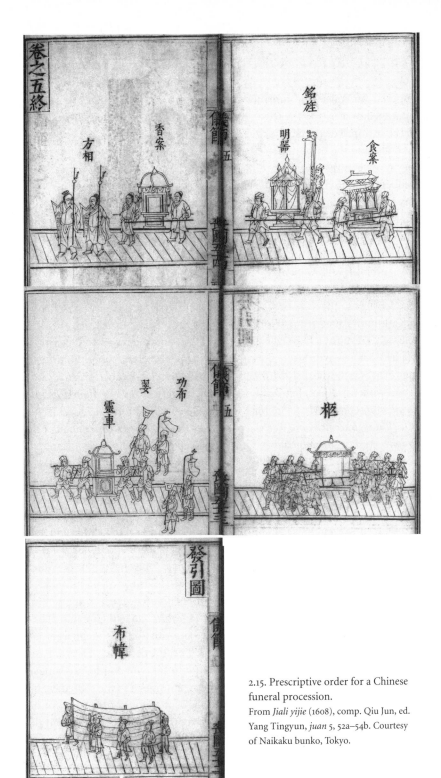

2.15. Prescriptive order for a Chinese funeral procession.

From *Jiali yijie* (1608), comp. Qiu Jun, ed. Yang Tingyun, *juan* 5, 52a–54b. Courtesy of Naikaku bunko, Tokyo.

REPORTS ON IMPERIAL FUNERALS

Imperial funerals—the mortuary rites for the emperor, the empress, the empress dowager, and the wives or concubines of the emperor—deserve special attention. They occupy a large portion of Dapper's description of Chinese funerals, and the importance attached to them corresponds to the emphasis they receive in the original Jesuit sources. Such funerals did not happen very frequently, but when they took place they caught the attention of the Jesuit missionaries, who were greatly impressed by them. The first imperial demise after the Jesuits had settled in Beijing in 1601 occurred in 1614. The imperial consort Lishi, natural mother of the Wanli Emperor, known after 1571 as Empress Dowager Cisheng, died on Wanli 42/2/9, or 18 March 1614.[80] At that time several Jesuits were active in Beijing, among them the aforementioned Álvaro de Semedo and Diego de Pantoja, as well as Manuel Dias junior (1574–1657), visitor to the missions, and Sabatino De Ursis (1575–1620).

Communication from China reached Europe relatively quickly; by 1620, six years after Empress Dowager Cisheng's death, an account of it appeared in Madrid. Francisco de Herrera Maldonado, a Spanish cleric and minor literary figure (he was the Castilian translator of Fernão Mendez-Pinto's *Peregrinação*),[81] reports extensively on her death in *A Short History of the Kingdom of China, Death of its Queen, Mother of the King who Reigns Presently, which Occurred in March 1617. Sacrifices and Ceremonies of Her Burial. With a Description of this Empire. And the Introduction of Our Holy Catholic Faith* (*Epitome historial del Reyno de la China, muerta de su Reyna, madre de Este Rey que oy viue, que sucedio a treinta de Março del Año de mil y seiscientos y diez y siete. Sacrificios y Ceremonias de su Entierro. Con la Description de aquel Imperio. Y la Introduccion en el de nuestra Santa Fe Catolica*).[82] This work, which by 1622 had already been translated into French,[83] is a compilation of information about China and Asia, drawn from more than seventy different sources that are acknowledged at the end of the work.[84] In chapters thirteen through seventeen—about one quarter of the book—the author discusses the death, interment, and burial ceremonies of the mother of the Wanli Emperor. This section is based on "three booklets," so far unidentified, that the Beijing Jesuits had in their hands. These apparently official sources provided detailed information on the different sacrifices and ceremonies from death to burial.[85] Yet the description is also based on what the Jesuits saw themselves. Semedo, in his own words, was an eyewitness[86] and Dias took active part in some ceremonies. On the sixth day after Cisheng's death, for instance, when officials went to the court to lament her demise and to present condolences to the emperor, Dias participated in this ceremony as well and the emperor received his letter of condolence in person.[87] The whole report may well have been partly composed in Macao, where the Beijing Jesuits, except for Dias, lived after they were expelled from Beijing in 1617.

The funeral is better known, however, through its description in chapter seventeen of Semedo's *The History of that Great and Renowned Monarchy of China*, which Dapper would later use.[88] Semedo's depiction may be read as a summary of the account in Herrera Maldonado's book, and both possibly had the same text as their source. Semedo first describes the funeral rites performed in the palace in the first five days after death, and then the different rules issued for the mourning of officials and commoners in Beijing and the whole country. Then follows the description of the burial rites: from the transfer of the coffin, which started on Wanli 42/6/9, or 15 July 1614, exactly four months after the death, till the burial itself on Wanli 42/6/15, or 21 July 1614. This section includes the instructions for the preparation of the funeral and descriptions of the coffin and chariot and the different steps of the transfer. All these events are recounted in much more detail than the account given in the official *Veritable Records of the Ming* (*Ming shilu*), which were compiled after the death of an emperor and were based on archival documents, especially edicts and memorials.[89] Semedo's chapter also contains a brief account of the death of the Wanli Emperor, who died on Wanli 48/7/21 (18 August 1620), and a translation of his last will and testament, which can also be found in *Veritable Records of the Ming*. There is no description of its ceremonies "because they are the same with those we have already related."[90]

The other funeral receiving extensive attention is that of the Shunzhi Emperor, who died on Shunzhi 18/1/7 (the night of 5–6 February 1661). In Schall von Bell's *Historical Narration*, it occupies chapter twenty-four, from which Dapper quotes extensively.[91] This account is based on Schall's eyewitness report. Schall's relation with the Shunzhi Emperor had been remarkably close and personal. The Manchu term *mafa*, meaning "master" or "teacher," the title the emperor used to address him, illustrates the nature of that relationship. Schall, who had visited the emperor a few days before his death, took part in several of the mourning ceremonies. His description is much shorter than the one of the funeral of Wanli's mother, but it contains all the principal stages of a funeral: the ceremonies of the first seven days, including the limits imposed on the ceremonies and the oath taken by the officials for the new emperor; the transfer of the coffin from the palace to the temporary repository on Shunzhi 18/2/2, or 2 March 1661; the end of the mourning on the twenty-seventh day; the continuation of the ceremonies and sacrifices till the hundredth day; and a brief reference to the proper burial in the grave two years later. In this case, as in the case of the earlier imperial funeral, the description is in several ways more detailed than in the official *Veritable Records of the Qing (Qing shilu)*, partly because of Schall's personal involvement.[92] In addition to this funeral, Dapper also selected Schall's short description of the funeral of one of the Shunzhi Emperor's concubines, Dong shi, who died on Shunzhi 17/8/19, or 23 September 1660, probably because it shows that it was "a very great Funeral" with many "wasteful ceremonies."[93]

These descriptions confirm modern analyses of imperial funerals.[94] The sequence of rites for the death of a member of the imperial family, from the initial public notification of death to the final expulsion of the corpse from the community, was fundamentally the same as the sequence of the death ritual for a commoner.[95] Though these descriptions mostly concentrate on the public rituals (which usually appear in the *Veritable Records*), they also contain a fair number of references to the private rituals conducted in the palace. The account of the funeral of Wanli's mother, for instance, describes in a day by day order the different initial rituals of dressing the corpse, encoffining, and putting on mourning dress, and how the Wanli Emperor was personally involved in several of these ceremonies.[96]

The rituals of state sacrifices and ceremonies receive the most attention. Semedo, particularly, brings them to the forefront of his descriptions through his explicit observations:

> On the eighth day, were made Sacrifices to Heaven, Earth, the Planets, Mountaines, and Rivers, with great Solemnitie, when these were ended, the King commanded, that the same Sacrifices should be made to the nine Gates of the Palace, through which the Corps of the deceased Queen was to passe, and to the Tutelar Angels of them, as also the six Bridges of the River, which runneth through the Palace offering in all these places living creatures, Aromaticks, wine made with severall Spices and ingredients, and diverse other perfumes.[97]

Such sacrificial offerings marked each of the rituals performed while the coffin lay in state, then moved to temporary storage, and was finally interred. In addition to the offering of animal sacrifices and wine libations, the Qing emperors also adopted the Chinese practice of the burning of paper replicas of such items as money, ingots, furniture, clothing, servants, and houses. The tremendous quantity of paper goods was a major expenditure, as was the loss of the deceased's clothing, furniture, and utensils that were burned as offerings together with the paper goods for the use of the deceased in the next life.[98] A description of the sacrifices on the twenty-seventh day, marking the end of the mourning period for the Shunzhi Emperor, illustrates the overall abundance of such sacrifices:

The next Morning, being the twenty-seventh day after the Emperor's Death, they all met again by the Corps, and every one standing in their appointed Places began their general Lamentation. Having perform'd all Ceremonies as on the day before, the Letter given by the Emperor to his Son, containing the Praise due to the Deceased, was publickly read; whereupon the Magistrates doubling their Shreeks and Cries, return'd into the base Court, whilst four of the chiefest Persons of Quality going to the Paper Mountain, cover'd with yellow Silk, carry'd in an open Cloth, a Sable Sute of the deceased Emperor, with his Hat rais'd on the Crown with Pearls and Diamonds, and likewise a Sable Quilt whereon to lay his Head. Others in ten Carpets bore ten several Sutes more of the Emperor's; and Saddles and Caparisons for Horses were also laid on the Heap, besides Flags, Fans, Gold Plates, and the Emperor's Sedan; all which being brought to the Heap of Paper, cover'd with yellow Silk, they set on fire, and threw in the Tables full of Flannel Clothes, many Gold and Silver Vessels, which being melted stream'd down the Hill like a Rivulet. Then the Governors unty'd their Girdles, which being of white Cloth, they had fastned about their Middle, and so throwing them into the Flame they were released of their Mourning. Lastly, they pull'd off all their Mourning Habit, and leaving it there went home.[99]

The original Latin version mentions that tables with "ten thousand pieces" of silk were thrown into the fire. The translator may have considered this to be an exaggeration, but the description of the same sacrifice in *Supplementary Regulations and Precedents to the Institutes of the Great Qing Dynasty* (*Qinding daQing huidian zeli*, completed 1764, printed 1768) confirms the extent of the objects being burned.

> On the third day [of the second month, or 3 March 1661], they performed the first sacrifice. The Emperor went in person to display the cap and vestments [of the deceased emperor], one red banner [with the names and titles] made in paper, two hundred and five thousand ounces of gold and silver [in paper], one hundred and forty-five thousand ingots of paper money, ten thousand *duan* of color painted tissue (in paper), fifty thousand pieces of paper silk, eighty-one tables of sacrificial banquets, twenty-seven mutton, and forty-one vessels of wine. The escort carriage was prepared before the main gate of the Shouhuangdian. The princes and the officials under them, the princesses and princes-consorts and the fourth-grade officials under them, up to the guards and court ladies of third class, all gathered together and knelt when the *jiwen* was read.
>
> After its reading, the Emperor offered a libation of three cups of wine, and all performed the kowtow three times and enchanted the lamentations. After the sacrifice, the reader of the *jiwen*, by order [of the emperor] went to set the fire,

and the three cups of wine of the libation were also burned. When this was finished, everybody retired. That day was the twenty-seventh day. The Emperor took off his mourning dress, and the others also took it off.[100]

In general, relatively little mention is made of the Buddhist and Daoist services that were performed on behalf of the deceased in the palace or in the temples. These private services are not mentioned in the official Chinese sources either. In Herrera Maldonado, reference to Buddhist monks or Daoist priests is sporadic and their actions associated with the Devil, but they earn scarce mention in Semedo's version of the events.[101] In Schall's description of Shunzhi's funeral, they are also only briefly mentioned, but in his account of the funeral of the concubine Dong, Schall takes greater note of them with a story that is not adopted by Dapper. Schall does not focus on Buddhist ceremonies themselves, but remarks instead on the introduction of a larger number of monks in court. He is of the opinion that concubine Dong's death was more damaging than anything she did when alive: "Through her death she made [the emperor] fall into a madness more repulsive than the one of Salomon, because he openly displayed himself as a disciple of the Bonzes, shaving his head, and living and dressing himself like them."[102]

Despite their similarities, these descriptions also bring to light two major distinctions between imperial funerals and those of commoners. The ceremonies surrounding imperial funerals are on a much grander scale, performed with great splendor, the observation of which compels Semedo to treat them in a separate chapter.[103] The material richness of the ritual objects and paraphernalia not only revealed the wealth of the reign, but also added lustre to the event. Jesuits were sensitive to the magnitude of these funerals, apparently never having experienced anything similar in Europe.[104] But the Chinese, too, rarely saw such an event: "If the people of the country itself find [such funerals] so agreeable to watch, how much more receptive then should foreigners be to their narration?" the French version of Herrera Maldonado's text rhetorically asks.[105] This may explain why the missionaries describe the events in such detail. While the official Chinese sources pay much attention to the ritual performances that are repeated day by day, recording all the bowings and lamentations, the European sources not only stress the different "ceremonies,"[106] but include precise descriptions of the material side of the ceremonies, such as the chariot prepared for Wanli's mother.[107] Such details are not found in the official Chinese sources. Another example is the detailed description of the procession for accompanying the coffin of the Shunzhi Emperor to its temporary location at Jingshan, outside the Forbidden City, on the second day of the second month. There it would lie in state and receive daily offerings until the final interment.[108] Schall participated in this procession, and describes its elaborateness in great detail:

> Thither came all the Grandees Habited [among whom Father Adam Schall for the reason of his office] in white Mourning, to accompany the Corps, before went nine Elephants with Turrets on their Backs; forty Camels, caparison'd with red Cloths and Bridles plated with Gold, and rich Symiters hanging down by their Necks, were loaden with Tents and other Furniture: then follow'd an hundred Horses, led by yellow Bridles, without Gold, except the Buckles, which were onely Gilded: next in order were Drums, Trumpets, and other with Instrumental Musick to the number of a hundred; behind which were carry'd fifty Gilded Hammers, and above an hundred Flags of several colours, with wild Beasts, Birds, and twenty eight Stars, stitch'd with Thred of Gold; then again fifty Hammers, after which were led a hundred Saddled Horses, the last thirty laden with rich Flannel, and the Emperor's Clothes condemn'd to the Fire; next these came twenty Youths, every one holding an Imperial Quiver, imboss'd with Pearls and Precious Stones, besides Bowes and Arrows, and just before them walk'd twelve Greyhounds; behind these came the Emperor's Sedan, born by sixteen Men, in which when living he us'd to be carry'd, richly Gilt, and on the top adorn'd with a Golden Ball; the Bearers were clad in a Livery of a Saffron colour, Embroider'd with Roses of Gold; next them were carry'd several Gold and Silver Chargers; behind which follow'd the Bier with the Emperor's Corps, cover'd with Cloth of Tissue, Embroider'd with blue Clouds and Flowers, supported by thirty two Bearers, all in a Saffron-colour'd Livery, and adorn'd with Golden Roses; behind the Corps came Soldiers with Pikes and other Arms; then the Emperor's Mother in a Sedan cover'd with Purple-Silk; next hers, seven more cover'd with white Cotton, in every one of which was a Queen, or Concubine of the Emperor's; then follow'd many Grandees on Foot; lastly, all the Magistrates, and those that shew'd Reverence by kneeling and bowing to the Corps as it pass'd by, follw'd disorderly one among another to the Grave, which was inviron'd with a Wall, but the multitude pulling it down, quickly made room for all comers.[109]

Although these details have so far only been found in European and not Chinese sources,[110] they nevertheless show that the many ritual signs that accompany the funeral procession affirm the central place of the emperor, even if only his corpse, in the Chinese realm of the living.

The second aspect that distinguishes imperial funerals from those of commoners was the number of the participants. In the case of imperial death, not only did immediate kin, the larger descent group, and officials observe the mourning practices, but every citizen was required to observe them as well.

The account in Herrera Maldonado contains an extensive description of all the regulations issued on the occasion of the funeral of Wanli's mother. Semedo gives a succinct list of them, which corresponds closely to the regulations found in *Veritable Records of the Ming*.[111] These give a very good idea of the totality of the mourning. Not only were different classes of people involved, but the external signs of grief were widespread, expressed through prescribed ritual ceremonies, dress, food, and sound. The regulations dictated:

> First, that all Mandarines, both of the Gowne and Sword, should make their appearance at the Palace the day following, to bewaile the deceased Queen: which done, without returning to their houses, they should go directly to their Tribunalls, there to remain and keep a fast for three daies, without eating flesh, fish, or eggs, or drinking any wine. That done, for the space of other three daies, they should come all to the gates of the Palace, and there in their order, one by one, should make foure accustomed reverences, with some other externall signes of griefe, and then returne home to their houses.
>
> The second: that all the wives of the Mandarines, from the first to the fourth degree, cloathed from head to foot in close mourning, should assemble at the same place, and for the space of three days lament in the like manner: and that afterwards, at their owne houses, for the space of twenty seaven days, they should not put on their Jewells, ornaments, etc.
>
> The third: that those of the Royall Councell, called Han Lin [Hanlin] should all make Poems, verses, and compositions in praise of the deceased Queen.
>
> The fourth: that they of the Quan Lo Su [Guanglusi], that is, the Officers of the Kings exchequer and revenue, should, with all diligence and liberalitie, provide what ever was necessary, for the sacrifices and other expences of the funerall.
>
> The fifth: that all the Bonzi, and ministers of the Idols, should ring their bells for a long time, as a signe of sorrow and griefe.
>
> The sixth: that for thirteen daies there should be no flesh killed, or sold in the shambles: but that all should fast, as the King did; who, for the first three days, did eat only a little rice boyled in faire water, and the rest of the time, pulse only.
>
> The seaventh: there was order given to the President of the Councell or rites and ceremonies, and to those of the chamber, that they should present mourning garments to all the Embassadours, who did then actually reside in the Court; and that they should be brought to the Palace and performe one day the ceremonies and compliments in like manner as the people of the Country did.
>
> The eighth: that all Mandarines, that had finished their government, and all new pretenders should come for three days to the Palace, to do the same reverence and ceremonies.

The ninth: that the common people, for a week together, should do the same, morning and evening, at the Palace of the Governour of the City.[112]

This is followed by instructions for the officials and common people in the provinces. By describing how the whole country had to mourn, the author reinforces the idea that funerals were a basic value for the whole country.

These descriptions of the imperial death rituals confirm the pre-eminent and unique position of the emperor in the Chinese world view.[113] Yet compared to accounts of European royal funerals, such as descriptions of the funeral for Philip II of Spain, the authors of these reports about the funerals of Chinese emperors make little attempt to develop concepts of royal sacredness that were so central in Europe.[114] Through the depiction of rituals that variously appear as superstitious or admirable in the eyes of the authors, the narratives underscore the human albeit sophisticated nature of the Chinese emperor rather than a sacred and divine one.

CONCLUSION

The descriptions by European authors of Chinese funerals are texts with many different layers, each of them originating within a different context and aiming at a different audience. For instance, Ricci's account is partly based on earlier notes compiled by himself and also on (travel) reports written by others, some of which served as internal communication within the Society of Jesus. His story in the Italian original had initially been written with a European audience in mind. Trigault not only translated it into Latin, but also, in the context of his propaganda tour, further adapted it for a broader European audience. In Dapper, this information is selected so as to document the Dutch East India Company's embassies to China with ethnographic descriptions. As a Protestant he is critical of ritualism, an attitude conveyed through small remarks such as the one in his comparative description of a Chinese funeral procession—"which is perform'd like the Romans Processioning."[115] Moreover, like other Protestant texts of his time, Dapper's book, unlike Ricci's, was not intended to support a call for a Christian expedition targeting the conversion of the Chinese. These changing contexts show that, together with changing rhetorical styles, very different interests were involved in the use of the same material.

Yet the depictions of funerals occupy a separate place in these overall accounts. Compared to the sections that describe the success or failure of the Christian or commercial expeditions, the sections on funerals belong to proto-ethnographic descriptions of China and give a fairly good insight into the funeral practices in seventeenth-century China. They also reflect the experience of "otherness" in which the authors were involved. As such they contain a dialogic element, since they not only reflect the authorial voice of the authors but also stage the distinct and diverse voices of the "other."[116] These descriptions can therefore be evaluated in terms of how their narrators perceived themselves in relation to the Chinese cultural tradition. According to cultural philosopher Tzvetan Todorov, there are three axes from which to approach the question of otherness.[117] First is the axiological level, the degree to which experiencing the other involves a judgment of values: the other is good or bad, liked or disliked, equal or inferior. In the many quotations above there appears, on the whole, little value judgment. The texts cited are mainly of a descriptive character; even in the description of the Buddhist and Daoist ceremonies to which the missionaries were opposed, authors' opinions barely surface. Certainly, value judgment is not absent in these texts, as is clear from small interruptions, such as "Funerals, which may rather be call'd glorious Show," or the disapproval of the Shunzhi Emperor's expenses for the funeral of his concubine Dong, which are indicative of a critical attitude toward outward shows of wealth at funerals. But taken as a whole, few such evaluative words appear. These texts rarely judge Chinese funerary traditions as being good or bad, liked or disliked. There is, however, one major exception. While these texts esteem the way the Chinese value funerals more than Europeans do, Chinese funerals often appeared to the missionaries as being too expensive, sometimes even extravagant. The sense of extravagance is polysemic. In the case of imperial funerals, the Europeans convey, through their lengthy and detailed descriptions, an attitude of admiration. But in another sense some aspects of funerals are considered too pompous, with the Chinese spending too much money on them, especially on the coffin, the tomb, and the paraphernalia of the procession.[118] Their reaction joins the attitude of some Chinese gentry who in the late Ming criticized the extravagance of funerals, though for different reasons.

The overall value judgment should rather be sought in the presentation of funerals within the broader depiction of Chinese culture. Inspired by the hierarchical classification of cultures from barbarian to civilized,[119] the authors of these texts made efforts to represent China as a civilized country, which in many regards was equal to Europe, and from which in some aspects Europeans could even learn. Though these texts concede that the Chinese funeral may contain some idolatrous components, it is nevertheless depicted as part of a very sophisticated ritual system.

The second of Todorov's three axes, the praxeological level, is the study of how human behavior is governed by the rapprochement with or extraction from the other: one adopts the values of or identifies with the other, or, having imposed one's own image, the other is assimilated; between submission to the other and submission of the other there is also the option of neutrality or indifference. Probably because of their descriptive and less evaluative character, the Jesuit accounts of Chinese funerals use few words that express identification and therefore are rather indifferent with regard to rapprochement. This is again due to the particular genre of these descriptions as reports or accounts; their distant approach is enforced, for example, by the fact that Dapper himself never went to China but compiled his book on the basis of descriptions by others. As will be seen later, other sources, such as personal letters on participation in funerals or reports on ritual debates, are less distant and more clearly express rapprochement or extraction. Again there are some exceptions in the texts that were analyzed above. Semedo, for example, notices that "Europeans make little ado about their Funerals, whereas the Chineses esteem nothing more."[120] This opinion is shared by at least Pantoja and Martini.[121] At the end of his description, Semedo becomes even more lofty and reveals his purpose of evangelization through an initial admiration of Chinese values:

> Truly there is nothing in China, so worthy to be imitated by Christians, as their piety towards their Parents, and God having given to this Nation such knowledge and inclination to vertue, it is [a] great pittie, that they should only want the foundation of faith. Hence we may see, with how great fruit and profit the Gospel might be preached in this Kingdome, or rather by the goodnesse of the Lord, it is already preached, as we shall declare in its proper place.[122]

In Todorov's third approach, at the epistemological level, there is no absolute but rather an infinite gradation between lesser and greater states of knowledge—acknowledging or ignoring the identity of the other. As Trigault's comments concerning his method and aims illustrate, the authors of these early texts exhibit a clear willingness towards gaining greater knowledge about the other. The information reported is based on various sources involving both Chinese and Jesuits: Chinese primary sources, information provided by the Chinese collaborators of the Jesuits, and eyewitness reports by the Jesuits themselves. The result is that even in shorter reports, such as Trigault's, the writers demonstrate an extensive knowledge about Chinese funerals. Dapper's accumulative style, without doubt, strengthens the idea that he wants to disseminate a thorough knowledge of his subject. Moreover, these authors clearly wanted to transmit their knowledge of the Chinese other to the European reader. For the Jesuits, their reports belonged to a whole system of information produced by means of annual letters, destined to reach both the inner circuit of the Jesuits and a wider European audience. The encyclopaedic way in which

Dapper treats his subject, and the fact that his work was less aimed at propaganda to support a mission of conversion, made this information even more available to the European reader. To transmit this information, the authors used the language and the categories appropriate to their European audience. But even if the contemporary universalistic classificatory schemes, dividing people into Christians and gentiles, were not far away, as will appear from a comparison with other depictions, such schemes do not come into view in these proto-ethnographic sections. As pointed out earlier, these descriptions of behavior rather tend to be independent from any serious analysis of beliefs, and are interpreted in terms of civility rather than Christianity.

These sources not only describe the "other," but in doing so, they also project an image of the "self." That the other and self can as such be identified is of particular advantage for a comparative approach: the sources highlight the differences between the Chinese and European funeral practices as they were practised in the seventeenth century, confirming a number of differences already noticed and which will be important for subsequent analysis. These differences can be summarized as follows. The time between the moment of death and burial is long in China (up to several months) and short in Europe (one or two days). In China the major location for the rituals preceding burial is the home of the dead; in Europe it is the church. The length of the pre-burial period explains the different attitudes towards the corpse: in China the corpse has to be preserved in an airtight coffin, while in Europe the corpse is transported in a reusable coffin and often wrapped only in linen for burial. In China rituals of condolence are offered in the period between encoffining and entombment, with family members the main actors in all these ceremonies while specialists play only a secondary role. Conversely, in Europe the main actors are the priests while family members play a secondary role. The corpse is transported to a place of burial outside the Chinese village or town in a grand procession; in Europe, the corpse is conveyed to its grave in a simple procession and is buried inside or near the church. These differences are exemplified by the imperial funerals in China.

3 / The Gradual Embedding of Christian Funeral Rituals in China

When Matteo Ricci settled in China in 1583, it was not clear what shape Christian funerary rituals would take in this new environment. Through different phases of cultural interaction over the course of the next century, Christian rituals gradually became embedded into Chinese society. In the initial period missionaries adopted a purist and exclusivist approach, stressing the necessity of sober and fundamentally Christian funerals. Next followed a time of experimentation, mainly by Chinese Christians, which led to various types of adaptation as well as to the reframing of Christian prescriptive texts. Finally, after the Manchu invasion, it was primarily Christian associations that were taking care of funerals.

FROM SEPARATION TO JUXTAPOSITION

Writing the history of ritual contacts between two cultures from the point of view of interaction could plausibly start with the experience of the receiving culture. Primary sources, however, impose a serious limit on this approach, since for the initial thirty years, corresponding to Ricci's arrival until his death in 1610, no relevant documents written by the Chinese have survived, only ones by the European missionaries. The major source, Ricci's and Trigault's account of the Christian expedition into China, contains no systematic discussion of contemporary Christian funerals that would be equivalent to its proto-ethnographic descriptions of Chinese funeral rites. References to Christian funerals in China are limited in number and are dispersed throughout the text.[1] This can be partially explained by the fact that, in this initial period, Christian funerals were infrequent because the Christian community in China was not large—two thousand five hundred Christians and sixteen Jesuits, of whom eight were Chinese, in 1610. In such a context, missionaries above all aimed at spreading the Christian faith, and in terms of ritual practices they separated themselves from the Chinese cultural environment, while focussing on the major sacramental rituals, such as baptism, confession, and Eucharist. Beginning in the 1620s, however, documents written by Chinese appear, and they illustrate a new juxtaposition of *Family Rituals* with Christian rituals.

Initial Purist Approach

In the beginning, the Jesuits were hardly aware that the importance of funeral rites in China would have consequences for themselves. For instance, when António de Almeida, SJ (1557–1591), died in Shaozhou, Guangdong, the Chinese could not understand why Ricci and his companions did not wear a mourning garb. The Jesuits, Ricci says, explained that "we religious, when we enter into religion, are like dead to the world, and therefore we do not make such a thing of this fate."[2] In the end the house servants were allowed to wear mourning garments during the condoling period. The only other accommodation the Jesuits made to local custom, apparently, was the purchase of a first-class coffin, "in order to show to the Chinese the quality of the Fathers, because herein they demonstrate their way of honouring the dead." The major reason for buying a coffin, however, according to Ricci's explanation, was that they could not bury him in a church, as would have been done in Europe. Chinese custom would prohibit anyone entering any building that had a body buried in it, but the Jesuits did not want to follow the Chinese practice of burying him "on a hill far away from the house." Using a coffin allowed them to postpone burial; the coffin was then kept in their residence for two years until the Rector of the College of Macao decided upon a burial place in Macao.[3]

As far as the specific funerary rituals are concerned, in these early years the Jesuits adopted an approach that can be characterized as purist concerning the Christian tradition and exclusivist with regard to the Chinese traditions. In general, Ricci and his fellow Jesuits were less tolerant in the early stages of their missionary activities than later, though they adhered to no specific regulation. If death occurred, the Jesuits' priority was to bury the deceased— Chinese Christian or foreign missionary—according to Christian rites. There was little intention of accommodating local custom. The Christian rites were based on a European template reflected in the major Catholic prescriptive texts: the Office of the Dead, Mass with absolution, and burial with Christian prayers. Interaction with Chinese funerary rituals was restricted. In the beginning years missionaries did not yet differentiate between Confucian and Buddhist or Daoist funeral rites. They were hardly able to do so, since in the majority of the cases that they could observe, these traditions were interwoven with each other. The abstention from local rites by Christians was therefore seen by the Jesuits as a sign that helped to strengthen and spread the Christian faith. For instance, in

1601, when there were about twenty neophytes in the Christian community of Nanjing led by the Portuguese Jesuit João Soerio (1566–1607), Ricci reports:

> These few Christians proceeded with much fervour, visiting the church to come for Mass on feast days, though it was at a distance of one mile and more. They used to submit their doubts and cases of conscience in order to know what they had to do, and they used to confess publicly to be Christians. And they used to abstain from gentile rites at the sepulture of the dead and other occasions. This helped a lot to spread more our Holy Faith.[4]

This passage, which is written like a summary, stresses in the first place the observance of the Christian rites by a small and rather exclusive community, wherein one abstained from "gentile rites." This exclusive attitude appears also on the occasion of the death of a certain Paul Qin in Nanjing in the same year.

> [His son Martin] did not engage in rituals that did not conform to the rituals of the Christians. It was something needed because of the good example given to others. This was not easy because it was never seen that a man of his quality held funerals without the display of the ministers of the idols, while Ours were not present in time to perform all the ecclesiastical ceremonies.[5]

Martin made a public announcement that could be read by everybody, stating that his father died a Christian and had forbidden the ministers of the idols to come to his funeral. When the Jesuits arrived a few days later, they held in their chapel "a beautiful funeral, in the presence of his sons, dressed in mourning, and other Christians, everybody remaining much consoled by it."[6] According to the Trigault translation, this was the first time these converts saw a Christian funeral, and they departed from the custom to keep the corpse in the house for a long time before burial.[7] The following year, still in Nanjing, a certain Zhu, who fell sick some time after he had been baptized, left orders for his wife that "at his burial none of the ceremonies of the gentiles should be used, but in everything follow what the Fathers ordered." This approach is also said to have had a very salutary effect on all the converts.[8] And at the funeral of Fabio, who died at the age of eighty-two in Beijing in 1605, "no rituals were used other than those which our Fathers had said were licit in Christianity."[9] The family members and Christians are said to have been admired by the neighbours for the "new way of funerals" (*modo novo di essequie*), and for having posted a statement at the door saying that "no bonze or priest of the idols should enter there." Moreover, Fabio's wife was edified by the fact that the Jesuits performed their rituals for free, thus saving her money that she otherwise would have had to spend on the "priests of the idols."[10] These short references are explicit concerning the rejection of gentile ceremonies in favor of the strict application of Christian ceremonies, but, with the exception of the vague reference to the mourning dress, they are silent about which Chinese rites were accepted. They depict a Christian community that is ritually separate from its environment.

Only gradually were some Chinese funerary customs accepted. This happened first through the initiative of the Chinese themselves and was largely due to the network in which the deceased Jesuit or Christian had been involved. As long as this network was very small, the funeral could be limited to an exclusively Christian ceremony. When this network was larger, however, the chances of interaction with Chinese funeral practices increased. For instance, when the Jesuit Soerio died in Nanchang in 1607, his fellow Jesuits did "not give expression to their sentiments, as was usual in China," because "it did not correspond to our profession." Yet their friends, dressed in mourning, came to their house to condole with them. These Chinese friends installed a bier and covered it as if his body was there. "They made four genuflections, and touched each time with their head the ground." Many are said to have mourned the death of this Jesuit. Some, possibly both Christian and non-Christian, wore a mourning dress for some time, "and when asked why they did so, they answered that it was for this Father, their teacher."[11] This story shows that while the Jesuits themselves opted for a limited funeral for their companion, the local Chinese environment forced them to adopt a more explicit mourning, including several Chinese customs such as the four genuflections and the mourning dress.

Similar imperatives towards accommodation occurred when Christians of relatively high social status died, as was the case with the father of Xu Guangqi (1562–1633) who passed away in Beijing on 23 May 1607, in the same year as the Jesuit Soerio. Xu himself, known as "Doctor Paul," was baptized as a Christian in 1603:

> At that time the father of Doctor Paul died. Therefore, following the usage of China, the whole capital came to wail at his house and to console him with very grave ceremonies. And while he showed much affection for his father and made him a coffin of incorruptible wood such as cedar, with a value of one hundred and twenty scuti according to his status, he nevertheless was very careful in these rites not to perform any ritual against the rules of Christianity, deliberating in everything with the Fathers. In this capital, this was something very new and not yet seen.
>
> After a few days Ours erected a catafalque in the house, covered with black damask; and with many candles and perfumes, which the son had offered, they

held the solemn Office [of the Dead], he being present, dressed in mourning, which consisted of a rough garment of heavy cotton, with beret, belt and footwear all rather fantastic in white, which is the mourning colour; next they also said Mass. With this he and all the Christians were very satisfied.

Afterwards Doctor Paul carried the coffin of his father back home [to Shanghai]; he remained there during the mourning according to the laws of this kingdom.[12]

This text makes several references to Chinese practices such as the extensive condolence ceremonies, the expensive coffin, and the white mourning dress. The author's specific mention that no rituals were performed "against the rules of Christianity" suggests that the openness to Chinese rituals was an approach of prudence. Central to this description of the ritual are the Catholic ceremonies, such as the Office of the Dead and the Mass, in which the European black is maintained as the mourning color. That Catholic ceremonies were important for the reporting Jesuit is also evident at the burial ceremony of Xu's father in Shanghai:

He celebrated the funeral of his father with all the display of the ceremonies of the Church, even though they could not be performed with such perfection because the Father [Lazzaro Cattaneo, SJ (1560–1640)] was alone without companion. But even in such a condition, it was of much consolation to all, showing that the Christians had lost nothing with the religion they had embraced, instead the funerals winning in solemnity with the beautiful ceremonies of the Catholic Church.[13]

As the Christian communities continued to grow, the interaction with local rituals increased as well. Two years later, at the death of Bartolomeo Tedeschi, SJ (1572–1609) on 25 July in Shaozhou, Trigault not only mentions the practice of Chinese condolence rituals, but also reflects on past experiences:

After his death, he was bewailed by all the Christians and friends following all the norms of the Chinese style, because the Fathers now knew the rites to be observed in such circumstances; due to ignorance, these had been unclear at the death of those who died at the beginning of the mission.[14]

The prudent approach of the past is here explained on the basis of ignorance, thus admitting that changes were to occur. Funeral practices show that in this initial period, Christianity in China resembled a voluntary society, composed of rather strict and committed Christian believers bound to each other by their participation in the same rituals. The exclusive membership policy, with an emphasis on adult conversion and commitment, was accompanied by exclusive ritual practice. While for certain rituals, such as the Eucharist, one could easily maintain the separation; for others, however, such as funerals, compromise was necessary.

The death of Matteo Ricci in Beijing in 1610 was a turning point in some ways, because his funeral and burial were the cause of the Jesuits themselves becoming involved with more Chinese funerary customs. The first critical step was the decision about his burial place. At the initiative of a Christian convert, the Jesuits asked the Chinese emperor to offer an appropriate burial ground.[15] The reason for this request was directly related to the difference between European and Chinese burial customs: whereas the Chinese traditionally buried the dead outside the city walls, in the European-Christian tradition burial preferably took place in or close to a church, and this, as had been the case for the burials of Almeida, Soerio, Tedeschi, and others, had so far always been the church in Macao.

> With the funeral service performed according to the ecclesiastical rites, [father Matteo's] body, enclosed in a coffin, was kept in our house, according to the Chinese custom, until a place beyond the city walls could be purchased for its interment (because it is not allowed among Chinese to do that inside the city). This caused the Fathers some concern, because of the lack of space in the house and also because of this unusual situation. Up to this time, no one of the Society of Jesus had been buried outside the plot of the College of Macao and it was an order to be followed, that they would die in the College, or would be brought to it after they had died to be buried in the common grave of their fellow fathers. This order could not be followed in the present instance, and even though it could be, it seemed better not to do so, because it was quite evident that in taking the common father [of the Mission], the Divine Goodness had ordained that something extraordinary and unexpected was to result from his death.[16]

Ricci's corpse was kept in a traditional Chinese coffin. While some Chinese practices, such as the habit of condolence, were accepted, others, such as the funeral procession, were only applied in a limited way, because the Chinese procession was considered to resemble an act of "triumph" and did not conform to Jesuit ideals of poverty and modesty:

> The Chinese frequently keep the bodies of their deceased in the home, hermetically sealed in a coffin, and sometimes for years, until they have built or discovered a suitable place for burial. The casket is covered over with a shiny

bituminous substance, rendering it absolutely impervious to gases. The casket containing the body of Father Ricci was kept beside the altar of the domestic chapel [in the Mission Center] for almost a year from the time of his death. When the Fathers came into the peaceful possession of the villa, the body was taken there, to await the preparation of a cemetery, according to ecclesiastical directions, and the instalment of a chapel. The transfer to the villa was made without the pomp exhibited by the Chinese on such occasions, because such display is more suited to a triumph than to a funeral. Such pomp, moreover, would have been out of keeping with our poverty and religious modesty. The transfer of the body [from the Mission Center to the new villa] took place during the morning hours [of 22 April 1611] and was attended by a large following of converts, carrying lighted candles, in procession behind a cross, borne beneath a canopy. The coffin was placed in a room adjacent to the house chapel and stationed, after Chinese fashion, to accommodate those who would come to pay their last respects to the departed.[17]

The order of this procession with cross and candles corresponds to the prescriptions of the *Roman Ritual*. On the day of the burial itself, 1 November 1611, all the regular Christian ceremonies were celebrated: the recitation of the Office of the Dead, the funeral Mass, an ecclesiastical procession (*ecclesiastico ritu processio*), and the prayers at the tomb in front of a painting of Christ. But in the end, there were also some Chinese rites:

When the ecclesiastical rites were finished, the neophytes did not omit the civil ones (*politicos suos*), and performed, following their custom (*ex more*), inclinations and genuflections first to the image of Christ the Saviour, and then to the tumulus. . . . Many days afterwards gentile friends came flocking in to perform their usual rites for the deceased.[18]

A prudent and hesitant approach is again apparent. These Chinese rituals are not integrated into the Christian ones but remain separate and are only occasionally juxtaposed when their chronology overlaps. As Johannes Bettray has shown, after thirty years of living in China, the Jesuit missionaries were apparently allowing the performance of these particular local customs: some condolence ceremonies including the bewailing of the dead; the wearing of mourning dress; the performing of four ritual prostrations before the corpse (also performed by the missionaries themselves); the offering and burning of candles and incense before the coffin; and, as in the case of Ricci's funerary ceremonies, the inscribing of tombstone eulogies. In addition, a length of time was set aside for mourning according to the Chinese custom, and the practice of buying an expensive coffin was adopted as far as possible. In other details, typical Christian things were displayed with the best possible pomp.[19]

What reasoning evolved to make the Jesuits more tolerant? Although Ricci himself did not give much systematic evaluation of the Chinese ancestral or funeral rites, his few insights played a major role in the policies that would be adopted later. In one key passage of his chapter on the Chinese sects, he describes the offering of food, incense, and silk or paper to the dead ancestors, and goes on to explain:

> The reason they give for this observance on behalf of their ancestors is this, "to serve the dead as if they were living."[20] Nor do they think that the dead come to eat these things, or have need of them; but they say they do it because they know of no other way of showing the love and gratitude they have for them. Some say that this ceremony was instituted more for the living than the dead, that is to teach children and the ignorant to know and serve their parents while alive by showing them that important people perform for [their parents] after their death the services they were accustomed to perform when [their parents] were alive. And since they neither recognize any divinity in these dead, nor ask anything of them, nor hope for anything for them, the practice is completely free from any idolatry (*idolatria*), and perhaps could even be said to involve no superstition (*superstitione*). Nevertheless, it would be better to replace this custom with giving alms to the poor for the souls of these dead, when they become Christians.[21]

Ricci thus concludes that the Chinese do not believe that the dead are actually present, or that they are divine. The practice is certainly not idolatrous and perhaps not superstitious.[22] But because of the danger of superstition, it would be better to aim at eventually replacing such customs.

These short references represent the birth of a categorization that would last for at least a century. In the first place were Christian rites. They are variously called "rite of the Christians" (*rito de' christiani*), "ecclesiastical ceremonies" (*cerimonie ecclesiastiche*), or "ceremonies of the Church" (*cerimonias da Igreja*) in Ricci's original text.[23] These were the rites the missionaries were accustomed to, and in contemporary theology these rites belonged to the "true religion" (*vera religio*), because they were offered to one whom they considered the true God. At that time, besides the restricted meaning of "entering religion" (i.e., entering a monastic order),[24] the term *religio*[25] also referred to "ritual practice,"[26] a "social fact," or an "articulated whole of institutions."[27] *Religio*, meaning the "careful and even fearful fulfilment of all that man owes to God or to the gods," mostly corresponded to the classical and Roman concept of the word.[28] This is probably also the meaning used by Ricci when he entitled the chapter of the book in which this passage occurs: "Of the various sects which in China are about religion" (*Di varie sette che nella Cina sono intorno alla religione*).[29] Generally speaking, in the sixteenth and early seventeenth centuries there was no real distinction drawn between religion and non-religion, or secularity, since, according to the theology, all people had an inborn knowledge of God. Neither was religion a generic term yet, and thus Ricci did not speak of the "three religions." A clear distinction, however, was made between true religion (i.e., latry) and false religion (i.e., idolatry), a value judgement in which the ritual aspect predominated over the doctrinal aspect of faith.[30] Christians considered their own persuasion the true religion (*religio vera*) because they worshipped the one true God, while others, such as Romans or in this case Chinese, were believed to be misled by demonic forces and therefore practicing idolatry.

This leads to the second type of ritual. Distinct from the Christian rites were the "rites of the gentiles" (*riti gentilichi*) or the "gentile ceremonies" (*cerimonia de' gentili; cerimonie gentiliche*).[31] Certainly in the beginning of the Christian mission in China, all non-Christian funerary rites, whether Buddhist, Daoist, or Confucian, seem to have qualified as "false religion" or "idolatry," because they were offered to wrong deities who, to the missionaries, were mere creatures. For instance, in the Latin translation Trigault rendered Ricci's chapter as "Various Sects of False Religion among the Chinese" (*Variae apud Sinas falsae Religionis sectae*).[32] The missionaries only gradually accepted certain Chinese funeral rites—those embedded in the Confucian tradition of the *Family Rituals* and referred to as "Chinese custom" (*ex more sinico, conforme ao custume da China*).[33] These rituals were thought to be in compliance with Christianity, or at least not opposed to ritual practice in the service of the one considered the true God. The food offerings to the dead, for instance, are made "as if" (*come*) or "as when" (*come quando*) "they were alive."[34] The passage refers to a sentence about the fulfilment of one's filial obligations (*shisi ru sheng, shiwang ru cun*) from *On the Practice of the Mean* (*Zhongyong*).[35] Because of its conciseness and the polysemic character of the words, various interpretations of this phrase exist. It can, for instance, be interpreted as a comparison between serving the dead and the living: "To serve the dead *as* one serves the living, to serve the departed just *as* one serves those still in this world."[36] Others interpret it as a supposition: "To serve the dead *as if* they were living, to serve the deceased *as if* they were present."[37] Even with such a translation there can be several interpretations. The sentence could mean that one presumes the dead are still living (even if one does not know it for sure). But the supposition could also be a pure hypothesis based on the fact that they are certainly no longer alive. It is the last interpretation that the Jesuits followed. To them, these are only "as if" rituals; in other words, one should not believe that the deceased are present. Yet, in the opinion of the Jesuits, there was still the danger of rituals containing what was labelled "superstition," which usually meant the improper worship of the true God. Such rituals should be purged and gradually replaced by Christian rituals. This explains the distinction Ricci makes between idolatry and superstition.

Negatively formulated, any ritual "that did not conform to the rite or rule of Christianity"[38] could not be practiced. Positively formulated, rituals could be performed that the Jesuits labelled "political," pertaining to the state, or "civil," pertaining to (the body of) citizens, categories they used to make certain gentile rituals acceptable. These terms most probably originate in the so-called threefold discourse about gods (theologia tripertita) by Marcus Varro (116–27 B.C.E.), as discussed in Augustine's (354–430) City of God (Civitate Dei). Varro distinguished between three discourses on the concept of god: mythical discourse, used by poets; physical, used by philosophers; and civil. The civil discourse "is that which citizens in the states, especially the priests, have an obligation to learn and carry out. It tells us what gods are to be worshipped by the state and what rites and sacrifices individuals should perform."[39] While Augustine was critical of the civil discourse, the expression "civil religion," as it was used by the Jesuits in China, was a rather neutral term usually not interpreted as idolatry and referring to ritual practices that the emperor and the officials accomplished as part of their civil or political function. The term "civil" was applied to most of the rituals of the "law" or "sect" of the literati (lex or secta Literatorum),[40] the terms that the Jesuits used for what in the nineteenth century became known as Confucianism.[41] The other laws and sects, such as Buddhism and Daoism, were usually considered "false or profane religion"[42] and Buddhist monks and Daoist priests were considered "ministers of the idols" (Ministri degli idoli).[43]

Besides these theological reasons there may be another reason why the Jesuits so strongly rejected Buddhist and Daoist rituals in particular. From an anthropological point of view, there is probably more correspondence between Catholic and Buddhist rituals than between Catholic and Confucian rituals. They are similar in the notions of a punitive underworld, the possibility of salvation, merit-making, and the intervention of ritual specialists (monks or priests) who recited sacred texts and performed rituals that required apprenticeship. Thus, because of the competition between Buddhism and Christianity within the Chinese religious context, the missionaries and their converts were in fact subjected to what Vernon Ruland calls the phenomenon of "inflated difference": the average (minority) group, pressed to consolidate its own identity, is prone to dis-identify with others and to play up otherwise negligible differences between those inside and those outside its boundaries.[44] This phenomenon may explain why missionaries purposefully dissociated themselves from Buddhist and Daoist funeral rituals and substituted them with Catholic rituals.

Implementation of Family Rituals

So far, the overall picture of funerals in the beginning years of the Christian mission in China is that of a practice in which Christian and European rites were affirmed as much as possible, with only limited acceptance of certain Chinese "civil" rites. It is difficult to assess to what extent funerals as they were actually practiced were as pure as they were presented in the Jesuit reports. They indeed may have been rather exclusive events given the small number of Christians: an identity as a distinct ritual community is easier to assert when the community is small than when it interacts with other communities. In addition, the reports had the added purpose, beyond simply reporting, of proving to the European reader that Christian rituals were being conducted in the orthoprax way. In the twenty to thirty years following the death of Matteo Ricci, Christianity spread to other regions in China, the number of Christian converts increased, and the first Chinese writings on the Christian mission appeared. They give not only a more nuanced picture of what happened to the funeral rituals, but they also show how local Chinese movements, especially the Confucian search for orthopraxy with its stress on Zhu Xi's *Family Rituals*, contributed to the gradual embedding of the Christian funerals.

This nuanced picture appears when one confronts European and Chinese sources. The case of the parents of Yang Tingyun, a well-known Christian scholar, is very illustrative in this regard. Like Xu Guangqi, Yang Tingyun originated from the Jiangnan region, the most dynamic area of Christian activity in the early seventeenth century. European sources attach much importance to the funerals of Yang Tingyun's father and mother, who died, respectively, in 1618 and 1619 at the ages of eighty-five and eighty-four. References to them appear in the annual letters (*litterae annuae*) written by the Jesuits for their superiors in Europe, and of which several were published in Europe for a wider public. In *Annual Letter 1619* (*Littera Annua 1619*), for instance, the following account of the funeral of Yang's father is provided:

> [Yang Tingyun] did not spare anything for the service and the solemn Mass; they
> were celebrated in our church, since he had parament of black damask made,
> and had the church draped with the same fabric, as well as the funeral chapel,
> the middle of which was dressed with several steps filled with candles; something

that was worthwhile seeing since it was not practised in China. This showed to everyone that the Chinese do not surpass us at all in the pomp of funerals, and this is no small praise, because they do not want to be surpassed by any country in the splendour and expenses of the obsequies.[45]

This description closely corresponds to the one of the funeral of Xu Guangqi's father cited earlier, including the stress on the pomp of the funeral Mass. The depiction of the funeral of Yang Tingyun's mother in *Annual Letter 1620* (*Littera Annua 1620*) is even more detailed:

> Her funeral was done conforming to the Christian Religion, and one of our Fathers participated in it. After having chanted the responsorials of the holy Roman Church, he elevated for [God] a trophy against the Chinese superstition in this city. In the eyes of other people, this [superstition] is very fertile among elevated people, so it also has resulted in Magistrates who are considered by all as very important observers of Chinese ceremonies. Consequently the corpse of the mother of Doctor Michael was buried with the same funeral pomp, and same concourse of Christians, and of Gentiles, as with which we have said, the father was buried last year; without forgetting the prisoners, to whom Michael sent a good dinner, this all to the edification of the Christians, and the Gentiles. An altar on the place where she would be buried had been dressed with the image of our Savior, to which the Christians and the Infidels made reverence, burning perfumes before it, just like the Chinese are accustomed to do as a sign of honor, and of veneration. But the funeral chapel, which was in the house of Michael, surpassed everything. It was fully covered with black damask, and the chasubles and the front of the altar were of the same fabric. The white color was strongly associated with mourning among the Chinese, but we did not want to dissociate ourselves from the European custom concerning the ceremonies of the holy Church. The Requiem Mass was solemnly chanted there, and Doctor Michael was present dressed in white sackcloth, which was fastened with a straw belt, and he followed the custom introduced recently in this Kingdom of similar actions of piety and of religion.
>
> This was done in the second city after the Royal city, at the moment when the preachers of the Christian law were banished from the Kingdom, and before the eyes of our adversary who remains in that same city: I do not know which of the two is more admirable: whether Doctor Michael who has given such heroic proof of constancy, by making so openly profession of our holy faith, or whether the Magistrates of the same city who conceived such a great opinion of the majesty and holiness of the Christian Religion.[46]

At Yang Tingyun's own death in 1627, many friends and "idolatrous" family members wanted to give him a traditional Chinese funeral ceremony presided over by Buddhist monks and with the pomp reserved for high officials. His son John sharply opposed the proposal. Instead, he gave his father a solemn Christian funeral as an example to all believers and unbelievers. The money that was saved was given to the poor "at the gate of the house" instead of to the monks.[47] As appears from these descriptions, funeral ceremonies "in the style of the Christians" seem to have been an important outward expression of Christianity, and for this reason the missionaries did not want to move too far away from European customs. The *Annual Letters* stress the importance of European customs in this sense in several instances.

That things were more complex can be inferred from Chinese sources. Fortunately, two different Chinese sources also refer to the funerals of the parents of Yang Tingyun. The first is a biography of Yang Tingyun's wife, written by Chen Jiru (1558–1639).[48] This well-known scholar from Huating (Songjiang) had renounced all political ambition in the early years of his career and spent his life writing and reading. His writings were in great demand, and he earned his living partly by composing texts for others. He was an acquaintance of Yang Tingyun and the biography of his wife, née Lü, contains valuable information about their life. For instance, reference is made to the fact that Yang Tingyun established a Benevolent Society (*renhui*). Besides feeding hungry people, dressing those who suffered cold, administrating medications to the sick, and caring for orphans and solitary persons, this association also "buried neglected corpses." In that same text is a brief reference to the funerals of Yang's parents. According to Chen Jiru, Yang Tingyun and Lady Lü, "in the way of prostrating and arranging the funerals, used the family method of Zhu Xi (*Ziyang jiafa*)."[49]

Chen's text does not make any reference to Christian practices, but the mention of Zhu Xi's *Family Rituals*, however, is significant. Allusions linking adherence to *Family Rituals* to gentry status appeared frequently in gazetteers and private texts since the sixteenth century, and the reference in Chen's text clearly shows the value attached to them by both Chen and Yang. While education administrator for Nanjing in 1608, Yang Tingyun, in fact, together with several other important local officials, supported the reprint of Qiu Jun's *Etiquette of the "Family Rituals"* (*Jiali yijie*). The revision (*ding*) of this edition is attributed to Yang.[50] This shows that Yang, both before and after his baptism, fully participated in the movement to restore Zhu Xi's *Family Rituals*.

An explicit reference to Yang Tingyun taking the *Family Rituals* as a guide appears in his Chinese Christian biography, *The (Extraordinary) Life of Mr.*

Yang Tingyun (*Yang Qiyuan xiansheng* (*chaoxing*) *shiji*), which was compiled after his death by a certain Ding Zhilin in collaboration with Giulio Aleni. This biography places the use of the *Family Rituals* in the context of Buddhist and Daoist services.

> Mr. Yang was very devoted and sincere in observing mourning for his parents. For a long time, Buddhist funeral services (*foshi*) had been practised in Hangzhou. [At these occasions] one gave alms to monks from far and wide, while they widely proclaimed their sutras and ceremonies, and they played cymbals and drums until late at night and burned mock money till early in the morning. Since one saw that Mr. [Yang] was alone [without monks], and since one did not hear any noise, one wondered what happened. Intimate relatives came to reprimand and remonstrate him. But Mr. Yang ordered to bring him a copy of the *Family Rituals*, and showing it to them, said: "Is not this [the book] that we commonly respect and observe? As regard rituals, nothing is more perfect than *Family Rituals*. The Song Confucians standardised the ancients' funeral sacrifices and handed them down and for numerous reigns, nothing more than this. How can one choose to gain merit through the present chanting of the Buddha name?" Everyone silently approved, but still one was privately of the opinion that Mr. Yang was too frugal in treating his parents. Thereupon, on the seven sevens, which are traditionally days of Buddhist services, he calculated the costs of a Buddhist service and gave the double in charity to the old, crippled, prisoners, orphans and widows. Then everyone understood that Mr. Yang was completely right in his vision. After leaving off the mourning apparel and having constructed the tomb, he observed and prepared everything according to the impressive ceremonies of the Holy Teaching, and it differed from the vulgar customs. As for the place, he merely chose a lofty and clean one and did not adhere to the theories of geomancy.[51]

These two Chinese sources are an important addition to the overall perception of the predominant Christian funeral liturgy. Christian gentry families, such as Yang Tingyun's family and probably Xu Guangqi's and others', were embedded in a tradition that adhered to the *Family Rituals*. Such dismissal of Buddhist and Daoist rituals and rejection of geomancy for funerals and burials were typical of a gentry who affirmed their status on the basis of Confucian funeral rites. It was characteristic of Christianity for its missionaries to be in contact with at least some of the members of this gentry class, and Christian rejection of Buddhist and other funeral rituals could be accepted by the Chinese gentry because the potential for such a rejection was already present in the Confucian tradition of that time. As is evident from Yang Tingyun's biography, it is on the basis of *Family Rituals* that the Buddhist and Daoist rituals are rejected. Furthermore, the rejected rituals are substituted not only with works of charity—"distributing to the poor what had been necessary if he had been buried in the way of the pagans"—but also, as European sources reveal, with Christian funeral rites, though the two Chinese sources do not mention this. The separate treatment of Christian and Confucian rituals in these sources also suggests that in practice they were implemented separately or juxtaposed to each other.

Yang Tingyun and Xu Guangqi originated from the Jiangnan area, the area where Christianity was most widespread in the early seventeenth century. The importance of the values and practices of the *Family Rituals* in the Chinese Christian's search for a gradual embedding of the Christian funeral ritual is also apparent in two other active Christian communities, in Fujian and Shanxi. There the networks were founded in the 1620s and were particularly active in the 1630s and until the early 1640s (before the fall of the Ming in 1644). The communities in Fujian and Shanxi were composed of two or three important local families that were interconnected with a much larger group and a missionary. The Fujian community was concentrated around the families Li and Zhang and the missionary Giulio Aleni. The other important community, in the southern part of the Shanxi province, was centered around the Han and Duan families and the missionary Alfonso Vagnone, SJ (1568/69–1640).

It was characteristic of these Christian groups to be involved in the local communities. Through most of the seventeenth century China lacked an effective central political authority, so that scholar-officials and local elites could not rely on the government to restore order.[52] Through the establishment of local benevolent societies and schools, the publication of morality books (*shanshu*), and the organization of community compacts (*xiangyue*) and relief efforts, these men took private action to do what had been previously considered the responsibility of the government. While in the early Ming, morality-book production was largely under imperial auspices, by the seventeenth century most new morality books and ledgers of merit and demerit were privately compiled and published. This was also the case with the leaders of the Christian communities in Shanxi and Fujian. It is worth noting that while higher gentry were more interested in the practicality of European sciences as an aid to save the country, the lower gentry were more interested in European moral writings, which became comprehensive blueprints for the reform of the society perceived as disordered and morally corrupt.[53]

In these morality books one also finds references to funeral practices. One example is Li Jiugong's (d. 1681) *Mirror for the Exhortation to Cultivation* (*Lixiu yijian*, 1639/1645), a Christian morality book. Li Jiugong, a candidate qualified to participate in the provincial examinations (*xiucai*) of Fuqing (Fujian), was baptized as Thomas by Aleni in 1628 at the same time as his elder brother Li Jiubiao, who was given the Christian name of Stephanus. Divided into moral categories, the *Mirror for the Exhortation to Cultivation* illustrates principal virtues by way of pious stories so as to encourage people to do good and avoid evil. This book contains a unique mixture of classical or historical stories and biblical or holy stories taken from the writings of the missionaries as well as from books by converts who related events that happened in the Chinese Christian community. It includes, for instance, the above-mentioned story of Yang Tingyun taking care of the funerals of his parents, given as an example of "serving one's parents" (*shiqin*), classified under the general category of "taking care of people" (*airen*).[54]

Yang Tingyun's story seems to have been quite popular since it appears also in Han Lin's (1600–1644) *Book of the Warning Bell* (*Duoshu*), another important morality book. Han Lin, who had successfully passed the provincial examination (*juren*) in 1621, belonged to the active Christian community of Shanxi, which was involved in charity works (especially during the Great Famine of 1633–1641) and in the revision of several writings compiled by Alfonso Vagnone.[55] In his *Book of the Warning Bell*, Han Lin attempted to introduce Christian ideas into the official Confucian system for the propagation of morality, which was a combination of the "community compact" (*xiangyue*) and the institutionalized explanation of the Sacred Edict (*shengyu*) of the founder of the Ming. His work was a collaborative initiative, since eighteen local scholars, seven of them with a metropolitan examination degree (*jinshi*) and six with a provincial examination degree (*juren*), participated in its compilation.[56] The message of *Book of the Warning Bell* is that the doctrine of the Lord of Heaven is a useful instrument for the improvement of society. Han Lin's explanations of the Six Maxims, found in the Sacred Edict, are based on both Confucian and Christian arguments that are juxtaposed so as to support each other. The interest of *Book of the Warning Bell* lies in that mixture of ideas, that process of cross-cultural sedimentation, which attempts to present Christian doctrine in a completely traditional context.[57]

In the first chapter of *Book of the Warning Bell*, which corresponds to the first maxim "to be filial and obedient towards one's parents" (*xiaoshun fumu*), Yang Tingyun is again taken as an example of someone who realized filial piety by leading his father to serve heaven. After mentioning that his parents died at an old age, the text gives recommendations for funerals:

> When parents die, one should go to the utmost in sorrow and effort so as to bury them according to the [appropriate] rituals; one should not cremate them and thus practise the customs of Western tribes; one should not call monks and thus

follow Buddha's teachings; one should not burn mock money and thus be misled by evil spirits; one should not be deluded by geomancy and thus believe the theories of the burial masters. These different points have been discriminated in the smallest detail by former Confucians, and contemporary wise people discussed them even more genuinely. Those who have clear insight into the principles surely do not behave in such a way.[58]

Some rituals were clearly rejected, as illustrated by the "do nots" of this text. Again, most of the rejected rituals correspond to those customs rejected by the Confucian elite at that time: Buddhist and Daoist funeral rites, cremation, and use of burial masters. The criticism of the burning of mock money is less explicit in Confucian texts, though not absent, and would become a specific object of Christian criticism.[59]

As such, the texts written by members of these Christian communities highlight the distinction made between Chinese rituals that were tolerated and Chinese rituals that were rejected. The tolerated Chinese rituals, often juxtaposed with European ones, were the traditional family rituals performed by the relatives themselves, several of which had already gained acceptance at the time of Matteo Ricci's death. Typical is the condolence visit, as appears from another text by Li Jiugong titled "My Rustic Opinion in Support of the Rites" ("Zhengli chuyi," undated), whose core ideas may be traceable to the 1640s, though it could also have been written later.[60] In it, Li Jiugong strongly defends the importance of the condolence visits.[61] Li is also of the opinion that writing a biographical note (zhuanzhuang) or an epitaph (zhiming) displays the conduct of the deceased so that those who read it may imitate it in admiration, and that installing a bamboo box allows the presentation of gifts to help console the grieving family in their sorrow.[62] Here the primary standard was that they should be in accord with the "Way" (dao), which also includes the Christian orthodoxy.

The arguments used by these local Christian community leaders to reject some rituals are made less about the idolatry or superstition that the missionaries objected to, but rather are made in terms of what corresponds to what is correct, zheng, often translated as "orthodox," according to the Confucian tradition. The focus of zheng is not on transcendent faith but on social morality, political legitimacy, and ritual correctness, thus on orthopraxy.[63] The template in this regard was clearly Zhu Xi's Family Rituals. His basic principle of "Do not perform Buddhist services" (buzuo foshi)[64] is one of the most often cited quotations in the Christian writings about ritual correctness. For instance, in "My Rustic Opinion in Support of the Rites," Li Jiugong points at three "do nots" for funeral rites: do not invite monks, do not burn mock money, and do not engage in geomancy with burial masters. In his opinion these practices had long since been rejected by Confucians of former times. He stresses that one should follow the orthoprax way and not engage in Buddhist services, as Zhu Xi had already clearly stated.[65]

A similar argument appears in "Record of Correspondences between the Family Rituals and the [Christian] Teaching" ("Jiali hejiao lu") by Zhang Xiangcan (who passed the provincial examination in 1648, from Xi'an) of the Shanxi community.[66] This work also points at another use of *Family Rituals*. Not only does *Family Rituals* support the Christian rejection of Buddhist and Daoist practices, but the text is also used in rebuttal against those who criticize Christianity for not practicing certain other rituals. In his "Record of Correspondences," Zhang includes seventeen criticisms of Christian marriage and funeral rituals, such as that Christianity does not invite yin-yang specialists to select a suitable burial place; that it does not use grave goods (*mingqi*), which are models of household objects buried in graves; and that it does not want the demon-quellers (*fangxiang*) to exorcise spirits at the grave.[67] Zhang then uses *Family Rituals* to defend against those criticisms. For instance:

> Some people in the world criticize Catholicism because at condoling and offering gifts it uses incense and candles but no paper ingots. But *Family Rituals* only mention that "Those who condole should all wear plain clothes; for gifts use incense, tea, candles, wine, or fruit; for contributions use money or silk." Where did it ever mention the ritual of using paper ingots?[68]

These are all arguments *ex silentio*: why should Christianity be obliged to practice certain rituals that are *not* mentioned in *Family Rituals*?

The Jesuits themselves would sometimes use *Family Rituals* to defend their position. For instance, in his rejection of mock money in *Questions and Answers Regarding the West*, Aleni clearly refers to *Family Rituals*: "The belief that false paper money and Buddhist services will help the dead in the other world is an absurd lie invented by the bonzes to deceive the people. In your country the *Family Rituals* of a famous Confucian scholar have clearly forbidden them."[69]

Independently of each other, Christians from Jiangnan, Fujian, and Shanxi all referred to the implementation of the *Family Rituals* in their discussion of Christian funerals. It thus appears that the fact that Chinese Christians originated in a culture in which funerals conducted according to the *Family Rituals* were regarded as orthopraxy, and the fact that the missionaries considered these rituals as merely "civil," contributed to the gradual embedding of Christian funerals within this tradition.

INTERWOVEN FUNERAL RITUALS

Although several local rituals were performed in juxtaposition with the European rituals, some rituals were transformed or substituted by interwoven ones. In such interwoven rituals, gestures of filial piety, reduced to mere acts of respect and commemoration, were combined with the adoration of God and with prayers for the well-being of a deceased parent.[70] This appears from Chinese sources describing the life of local Christian communities in the 1630s, as well as Chinese translations of European prescriptive texts from the same period.

Experimentation and Mutual Accommodation

What Christian funerary rituals should look like in China was not preordained. In Ricci's time, only at the end of his life was an approach adopted in which some variation was allowed. According to different Chinese Christian sources emerging from the Fujian and Shanxi communities, in the 1630s there was still room for experimentation and creative adaptation, often initiated by the Chinese Christians themselves. The most important source for information about the Fujian community is the *Diary of Oral Admonitions* (*Kouduo richao*), an extensive record of missionaries' conversations with converts and interested literati in Fujian selected from the ten-year period of 13 March 1630 to 4 July 1640. More than twenty-five Christians, including the brothers Li Jiubiao and Li Jiugong, participated in the recording and editing of this work.[71] Besides theological or moral questions, it also contains exchanges about practical matters such as funerals. They are grouped in one passage.

Chongzhen 10/3/24 [18 April 1637, probably in Quanzhou].

On the twenty-fourth our fellow believer Mark Zhang had passed away, and his son had invited a number of friends to come to his home to recite the prayers. The master [Aleni] said: "In what we undertake to do today we must heed the Way rather than worldly customs. Even the slightest inability [on our part] to free ourselves from worldly [customs] will remove us far from the Way. Please let us go early and return early, lest we burden the host with our presence." The friends all agreed.

After some time they came to talk about the subject of [food] offerings. The master said: "I have observed how in accordance with Chinese ritual after a parent's decease a posthumous portrait and a wooden tablet are displayed, and that respectfully an offering is made of wine and food. I suppose that this is an expression of the son's sincere intention to treat the deceased one 'as if he were present.' However, it is essential that the 'flavor of the Way' and the feeling of filial piety be combined—nothing could be better than that. Lately there was a fellow believer here in your prefecture who, when one of his parents had departed from this world, realized that sacrificial animals and other offerings have nothing to do with the body and soul of the deceased one. He only had a cross made, on the side of which the name of the deceased one was written; he placed it in front of the bier [carrying the coffin] and worshipped it. Every seventh day he would treat his relatives to all kinds of food and delicacies, but he first would offer these, [standing] in front of the Lord, and recite the *Scripture of Blessing the Food and Drinks* (*Jiangfu yinshi jing*), praying for the Lord's protection. Then he would pass [the food] on to the others, as a means to obtain happiness in the hereafter. In this way justice was done both to the sincere expression of filial piety towards the deceased one, and to the intention of the Way according to [our] religion. Moreover, in the book *Very Strange Things* (*Haoguai shi*) written by His Honor Mr. Zhang [Zhang Geng], there is one entry that reads: 'During his life a man does not dare to receive other people's homage; once a guest is bowing down he will refuse to accept such a sign of subservience. How then would he be willing in the hereafter to accept the prosternations of the whole group, old and young, close and distant relations?' Therefore placing a cross is convenient for both the living and the dead."[72]

These newly invented rituals sought to preserve equilibrium between the traditional ways of expressing one's filial piety and the orthodoxy of the Christian "Way": the deceased parents are being commemorated but not worshipped. The deceased is only treated "as if" he or she were present. The passage also shows that there was not yet a clear-cut policy with regard to important matters such as the offering of food. An equilibrium was achieved by combining the traditional paraphernalia with a crucifix, so that the bowing and prostrations were always done before the crucifix, and by blessing the offerings with a Christian prayer.

Other adaptations concerned the consumption of the food that was offered. According to Chinese custom, it was to be consumed by those who had offered it. Instead of consuming it oneself, the accommodation consisted of distributing it to the mourners. In other cases, it is to be distributed to the poor. This is what Aleni recommends in a letter he wrote to Christians in Fuan probably in 1635 or 1636. He not only refers to the European experience, but also argues on the basis of the "as if" quote from *On the Practice of the Mean* (*Zhongyong*), here attributed to Confucius himself:

In the inferior kingdoms [of Europe] sacrifice is a matter of great weight and importance. One should not make offerings and ask for good things for sure, but there [in Europe] they also have offerings at the sepulture of the main ancestors and relatives. What people intend and want in doing this is to express a way to commemorate the fact that their ancestors received mercy themselves, and [thus] they do those deeds on their behalf. This is what Master Confucius says, *su su ju seng su vang ju chun* [*shisi ru sheng, shiwang ru cun*], that is, "serve the dead as if they were living, serve the deceased as if they were present." If one considers this sentence of Master Confucius, [one will see that] it expresses the same doctrine of our kingdoms of Europe, namely that one should not forget the dead. Therefore following the doctrine of Master Confucius, which aims at remembering the deceased, it will be possible to continue doing such offerings to the ancestors, because it is not illicit and something that cannot be done. And having done all these offerings it will be better to give them to the poor.[73]

A similar reference to the practice of offerings at tombs can be found in Aleni's *Questions and Answers Regarding the West*, where he mentions that in European practice, "Sometimes food and drink are placed on the ancestors' graves; when the ceremony is over, the offerings are given to the church for distribution among the poor."[74] While so far no reference to the practice of placing food on tombs in Europe has been found, offering a meal to the poor was the most common form of funeral almsgiving.[75] Thus some selection and reorientation of a specific ritual practice developed: distribution to the poor is used as an alternative to allowing food offerings but the consumption by those who offered them is not allowed. Distribution of food to the poor was also encouraged in China by Chinese Christians such as Li Jiugong.[76]

There were other forms of accommodation involved in funerals. In the next passage of the *Diary of Oral Admonitions*, Aleni refers to a certain Mr. Li who designs a funerary portrait to try to guarantee that his descendants will go on practicing Christianity:

And again, in Chu [Hubei] a certain friend named Li has designed his own [posthumous] portrait, as follows. At the top the Holy Sign [of the cross] is drawn, supported by "clouds of good luck." It is flanked by a portrait of himself holding a rosary, wearing a Holy Casket [an *Agnus Dei*], and turning towards the cross. In addition he has stipulated in his testament that those of his sons and grandsons who are believers will be represented in this painting, according to the alternating order of *zhao* and *mu*. But[, he said,] "Those who are non-believers I do not consider to be my sons and grandsons, and they are not allowed to figure on this picture together with me. If after my death some want to condole and bow before me, it will be as if together with me they respectfully worship the high Lord." By this arrangement he surely has complied with both the Way as well as with popular custom, both being practised without any obstruction.[77]

This case constitutes a Christian variant of the well-known tradition of hanging a funerary portrait in either the ancestral hall or the family home after a funeral. Normally, this type of portrait follows an extremely common stereotype, with the deceased represented in ceremonial attire in a rigid frontal position. Li's picture obviously is different, and appears to be a Christian variant of another type of ancestral portrait, in which the deceased is represented in non-official attire together with his wife and children and occasionally other relatives. The exclusion of non-Christians from the family group is a rather exceptional case.[78]

These interwoven ceremonials appear to have been created by the believers themselves. As Erik Zürcher explains, they are referred to in the *Diary of Oral Admonitions* not as procedures imposed by Aleni but as laudable solutions invented by individual converts.[79] Because of the distance from missionaries and, therefore, a lack of contact with them, apparently all kinds of local experiments were being made. Accommodation was a two-way process in which the believers themselves played a role.

These accommodations affected both Chinese and European rituals. The adaptations were caused by material circumstances, such as the availability of a priest and the financial welfare of the family. One finds the depiction of such variation in funerary practices in Li Jiugong's "My Rustic Opinion in Support of the Rites" ("Zhengli chuyi"):

> Fortunately the Christians of today already completely reject the above-mentioned three corrupt practices [inviting monks, burning mock money, and engaging in geomancy with burial masters]. However, if one wants to go to the utmost of the way of filial piety for one's parents, one should follow the ritual rules of the Holy Teaching. In short [it means] that with regard to his Christian parents a son should within the first hundred days of mourning, as an expression of earnest grief, ask many times on their behalf that the priest offer Mass to God and also that the fellow Christians transfer merits (*tonggong*). This can be done in a church or at home, according to the convenience of the principal mourner.
>
> As for the burial itself, one needs to be even more attentive. But it is also difficult to outline in one sentence the funeral practices for all families. Poor families, in the period approaching burial, only call a priest and fellow Christians to the church on the Sunday before the burial to chant and pray for a peaceful repose. On the day of the burial only the closest family members accompany [the corpse] to the mountain, they respectfully honour the dead body of the ancestor and inter it. They limit themselves to what their means allow and this is also called "ritual behaviour."[80] That is, not to deploy any extra goods or extravagant ornaments is also possible.

As for more wealthy families, it may be that because they do not tolerate the idea that family members are treated in a thrifty way, they conduct the funeral according to the worldly customs. That is, they cannot entirely renounce every exposure of ornaments, and so should select what is conforming to ritual behaviour. It should be close to the Way[81] and should not involve Buddhism or Daoism, and only then it will be appropriate. If on the very day [of burial] when the family members accompany [the corpse] for burial outside [the village], and they particularly want the priest and fellow Christians to climb the mountain to offer Mass and transfer merits for the deceased, then, following the invitation of the principal mourner, one distributes candles to the Christians who escort the funeral, and after lighting they carry them in order to increase the luster. This is not at all contrary to ritual behaviour. Only on the mountain, when one arranges a banquet to treat [the guests], it should be different from the worldly customs. Food should be limited to four to six dishes and one should not allow more. And the wine should be limited to five to seven rounds and not go into excess. In this way one will not reject anyone when inviting guests, nor treat them stingily. Especially when the way is rather distant [from the home to the mountain], and at the funeral procession one accompanies the principal [mourner] in his grief, [and one eats and drinks out of hours], ritual behaviour should take into consideration what can be easily performed, and one only practices it in accordance with human feelings.[82]

Besides this, on the day of the burial, one might also distribute food and goods to the poor, so as to obtain merit for the [deceased] parent, and this will be an even greater expression of the love for one's parents. But filial piety cannot be enforced upon people. If these more or less can be adopted as fixed rules, they will give insight into the real principles and real matter of the burial of parents. Then one can observe [the rules] forever, and both the dead and the living will be without resentment.[83]

This quotation confirms several other aspects of the embedding process already identified: the use of candles by the participants in the cortege "to increase the luster," and the importance of the banquet, which in this case is held not at the home of the deceased but at the place of the burial. The instructions also indicate the efforts to keep the catering of guests under control. In addition, the passage indicates that Christians observe the traditional mourning period of one hundred days, during which they obtain and transfer merit (*tonggong*); the help that the living can offer for the salvation of the deceased through prayers and works of charity is considered an expression of filial piety. The term *gong* that is used by the Christians was a central concept in the Chinese religious experience as a whole and in particular in lay Buddhism.[84] In Mahāyāna lay Buddhism, the primary aim of all religious acts was the production of merit (puṇya, gong) that by its positive force will eliminate evil karma, bring well-being to the present life, and lead to a better rebirth both for the devotee and for other beings. Such merit could be produced in many ways, such as devotion, recitation, prayer, pious vows, self-mortification, alms-giving, and pilgrimage, as well as rituals performed by monks on the devotee's request. Buddhist and some Daoist funeral services included special merit-making rituals (zuogongde) during which the monks or priests would chant scriptures to accrue more merit for the deceased so that they would receive fewer punishments in the courts of hell and be reincarnated in better stations.[85] In late Ming times the conception of karmic retribution as a kind of balance of positive and negative acts had given rise to the widespread custom of daily recording one's good deeds and transgressions in a "ledger of merit and demerit" (gongguoge), also practiced by Confucians.[86] As such, with their stress on merit, Chinese Christians were part of a movement that was very much alive at that time.

Another aspect of Li Jiugong's text also participates in a contemporary intellectual trend. At the end of "My Rustic Opinion in Support of the Rites," where he writes that his discussion addresses the "real principles and real matter" of the burial of parents, he uses the word shi, meaning "real, solid, concrete" as opposed to xu, "false, empty, void." This was a key term for expressing the idea of "concrete studies" or "real learning" (shixue) that was characteristic of a movement involving many late Ming and early Qing thinkers. With their stress on practicality and looking into things in the world, they criticized the void theories of Wang Yangming (1472–1529), according to whom there was nothing to be investigated in the things of the world. This concrete vocabulary was also adopted by the Jesuits and used in discussions of theology, science, and ritual. Manuel Dias applies it to funeral rituals in his Direct Explanation of the Holy Scripture (Shengjing zhijie, 1636–1642). Commenting on the passage from Mark 16:1 about the women who brought spices to anoint the body of Jesus, Dias distinguishes between "real and false rituals":

> The Holy Teaching rejects the false and values the real. Wrapping the body, making up the corpse, encoffining, burying, and others, are all real rituals, which are valued by the Holy Teaching. Burning mock money, Hades money, geomancy, selecting an auspicious day, and others are all false and rejected by the Holy Teaching.[87]

When the Dominican and Franciscan friars arrived in China they were faced with these interwoven rituals and with these types of experimentation. Some of the texts mentioned above may have been written in the midst of the controversies evoked by the presence of these newcomers. The permanent presence of Dominican missionaries in China began in the 1630s when Spanish Dominicans arrived in Fujian from Manila. It was soon evident that their views on Chinese rites differed from the Jesuits', who at a meeting in Jiading (Zhejiang) in 1629 had more or less found grounds for common agreement among themselves.[88] An important event for the Dominicans was their discovery of ancestral rituals, in which Christians from the Miao lineage participated in Mindong in 1635. The friars were scandalized, in particular, by the rituals of sacrifice (*ji*) offered twice a year by the assembled lineage. Not satisfied by the response of the Jesuits with whom they discussed the matter, nor by the Chinese Christians whom they interrogated, they produced voluminous papers that on their way to Manila and Rome would mark the beginning of the Chinese Rites Controversy.[89] Though there is a close link between ancestral and funeral rites, however, the focus of the discussion was more on ancestral practices than on funerals. But even the Dominicans did not reject all Chinese customs, as is shown in the case of Juan Bautista de Morales (1597–1664), whose corpse was kept in a coffin for a long time before being buried, "which is inevitable because of the ancient and permanent custom in the empire."[90] Moreover, not all Jesuits accepted unhesitatingly the majority line among them. For instance, in a letter of 19 September 1635 addressed to Antonio de Santa María Caballero (1602–1669), who was the first Franciscan who arrived in Fujian, the Jesuit Inácio Lobo (1603–?) gave lively expression to the physical effects of his fears at the time of condolence:

A few days ago I went to such [a condolence rite], and honestly, when I saw the image of the deceased in whose presence I would have to kneel down, my limbs trembled, my hair stood on end, my face turned pale without any blood in it, because it had all withdrawn in the heart, which would not allow me to prostrate myself before the one whose soul is burning in hell. I was on the point of retiring, feigning some accident or sudden colic. But two friends, great officials, who stood on my side told me that my vice-provincial [Manuel Dias or Francisco Furtado] and Father Giulio Aleni, had done this act many times, the one in Beijing and the other in Zhejiang. And so I did it against my will, and I do not know whether I should say so even with some scruple.[91]

Despite such individual reservations, by the 1640s some agreement existed between Chinese converts and Jesuit missionaries with regard to Chinese funeral practices. Some were clearly rejected, such as the Buddhist and Daoist services and geomancy. The rhetorical reasons for this rejection differed among Chinese and Jesuit believers: in the eyes of the Chinese converts it was primarily because those practices did not accord with the *Family Rituals*, while in the eyes of the

Jesuits, they were idolatrous or superstitious. As for the rituals prescribed by the *Family Rituals*, various attitudes were adopted. Some, such as genuflections, were already integrated in Chinese Christian funerals. Bringing these practices into accordance with the Christian orthodoxy could occur in several ways, such as by setting up an image of Christ. For other practices, whether or not in juxtaposition, there was nevertheless room for experimentation. For still other rites, such as food offerings, the method for practice was not clear. Food offerings were generally avoided, but if offered, instead of being consumed by family members the food was distributed to the poor. The Dominicans, however, eliminated most of the latitude for experimentation.

Reframing European Prescriptive Texts

To what extent did these accommodations affect the Christian prescriptive texts on funerary rituals? That they were affected at all is clear from the reframing that occurred when the missionaries translated these texts into Chinese.

Prescriptive liturgical texts in general were not a major concern for the young China mission. Even after having received permission in 1615 for future Chinese priests to use (literary) Chinese for the celebration of the Mass, the recitation of the breviary, and the administration of sacraments and other liturgical functions,[92] a long time passed before a systematic translation of liturgical texts was undertaken. This was also the case for such non-sacramental rites as the funeral.

The earliest Chinese Christian work specifically devoted to the assistance of the dying and to funerals is *Rules for Helping to Obtain Merit Towards a Good Death* (*Shanzhong zhugong guili*) by João Fróis, SJ (1591–1638), completed sometime before his death.[93] Most of this book concerns assistance of the sick and the dying. It is a translation of part of the *Manual for the Celebration of the Sacraments of the Church* (*Manuale ad sacramenta Ecclesiae ministranda*, 1605), the ritual handbook that the Jesuit bishop Luís Cerqueira had compiled for the Japanese mission. Fróis and his fellow Jesuits opted for Cerqueira's *Manual* rather than the more official *Roman Ritual* of 1614, possibly because at that time the Jesuit Mission in China did not yet own a copy of the *Roman Ritual*.[94] Fróis translated most of the section "On helping the dying and commending them to God" (*De iuvandis, et Deo commendandis morientibus*).[95]

The most prolific author with regard to translation of official liturgical texts is without doubt Lodovico Buglio, SJ (1606–1682), who arrived in Beijing in 1648 and remained there even during the exile of most missionaries to Canton (1666–1671). He himself was in favor of the ordination of Chinese priests and the celebration of Catholic rituals by them in the Chinese language.[96] By order of his superiors he translated the *Roman Missal* as *Canonical Texts for the Mass*

(*Misa jingdian*, with Latin title *Missale Romanum, auctoritate Pauli V Pont. M., Sinice redditum*, 1670),[97] the *Breviary* as *Prayer Book for Priests* (*Siduo kedian*, with Latin title *Breviarium Romanum Sinice redditum*, 1674),[98] and he is also said to have translated the *Roman Ritual* (*Rituale Romanum*).[99] The latter was published as *Ritual for the Sacraments* (*Shengshi lidian*) in Beijing in 1675.[100] The volume also bears the Latin title of *Manuale ad Sacramenta ministranda iuxta ritum S. Rom. Ecc. Sinice redditum*, a title very like that of Cerqueira's book. Indeed, it appears that Buglio's work is not a translation of *Roman Ritual* itself but of Cerqueira's *Manual*.[101] The sections on the assistance of the dying and on funerals clearly confirm this.[102] For the section on the assistance of the dying, Buglio undoubtedly had Fróis at hand, copying it and making small changes.[103] For the funeral itself, in contradistinction to Fróis, Buglio opted to follow rather closely the section "On the office of the sepulture" (*De officio sepulturae*)[104] of Cerqueira's *Manual,* including the "Ordo recitandi responsoria pro defunctis" which are the responsorial prayers for Mass and at the tomb.

While Roman authorities accepted the ordination of mature Chinese—the first Chinese priests were ordained in mainland China in 1688—these priests did not get the permission to celebrate Mass or other sacraments in Chinese, since they were supposed to know sufficient Latin to pronounce the liturgical words in Latin.[105] Likewise the Chinese translation of such liturgical books as the *Roman Missal, Roman Ritual* (*Manual*), and *Breviary* did not receive Rome's approval. Though they were published in Beijing, they were not used in liturgy. There seem to have been some exceptions, as appears from Buglio's *Ritual for a Good Death and for the Sepulture* (*Shanzhong yiying lidian*), a separate publication of sections on the assistance of the dying and on funerals from his *Ritual for the Sacraments* (*Shengshi lidian*).[106] When this text was first published and whether Buglio, who died in 1682, penned its final strokes are not known.[107] However, despite the lack of approval from Rome for the *Ritual for the Sacraments* as a whole, it is significant that the ritual of the funeral was still published in this separate edition.

The final text related to the funerary liturgy that Buglio translated is the *Office of the Dead*, which he called *Yiwangzhe rikejing*.[108] Buglio's translation includes the prayers, psalms (around twenty-three in total) and scripture readings (nine selections from the book of Job) to be read during the prayer sessions at a funeral and on certain fixed days of commemoration.[109]

The language used in these translations is literary Chinese. This choice conforms to the Roman instructions of 1615 that allowed Chinese priests to administer sacraments and fulfill their liturgical functions in "erudite language that was proper to the literati."[110] In general, the Christian language related to death was mostly based on the (Neo-)Confucian vocabulary picturing death as a final ending (*zhong, zu*) and as loss (*sang*). The Buddhist and Daoist vocabularies, on the other hand, speak of death in terms of awakening (*jue*), returning (*gui*), and going on (*qu*).[111] Much of the technical language related to Christian funerals, such as *lian* for wrapping the body and encoffining or *zang* for entombment can be found in classical works such as *Family Rituals*. Noteworthy is the consistent use of the term *zhuwen* for the prayers for the deceased in *Office of the Dead* (*Yiwangzhe rikejing*), which is the traditional Chinese name for an invocation or prayer at funerals and sacrifices.[112] As for the language of the prayers, like other Christian texts of that time they employ a combination of translation, sometimes leading to the creation of neologisms (i.e., *zhubao shengren* for patron saint, or the saint after whom one is named), and transliteration, which is also used for rendering personal names. In one of the most important recitative prayers, the Litany of the Saints, in which the names of at least twenty-five saints recited by the intoner are alternated with the response of the faithful, the use of Chinese sounds results in an ensemble that resembles the Buddhist chanting in which transliterated Sanskrit words are commonly used. This inclusion of foreign names and language likewise opened the liturgy up to a universe broader than Chinese.

A comparison of the translations by Fróis and Buglio with the original versions makes it possible to discover the adaptations they contain. One of the first changes concerns the order of the funerary ritual. The translators clearly have adapted the texts to the elementary structure of the Chinese funeral in which encoffining and burial were the two principal moments.[113] This appears first in Fróis' text, in the section on assisting the dying. In Cerquiera's *Manual*, the original on which Fróis based his translation, this section is followed by the long section, "On the office of the sepulture" (*De officio sepulturae*), which describes the actual funerary liturgy.[114] Fróis' *Rules for Helping to Obtain Merit Towards a Good Death*, however, leaves out this section and only has four short subdivisions of prayers to be read before and after encoffining (*rulianqian, rulianhou*), and before and after entombment (*anzangqian, anzanghou*).[115] Though no explanation is given for this change, it seems to be a first indication of the adaptation of prayers of the funeral office to Chinese practice. As mentioned before, encoffining as such does not appear in Cerquiera's *Manual* or the *Roman Ritual*, since the concealment of the body was still a relatively new practice in Europe. The same change as in Fróis' text can be observed in Buglio's *Ritual for a Good Death and for the Sepulture*. Compared to his *Ritual for the Sacraments* (*Shengshi lidian*), which was meant as a precise translation of the *Roman Ritual* (*Manual*), *Ritual for a Good Death and for the Sepulture* accords a more prominent place to the encoffining and entombment. The newly added subtitles, "Ritual of encoffining" (*Rulian lijie*) and "Carrying of the coffin and entombment" (*Taiguan rumu anzang*),[116] indicate that they were recognized as key moments. The Chinese Christian funerary liturgy was purposefully restructured within an elementary framework in which encoffining and burial became the principal events.

A second change, closely related to the first, concerns the main officiant of the funerary liturgy. Though the *Roman Ritual (Manual)* is primarily intended for the priest, Fróis' *Rules for Helping to Obtain Merit Towards a Good Death* does not explicitly mention the possible officiants. His work is not priest-oriented and can be used by both priest and lay person. Moreover, it is significant that his text does not mention the celebration of the Mass as part of the funeral service. *Rules for Helping to Obtain Merit Towards a Good Death* was apparently also designed specifically for Chinese Christians in charge of funeral rites. The change from priest to lay person is more evident in Buglio's translations. Buglio's *Ritual for the Sacraments* (*Shengshi lidian*) was made in the hope of obtaining permission for Chinese priests to celebrate Mass in Chinese. His text explicitly mentions the main officiant, i.e., the priest (*duode*), every time he plays a part in the liturgy. The importance of the clergy in this text is confirmed by the fact that it includes prayers for bishops and priests.[117] The destined audience for the *Ritual for the Sacraments* clearly was future Chinese priests. A notable difference, however, appears when one compares this work with its later edition of the selected aspects of the funeral ritual in Buglio's *Ritual for a Good Death and for the Sepulture*. In the latter, the references to the priest (*duode*) have been left out, while the voice of the people (*zhong[ren]*), left implicit in the *Ritual for the Sacraments*, has been added. The later *Ritual for a Good Death and for the Sepulture* seems to have been intended for those in charge among the Chinese laity and no longer for priests alone.[118] It seems likely, therefore, that while waiting in vain for the approval of Mass to be said in Chinese by Chinese priests, the missionaries were actively encouraging the transfer to the Chinese of responsibility for the celebration of non-sacramental rites such as funerals.[119] This shift is also confirmed by the publication of the *Office of the Dead* as *Yiwangzhe rikejing*, and in fact, as a separate booklet it was easily accessible to associations of lay Christians. In this work references to the priest are left out as well.[120]

Unlike the *Roman Missal* (*Missale Romanum*) and the *Roman Ritual* (*Manual*), which were translated by Buglio but never approved by the church authorities for practice, Buglio's two works concerning the funerary rituals, *Ritual for a Good Death and for the Sepulture* (*Shanzhong yiying lidian*) and the Chinese version of the *Office of the Dead* (*Yiwangzhe rikejing*), seem to have been widely used in the Chinese Christian community. Several early twentieth-century sources confirm that these were still very popular at that time.[121] In contradistinction to many countries where the recitation of the Office of the Dead had more or less disappeared (though had never been completely abolished),[122] in China it had been kept alive until the twentieth century.

CHRISTIAN ASSOCIATIONS AND FUNERALS

The procedure for funerals as described by these prescriptive texts may partially reflect the actual practice of funerals in the 1650s and 1660s. Yet, descriptive texts informing us about funeral practices in this period seem to be less numerous than in the preceding period, and the overall situation of the Catholic Church in China seems to have been in decline. On the one hand, the Christian communities had been affected by the Manchu invasion. This was true for the Shanxi–Shaanxi region where civil war and unrest, with the bloody intermezzo of Li Zicheng (1606–1645), took place in the late 1630s and the 1640s, but also for Fujian, where the Manchu invasion and the association of Christians with Ming loyalists led to conflicts.[123] Moreover, Christian contact with literati circles had diminished since the 1630s and, as John Wills points out, "there were no more Xu Guangqis and Yang Tingyuns, no more members of the high scholar-official elite making a desperate leap into a new foreign religion in the hope of thereby saving some of the core values of the Confucian tradition."[124] On the other hand, the Jesuits had quite remarkably survived the transition from Ming to Qing. This was largely thanks to Johann Adam Schall von Bell. His almost immediate appointment to the post of Director of the Astronomical Bureau was due to the fact that he could supply the court with a complete Western-style calendar system, which was interpreted as an auspicious sign for the new dynasty. It is partly because of the connection with this Bureau that the Jesuits survived the Ming–Qing transition without many setbacks, though the role of the Jesuits gradually shifted from intellectual companions of the gentry into expert advisers to the throne.[125] Moreover, despite damage to several Chinese Christian communities, others survived and even flourished. This was especially true for the Jiangnan area, where there were around fifty-five thousand Christians in 1663, representing about half of the total number of Christians in China at that time.[126] It was also in Jiangnan that Christian communities were most clearly organized in "congregations" (*hui*).

These congregations, by playing a major role in the care for funerals, became important institutions for the embedding of funeral rituals. They illustrate how the combined societal and church organization incorporated the Chinese Christian funeral liturgy that had come into being in the previous decades. From the beginning, the organization of associations or societies had been an important activity of the Chinese Christians. In the seventeenth century, several types of Christian organizations received the label *hui*. Sometimes the term refers to a select group with a relatively specific or formal membership, similar to a sodality, and in other cases it refers to an important way for the church to organize and administer the larger group of people in the area (a *christianitas* or congregation, similar to a parish). The activities of the groups also differed, from exercises in personal cultivation or devotion to works of charity, or, as was most common, some combination of all of these. Finally, the groups were established at the initiative of either Chinese Christians or Western missionaries. As a result, they represented many traces of the interweaving of traditional Chinese and Christian elements.[127]

Lay organizations and benevolent societies that aimed at mutual help, charitable works, and moral improvement had a long tradition in China and flourished at the end of the Ming. Especially important were the charitable organizations called *tongshanhui*, which served many purposes, such as aiding impoverished widows, burying the unclaimed dead, and setting up soup kitchens. They functioned through the voluntary support of local elites, which included merchants and farmers as well as scholars and members of the gentry.[128] Moreover, in Europe there was a tradition of confraternities, which were voluntary rule-governed associations of people promoting their religious life in common. Jesuit missionaries themselves were also well acquainted with societal life. In Europe, the Sodality of Mary, established by the Jesuit Jan Leunis (1532–1584) in Rome in 1563, was a widespread organization for the spiritual and religious cultivation of students at Jesuit colleges, in line with the spiritual path of Ignatius of Loyola (1491–1556). It was by way of these confraternities that Jesuits promoted rituals, especially the Mass; that the Jesuits encouraged the establishment of similar associations in China is therefore not surprising.

From the start, Christian organizations in China maintained a close connection with funerals, just as European associations did. One of the major activities of the Confraternita della Madonna, established in Beijing in 1609, was to bury Christians with solemnity and display.[129] Jesuits were not only continuing their own traditions, but were also simply reinforcing a traditional pattern within the Chinese context; their converts needed little encouragement to set up such bodies by themselves.

Some of these associations were established by Chinese converts who had been participants in Buddhist lay associations, such as the societies for reciting Buddha's name (*nianfohui*) or the societies for releasing life (*fangshenghui*). Particularly noteworthy are the late Ming benevolent societies (*renhui*) established by famous converts like Yang Tingyun, who had been a member of a *fangshenghui* before his conversion, and Wang Zheng (1571–1644), a degree holder of the metropolitan examination who was baptized as a Christian around

1616.[130] As appears from statutes (*huiyue*) and descriptions that have been preserved, the major aim of these societies was to collect money to help the poor, in observance of the seven material works of mercy: to feed the hungry, to refresh the thirsty, to clothe the naked, to attend the sick, to lodge travellers, to ransom prisoners, and to bury the dead.[131] They particularly focused on the burial of the dead and were especially involved in the burial of abandoned corpses by providing a graveyard and supplying coffins. For some associations, such as the "Sodality for Achieving a Good End (of one's life)" (*Shanzhonghui*) in Fujian, their sole purpose was the arranging of funerals.[132] Unlike the associations established by the missionaries, such benevolent societies provided few liturgical activities (such as prayer). It is not known whether membership was reserved for Christians only, though they seem to have been voluntary associations open even to people without any scholarly affiliation. Benevolent societies, therefore, appear to have been a unique combination of the doctrine of Christian charity and typical late-Ming institutions by which the local elite used its wealth for doing good.[133] These benevolent societies demonstrate how Christian notions became operational within a purely Chinese context, reinforcing traditional values along the way.[134]

Another type of Christian organization, or *hui*, which had appeared in the late Ming but only became dominant in the early Qing, was the congregation. Because the number of Christians increased much more rapidly than the number of priests to serve them, Christian communities could only be visited at irregular intervals. Therefore, the missionaries organized Christians not into the type of parish that appeared in Europe but into congregations within small communities, which gathered for prayer and instruction even in the absence of a priest. The congregation became one of the most important means of church organization, resembling to a certain extent the associations through which most European Catholics had experienced the rituals of the Catholic Church before the Council of Trent.[135] In China, they were lay associations headed by a community leader (*huizhang*). Splitting up the believers into smaller groups helped them avoid the suspicion that large gatherings aroused, but small groups also facilitated better instruction.[136] Most congregations were open to people from different classes, but there were also special ones for women, for children, for literati, and for catechists. Congregations seem to have been widespread. Around 1650, for instance, Shanghai counted seventy-nine congregations of Our Lady and twenty-seven of Our Lord; by 1665, there were around one hundred and forty congregations in Shanghai and more than four hundred Christian congregations in the whole of China. The most active missionary in establishing such congregations of Christians was Francesco Brancati, SJ (1623–1671).[137]

Congregations in the early Qing period served primarily religious aims.[138]

Members gathered regularly in a church or hall for prayers, sacraments, and religious instruction. Works of mercy, especially the burial of the dead, were an important component of their activities. In taking care of the funerals of their own members and other Christians, they resembled their European counterparts, whose members fulfilled this obligation by offering prayers for the deceased and taking part in the funeral cortege.[139] The statutes of several of the Chinese Christian associations that have been preserved give a fairly good idea of the actual organization of funerals. One example is the rules of the Hangzhou congregation of Mary (*Shengmu huigui*), a congregation organized by Humbert Augery, SJ (1618–1673) some time between 1660 and his death in 1673.[140] They stipulate:

> When one of the brothers has left the world, the community leader (*huizhang*) asks the priest to offer two masses, in order to accomplish on his behalf the merit of atonement and purification of sins. Moreover, together with the brothers, he will chant the prayers for a good death (*Shanzhongjing*) or three strings of the rosary. Everybody contributes according to his means and according to his effort practices the one or two of the fourteen works of mercy in order to beg the Great Lord to grant his soul a peaceful repose.[141]

This description shows that the community leader (*huizhang*) and not the priest played the major role in the organization of funerals. Moreover, it shows that the rituals were organized around the notion of communication between the survivors and God in favour of the deceased person. Prayers and deeds of charity performed on their behalf had the power to speed the soul through Purgatory. These elements also appear in the possibly contemporary rules of another benevolent society ("Renhui huigui," author and dates unknown):

- As for the works of mercy to be practised by the association, at the moment, since it has just been established, they cannot be fully listed. The first thing is to perform the burial rites; as for the coverlet and coffin, let one do it according to one's efforts; it has already been discussed in detail in the *Ritual Sequence for Funerals* (*Sangli yishi*). But these [funeral rituals] should fully accord with the various rites of Holy Teaching and there should be no discrepancy.
- If a Christian dies, let his family ask someone to notify the community leader. If it happens that he is busy, then notify the vice-leader. If this vice-leader is also busy, rely on the treasurer to notify the Christians to gather at [the family's] home.
- The rules for chanting the prayers should follow the relevant section in the *Ritual Sequence for Attending Funerals* (*Linsang yishi*).
- While chanting the prayers, the voices should not be some first and others later, but all uniform, like when [those on] the left chant, the right responds and

when the right chants the left responds; one should not chaotically mix them with local dialect.

- Every time a Christian dies, let the priest know that during the Mass he should pray the Lord for his soul. And the Christians will either at the church or at home implore [the Lord] on his behalf, chanting either thirty-three Our Fathers or sixty-three Hail Marys. And the filial sons will lead the members of the house to do the same.
- If it happens that a member of the association dies, all fellow-members will either pray three strings of Our Father or three strings of Hail Mary, to implore [the Lord] on his behalf.[142]

This description also shows that there was already a set of fixed prayers to be used at funerals, and that some Christian sequences for funerals were being established. While this set of directives stresses the Christian side of the funerals, it tells us little about the practice of Confucian family rituals, which, as shown earlier, were probably also present.

Some congregations had a very specific purpose. Among the congregations established by Schall von Bell in the church he constructed in Beijing from 1650 to 1651, there was a congregation "for funeral pomp" (*pro pompis funeralibus*) with a male and a female branch.[143] According to Schall, it was the most needed one among his congregations:

> Indeed, the gentiles among the Chinese falsely accuse the Christian law that it has no due funeral ceremonies and that it takes no care of the dead; that it omits the ceremonies for the deceased parents just like barbarians forgetful of parental honour; that it buries its own members without pomp or decorum, while before [their baptism] they cared for them very much with honour and kindness.[144]

Schall explains that on the day that the members gather, each according to his or her means deposits on the incense table a gift for the expenses of the association. Next they attend Mass that is followed by a sermon, and then litanies and other prayers are recited in common. They also accompany the dead to the sepulture.

These various types of congregations became the core of the Christian communities during the long absences of priests. They proved their operational significance especially during the exile of the missionaries during the years 1665 to 1671, when they guaranteed to a large extent the continuance of religious life. In regions where the communities were not very well developed, Christian membership and practice waned. In others, such as the Jiangnan region, they seem to have remained stable.

These associations seem to have functioned outside the sphere of the family. However, the first indications of the place of Christian rituals in the development of lineages can be traced back to this period. As Zhang Xianqing has shown, there were two possible relationships, depending on the type of lineage. Some lineages combined traditional Confucian rituals with Catholic rituals. Since a considerable number of members of these lineages had converted to Christianity, Christian members lived together with non-Christian members in the same lineage. In terms of ritual practices there was a coexistence of rituals since non-Christians and Christians separately employed the Confucian family rituals and the Catholic rituals. Yet the combination of these rituals did not split lineages nor weaken the lineages' potential for expansion. Some lineages even made a transition from a traditional religious culture to a Catholic ritual life; such a lineage was usually rather small at the moment some members converted to Christianity, so Christian faith and practices were more easily accepted as the lineage's main religious tradition. Consequently, for those lineages having made the transition, Catholic rituals, including funerary rituals, superseded Confucian family rituals, and became the main rituals for preserving lineage identity and sustaining further development.[145]

CONCLUSION

The history of these first nearly one hundred years of interaction shows the gradual embedding of Christian funeral rituals in China. This happened through a long process with different phases of cultural interaction: first an initial purist position from the side of the missionaries who, after insisting on separation, gradually came to tolerate some forms of juxtaposition; next a time of experimentation by Chinese Christians that led to various types of interweaving, as well as the reframing by the missionaries of Christian liturgical codes into the elementary structure of the Chinese funeral; and finally the embedding of funerary rituals into the activities of lay associations. An important factor enabling this evolution is the nature of the funeral rite itself. Funeral rituals tend to be open rituals: though they can be limited to the in-group, usually they are inclined to be open to all people who were associated with the deceased or the relatives of the deceased. As long as a ritual community was a small minority group, as was the case with the Christian community in the first thirty years, it was possible to maintain a certain exclusivity, with a limited number of participants in an established set of Christian rituals. At that stage Christianity offered an alternative way of funerals that apparently was separated from the practices of the ambient culture. The new Chinese Christian community clearly adopted new practices, such as the celebration of a Mass and the chanting of specific

Christian prayers, for which there was no equivalent in Chinese culture. But once the group of Christians grew, the social connections with people outside the group increased as well. As a result, after a death, more people who were not members of the initial ritual community wanted to express condolence and use their own non-Christian rituals for it. Thus the Chinese who were not directly involved in the Christian community became a primary agent in the change that was to occur in the funerals celebrated by that community. Therein funerals differ from other rituals, such as the Christian Eucharist or confession.[146] The latter are "closed" or exclusive rituals, since they are only for the participation of in-group members; they are not so easily affected by people from outside the community and over the course of time, as was the case in China, largely retained their European characteristics.

There are different ways of analyzing the changes funerals underwent, depending on which template one takes as reference: the European Christian rituals the missionaries wanted to transmit or the rituals in which the Chinese converts were involved. For the initial more purist and exclusivist phase of Christian funerary practice in China, the historian can rely only on missionary sources. They convey the idea that the Chinese converts underwent a major ritual change because, by becoming Christians, they fully integrated European rituals dealing with death and rejected nearly all the original indigenous funerary practices, especially the Buddhist and Daoist ones. The case of the funerals of the family of Yang Tingyun, however, makes clear that the situation was more complex. It appears that many Chinese Christians preserved the tradition of conducting funerals according to the Confucian *Family Rituals*, while Christian rituals replaced Buddhist and Daoist rituals. Moreover, like those of other local communities in China, the members of the Christian communities created new rituals from existing ones.[147] Their template was the *Family Rituals*, but instead of inviting Buddhist monks or Daoist priests to recite scriptures and perform rituals with merit-making purpose, Catholic priests were now invited. In other words, in the eyes of contemporary Chinese, the Chinese Christian funerals may well have looked like a new variation formed around the Confucian core.[148] An important factor in these changes was that the trend among the elite toward upholding the exclusive *Family Rituals* and rejecting Buddhist and Daoist practices actually favored the acceptance of the Christian rituals; the basic premises of that movement were easily taken on by Chinese Christians. The acceptance of European funerals by some Chinese thus confirms a generally accepted interpretation of cultural exchange: when a foreign element is introduced into a culture and is then relatively easily absorbed, usually some pre-existing internal movement within the culture enabled that acceptance.

Although some local funerary rituals were rejected, some were gradually integrated into the Christian template. Much of this happened through experimentation undertaken mainly by the Christians themselves, the result of which exhibited a wide variety of interwoven patterns. One type of interweaving is integration without much change. The color used in mourning is a clear example. Chinese Christians accepted the use of black damask that decorated the catafalque and chapel for the funeral Mass, while missionaries accepted the white dress of mourners attending the Mass: both aspects were juxtaposed within one and the same liturgy without change of form or meaning, because both colors were considered a sign of mourning. In most cases, however, integration of a specific new form was only possible when the meaning changed or a new meaning was applied. Genuflections before a funerary table were only acceptable for the missionaries if they expressed filial piety, and not the belief that the soul of the ancestor was present in the tablet. In order to avoid a wrong interpretation, a crucifix was put on the table so that veneration was oriented toward God. To Chinese Christians, candles could be distributed to the participants in the funeral procession because they could enhance its luster. There could also be new meanings attached to an existing form. For instance, the distribution of food to the poor, and other works of charity, while still maintaining their old meaning of expressing filial piety, became aids in helping the soul of the deceased to be saved (*tonggong*). And the epitaph and biographical notes were now used to spread the Christian virtues of the deceased.

Not only were Chinese elements integrated into the Christian ritual, the Christian ritual itself was integrated into the Chinese template. In the process, some structural and institutional changes occurred. That the organization of the church in China took on the shape of a Chinese social organization is of particular significance. Christianity in China was not constructed around a basic structure of parishes, but around associations that, with important lay leadership, became the major institutional factor in the organization of funerals. Cultural changes also pertained to the general frame of funerals, of which Chinese translations of European prescriptive texts are the clearest examples. Instead of being primarily texts addressed to the clergy, several of them are clearly addressed to lay people. Moreover, they were adapted to the two major moments in the elementary structure of Chinese funerals: the encoffining and the entombment. These changes show that Chinese funerary practices were not only adapted to European practices as transferred by the missionaries into China, but that the Christian rituals too were reframed by the Chinese funerary tradition. This adaptation bears some similarity to the pre-tenth-century European situation, especially with regard to the role of the laity. These changes are confirmed later by the history of the effect and reception of the Christian texts that were introduced.

4 / Funerals as Public Manifestation

In the middle of the seventeenth century the practice of Christian funerals in China had apparently become more solidified, yet missionaries and Christian converts were still searching for practical agreements on the forms of actual funerals. The period of exile in Canton (1666–1671) represents a kind of caesura in the liturgical development of the mission. Missionary documents show that after the exile, the approach of missionaries and converts toward the embedding of rituals shifted from one of simple adaptation to one of incorporating more significant changes because the Chinese cultural tradition was so compelling—a "cultural imperative." Moreover, they transformed their attitude into a real "policy" with regard to the public manifestation of funerals.

THE CANTON CONFERENCE

The Canton exile was the outcome of the "Calendar Case" that took place in Beijing in the years 1664–1665, in which a dispute about funerals played a role. In order to remove the foreigners in charge of the Astronomical Bureau, Yang Guangxian (1597–1669), in three petitions between 1660 and 1664, accused the Europeans of falsifying the calendar, promoting a heterodox sect, and preparing an invasion by Europeans. It was only in September of 1664 that a memorial submitted by Yang was accepted by the court, because it accused Johann Adam Schall von Bell of having selected an inauspicious date and site for the burial of Prince Rong, an infant son of the emperor's favorite consort Dong.[1] This selection had been made by the Water Clock Section (Loukeke), a unit in the Astronomical Bureau (Qintianjian) of which Schall was director.[2] According to Yang, this unfavorable selection had caused the death of both the consort (September 1660) and the Shunzhi emperor (February 1661). These circumstances provided the regents with concrete evidence to substantiate Yang's accusation that the missionaries were plotting a rebellion and subverting Chinese ideology, as their writings on Christianity and Western astronomy and geography already suggested. In April of 1665, after a seven-month-long investigation of the matter, Schall and seven officials in the Astronomical Bureau, five of whom were Christians, were sentenced to death. Although Schall was pardoned, the five Christian officials, including one Li Zubai (baptized 1622), were executed on 18 May 1665.[3] In addition, all missionaries in the country were to be exiled. Only four Jesuits remained in Beijing: Schall von Bell, who died in 1666; Lodovico Buglio, who would spend the years of isolation translating several Catholic prescriptive texts; Ferdinand Verbiest (1623–1688); and Gabriel de Magalhães (1610–1677). Except for a small number of missionaries hiding mainly in the Fujian and Jiangnan regions, all other missionaries who had been summoned to Beijing were sentenced to confinement in Canton.[4] They arrived there on 25 March 1666 and remained until 1671. Meanwhile, the churches in the provinces were closed and Christianity forbidden.

This exile was to a certain extent a turning point for liturgical praxis; the confinement of priests had a twofold consequence. First, the Christian communities were left all alone and had to maintain certain ritual practices on their own. Second, the missionaries of different orders were enclosed in the same compound in Canton and thus compelled to negotiate with each other their disagreements about liturgy.

While in exile, the missionaries staged an important event—the Canton Conference. For six weeks, from 18 December 1667 to 26 January 1668, nineteen Jesuits and four Dominicans discussed several practical issues concerning Christian liturgy and rituals.[5] A tacit agreement to avoid major problems, however, explains why the conference's forty-two final resolutions contain almost no reference to any issue related to the practices at the core of the Chinese Rites Controversy—namely, the sacrifice to Confucius and ancestral worship.[6]

After the Canton exile, funerals apparently became part of an explicit and conscious Christian policy. Certainly, before the exile, funerals had taken a certain shape but it is after the exile that funerals became a means for the public manifestation of Christianity. At first sight, however, funerals are not a major issue in the resolutions of the Canton Conference. Aside from the prohibition in article 40 against burning or making paper money,[7] only one article, number 34, is devoted to funerary rituals:

34. Neophytes are encouraged to assist frequently at the funeral obsequies of Christians, and, as much as possible, to display a Christian procession (*pompa*) while in a decent way holding a funeral. In the church the minister should recite the usual responsorial prayers (*Responsoria*) before an available substitute of the coffin together with the funeral apparatus, and offer [Mass] at the altar. Concerning the benediction of the coffin itself in the house of the deceased and its burial at the place of sepulture, however, it is not possible to give a fixed regu-

lation, but it is left to his prudence to judge what is profitable according to the circumstances of place, time and persons.[8]

This regulation indicates a distinction was made between rituals performed by the priest in the church and rituals that take place around the body in the house of the deceased and at the tomb. Moreover, it is noteworthy that the Canton Conference was of the opinion that no "fixed regulation" could be given, which seems to indicate that the established practice thus far had been one of variety rather than of uniformity. Yet the most significant indicator for the analysis of how missionaries turned funerals into a policy is the appeal to Christians that they should assist at funerals and as much as possible to display a procession.

This regulation by the Canton Conference requires an insight into its background. Why should Christians be asked to participate more in funerals? What opinion did the Chinese have about Christian funerals that made it necessary to make such a rule? Thomas-Ignatius Dunyn-Szpot, SJ (1644–1713) provides some answers in a section of "The History of Christianity Between 1641 and 1700" ("Collectanea Historiae Sinensis ab anno 1641 ad annum 1700").[9] Dunyn-Szpot compiled this manuscript in 1700–1710 on the basis of all materials available in the Society's archives in Rome. His account of the years 1677–78 includes a section called "The settlement for Christian funerals and obsequies as fixed by the Fathers in exile in Canton, and as put into praxis"[10] that explains:

> As far as the funerals are concerned: the most important among the false accusations that the gentiles hurl at the Christian Religion is that they [Christians] abrogate the care for the deceased and that they forbid exhibiting to them the honour that they deserve. This false accusation went so far that in the rescript by the Tribunal of Rites this was the most important reason for not granting to the Fathers who were in exile in Canton the faculty to return to their churches.[11]

The Chinese accusation of the neglect of funerals probably encouraged the participants in the Canton Conference to include an appeal for a more visible Christian involvement in funerals.[12] This would have several benefits:

> Although burying deceased Christians following the Chinese custom (*ad morem Sinicum*), but with a Christian ritual (*Christiano tamen ritu*), according to their financial means, had been put into practice earlier, nevertheless, in order to increase the majesty of the Christian religion among the gentiles; to banish by concrete facts the opinion that had wrongly taken shape about the neglect of the dead; and to increase the suffragia[13] by the faithful for the souls after being divested of the material corpse, [Christians] now had to attend to the following: there

was to be one and the same place to bury the dead, which should be purified by blessing, holy water, and other Christian rituals on a field outside the walls of cities or villages and even hamlets, in the shape of some garden enclosed by a fence, as it is the custom of the Chinese to bury their deceased.

To these places the funeral procession of the poor should be conducted, with certain expenses that the mercy and charity of the other richer Christians would supply for. In the funeral procession, a statue of Our Saviour nailed on the cross should lead, followed by an image of the Most High Mother of God, and finally an icon of St. Michael, the first among the angels, all carried with the splendour corresponding to the richness or poverty of the place. Thereafter the Christians should accompany the procession in long rows with illuminated wax candles, and with this rite, [the funeral procession] is led to the church, if there is one; and from there, after saying the prayers (*orationes*) the Church prescribes in the case that there is a priest, and if not, after the prayers (*preces*) said by the prefect of that *christianitas* [i.e., by the leader of that Christian community], it is conducted outside the walls to the place of burial where [the coffin] is entrusted to the earth accompanied by the same prayers (*orationes*). In every month certain days have been determined when Christians should convene in cemeteries to address prayers for the deceased to God and to support each other with alms and other pious suffragia.[14]

Dunyn-Szpot adds that a bit later Ferdinand Verbiest, then vice-provincial of China, asked to build on each cemetery a house, like a house of prayer, "where the Christians who still fell under the prohibition of the emperor could gather under the pretext of venerating the ancestors who rest there, which can happen on the basis of the Chinese laws, and at the same time sacraments can be administered to the faithful even during persecutions when they occur."[15]

A FUNERARY POLICY

Dunyn-Szpot's description demonstrates in a nutshell that following the Canton Conference, missionaries conceptualized funerals as practice based upon "policy"—a new standard for practice. This policy contained several aspects. In the first place the observance of funerary rites and the maintenance of tombs were perceived as a means to return to places that had been abandoned and to ensure the survival of a Christian community in future times of persecution. Secondly, paying attention to funerals and spending more on them was considered a way to counter the accusation of lack of filial piety. Thirdly, some rituals, such as the condolence rites, which had been previously treated with suspicion because of the possible danger of superstitious actions, were now praised as ceremonies displaying filial piety. Finally, the funerary procession became an excellent opportunity for a public manifestation of Christianity.

These four aspects emerge from contemporary European and Chinese sources written by missionaries after the Canton Conference. One such source is the *Life of a Christian Woman in China, Madame Candida Xu* (1688, 1691, and 1694) by Philippe Couplet, SJ (1622–1693), himself a participant in the Canton Conference. This book relates the life of Candida Xu (Hiu) (1607–1680), granddaughter of Xu Guangqi (1562–1633).[16] It gives a lively description of the daily life in the Songjiang mission where Couplet was active after the Canton exile until his return to Europe in 1681. Another text is the undated "Rules of the Sacred Teaching" (*Shengjiao guicheng*), possibly by Feliciano Pacheco, SJ (1622–1687) or even Philippe Couplet.[17] This is a short text with forty-five practical rules for Christian liturgy. Though it is undated, its composition can probably be situated in the aftermath of the Canton Conference, and to a certain extent its content overlaps with the final resolutions of the Canton Conference.

Facilitating a Return to the Missions

In Couplet's *Life of Madame Candida Xu*, the author confirms the first characteristic of the funerary policy by stating clearly that the care for the dead contributed to the return of missionaries to their original missions:

> Nothing has contributed more to the establishment and development of our religion than these final works of charity toward the deceased. When one wants to bring new priests and new missionaries to China from Europe, then one says that they come to show the final service of piety and gratitude to their friends. It is also an honest reason to have easy entrance into these Provinces, where so many who proclaimed the faith have been buried, and where these final services of charity are welcome. For the same reason we are obliged to renew the graves that were destroyed or had decayed during the persecutions, and also to move the corpses to places where we want to found churches, or to keep those that are now built.[18]

A clear example of missionary expansion through funerals and tombs took place in 1671 immediately after the Canton exile. On his way back to Shaanxi province, Francesco De Ferrariis, SJ (1609–1671), died near Nanjing. Although missionaries were allowed to return only to their original mission bases and no new missionaries could join them, Giandomenico Gabiani, SJ (1623–1694), from the mission in Yangzhou, accompanied the corpse to Xi'an. The official request by Verbiest to allow Gabiani to remain in Xi'an, instead of returning to his former base in Yangzhou, "so as to take care of the sepulture of his brother De Ferrariis," was answered positively because the Court of Rites was of the opinion that "one could not refuse the Fathers' [request] to render these duties of piety."[19]

The importance given to burial grounds was not unusual, though the advice to have "one and the same place to bury the dead" seems to have been a new phenomenon for Christians.[20] According to Couplet, it was Xu Guangqi himself who in the past had advised the missionaries to buy burial grounds and to build a chapel that would protect them during unforeseen persecutions.[21] It is not impossible that Christians and others considered these chapels a kind of ancestral hall (*citang*):[22] "In the whole of China tombs are privileged places, which one does not dare to touch. Positioning some people to maintain them and to give to the deceased the honours they deserve is allowed."[23] For the same reason, after the exile in Canton the ancient tombs of missionaries were restored in Nanjing (outside the walls of the city) and Hangzhou.[24]

The funeral policy concerned not only deceased missionaries but also deceased Chinese Christians. One gets a glimpse of this aspect from an account book compiled by the Jesuit missionary François de Rougemont (1624–1676). After the exile, he had returned to the Jiangnan region, where he was based in Changshu; the account book is a record of all his expenses there during the last two years of his life. They include funeral expenses for ordinary Christians. Not only did de Rougemont sponsor funerals by assisting with the costs of candles and incense, but he also supported the acquisition of land for a private graveyard and the payment of the related land tax.[25]

It is also in the Jiangnan region that new funerary practices originated, especially through the efforts of Couplet and de Rougemont. For instance, the cross that during life had publicly manifested one's faith was now placed inside the coffin at one's death. "Rules of the Sacred Teaching" gives precise instructions:

> 26. At the moment of encoffining, one should place a rosary and a cross in the coffin. On the cross one writes an inscription conforming to the picture below. The encoffining and entombment should follow the "Rules and prayers for assisting the dying" (*Zhuzhong jinggui*) without attempting to change anything.

The quote refers to a picture of the cross that includes the following instructions:

> One should make this cross in advance: cast it in copper; engrave it with the inscriptions; and expose it in the house, only leaving blank the date of decease in order to inscribe it after death. In this way it will be kept for ever and will not decay. If, however, this is not possible, then there is no problem in using wood to make it.
>
> For making this cross one should go to the church to get a model.

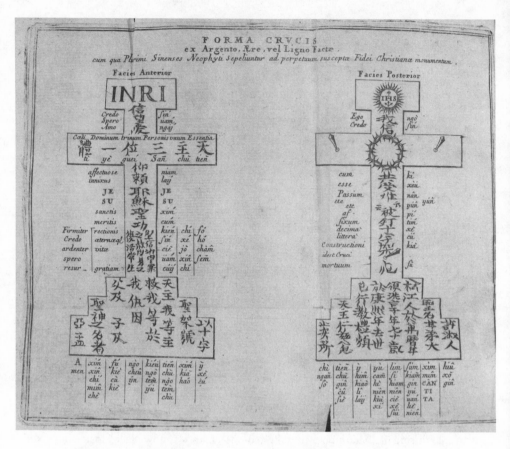

4.1. Funerary cross of Candida Xu (d. 1680), front and back.
From Philippe Couplet, *Historia de una gran Señora christiana de la China* (1691), between 158–159.
Courtesy of Maurits Sabbe Library, Faculty of Theology, K. U. Leuven.

According to the same instructions, the text on the cross should read:

Faith, Hope, Love

Master of Heaven, Three Persons in One Substance

Relying on the holy merits of Jesus, I believe in the forgiveness of sins, the resurrection of the body and the hope for eternal life in heaven.

Name . . . , district . . . , baptised on . . . (date), Christian name . . . , lived . . . years in the world, died on . . . (date), after having received the Christian rituals.

Trusting in God's mercy, may [the person] repose in peace.[26]

4.2. Funerary cross and portrait of Candida Xu, in which the traditional seated pose for funerary portraits is here transformed into a standing figure.
From Jean-Baptiste Du Halde, *Description . . . de la Chine* (1735), vol. 2, between 78–79 / (1736), vol. 2, between 120–121 / (1738–1741), vol. 3, between 12–13 (cross), 16–17 (Candida Xu). Courtesy of Maurits Sabbe Library, Faculty of Theology, K. U. Leuven.

In his *Life of Madame Candida Xu*, Couplet reports that in the Songjiang and Shanghai area, "which includes more than four thousand families," the Jesuits introduced the custom of preparing crosses in silver, copper, or wood. Following this custom, "Madame Candida had one made in silver"; at her death, the missing information in the text about her death was added to her cross.[27] An illustration of this funerary cross is included in the account of her life, and has been reproduced in other European sources (figs. 4.1, 4.2).[28] Another contemporary European source contains the reproduction of the funerary cross of Philippe Xu Yongchang from the same Songjiang region, who had been baptized on 24 September 1644; he died on 7 June 1686 at the age of forty-one years (fig. 4.3).[29]

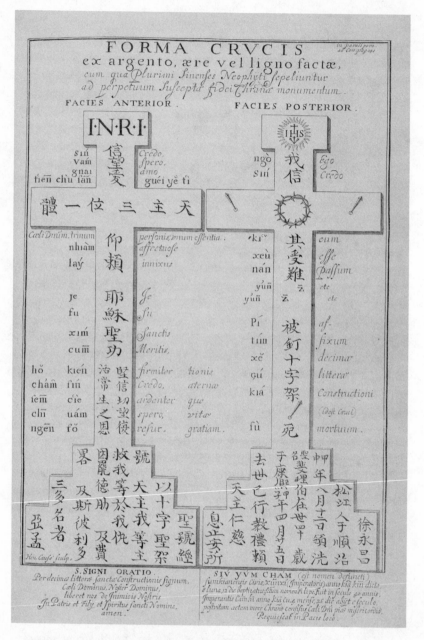

4.3. Funerary cross of Xu Yongchang (d. 1684).

From Godefridus Henschenius and Daniël Papebrochius, *Acta sanctorum* (1685–1688), in section *Danielis Papebrochii . . . Paralipomena Addendorum*, one folio after 141. Courtesy of Maurits Sabbe Library, Faculty of Theology, K. U. Leuven.

The preservation of tombs, the acquisition of burial grounds, and the creation of new funeral practices illustrate how, after the missionaries' return from exile, both missionaries and Christians implemented the new recommendations.

Increasing Funeral Expenditures

The Europeans believed funerals to be the most important of the rites of passage for the Chinese. The different descriptions in European sources of Chinese funerals reveal a general opinion, however, that not only did the Chinese value funerals more than the Europeans, but that Chinese funerals were sumptuous, sometimes even extravagant. To the Europeans, the Chinese funeral contrasted with the much more sober European burial tradition. Before the Canton exile, the question that arose from this contrast was whether missionaries should insist on continuing with their rather sober funerals, or whether they should adapt Christian funerals to the more expensive local practices,[30] given the fact that the show of material abundance at a Chinese funeral was interpreted as an expression of filial piety. After the Canton exile, the balance in attitude leaned toward funerals that would facilitate Christians' stronger public expression of honor to their parents.

This second characteristic of a more clearly defined policy about funerals is described in the "Rules of the Sacred Teaching." Aside from the usual prohibitions against burning money, the text insists that Christians should incur more expenses for funerals, without becoming extravagant, as part of a public manifestation of piety that also extends to the care of the tombs:

28. When in a Christian family the father or mother dies, the funerary and sacrificial rites should necessarily be distinguished from the non-Christian ones. At this moment, even if people do not invite Buddhist and Daoist monks and do not burn ingots and silk, and other vain expenses, for the rest they generally follow the ancient rites. Non-Christians often suspect us Christians of not honouring our ancestors and of being parsimonious with regard to our parents. Your priest has already discussed several times with you all that one should incur some practical expenses for parents, so that because of God our great father-mother, we manifest our filial piety and respect to our bodily father and mother. With regard to the cleaning of the tombs in spring and autumn, except for incense and candles, one should spend some more on composing a wreath or corona made of natural flowers or of wool or paper, or on making a cross to be fixed on the tomb, so that people clearly see and know that we Christians love and revere our parents, but unlike the non-Christians we do not engage in extravagant and useless expenses.[31]

The theme of spending more money on funerals appears also in Couplet's *Life of Madame Candida Xu*. The latter is clearly written for a European audience. The author highlights aspects of funeral rituals in China by comparing them implicitly or explicitly with certain European customs at that time. Moreover, Couplet not only draws out the differences between Chinese and European practices, but also makes reference to differences between Protestant and Catholic practices within Europe:

> It can be observed that the care for the dead and the pomp of the funerals, which the heretics of our times have tried to abolish with force against the Catholics,[32] are so well received by the Chinese that they appreciate with pleasure the funeral ceremonies of the Church. These ceremonies have contributed much to making our holy Mysteries and our religion respected among a people that makes such considerable expenditures for funerals, that the coffins of important persons usually are worth more than six hundred Chinese *ecu* (*liang*). These coffins are made of large planks of cedar wood, or another precious wood coming from Sichuan province. They enclose this first coffin in another made of rather thick planks, so well covered with pitch and beautiful lacquer, that they are not less beautiful than the cabinets that come to us from China and Japan.[33]

The use of a single or multiple coffins contrasted with the European praxis where the concealment of the body by a coffin was of only recent date and the preservation of the corpse through the use of a coffin was less necessary because the deceased person was usually buried within a short time after death. The sealing of the corpse in an airtight coffin, on the contrary, was considered by many Chinese to be the most important feature of the traditional funerary ritual.[34] This difference in praxis appears in several contemporary European sources. Couplet arouses the amazement of the European reader as he describes the offering of a coffin for one's parents:

> Madame Xu prepared for herself everything necessary for the funerals, and she had a coffin worth eight hundred *ecu*, which her son, the Lord Basilius, had offered to her. What in Europe would be considered a strange thing, if one would imagine offering such presents to one's parents, is considered in China to be an action of respect and piety. What is considered in one place contemptible and improper is considered in another place very reasonable and honourable.[35]

The final remark reflects a certain degree of adaptability to different rituals.

Condoling Practices

The description of the condoling on the occasion of Candida Xu's death in 1680 in the Shanghai region offers an insight into the concrete practice of condolence. As related by Philippe Couplet, the main role at this condoling was assigned to the son of Candida, Xu Zuanzeng, baptized as Basil (1627–1696?), who passed the metropolitan examination in 1649 and held several official posts during his life:

> Her son, Sir Basile, who had been with her since some time, and who disposed of all his assignments with permission of the emperor in order to express the final duties to her, went into mourning, which lasts for three years: it is a dress of coarse tissue in white, which is the colour of mourning in China, with a cord as belt and grass sandals. In this lugubrious dress he prostrated himself three times before the body of his good mother, and touched the ground with his forehead nine times,[36] shedding tears over the loss he came to experience, and the whole family did the same after him.[37]

The description of mourning dress and period shows that Xu Zuanzeng was observing the first degree of mourning that was commonly practiced among the elite in late Ming and early Qing times. After his personal condoling, Xu Zuanzeng took the necessary preparations for the final laying out of the body.

> After the body was put in the magnificent coffin that he had prepared, he composed a eulogy, or[38] a necrology, which he had printed to be sent to all mandarins, and to literati. At the same time a table covered with a large white cloth, burning candles and incense was installed in the room where the body was laid out behind a white curtain, which also covered the place where the women were crying. The Portrait of the Lady [Candida Xu] was spread out on the white curtain; it is this image that is also carried in the funerary ceremony. Several painters usually offer their services to make these portraits: they all work together, as one does here in the academies, after models, and the one that appears to most resemble the deceased is chosen.[39]

The Xu family followed most of the norms provided by Zhu Xi's *Family Rituals*, not only with regard to mourning dress or the practice of kowtow, but also with regard to the other material and social actions: eulogy or necrology, table with candles and incense, the use of a white curtain, portrait, etc.[40] These were all commonly practiced in the seventeenth century, and can be found in contemporary novels such as *The Golden Lotus* (*Jinpingmei*).[41] The attention the European author gives to the portrait is noteworthy.[42] An ancestor portrait was a pictorial genre that had little equivalent in Europe, even if Aleni in his *Questions and Answers Regarding the West* mentions that the ancestors' portraits "are also painted and hung up in the house to serve as examples to their descendants, so that by looking at them these [descendants] may be induced to imitate their ancestors' virtues."[43] In China such a portrait is always in the hanging-scroll format and depicts a forebear shown full-length, customarily in a rigidly frontal and symmetrical pose seated in a chair, and wearing formal, highly decorated clothing. In theory, the figures in ancestor portraits are always pictured in their finest, most formal clothing, which, if they held high rank, meant court dress.[44] The picture of Candida Xu included in Couplet's *Life of Madame Candida Xu* is one such ancestral portrait.[45] She is shown in the dress and headgear that she received when she was given the honorific title of Lady of Virtue (*Shuren*), a title of honor sometimes conferred on wives and mothers of officials.[46] Just like in portraits of other female forebears, the sitter here is depicted in a demure pose, hiding both her hands and feet, as is typical. The Christian rosary in her hand is probably the most personal detail such a portrait type would ever reveal, equivalent to and taking the place of Buddhist prayer beads (figs. 4.4, 4.5).[47]

Couplet then gives a detailed description of the process of condoling:

> Officials of all classes came with ceremony to pay the last honors to this corpse, following the practice of China. They first entered in a hall, where, after having left their ceremonial clothing for a white robe, they advanced with presents, which are incense, pieces of white silk, candles of particular wax made by ants, and which is strongly odoriferous, and more precious than those of the bees. They prostrated themselves before the white curtain, beating their head against the earth; consequently Sir Basile came from behind the curtain and prostrated himself before them, beating three times his head on the earth; and the officials, preceded by the master of ceremonies, returned to the hall to take back their ordinary clothing and to retire. This ceremony lasted several days, after which Sir Basile went in his mourning clothes all over the city of Songjiang, preceded by a master of ceremonies, to make the same genuflections, and same beatings of the head, only at the door of the palace of each mandarin on a white carpet spread to this effect.[48]

This condoling sequence corresponds closely to the Chinese depictions of condoling that can be found in various descriptive and prescriptive sources of that time.[49] As it is depicted here, however, it is no longer a distant report transcribed as it may have been from a book, but a report by an eyewitness, who

Candida HIV Doctoris Pauli SIV Imperij Sinarum Cancellarij neptis, pietate ac fidei zelo illus-
tris obijt 24. octobris 1680. Ætatis suæ 73. in
Vrbe SumKiam Prouinciæ NanKim.

4.4. Ancestral portrait of Candida Xu, depicted with Christian rosary.
From Philippe Couplet, *Historia de una gran Señora christiana de la China*
(1691), opposite 1. Courtesy of Maurits Sabbe Library, Faculty of Theology,
K. U. Leuven.

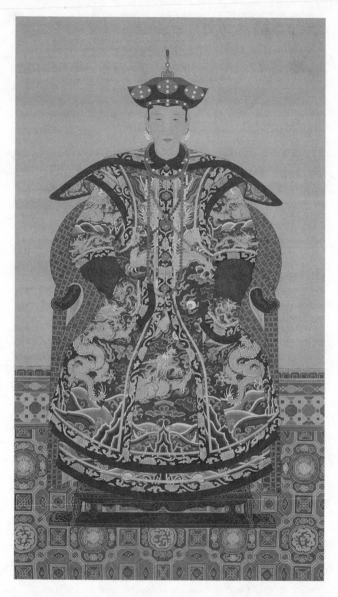

4.5. Ancestral portrait of Lady Guan, depicted with Buddhist prayer beads.

From hanging scroll, ca. mid-seventeenth to early eighteenth century. See also Stuart and Rawski (2001), 58, illustration 2.1. Courtesy of Arthur M. Sackler Gallery, Smithsonian Institution, Washington, D.C.

was probably also a participant, submitting himself just like all the others to the orchestration by the master of ceremonies. The description also confirms the fact that such condolence ceremonies contributed to making funerals an open ritual, in which Christians as well as non-Christians participated. It is because of ceremonies of this type that the Christian rituals were challenged. Yet these ritual actions do not include ceremonies that can be qualified as typically Christian. They are instead juxtaposed with Christian rituals performed at another time. However, the rituals of condolence are not described as being in contradiction with the adaptation method of the missionaries. This leads Couplet to the following observations that correspond to the categories of permissible activities that Ricci had already used:

> Our missionaries performed their ceremonies following the ways of the Christians; while cutting off everything that had the slightest smell of idolatry or superstition, they kept the incense and the candles, which are in use in the Holy Church. If they allowed genuflections and the bowing of the head on the earth, it is because these honours are merely civil in the whole Empire of China, and one also does them before the parents, the officials, and the emperor during their life.[50]

The Dutch version of the *Life of Madame Candida Xu* includes at this point the names of several missionaries who performed these rituals on the occasion of the death of the parents of important officials: Francisco de la Concepción, OFM (1635–1701) and Francesco Saverio Filippucci, SJ (1632–1692), who performed them for the father of the governor of Guangdong; and Francisco Varo, OP (1627–1687), for the mother of the governor of Fujian. Though the rituals were for "the dead bodies of gentiles," Couplet says, the missionaries participated "in appreciation of the favours that the children of these governors had conferred upon them. There is no reason to punish this [performance of rituals] and it should not be forbidden. Practices are not the same in all places; in every country one should live according to its customs, as long as it is not a reprievable evil."[51]

Funeral Processions

The fourth and probably most important characteristic of the policy concerning funerals after the Canton exile is that funerals became a public manifestation of Christianity and the Christian community. Most Christian rituals (i.e., Mass, prayer sessions) were not necessarily hidden, but were performed in the private confines of a church, chapel, or house. The funerary procession, on the other hand, became a rare occasion for a public event.

In China, funeral processions, which could take place months or even years after the death, were important public and social events. As shown in lively depictions in contemporary literary sources such as *The Golden Lotus* or *A Dream of Red Mansions* (*Hongloumeng*), they could be of immense size in their fullest form, involve large numbers of people hired for the occasion, and cost a great deal of money.[52] The descriptions in contemporary European sources indicate that both the ordinary funeral processions and the extraordinary, such as those for imperial funerals, made a great impression on the missionaries. In rare cases missionaries even participated in such processions. For instance, when the Shunzhi Emperor died in 1661, Schall participated in several ceremonies and took part in the procession "by reason of his function" (*pro ratione officii*).[53] So did Ferdinand Verbiest in 1681 when the Kangxi Emperor ordered the entombment of the two empresses who had died a few years earlier but were still not buried because the emperor's mausoleum was not yet finished. Verbiest reported to Europe that he had been amidst the "great and noisy" funeral procession organized for that event.[54] These short references, just like those of the condolence visits, clearly illustrate how social duties obliged the missionaries to participate in the rituals of non-Christians.

Not all funeral processions were as sumptuous as an imperial procession, but most of them, by demonstrating wealth and influence, were a means of reasserting the status of the family weakened by death, as C. K. Yang has pointed out. The spectacular display of a funeral procession could include thundering vanguard drums, elaborate banners, signs of honorific titles bestowed on the deceased by the imperial government, glorifying praises written on banners and scrolls sent by individuals and organizations, bands playing funeral music, troupes of Daoist and Buddhist monks in full, colorful religious costumes, long marching lines of mourners from relatives to friends and representatives of civic organisations, the massive decorated sedan chair for the spirit tablet, and finally the coffin, the quality and cost of which frequently served as a measurement of the wealth of the mourning family. This was the way of the rich, but less well-to-do families often ran into debt to have an elaborate funeral that might require years to repay.[55]

Given the positive and public meaning of these funeral processions, after the Canton Conference missionaries apparently no longer just passively tolerated such processions but actively promoted them and adopted them into Christian practice.

The days of these funerals are days of triumph for the religion. During these, the Cross, the images of the Saviour, of the Blessed Virgin, of Saint Michael are solemnly carried. The Christians follow in a notably modest way, two by two and dressed in mourning clothes. They carry lighted candles, incense, and perfumes. Several musical instruments are being played. The public funerals that are so solemn show to the Chinese that we are not ungrateful or impious towards the memory of the dead, as the Chinese idolaters had accused us of, so as to make us hateful.[56]

Chinese and European elements are interwoven: the mourning garments, the carrying of candles, incense and perfumes, and the playing of music. The description of this procession corresponds closely to the description given by Dunyn-Szpot in line with the resolutions of the Canton Conference. These stipulations were not a complete innovation, but rather a confirmation of a practice that had been growing in China gradually. Some early Christian funerals had already been pompous public manifestations. The burial of Xu Guangqi, for instance, was accompanied by a "procession not seen in Europe," according to Dunyn-Szpot.[57] Moreover, a funeral procession already played a role in the symbolism of the funeral in Europe, though it was mainly seen as a solemn ecclesiastical procession. After the Canton exile, however, the funeral procession came to be seen as a conscious means not only to manifest respect of the living for the ancestors but also to manifest the Christian faith and community (a "triumph for the Religion").[58] The various images that are carried, in contrast with the European practice where usually only a crucifix is carried, substitute for the many objects and paraphernalia (including images of elephants, camels, and tigers) that were carried in traditional Chinese funerals of that time.[59] They also exhibit the importance of these Christian figures for the Catholic faith. In addition, in Europe processions were mainly clerical demonstrations. Given the limited numbers of priests in China, it was not the clergy but the Christian community who occupied the most important place in the Chinese Christian processions.

The new attention paid to Christian funerals was not only an initiative of missionaries and Chinese Christians, but was, unexpectedly after the exile, encouraged by imperial decisions. In the post-exile period there were three funerals that received imperial sponsorship and the participation of imperial representatives: those of Gabriel de Magalhães in 1677, Lodovico Buglio in 1682, and Ferdinand Verbiest in 1688.[60] Both Chinese and Western documents produced by the missionaries make much of this imperial support. They clearly wanted to see the emperor's sponsorship of funerals as his recognition of Christianity itself. The extended processions organized for these occasions were thus considered public manifestations of Christianity with imperial sanctioning. The many documents that exist about these funerals demonstrate the significance the missionaries attached to them.

CONCLUSION

The above mentioned texts show how, especially after the Canton exile, the practice of a Christian funeral underwent further changes in China. The contrast with the initial period is significant. In the early years missionaries pleaded for sober funerary rituals and opposed the processions that resembled more a "triumph" than a funeral, whereas after the Canton Conference they considered these processions a "triumph" for Christianity. The same word shifts from a negative to a positive connotation. These changes came about partly because of the nature of the funeral ritual itself and missionaries' claims for Christian orthodoxy, but also because of what Erik Zürcher calls the "cultural imperative." In "Jesuit Accommodation and the Chinese Cultural Imperative," Zürcher explains that no marginal religion penetrating from the outside could expect to take root in China (at least at the social level at which the Jesuits functioned) unless it conformed to what was considered "orthodox" and "orthoprax" (*zheng*), in a religious, ritual, social, and political sense. In order to avoid being branded as "heterodox" or "heteroprax" (*xie*) and treated as a subversive sect, Christians had to prove that they were on the side of the orthodox, or *zheng*—that part of Chinese culture that is imperative and unavoidable for any people who wish to function within it.[61]

From the earliest times, Christians had been accused of lacking in filial piety because of the mediocre way in which they buried their dead. During the Canton Conference the missionaries realized they had to take action against the accusations that Christians deny any need to care for the dead and that they prevent the demonstrations of respect the dead deserve. Through the interaction with Chinese converts, missionaries resolved the problem by transforming funerals into an active "policy"; rather than maintaining a reserved and discreet attitude toward the funerary ritual, they would approach it as a strategy whose practices were now policies. This approach resulted in several changes in funerary practices that went beyond the simple toleration or adaptation of the earlier period. The observance of funerary rites was used as a means towards another end, as was the case when this observance was used as an argument to return to places that had been abandoned. In certain cases Chinese Christians were even encouraged by the missionaries to use the cemeteries as a place to celebrate their sacraments "under the pretext of venerating the ancestors who rest there," as Verbiest suggested.

In the middle of the seventeenth century quite a number of Chinese ritual expressions were already interwoven with the Christian funerary rituals: genuflections, incense offerings, expensive coffin, white mourning dress, etc. Others became more manifest during this period, such as the use of a funerary painting, with an interesting case of substitution of the Buddhist prayer beads by the Christian rosary in the painting of Candida Xu. In some cases these adoptions were restricted, such as the use of natural flowers or of wool and paper on the tomb. In addition, there were shifts in the meaning of certain concrete rituals; notions, symbols, and practices acquired a new meaning because they functioned in a different context. Whereas the missionaries in the first half of the seventeenth century were concerned with the ways in which several Chinese rituals could be interwoven into the Christian ritual without being considered idolatrous or superstitious, the major question in this later period was how to use or at least tolerate these Chinese rituals so as to show that Christians also practiced filial piety. The condolence rites paid to Candida Xu are a clear example of this shift: they include a large number of practices, which at that time were fully accepted, and were all favored as expressions of filial piety by Christians. Thus to a certain extent the concern about the manifestation of piety by the relatives became more central than the concern about the salvation of the soul of the deceased. Determining this acceptance is the missionaries' awareness that several of these practices can have a completely different meaning, as so clearly expressed by Couplet: "What in Europe would be considered a strange thing, if one would imagine offering such presents to one's parents, is considered in China to be an action of respect and piety. What is considered in one place contemptible and improper is considered in another place very reasonable and honourable." This tolerance made such practices possible.

The change of emphasis clearly occurs in the public manifestation of the funeral. The model of a sober funeral was initially exported as a Catholic model to China, where it contrasted with the model of a luxurious and pompous funeral—or thus it was felt by the missionaries. Gradually the missionaries changed their attitude toward the funeral, from seeing it as a rather sober affair to a more solemn one; it had to accommodate the deeply internalized sense of obligation among the Chinese that caused Chinese funerals to become more expensive. Christianity could not escape this tendency. The most significant example of change was the funerary procession. Here the missionaries joined a dynamic cultural element present in China: funerals in general but funeral processions in particular had an uncontested significance in their public expression of filial piety. By joining with the strength of the funeral's public reputation, missionaries transformed the meaning of the funerals in a twofold way. A funeral was first considered an expression of respect for the parents, a meaning that was only implicitly present in a European funeral, but was the explicit focus of the Chinese Christian funeral. Next, the missionaries also saw the display in funerals of both Christian images and the Christian community itself as a public manifestation of the Christian faith. Given the positive ritual strength of a funeral procession in China, this rare occasion of public manifestation of Christianity could hardly be challenged. While in these changes the missionaries seem to have taken the initiative because of the policy decided at the Canton Conference, just as in the previous period these changes could not have been possible without the Chinese, both Christians and non-Christians.

These evolutions highlight another consequence of Zürcher's cultural imperative. The latter transformed what had been a predominantly didactic mode of transmitting values of Christianity into a ritualistic mode. As pointed out by Chow Kai-wing, the didactic mode transmits cultural values by engaging the participants in a dialogue, a conversation, or a discussion in either a personal or a textual encounter. In contrast, participants in a ritual learn values experientially through witnessing or performing ritual acts. By following the formal procedures of a ritual, one either accepts its symbolic meaning or willingly suspends any doubts regarding its professed meaning.[62] Though they often acted as ritual masters in Christian liturgy, the Jesuits more often acted as teachers who tried to convey their message by way of the didactic mode. Their "apostolate through books" in China is a clear example of this method. The cultural imperative, however, forced them into the direction of the ritualist mode: it was not enough to write or teach that Christians practiced filial piety. "In order to banish by concrete facts the opinion that had wrongly taken shape about the neglect of the dead," as Dunyn-Szpot writes, the cultural imperative also had to be ritually manifested. And funerals were an appropriate ritual expression of it. This change also influenced the specific role of the Jesuits. In the didactic mode of communication, an authority figure—the teacher or instructor—always plays the key role in imparting knowledge and values, and the students "receive" the teachings. Even in the most important Christian rituals, such as Mass and confession, these didactic roles of authority are preserved since the priest usually delivers a homily to the assembly or moral instruction to the penitent. In the ritual mode of transmission, the role of participant ranges from mere presence as audience or witness to full participant as performer. Despite this difference in degree of participation, the participants in a ritual do not play the roles of teacher and student. They only have to perform the proper ritual sequence. Such a shift in roles can also be observed in what happened to the Jesuits in this period. Both in the condolence rites, which were orchestrated by the master of ceremony, and in imperial and sometimes other funeral processions, the Jesuits themselves merely played the role of participants. During these rituals their status as teachers was temporarily suspended and they experienced what Victor Turner has called a *communitas*, a relatively undifferentiated community or even a communion of equal individuals who submit together to the general authority of the ritual elders.[63] As such, they were no longer transmitters of values, but they submitted to the authority and values encoded in this Chinese ritual structure.

5 / Funerals as Community Practice

In the post-Canton period, at least as important as the development of a mission policy regarding funerals was the creation of a systematic Chinese Christian funeral liturgy. As illustrated by a guideline of rituals for funerals in thirty-two articles that was drafted in Guangdong in 1685, the Chinese and Christian funerary traditions were interwoven within one and the same ritual process.[1] From this unique document, two major functions of the funeral ritual emerge: first, it allows the transformation of a deceased individual into an ancestor by the family and into a member of the community of saints by the Christian community; and second, it strengthens the cohesion and solidarity of both the family group and the Christian community. The Chinese Christian funeral ritual is framed into the elementary structure fundamental to the Chinese funeral, and upon this core framework are grafted key elements of the Christian ritual.

A GUIDELINE FOR CHINESE CHRISTIAN FUNERALS

The ritual guideline for Christian funerals stipulates the different actions to be performed by the participants from the moment of death until the entombment of the body. There are four different versions of this guideline:

A. "Ritual Sequence for Attending Funerals and Organizing the Procession" ("Linsang chubin yishi") (earlier version)[2]
B. "Ritual Sequence for Attending Funerals and Organizing the Procession" ("Linsang chubin yishi") (later version)[3]
C. "Ritual Sequence for Funerals and Burials" ("Sangzang yishi") (earlier version)[4]
D. "Ritual Sequence for Funerals and Burials" ("Sangzang yishi") (later version)[5]

These four versions of the "Ritual Sequence" guideline, which are here labelled "text A," "text B," "text C," and "text D," are interrelated and were probably produced in this chronological order.[6]

Text A is anonymous, but notes written on the cover of texts B, C, and D give information about their textual history.[7] Text B contains a short note in Latin and Portuguese by Francesco Saverio Filippucci, SJ (1632–1692): "I had Antonio Ly, *xianggong* [i.e., local catechist] of this house, compose this paper in the first month of 1685."[8] This note is important because right from the start it acknowledges the Chinese collaborator, (Antonio) Li Andang, as main author of the text, Filippucci being the one who ordered the document. The note on text C, also signed by Filippucci and dated 16 May 1685, gives information about the subsequent transformation of the text: "This paper is drawn from the other one that I had composed by Antonio Ly, *xianggong* of this house. It was revised by Leontio Ly, *xianggong* of His Lordship the Bishop of Basilitano, who wished to approve and sign it. The Reverend Friar Agostinho de S. Pascual retained it, because he wished to add the obligation of a statement of clarification in number eleven."[9] The Bishop of Basilitano was Luo Wenzao or Gregorio López (1617–1691), a Dominican (OP) ordained as a priest in Manila in 1654 and consecrated as a bishop in Canton on 8 April 1685. Agustín de San Pascual (ca. 1637–1697), was a member of the Franciscan Order of Friars Minor (OFM) who came to China in 1671. He first served in the Dominican mission in Fujian, and then from 1677 to 1683, he reopened the Franciscan mission in Shandong. By the close of 1683, he was active in Canton, where he had also served as assistant priest at the episcopal ordination of Luo Wenzao. He authored several treatises in Chinese and drew up pastoral norms for the Spanish Franciscans in China. At the end of 1685, de San Pascual was elected to a five-year post as their provincial commissar.[10]

The note on version D indicates the suspension of the publication project through Filippucci's withdrawal of his signature:

This paper, revised by Ly Leontio, *xianggong* of the house of His Lordship the Bishop of Basilitano, has an addition to number eleven dealing with the statement of clarification on offerings to the dead and, without my knowledge, it was signed by His Lordship the Bishop and by the reverend Fathers Friar Jo. Francisco de Leonessa[11] and Friar Agostinho de S. Pascual. I disclaimed this, and with the consent of all, my name was withdrawn from the head of the paper and likewise my signature from the bottom of the same together with the seal of His Lordship the Bishop and the signatures of the aforesaid fathers so as to invalidate the foregoing signatures.[12]

It seems that the "Ritual Sequence" guideline was never printed.[13]

As appears from this history and also from the content, the guideline was intended as a local prescriptive text, destined for basic Christian communities, including the lower layers of society. It is also clear that the text was not detached from practice. Not only was it composed and revised by two local catechists, but the major reason why the text was not published was that the amendments by de San Pascual would have altered the practice current among Chinese Christians.[14] It is not a text with the same status as the European *Roman Ritual*, which was the result of long negotiations among theologians who not only took into account a praxis, but also the long tradition of written sources. The Chinese text in four versions is rather a guideline that was drafted close to the place of action and that tried to bring order to already existing practices. Taking into account these limits, the guideline is also a descriptive text that can inform us about certain funeral practices at the end of the seventeenth century. The rules of the longest text, version B, are translated here:[15]

"RITUAL SEQUENCE FOR ATTENDING FUNERALS AND ORGANIZING THE PROCESSION"

[Introduction]

1. The rituals of the Holy Teaching and the non-superstitious local rituals are different in meaning. Therefore they must not be mixed inappropriately. One has to perform the rituals of the Holy Teaching first and only then can one apply the non-superstitious local rituals.

[The beginning of the end: Immediately following a death]

2. When a Christian has left the world, the family members should immediately report it to the priest and ask the priest to say Mass for the soul of the deceased ancestor. To avoid harm to the soul, the report should not be delayed.

3. Through the community leader (*huizhang*), the community members should be informed so that they gather at the home of the deceased ancestor to chant prayers.

[The preliminary laying out][16]

4. When the community members have been gathered together, then first the corpse is received in the central hall. Wooden planks serve as a bed, with a white cloth placed on top, and the corpse then placed on it. In front of the corpse, there is a table on which are arranged incense and candles.

5. A holy image should be placed. The table, the table cloth, the incense, flowers, wax candles, and other things that have been arranged on it should all be very clean.

6. The community members gather together and kneel before the holy image. They make the sign of the cross and pray the introductory prayer, the Our Father, the Hail Mary, the Litany of Mary, all these prayers once. Next a string of sixty-three Hail Marys, the prayer after death, and the closing prayer with the sign of the cross. When done they rise.

7. The community members bow four times and rise four times before the corpse. Next they prostrate themselves and accomplish the ritual of weeping; it should be done in a restrained way.

[Encoffining: The final laying out]

8. Concerning the preparation of the wood for the coffin, the thickness will depend on the economic means of the family.

9. After the preparation of the coffin, the community leader and community members are invited to gather together to chant prayers. Moreover, at the moment of preparing the body for the coffin, together they kneel towards the holy image and with the hands folded in front, they make the sign of the cross, pray the introductory prayer and the Litany of the Saints, the prayer before the encoffining, and the closing prayer, and again make the sign of the cross. When it is finished, the community leader alone stands up. Then he uses holy water to sprinkle the corpse. Together they all pray the prayer for the sprinkling of holy water. When done they all rise.

10. When things are appropriately put in order, the corpse is placed in the coffin, then the coffin is closed completely and nailed shut. The community members kneel towards the holy image, make the sign of the cross, and pray the introductory prayer and the prayer after the encoffining. When done, they rise.

11. The coffin is placed in the middle of the family hall. In front of the coffin the incense altar is installed with objects displayed on it in neat rows according to their greater or smaller number. The filial sons kneel down, burn incense, and offer a libation of wine. When this activity is finished, the community members retire with the hands folded in front. The filial sons lead the people living in the family in raising the wailing. When it is finished, the filial sons kneel in front and thank the community members with a kowtow.

[Ancestral tablet]

12. When inscribing the funerary tablet, do not use the characters *shen* (spirit),

ling (soul) and the like; rather, write "the seat of our late father so and so" or "the seat of our late mother so and so."

13. Before the funerary tablet of the deceased, it is not appropriate to chant prayers, but only to perform the local rituals so as "to serve the dead as one serves the living, and to serve the deceased as one serves the surviving." If Christians want to chant prayers for the soul of the deceased, they should chant before the holy image.

[Various ways of condoling]

14. If relatives and friends who are not Christians come to condole, one can accept the incense and candles they present as a gift. If there are golden ingots and money in paper, since it is emotionally difficult to refuse them, immediately moisten them with water so that they decay. Do not order someone to burn them, and they certainly should not be kept in the house. When the relatives and friends who are not Christians have finished performing the rituals of bowing with the hands folded in front, of kowtowing, and of weeping, the filial sons kneel in front and express their thanks by kowtowing.

15. If Christians go to condole to non-Christian people, they are allowed to present incense and candles as a gift, to bow with the hands folded in front, to kowtow and to weep, but they are not allowed to perform any non-Christian ritual that is superstitious, and also they are not allowed to perform any Christian holy merit making acts.

16. Since Christians take great pains to encourage their parents to become Christians, if these parents remain stubborn and until their death they are not able to open their hearts and submit to orthodoxy, then they themselves are responsible for the destruction of their soul; the filial sons cannot do anything about it. Since they are not permitted to perform the rituals of heterodox teachings, and nor are they to use the rituals of the Holy Teaching, they can only perform the ancient non-superstitious rituals.

[The seven sevens]

17. The ritual of the seven sevens can be used except for the blended and superstitious things.

18. When the time of doing the sevens happens to coincide with a Sunday or feast day, one should first go to church to attend Mass and only afterwards go to that family to perform the seven sevens ritual.

19. According to the local rituals, among the seven sevens, customs and habits are only put into practice on the first, the third, and the final sevens. The first seven is the day that the filial sons and filial relatives put on mourning garments and stop condoling; the third seven is the day that close and distant relatives and friends come for a banquet; the final seven is the end of the funeral rituals after which the filial sons go out in the street to thank the guests.

20. If Christians want to perform these rituals and ceremonies, it is appropriate that on that day they invite the community leader and community members to their home. They first perform the holy merit making before the holy image, then the filial sons can offer provisions and burn incense before the ancestral tablets, and together with the people living in the family they all perform the rituals of weeping and of the libation of wine. When done, the relatives and the community members consecutively bow with the hands folded in front, kowtow, and weep, so as to express wholly the idea that the old man who died is like their own father. When the ritual is finished, the filial sons kneel in front and thank the relatives and friends with a kowtow.

[Offering of food]

21. Concerning the wine and the food that the filial sons have arranged, how could the deceased ancestor really be able to enjoy it? They are only small testimonies of the civility of a filial heart. One can detain relatives and friends to distribute the food to them, but it is not appropriate that the filial sons drink the wine. The food and wine can also be distributed as a gift to poor people so as to extend benevolence on behalf of ancestors and help them to obtain the happiness of heaven.

[Funerary eulogy]

22. If among the relatives who are not Christians there is someone who has a funerary eulogy to express condolence, it is appropriate that the bereaved family in advance sends a necrology of the dead, so that the other will not introduce heterodox words.

23. Model for the necrology: First, introduce the deceased, saying: lordship so and so—personal name, birth name, Christian name, date of birth, date of death—was very fortunate to enjoy the Lord's grace to die peacefully after having attained the respectable age of so many years. Next, describe the good virtues of the life of the deceased ancestor: from which year he followed the Holy Teaching and venerated the Lord of Heaven; how he respectfully observed the rules and commandments; how filial and obedient he was towards his parents and charitable towards the young and orphans; the prosperities and adversities he

encountered in his life; and the different sort of beautiful deeds he did—they all can be described in truth. Next could be described how the filial sons and grandchildren who are still alive all follow the Holy Teaching, and are able to continue the good pursuits of the father and ancestors, etc. Finally, address the relatives and friends, saying: in the event you respectfully receive the necrology with which he was favoured, make it widely known. Fortunately they taught us uncles and children and grandchildren which direction to go so as to imitate the good virtues of the ancestors. My feelings are unequal to this sorrow. Respectfully written by me, so and so, committed to writing, while wiping away my tears.

[Preparing for the burial]

24. The day of carrying the coffin to the grave can be decided by the filial sons themselves, but it should not interfere with Sundays and feast days when one has to go to the church to attend Mass.

25. A few days before carrying the coffin to the grave, it is appropriate to invite the community leader and several members.

26. If there are people who invite Christians to keep watch during the night, prayers should be chanted at three times during that night: once at the beginning of the night, once in the middle of the night, and once at dawn.

[The procession]

27. On the day of carrying the coffin to the grave, Christians go to the family of the deceased, and before the holy image, they chant prayers according to the rules formerly explained. When the chanting is finished, the elements of the procession should be arranged in proper order for carrying the coffin to the grave. First should come musicians and banners, then a baldaquin [canopy] with the cross, a baldaquin with a holy image of the Lord of Heaven, and also one with Saint Michael, and then the one with the holy name. A stove can be carried by hand, and a palace lantern. Christians should [proceed] on the left and the right, in mourning dress, carrying incense and candles. At the end is the coffin, which is covered with fine silk. All the community members, old and young, walk in order, the filial sons lean upon the coffin and bow. The other filial relatives all follow behind the coffin.

[The burial]

28. When the coffin has arrived on the hill, [the procession] stops. The community members kneel down with their hands folded in front in the direction of the cross baldaquin. They make the sign of the cross, pray the introductory prayer,

the Litany of Mary, and the prayer before the entombment, all once, and the closing prayer. When done, the community leader stands up and sprinkles the grave and the coffin with holy water. The prayer for sprinkling holy water is chanted, and then the coffin is lowered into the tomb and covered with earth. When it is finished, the community members make the sign of the cross in the direction of the cross baldaquin, perform the introductory prayer, the Litany of All the Saints, the prayer after the entombment, and the closing prayer. When done, they rise, and the filial sons kneel in front and thank the community members with a kowtow.

29. When the ritual of entombment is finished, they immediately invite [the carriers of] the cross and the other baldaquins to return home in the same arrangement as before. The community leader and community members go together to the home of the deceased. They kneel before the holy image. They express their thanks to the Lord of Heaven. When done, they rise. Afterwards the funerary tablet of the deceased ancestor is installed on the incense altar, and the different objects are arranged in proper order. The filial sons kneel down, present incense, offer a libation of wine, and lead the family members in paying respects. When done, the filial sons thank the community members by paying respects.

30. If the filial sons want to entertain the community members who will return, they can ask them to stay, and as it seems fit to them, detain and entertain them, and they can also offer them refreshments.

[Paying respects to the dead]

31. Every year on the day of the *qingming* festival, Christians can go up the hill to pay respects to the tombs. When it is a tomb of a Christian, one first chants prayers, praying to the Lord of Heaven for the soul of the deceased. Afterwards one can light candles, burn incense and offer provisions. If it is a tomb of a non-Christian, one is not allowed to chant prayers, but one should limit oneself to lighting candles, burning incense, and offering provisions.

32. In paying respects to the tomb, cover paper does not matter, but one cannot use paper money. One can only use plain white paper and weigh it down with earth on top of the tomb, letting people know that someone is taking care of this tomb.

CHRISTIAN RITUALS AND LOCAL CUSTOMS

While the "Ritual Sequence" guideline is clearly meant for Christians, it is significant that right from the beginning it is not intended to present only

Christian funeral rituals. Though the text warns against the inappropriate mixing of Christian and (non-superstitious) local rituals, the whole text shows how these can be combined. "Local customs" in the text primarily mean the customs from the province of Guangdong, whose capital city is Canton.[17] Yet the local customs mentioned are clearly a mixture of different traditions.

The basic structure of the funeral as proposed in this guideline corresponds to the uniform Chinese structure that emerged in Ming and Qing times. This was based roughly on classical models outlined in the *Book of Rites* and later simplified by Zhu Xi and others in *Family Rituals*.[18] In text A (article A2), there are explicit references to some of the major events in the Chinese ritual sequence, such as the preliminary laying out or dressing of the corpse (*xiaolian*) and the final laying out or encoffining (*dalian*) as mentioned in *Family Rituals*.[19] As they were in the late Ming, Chinese who became Christians in the 1670s and 1680s were most likely well acquainted with this classical structure. This can be deduced from other works by Chinese Christian authors that date from the same period. For instance, Paul Yan Mo's "Successive Questions of Fr. Li" ("Lishi tiaowen") (ca. 1694), written in collaboration with his father, Ambrosius Yan Zanhua, is a very systematic work in which, on the basis of classical writings, they answer questions raised by Fr. Li (possibly Simão Rodrigues, SJ (1645–1704)). At the question "What are the different rituals involved in funerals?" the authors quote extensively from the chapter on funerals in *Family Rituals*.[20]

In the seventeenth century, commitments to Neo-Confucian ritual systems were neither total nor exclusive. In many places, indeed, the classical ritual sequence was supplemented by rituals of Buddhist or Daoist origin. This was, for instance, the case in the "doing the sevens" (*zuoqi*) or seven sevens ritual, when families engaged Buddhist monks or Daoist masters to chant scriptures every seventh day since the hour of death until the seventh seven (the forty-ninth day). Though mainly of Buddhist origin, seven sevens feasts had become widely accepted as particular days of condoling and paying respects to the deceased parents. "Doing the sevens" therefore refers to a wider set of practices on every seventh day, even without the presence of monks. The concrete rituals of doing the sevens were numerous and differed from place to place. As appears also from these texts, according to the local Guangdong practice, rituals are performed only on the first, the third and the seventh seven (B19).[21] Texts B, C and D (B17) allow Christian funeral rituals to be supplemented by the seven sevens ritual, as long as no superstitious words (C and D) or practices (B) are involved. In all these cases, the seven sevens ritual supposedly does not include the visit of Buddhist or Daoist monks. Chinese Christian funerals at the end of the seventeenth century were clearly based on *Family Rituals*, while they rejected most of the explicit Buddhist and Daoist practices.

From the outset the four versions of the "Ritual Sequence" guideline appear to be a mixture of different traditions. The basic structure is that of the traditional Chinese funeral sequence. Within this structure specific rituals of Christian, Neo-Confucian, or Buddhist origin are combined. Along with this variation, which will be developed further, it is important to stress the fact that this guideline was built on a package of actions, routines, and performances that constituted the "elementary structure" of Chinese rites. The actions belonging to this elementary structure were performed with minor variations throughout China during the late imperial era, irrespective of class, status, or material circumstance.[22] This guideline, with its stress on encoffining, procession, and entombment, confirms the existence of this elementary structure, albeit one interwoven with Christian rituals.

THE ACTORS AND THEIR ACTIONS

Beyond the differences among the versions of the "Ritual Sequence" guideline, their common characteristics are reflected in the findings of anthropological studies of funerals. The following survey first analyzes these common characteristics on the basis of three major questions: Who are the actors? What actions do they perform? What is the place of action? Next, on the basis of the results of this survey, analyzing the meaning and function of these Chinese Christian funerals shows to what extent these rituals contribute to building communities of effective rituals (see Table 5.1).

The Priest

The most obvious actor in the European prescriptive texts is the local priest. He clearly occupied the most important place in the funeral rituals as practiced in Europe in the seventeenth century. In this Chinese adapted local ritual guideline, however, his role is reduced to a marginal one. Explicit reference to him is made only once. Right at the beginning of the ritual sequence, just after a death, "the family members should immediately report it to the priest [A1—*duode*; B2—*shenfu*] and ask the priest to say Mass for the soul of the deceased ancestor." In two mentions of the Mass whose attendance should not be compromised by the observance of local funeral rituals, the role of the priest is implicit: "When the time of doing the sevens happens to coincide with a Sunday or feast day, one should first go to church to attend Mass and only afterwards go to that family to perform the seven sevens ritual" (B18) and the day of burial "can be decided by the filial sons themselves, but it should not interfere with Sundays and feast days when one has to go to the church to attend Mass" (B24). The marginality of the priest is thus further indicated by the location of his ritual action: contrary to the European prescriptive texts, according to which the corpse is moved from the house of the deceased to the church, where a funeral Mass takes place, and then from the church to the tomb, this Chinese ritual guideline locates the ceremonies merely at the home of the deceased and at the tomb. In these ceremonies the priest does not intervene. His celebrating a Mass for the deceased takes place in the church and does not require the attendance of the mourners.

The "Ritual Sequence" guideline thus corroborates the marginal role of the priest as already observed in the Chinese translation of European prescriptive texts, especially Fróis' *Rules for Helping to Obtain Merit Towards a Good Death* (*Shanzhong zhugong guili*) and Buglio's *Ritual for a Good Death and for the Sepulture* (*Shanzhong yiying lidian*), the rules for the associations of Christians, and the decisions of the Canton Conference (especially article 34). The reduced number of available Catholic priests could explain their marginal role, as may the minimal role of the ritual masters (also often called "priests" in modern Western texts) in traditional Chinese funeral ceremonies. Ritual masters occupy an ambiguous position, an "institutionalised marginality" according to James Watson, because of their constant exposure to death pollution (i.e., the danger of being contaminated by the airs emanating from the corpse according to the Cantonese concept). Therefore, they avoid exposing themselves too much to the influences of such pollution during burials. In addition, the ritual masters in a Chinese funeral never accompany the coffin to the grave, even though all other male participants normally join the procession.[23]

The Chinese Christian "Ritual Sequence" also contains elements that show that the community feels threatened because obvious danger is involved. Traditional Chinese ideas about the potential for pollution or chaos are partly the source of the threat; the text recommends that the offering table be clean (B5); weeping restrained (B7); and holy water used (B9). Another source is the new threats introduced by the Christian conceptions of superstition and idolatry, especially as identified in the actions performed by non-Christian relatives and friends (B14, B16). A comparison between the role of the Catholic priest and the Chinese ritual master cannot be extended too far, since the concept of priesthood in the Chinese tradition, where most of the ritual specialists are married and raise families in the communities they serve, is rather different from the Catholic concept.[24] Moreover, in the Christian tradition death is not really considered to be pollution. Still, it is significant that many ritual texts, such as the above-mentioned rules for associations, attribute only a marginal role to the Catholic priest in the funerary ritual. Such marginality corresponds to the role of ritual masters in Chinese funerals, but this role is similar to the funeral tradition of pre-tenth-century Europe.

The Christian Community

The marginal role of the Catholic priest contrasts sharply with the dominant place of the Christian community in these texts. The most central role in the funeral seems indeed to be occupied by the members of the Christian community, who are usually designated as *zhongyou*, as in B6, *jiaozhong zhongyou* in C6, or *jiaoyou* in C7.

The members of the Christian community are the main officiants during the crucial ceremonies: the first laying out (B4–7), the encoffining (B9–11), the adapted ceremonies for the seven sevens ritual (B20, A15), keeping the watch before burial (B26), the different ceremonies on the day of burial (B27–30), and the ceremonies of the *qingming* festival (B31). The action occurs in the house of the deceased and at the tomb. This community, always mentioned as a collective (the only individual mentioned being the community leader), and the community's actions are where the Chinese Catholic funeral ritual differs most clearly from the Chinese Confucian tradition, and also where it resembles to a certain extent the sectarian tradition.

The actions of the community members are significant for determining their role. In addition to wailing and bowing, their most important role is the chanting of prayers. In the Chinese tradition chanting is usually performed by the ritual master or by a group of monks who were invited for that purpose.[25] In the "Ritual Sequence" guideline, as in the rules for associations, it is the collective group of lay Christians that assumes this role. Herein Christian funerals resemble those of Chinese traditional sectarian funerals, at which lay members of the sectarian groups chant.[26] The different versions of this guideline allot a significant portion of the text to the prayers that have to be chanted. Text B has in total four articles with detailed instructions for the prayers, first described at the initial laying out of the body in B6, then at the encoffining in B9 and B10, and finally at the entombment in B28; text A contains three additional articles of prayer instructions for keeping watch in articles A8, A9, and A10.[27] These prayer sessions follow the usual order of a prayer session as instructed in the prayer book (*rike*) that was in the hands of many faithful for daily prayers: kneeling, sign of the cross, opening prayer (*chuxing gongfu*), various prayers, closing prayer (*yiwan gongfu*). Most of the prayers are well-known and are not funeral-specific: Our Father (*Tianzhujing*), Hail Mary (*Sheng-*

mujing), Salve Regina (*Shenerfu*), Creed (*Xinjing*), Litany of Mary (*Shengmu daowen*), Litany of the Saints (*Shengren liepin daowen*), as well as the repetitive prayers (the Our Father repeated thirty-three times, the Hail Mary sixty-three), and the fifteen mysteries of the rosary (*meigui shiwuduan*).[28] This indicates that the community could actively participate in the chanting of prayers, since most of the Christians knew these prayers by heart. The "Ritual Sequence" guideline also mentions the prayers that are related in a special way to this specific ritual action: the prayer after death to be said before the first laying out (*zhonghou daowen*), the prayers before the encoffining (*lianqianjing*) and after the encoffining (*lianhoujing*), at the moment of encoffining, the prayer before the entombment (*anzang qianjing*) and after the entombment, at burial (*anzang houjing*). These prayers can also be found in the Chinese translations of the European ritual handbooks, such as those compiled by Fróis and Buglio. The titles of the prayers in "Ritual Sequence," however, are not always identical to those in these ritual prescriptive handbooks.[29] Therefore it is difficult to assess if either of these two books, or even a different one, had been actually used as reference.[30] It is also unclear whether the prayers in these handbooks would have been known by heart.

As for the specific location of the ritual action by the Christian community, their chanting always takes place while kneeling before a "holy image," which may be a cross or an image of the Lord of Heaven or possibly of the Virgin Mary. Besides kneeling, the Christian community also participates in traditional forms of expression of respect and sorrow: bowing four times (*sibai*), prostrating themselves (*fufu*), bowing with their hands folded in front (*zuoyi*), kowtowing (before the corpse) (*koutou*), and weeping (*ju'ai*).[31]

The visits by these prayer groups were an important element in defining who was a member of the Christian community and who was not.[32] Moreover, they were an important forum for spreading Christian ideas and practices, because the Christian community as a group had access to the inner family sphere at these occasions.[33] Finally, these ritual actions provided the occasion for the participants to reinforce their intra-communal relations.

The Community Leader

A central role within the Chinese Christian community, as was already the case in the Christian associations from before the Canton exile, is attributed to the community leader (*huizhang*). The guideline makes clear that it is through the community leader that community members are informed about the death of someone (A1b, B3) and about the date for burial (A6b, B25). In addition to joining the community in its prayers (B9, B20, A12b=B29, A15), the community leader also plays a central role in the ceremonies of encoffining and entombment. He alone stands up and sprinkles holy water on the corpse in the first ceremony (B9), and he reads the prayer of sprinkling holy water (*Sashengshuijing*; i.e., *Asperges me*[34]) and sprinkles the corpse in the second ceremony (A12=B28). There is, however, no mention of incensing.

The central role of the community leader confirms the central role of the Christian community itself in the funeral ritual.

The Filial Sons

The Christian community and its leader to an extent overshadow the role of the "filial sons" (*xiaozi*) in hosting the event. The term is first mentioned after the encoffining description. It is not clear whether *xiaozi* means all filial sons or even all descendants, or whether the term refers merely to the chief mourner, who in Chinese tradition is always the eldest surviving son or designated male heir.[35] In traditional Chinese funerals, he is responsible for ensuring that the rites are performed to the satisfaction of the community. The structure of Cantonese funeral rites, however, is such that the chief mourner performs only the acts dictated by the presiding ritual specialist.[36]

The role of the filial sons demonstrates that the major place of ritual action of a Christian funeral in China was indeed the home of the deceased. In the Chinese Christian "Ritual Sequence" guideline the filial sons play a role in the rituals conducted in the home of the deceased: the ceremony after encoffining (B11), at the occasions of condoling (B14), and at the seven sevens ritual (B19, B20, A15). A partial explanation for the home being the main location of funeral action for Chinese Christians lies in the difference between the European Catholic and the traditional Chinese funeral. In the European ritual, entombment follows relatively shortly after death (one to three days later) and therefore the corpse is removed quite quickly from the home. In contrast, in the Chinese tradition, the coffin may remain in the central hall of the house of the deceased for several months before it is entombed. The Chinese Christian funeral rules in the "Ritual Sequence" correspond to the prevailing ideology in which the major rites of passage in China—capping, wedding, funeral—are considered "family" rites (*jiali*). Hence, this guideline is similar to the earlier European tradition when the principal locus of the funeral rite was also at home, and not in the church.

While the community members perform their actions before the "holy image," the filial sons are the only ones who perform actions before the funerary or ancestral tablet (B13, B20, B29). The "Ritual Sequence" guideline prescribes the holy image and funerary tablet to be put in two separate places, and not one behind the other as was the solution in some interwoven rituals in Fujian in the late Ming. These separate locations indicate separate ritual roles and domains. Filial sons are also the ones who, together with other filial relatives, don mourning garments on the first seven day (B19), thereby expressing both their particular relationship to the deceased as well as their altered position in the family structure. Members of the Christian community, however, only wear mourning garments during the procession (B27).

The actions of the filial sons are those traditional actions of Chinese funeral (and other) ceremonies that were not considered "superstitious" by the missionaries: the burning of incense (*shangxiang*) and the offering of provisions (*gongyang*) and libations (*dianjiu*) (B11, B20, A12, B29). The filial sons are the only ones mentioned in the guideline as performing these rituals; the only exception is during the *qingming* festival, when all Christians may light candles, burn incense, and offer provisions on the tombs of Christians (B31). The filial sons also lead the other family members, guests, and the Christian community in bowing with hands folded in front, kowtowing, and wailing. Moreover, they are responsible for the reception of the guests, for entertaining the guests after the burial (B30), and for saying farewell to the guests by kneeling and thanking relatives and friends with a kowtow—the action with which several articles of the guideline close (B11, B14, B20, B28). Finally, the sons decide the date of burial (B24), and have a special place beside the coffin during the funeral procession (B27).

The ritual actions of the filial sons at a Chinese Christian funeral indicate that they perform the principal actions that are prescribed for them in the traditional Chinese ritual handbooks such as *Family Rituals*.

The Relatives and Friends

Actors in the funeral ritual also include the wider group of people who knew the deceased. Members of the extended family—those who live as part of the family (*jiazhongren*) and other relatives (*qinqi*)—participate at the various funeral ceremonies with the traditional forms or expression of respect and sorrow: bowing with their hands folded in front, kowtowing, and wailing (B11, B20). The third seven is a special day on which close and distant relatives and friends, both Christian and non-Christian, come for a banquet (B19). Relatives and friends also express their sorrow and respect with the traditional bowing with their hands folded in front, kowtowing, and wailing (B14). Though these external participants may have been quite numerous, their role is not stipulated in great detail.

Among the relatives and friends, however, there may be a number of non-

Table 5.1. Structural Analysis of the Chinese Christian Funeral Ritual

	Rituals of the "Holy Teaching"		Local "non-superstitious" rituals		Local "superstitious" rituals
Location	Church Before a holy image		Home At the coffin of the deceased in the central hall Before the ancestral tablet		
Agent	Priest Christian community		Family		
	Leader	Community	Filial sons	Christian relatives	Non-Christian relatives
Ritual action	Mass Sprinkles holy water Chant prayers		Burn incense, offer provisions and libations		Burn paper money
	Bow, kowtow, wail				
Transformation of the corpse into	Member of community of saints		Ancestor		

Christians who want to perform "rituals of heterodox teaching," and Christians who go to condole at the home of non-Christians also may witness such rituals. In these interactions conflicts may arise between Christian rituals and rituals that are considered superstitious.[37]

TRANSFORMATION THROUGH RITUAL ACTION

This overview of actors and their actions shows that there are three major circles of participants involved in three characteristic groups of activity within the funeral ritual. The first circle comprises the members of the Christian community and its leader (with the priest in its margin). The action of this first circle is *verbal*, involving written texts: prayers chanted or read aloud before the holy image. The second circle is composed of the filial sons, whose action is characterized by *service*: the offering of food, wine, and other provisions and also the burning of incense before the funerary or ancestral tablet. The third circle is the wider community of relatives and friends. Its action, also shared by the other two circles, is one of *physical expression*: prostrating, bowing with the hands folded in front, kowtowing, and weeping.

How these different groups interact is exemplified in article B20, where Christians are given instructions for implementing the seven sevens rituals:

> If Christians want to perform these rituals and ceremonies, it is appropriate that on that day they invite the community leader and community members to their home. They first perform the holy merit making before the holy image, then the filial sons can offer provisions and burn incense before the ancestral tablets, and together with the people in the family they all perform the ritual of weeping and of the libation of wine. When done, the relatives and the community members consecutively bow with the hands folded in front, kowtow, and weep, so as to express wholly the idea that the old man who died is like their own father. When the ritual is finished, the filial sons kneel in front and thank the relatives and friends with a kowtow.

The ways for Christians to perform the seven sevens rituals, and the many other rituals in the guidelines under discussion, are carefully described, but what do these different rituals signify, and how do the actions of the rituals in the Chinese Christian funeral make that meaning manifest? Generally speaking, ritual is about transformation, especially rites of passage such as a funeral.[38] In particular, the funeral rite relates to the transformation from one state of being to another. The meaning of a ritual transformation, however, is very often not expressed. This is also clear from these ritual texts. They make explicit what to do, rather than offering the meaning of the rituals. They are concerned with orthopraxy (correct practice) rather than orthodoxy (correct belief).[39] Although prudence is needed to go beyond what these texts tell us, it is possible to investigate what kind of transformation they imply. The procedure followed here is to try to recreate meaning by reassembling the actors, their actions, and their place of action into a coherent set of messages.

The most apparent transformation is the transformation of a dead person into an ancestor. It is about the transformation of a biological death into a social continuity, in which the family holds the primary place. Food offerings play a crucial part in this process.[40] This transformation is signified by the role and actions of the filial sons. In the "Ritual Sequence" guideline, the filial sons are the only persons who offer libations of wine and food. These actions are performed before the funerary or ancestral tablet, which is the exclusive domain of action of the filial sons; the Christian community, for instance, is not allowed to chant prayers before the funerary tablet. Before the latter, the performance of only local rituals is allowed, so as "to serve the dead as one serves the living, and to serve the deceased as one serves the surviving" (B13). This quote is a slightly adapted version of the one in *On the Practice of the Mean* (*Zhongyong*) mentioned in chapter three, since the instruction "one serves" (*shi*) is added twice. As such, the sentence establishes a simple comparison between service to the dead and service to the living. This joins the "as if" interpretation the earlier missionaries made to emphasize the conviction that the soul is not present in the funerary tablet.[41]

The transformation from the deceased to an ancestor only offers a partial explanation of the ritual action that takes place. Given the importance of the Christian community, it appears that the transformation from biological death to a social continuity occurs in more than just the family; the Christian community is conceived as part of that social continuity, qualified with the classical idea of "community of saints" (*communio sanctorum*) of the Apostles' Creed.[42] Without doubt, the Chinese Christian funeral rituals were influenced by the dominant Christian European view on death, which at that time was a pessimistic one that required the chanting of prayers of intercession or the offering of masses for the "soul of the deceased" (B2, B13).[43] Yet in addition to the need for this individual salvation, there was also the Christian belief that the individual is ultimately incorporated into the immense family of saints, redeemed, and saved (*universa fraternitas*).[44] Moreover, it was believed that the mourners could address the community of saints, requesting intercession for the deceased. There was a kind of spontaneous solidarity of the living with the dead. It is noteworthy that the Chinese translation of these European concepts is built on the key notion of "merit" (*gong*). The reciting of Christian prayers for the dead is called "holy merit making" (*zuoshenggong*; B15, B20), "community of saints" is translated as *shengshen* (or *zhusheng*) *xiangtonggong*, and the leaflets announcing the death of Christians and asking the community of the living to pray for them were later called *tonggongdan*.[45]

In the "Ritual Sequence" guideline, this communal ideal of the life beyond death is expressed by the actions of the Christian community. The prayers of intercession, for instance, establish a link between the living, the dead, and the saints since the community of saints is invoked both in the content and in the expression of the prayers. These prayers include the Litany of Mary and the Litany of the Saints (B6, B9). Moreover, the chanting is always done before a holy image, which is an image of God, Mary, or a saint, and as just mentioned, not before the ancestral tablet. The community of saints is also invoked in the procession, when the corpse of the deceased is carried in succession with the image of the Lord of Heaven and of Saint Michael. Contemporary missionaries would not go so far as to state that the deceased is immediately integrated into the community of saints in heaven. Nevertheless, these actors, their actions, and place of action signify that the ancestral community is complemented by a Christian community of living and dead in which an individual is helped and supported by the saints.

The solidarity of the Christian community, in deeds of charity and in prayers of intercession, also leads the dead into the communion of saints. This is made very explicit by one of the regulations of the "Rules of the Sacred Teaching" (*Shengjiao guicheng*) concerning the solidarity with the dead of poor families:

> 25. When poor Christians die, the Christians, for the transfer of merit to them (*tonggong*), say prayers and perform a [rite of] commemoration. In case there are not enough resources for the coffin and burial, they should pay attention to supplying [the costs of] the burial. All this is putting into practice one of the fourteen works of mercy, namely the merit of "burying the dead," and certainly it achieves the solidarity [of merit] of the *communio* [community between living and dead (saints)].[46]

Christian merit-making in the form not only of prayers but also of financial solidarity thus established the spontaneous solidarity of the living and the dead.

In these Chinese Christian funerals there appears to be a double transformation: the transformation from the dead to an ancestor through the family and to a member of the community of saints through the Christian community. Moreover, by actively taking part in the funeral rituals, and entering into the family sphere, the living Christian community enlarges the family community into a wider community. Participation in Catholic rituals connects people to a much wider Catholic community that in earlier times and other places all participated in similar rituals.[47]

STRENGTHENING GROUP COHESION

Rituals function not only as vehicles for the transformation of the deceased, but also as reinforcement for the cohesiveness of social groups.[48] In his study of Chinese religion, C. K. Yang pointed out that one of the most important functions of the traditional Chinese death rituals is reaffirming the cohesion and solidarity of the family group.[49] In the "Ritual Sequence" guideline for a Chinese Christian funeral, the role of the inner family—of the filial sons—is clearly affirmed. The filial sons are identified as a specific group who perform specific ritual acts. When the sons fulfil their specific ritual role, the ritual has served as an integrative force that reinforces emotional bonds among the close family members.

This reaffirmation is mediated by certain specific ritual acts. One example is ritual weeping, which is common to many cultures. It is a demonstration of group cohesion and solidarity, whether the weeping is spontaneous or not, and an expression of concern over the loss of a member of the group. Ritual weeping either restores an affective relationship or creates a new one in the light of changes in the participants' social positions or roles. Whoever does not weep is regarded by the family as being disloyal not merely to the dead but also to the group.[50] European sources describing Chinese funeral rituals often make explicit reference to weeping as an important feature of these rituals, also pointing out the occasionally excessive lamentations,[51] sometimes opposing the "feigned tears" of the gentiles to the "real ones" of the Chinese Christians.[52] Weeping is also mentioned in the "Ritual Sequence" guideline. It is considered an explicit ritual, as described in A2 and B7 with the phrase, *ju'ai zhi li*.[53] The filial sons, for instance, lead the people of the family in raising the wailing (B11). In text A, it is stipulated that the weeping should be "moderate and not too grievous" (A2). External participants such as the Christian community perform this lamentation too. Weeping is also a part of funerals in Europe, but the fact that a *ritual* of lamenting is mentioned in this guideline, in contrast with the European prescriptive texts where it is not mentioned, shows the particular importance attached to it in China.

C. K. Yang further points out that the family group was consolidated not only by the mourners' demonstrative behavior but also by reaffirming relations with the wider social circle beyond the immediate family and by reasserting the status of the family in the community. This was an effort to reinforce the social and economic position of the bereaved family. As appears in the "Ritual

Sequence" guideline, acts to fulfil this function began with the sending of the obituary to relatives (B22, B23), not merely to inform them of the tragic event but also to invite them to participate in the funeral procession and mourning feast. Assembling the social group of relatives and friends, and the size of the group thus assembled, demonstrated the social and the economic status of the family.[54] This social function is also manifested in the banquet that is organized on the third seven (B19), the entertainment of the guests after the burial (B30), and the thanking of the guests by the filial sons who go out into the street for that purpose on the seventh seven (B19). Since the guideline is a ritual-procedural text, only limited attention is given to activities such as banqueting, catering, or socializing, but that does not mean that hosting was not an important aspect of funerals.[55] Another way of reasserting the status of the family in the eyes of the community is the demonstration, through the funeral procession, of wealth and influence.

The cohesiveness of a group affects not only the family but also the Christian community. In traditional Chinese funerals, a wider community of specialists—ritual masters, musicians, corpse handlers, monks and nuns, actors—and non-specialists participate in large numbers. What is significant in the "Ritual Sequence" text, however, is that the Christian community is mentioned as a collective body. It distinguishes itself from the family and the group of relatives by one major specialized role: the chanting of certain specific prayers. But it distinguishes itself also by the fact that it is not allowed to perform certain rituals at certain places.

CONCLUSION

In previous chapters, descriptions of funerary rituals early in the Jesuit mission to China give the impression that a Chinese Christian funeral rite developed that was characterized by a kind of juxtaposition of certain European and Chinese rituals without much interaction between them. The "Ritual Sequence" guideline produced in Guangdong in 1685, however, shows that at least by that date a new funeral liturgy had been created out of the "Chinese" and "Christian" funerary traditions and that they could indeed be interwoven in one and the same ritual process, even if certain parts were only performed in juxtaposition with each other in time or place. The result can best be compared to a botanical graft. The new element, the scion—the European funeral ritual—is grafted on a preexisting stable element, or the stock—the Chinese funeral. In the new Chinese Christian funeral, the elementary structure of the Chinese funeral is kept and serves as a rootstock for new elements. Characteristics of the newly grafted ritual that differ from the original European Christian tradition demonstrate that in China they were framed into the Chinese structure, with encoffening, condolence and entombment as major events. In the new Chinese Christian funeral, the time between death and burial was no longer short, as in Europe, but was now relatively long, as in the local tradition, with the corpse now preserved in an airtight coffin. The major place of the rituals preceding the burial was the home of the dead, not the church. The main actors of the funeral ceremony were the family members and the community, not the priest. Unlike the church graveyard in Europe, the place of burial for Christians in China was outside the village or the town and the corpse was transported to it in an elaborate procession. But there was also a scion, a new element that brought about some changes to the original stock: the Christian community ritual that expanded the Chinese family ritual. The two major functions of this Chinese Christian ritual reveal the effects of the new, Christian element on the preexisting ritual: first, the transformation from the dead to an ancestor by the family and to a member of the community of saints by the Christian community, and second, the strengthening of the cohesion and solidarity of both the family group and the Christian community. A distinctive new aspect of the graft was the predominance of words over deeds in the ritual activities of the community. It is also through the grafting, the missionaries realized, that certain Christian elements could be publicly manifested. Just as it is difficult to identify a botanically grafted specimen according to either of its earlier forms, the new ritual cannot be called exclusively Christian or Chinese; rather, it is Chinese Christian.

The "Ritual Sequence" guideline in addition clarifies several aspects of the interwoven rituals that have been touched upon earlier. The structural changes, such as the reframing of the Christian rituals around encoffining, condolence, and burial, substantiate the place of the elementary structure in the Chinese funerary ritual, because this elementary structure is maintained even after contact with European rituals. Another aspect is the institutional organization. The guideline shows the major role played by the local community of Christians and the specific role of the community leader—roles that could already be observed in the descriptions of the associations of Christians that took charge of funerals. A selection seems to have taken place in the borrowing of funerary rituals from Europe: the role of the priest was tolerated but marginalized, while the role of the laypersons was promoted and amplified. Finally, concrete ritual expressions, which, as already noticed for the earlier periods, were fully accepted, were now managed in specific ways. Roles are clearly distributed for certain rituals, some only performed by the filial sons, others by the community members, others by all.

The "Ritual Sequence" guideline clearly reveals the role of the community and the place of ritual in this community. The Christian communities that manifested themselves during funerals seem to share some essential characteristics of Chinese religiosity, exhibiting similarities with other communities, especially those of the Buddhist and Daoist traditions, that are striking. Such a community can be labelled a "community of effective rituals." In such a community, people are brought together and united in a group whose rhythm of life is modulated by certain rituals. These rituals were usually patterned according to a liturgical calendar, in the case of Christianity a Christian calendar. By introducing a new calendar to China, therefore, the missionaries were not just accommodating some technical aspects of a neutral division of time. They were challenging, whether consciously or unconsciously, the basis of ritual life itself: the transformation of natural time into a cultural framework and therefore into time that is not only culturally but also "cultually" defined. The introduction of a Sunday and of other Christian religious feasts, when converts were supposed to go to Mass and prepare themselves in advance by fasting, made them live according to a time rhythm different from the one practiced in Buddhist or Daoist communities of effective rituals. These practices may not have been introduced effectively in all places, but it is at this ritual level that itinerant missionaries most strongly competed with Buddhist monks, Daoist priests, or local shamans and that their differences were often inflated. Funeral rituals, however, are not patterned according to a calendar, since they happen occasionally, even if at these occasions the Christians still had to respect Sundays and feast days.

As the "Ritual Sequence" guideline and the rules for associations show, the organization of funerals depended on a more or less stable community that met regularly at other occasions. The rituals that were practiced were "effective" in the sense that they both built a group and were considered by the members of the group as giving meaning and effecting salvation. These were communities of mutual support in the general fight against all kinds of fear—fear of death, but also of disease, demons, and natural disasters—and the proven efficacy of these rituals, the happy discovery that "they work," appears to be a primary motive in joining and maintaining the community.

As appears from the above analysis, these communities also represent other characteristics of Chinese religiosity: They are very much lay oriented and have lay people in charge; though not always explicitly mentioned, it is quite probable that women played a major role as transmitters of the rituals, such as in the chanting of prayers. These communities also have a service-oriented concept of priesthood—priests are only needed to celebrate Mass. The doctrine that the community professes is expressed in a simple way; the belief in the afterlife is clearly conveyed by recitative prayers. Community members share a belief in the transformative power of rituals, whereby there can be intercession for the dead. All these characteristics reveal the extent to which these Christian communities were imbedded in a Chinese environment on the occasion of a funeral. It thus seems that in the same way that Chinese popular devotions and rituals were shaping the life of common people, Christian practices also provided awe-inspiring ceremonies which mediated salvation in daily life.

6 / Christian versus Superstitious Rituals

The funerary guideline, "Ritual Sequence," shows how the Chinese and European traditions could fuse more or less harmoniously into one Chinese Christian funeral rite. Yet ritual exchange is often accompanied by tension and conflict, such as appear with the shifts taking place in Chinese rituals as the missionaries imposed their own "imperatives." Christians would always encounter what were considered "rituals of heterodox teaching," because non-Christian friends and relatives would want to perform them while attending funerals of Christians, and Christian friends and relatives would condole at the home of non-Christians who had died where such rituals were performed. In these interactions, where Christian rituals appeared alongside rituals considered superstitious or idolatrous, conflict was bound to arise. Could non-Christian rituals be allowed at Christian funerals, and could Christians engage in non-Christian rituals at the funerals of non-Christians?

This question touches upon some aspects of the Chinese Rites Controversy, though this controversy as such will not be my focus. In general terms, the controversy turned around two major sets of problems.[1] The first concerned the name of God and such important concepts as angels, the soul, and others. The major question here was whether terms taken from the Chinese classics, like *tian*, meaning heaven, and *shangdi*, meaning high lord, could convey the Christian concept of God. The second set of questions was related to the ceremonies in honor of Confucius and the cult of ancestors, which comprised such forms of piety as prostrations, or kowtowing, incense burning, the serving of food, and so on, in front of the corpse, grave, or commemorative tablet. Here the question was whether Christians should be forbidden to participate in these acts, or if these ceremonies should be regarded as gestures of piety, or at least as not being contrary to Christian belief, and therefore should be tolerated. The missionaries could take still a third position: while condemning some features, they could permit converts to perform the rites with modifications and hope that the Christian conscience would eventually abandon or still further modify them. These questions received a wide variety of answers that can be classified in two approaches. The first, to which most Jesuits adhered, called the "Ricci method," was based on accommodation to the Confucian elite culture. Ricci and most of his successors defined these rituals not as idolatrous but as "civil" and "political" ones, and thus acceptable. They also opted to use Chinese terms from the classics for key theological terms such as God. The other approach, followed mainly by Dominican and Franciscan friars, considered the rites as superstitious and the chosen terms as not representing the Christian God. The controversy began when the first Dominicans reported directly to Rome what they had observed of Jesuit actions. These and subsequent interventions resulted in several Roman instructions in 1645, 1656, and 1669, but the discussion would eventually remain localized, within China. The conflict between the two visions intensified when Charles Maigrot (1652–1730), of the Society of Foreign Missions of Paris (Missions Etrangères de Paris, or MEP) and Vicar Apostolic of Fujian, launched an indictment of the rites in his mandate of 26 March 1693.[2] From that time the Holy See became involved in a juridical process of extraordinary complexity, while Jesuits' books about China became the subject of stormy debates and condemnations at the Sorbonne in Paris. The deliberations of a commission of cardinals in Rome resulted in the decree *Cum Deus optimus* of 20 November 1704, forbidding the use of *tian* and *shangdi* while approving *tianzhu* for the concept of God, and forbidding Christians to take part in sacrifices to Confucius or to ancestors. This condemnation was repeatedly confirmed in 1707, 1715, 1721, and 1742. Though some of the condemned rituals formed part of the funerary rite, funerals themselves were less affected by the controversy.

ALLOWING "NON-SUPERSTITIOUS" LOCAL RITUALS

When missionaries came to China and were confronted with funerals, their initial concern was to introduce "Christian" funerals. Such funerals consisted of rituals, such as Mass and prayers, which were oriented towards the salvation of the soul of the deceased. Since the funeral practices they encountered in China were quite different, and since funerals were public events that were attended by non-Christians, the missionaries very soon realized that it was not possible to hold purely "Christian" funerals, unless they confined Christians to a very reduced and exclusive community. By the 1670s, their method of accommodation had led to a combined practice: the dead were buried "according to the Chinese custom but with a Christian ritual," as described in Dunyn-Szpot's account of the decisions of the Canton Conference.[3] The "Ritual Sequence" guideline established by (Antonio) Li Andang and Francesco Saverio Filippucci adopts a similarly tolerant attitude toward the two types of rituals. In the opening article of the "Ritual Sequence," the relationship between them is described as a successive practice: "The rituals of the Holy Teaching and the non-superstitious local rituals are different in meaning. Therefore they must not be mixed inappropriately. One first has to perform the rituals of the Holy Teaching and only then can one apply the non-superstitious[4] local rituals."[5]

Which non-superstitious rituals could participants then perform at Christian rituals and which could Christians perform at the funerals of non-Christians? Missionaries had been discussing this question since the early seventeenth century.[6] The negotiations among themselves and with Rome had led to some important instructions on which missionaries living in China in the 1670s and 1680s could rely. One of the most important instructions was the "Decree of the Sacred Congregation of the Propagation of the Faith, dated September 12, 1645," issued by the body that was charged with fostering the spread of Catholicism and with the regulation of Catholic ecclesiastical affairs in non-Catholic countries. This decree was the answer of the Sacred Congregation to the questions presented by Juan Bautista de Morales, OP (1597–1664), who was one of the first Dominicans to arrive in China in 1633 and who had been scandalized by the practices in the Christian communities organized by the Jesuits in Fujian. He had returned to Rome in 1643 to present a list of seventeen questions in which he expressed his apprehension about these practices. Several of the questions attacked the Jesuit position concerning the names to be used for God or the rites offered for Confucius. Concerning the funeral rites, however, there does not seem to have been a fundamental difference between the practice in the Jesuit missions and the Roman response to Morales' questions issued in 1645:

12. When someone dies in China, whether he is a Christian or a pagan, the religiously observed custom is to prepare an altar in the home of the deceased, and to put on it an image of the deceased, or a tablet as described above, decorating it with incense, flowers, and candles, and laying the corpse behind it in a coffin. All who enter those homes to mourn genuflect three or four times before the decorated altar and the image of the deceased. They lie flat, their heads touching the floor. They carry candles and incense to burn on the decorated altar before the image of the deceased.

The question: Is it permissible for Christians, and especially for ministers of the holy Gospel, keeping in mind that this is a reciprocal sign of love and good will, to do these things, especially when the deceased are rather prominent persons?

The decision: This can be tolerated as long as the table is an ordinary piece of furniture and not a true altar, and if the actions performed are within the bounds of civil and political obsequies (*obsequii civilis et politici*).[7]

The decision taken with regard to this question is rather tolerant. Because these rituals merely addressed the deceased parents, they were regarded as "civil" or "political," terminology characterizing acceptance of rituals that had been in use since the beginning of the seventeenth century.

Other questions, however, received more negative responses. In reaction, the Jesuits dispatched Martino Martini (1614–1661) to Rome in 1651 to communicate that de Morales had not described their missionary practices accurately. A favorable decree followed on 23 March 1656 sanctioning the practices as described in a statement by Martini. Concerning the funeral rites, however, the position was basically the same tolerant one as stated in the decree of 1645:

4. The question: Could Christians be allowed the ceremonies which philosophers propose for the deceased as long as nothing superstitious is involved?

Another question: Could Christians perform permissible ceremonies together with pagan relatives?

Still another: Could Christians be present even when pagans perform superstitious actions, especially after having made a declaration of their faith (*praecipue facta fidei protestatione*)? They would not be cooperating, nor endorsing what the pagans do. But it would surely be noticed, if blood relatives were absent. It would cause enmity and hatred. The Chinese do not think that souls of the deceased are gods. They do not hope or ask anything from them.

There are three ways in which they honor their dead. First, when someone dies, whether a Christian or pagan, they always prepare a sort of altar in the home of the deceased. They place on it an image of the deceased, or a tablet on which the name of the deceased is inscribed. They decorate the altar with incense, flowers, and candles. Behind the altar they lay the body of the deceased in a coffin.

All who enter those homes to mourn genuflect three or four times before the inscribed tablet, or before the image of the deceased. They lie prostrate, their heads touching the floor. They carry candles and incense to burn on the altar, or rather before the tablet or image of the deceased.

The second way takes place twice a year in the halls of their ancestors. The Chinese call them halls, not temples, by the name of *Tsu tang* [*citang*]. These are really family remembrance places or even monuments. Only persons of high station or wealthy relatives have them. No deceased person is buried in them, but in the mountains. Within there is just an image of a distinguished ancestor. Then on steps, some higher than others, tablets are arranged to a span's height. On these the names of all the deceased in that family are inscribed, their rank, their dignity, their sex, the age, and the date of their death, even of infants and of girls. Twice a year all the relatives gather in this hall. The more affluent of these offer meats, wines, candles, and incense.

Poorer people are not able to have these halls. They keep the tablets of their deceased at home, either in a special place, or even on the altar where saints' images are kept, for lack of space, because the house is small. They do not venerate these tablets. They do not offer them anything. They are there because there is no room for them anywhere else. The Chinese ceremonies described above take place only in a hall for the deceased. If they do not have a hall, they omit the ceremonies.

The third way is what takes place at the graves of the deceased. In accordance with Chinese law these are all in the mountains, away from the cities. Children or relatives come to these at least once a year around the beginning of May. They tidy up the graves, uproot the weeds and grasses that have sprung up. They weep, they wail, they genuflect, as was stated in the first way. They set out cooked foods and wine. After they have finished weeping, they eat and drink.

In the light of what was said above, the Sacred Congregation ruled that Chinese converts could be allowed to use these ceremonies honouring their deceased, even with pagans, as long as they are not doing anything superstitious (*sublatis tamen superstitiosis*). They can even be present with pagans when they are doing superstitious things, especially after having made a declaration of their faith (*praesertim facta fidei protestatione*), and if there is no danger of subversion, and when hatred and enmities cannot otherwise be avoided.

His Holiness approved these answers and decisions.[8]

That these norms were accepted by most missionaries is also evident from the "Pastoral norms established for the China mission [of the Spanish friars]" that had been compiled by the Franciscans Agustín de San Pascual and Miguel Flores de Reya, (1644–1702), in 1683.[9] The instruction about condolence makes explicit reference to the norms of 1645:

3. We determine that the ceremony *diao* (that we call "condolence" (*pésame*) in our Spanish) can be allowed to a Christian, as long as one only offers incense, candles, and silver; these things as such are indifferent, and cannot be argued to be a religious action. As for performing bows, genuflections, and prostrations in front of the table on which rests the [funerary] tablet or the image of the deceased, or even the deceased in his coffin,[10] there is no obstacle, because for such a circumstance these actions had been proposed to the S. C. of Prop. in 1645 and were said to be licit.[11]

PROHIBITIONS OF "SUPERSTITIOUS" RITUALS

What funeral rites did missionaries consider "superstitious"? The clearest rejection of funeral rituals possibly considered superstitious concerned three domains: the inscriptions on the ancestral tablet, the usage of food offerings, and the use of paper money.[12]

Ancestral Tablet Inscriptions

The four versions of the "Ritual Sequence" guideline all prescribe, without explanation, the use of a funerary tablet and the omission of the words *shen* (spirit), *ling* (soul), and the like (B12). In fact, the phrasing of this article is almost the same as that of article 27 in "Rules of the Sacred Teaching" (*Shengjiao guicheng*), the set of forty-five pastoral rules that was probably established in the aftermath of the Canton Conference: "For the funerary tablet of a deceased Christian, the characters *shen*, *ling* and others should not be written, but only 'the seat [*wei*] of Mr. so and so' or 'Mrs. so and so.'"[13] The reason for this prohibition was that, according to the Catholic faith, the tablet could not be considered the seat of the soul of the deceased. It seems that by the 1680s, this had become a generally adopted practice, which apparently did not give rise to much controversy among the missionaries at that time.

Food Offerings

The second controversial issue concerns the suspicion of superstition in the usage of food and wine. The first part of the problem was the consumption by the mourners of the edible offerings to the deceased. Article 21 of the "Ritual Sequence" guideline explains that food and wine "are only small testimonies of the civility of a filial heart. One can detain relatives and friends to distribute the food to them, but it is not appropriate that the filial sons drink the wine. The food and wine can also be distributed as a gift to poor people so as to extend benevolence on behalf of ancestors and help them to obtain the happiness of heaven." The adopted solution of distribution to the poor is the same as the one already practiced by the Fujian community in the 1630s.

The second suspicion of superstition arises from the question of whether the deceased persons themselves are able to accept the food. That the solution to this question was a point of serious contention emerges in the four different versions of the ritual guideline, particularly disputed through the various permutations of article 11. The notes on the cover of the different versions explain that the Franciscan de San Pascual wanted to change this article, which he did in text D. The Jesuit Filippucci, however, refused the alteration and consequently refused to allow the text's publication. In the different versions of article 11, which fortunately have been preserved, the degree of accommodation clearly varies from texts B to C to D. Comparison between these versions illustrates the different attitudes towards this question. The version in text B, proposed by Antonio Li Andang and Filippucci, stipulates the following:

> The coffin is placed in the middle of the family hall. In front of the coffin the incense altar is installed with objects displayed on it in neat rows according to their greater or smaller number. The filial sons kneel down, burn incense, and offer a libation of wine. When this activity is finished, the community members retire with the hands folded in front. The filial sons lead the people living in the family in raising the wailing. When it is finished, the filial sons kneel in front and thank the community members with a kowtow.

The version in text C includes an explanation (indicated here in italics) by way of a quote from the "Tangong" chapter of the *Book of Rites* (*Liji*):

> The coffin is placed in the middle of the family hall. In front of the coffin the incense altar is installed with objects displayed on it in neat rows according to their greater or smaller number. *It is exactly as it is said in the chapter "Tangong" in the* Liji: *"Immediately after death, there is an offering of dried flesh and minced meat . . . but the dead have never been seen to partake of these things."*[14] *This does not prevent the filial sons from expressing their feelings and in this case* to kneel down, offer incense, and offer a libation of wine. . . . [same as previous version].[15]

The final version in text D, proposed by de San Pascual, suggests that Christians actually profess their position with a "statement of clarification":

> The coffin is placed in the middle of the family hall. In front of the coffin the incense altar is installed with objects displayed on it in neat rows according to their greater or smaller number. It is exactly as it is said in the chapter "Tangong" in the *Liji*: "Immediately after death, there is an offering of dried flesh and minced meat . . . but the dead have never been seen to partake of these things." This does not prevent the filial sons from expressing their feelings and in this case *while displaying the objects they should make a declaration before their relatives and friends of their understanding of the meaning of the matter. Or, if they so wish, they may write a couplet beside the offering, such as: "How could [the deceased] ever partake in such delicious food; nevertheless we wish to express our filial piety." Hereafter,* they kneel down, offer incense, and offer a libation of wine. . . . [same as previous version].[16]

As explained in the notes by Filippucci on the covers of texts C and D of the "Ritual Sequence" guideline, it is the adding of this "statement of clarification" (*protestação* in Portuguese, *protestatio* in Latin)[17] to article 11 that prompted him to refuse to sign the text and finally to refrain from publishing it. As appears from version D, this statement refers to a declaration Christians should make of clarification or opposition (protest) about the meaning of the use of food at funeral rituals.

From another report by Filippucci on the incident, we know that he believed de San Pascual to have been "only instructed in theology in a mediocre way." He thought de San Pascual had in a light way, presumably through some superficial argument, convinced Bishop Luo to ask Filippucci to include a statement of clarification against these "superstitious" Chinese rites. Filippucci refused to do so for two major reasons. He was of the opinion that it was difficult to condemn, on the basis of one protest, a practice that had been established by the Jesuits many years earlier and that had long been practiced by neophytes without any stigma of error in faith. Moreover, he did not want this event to turn into a "triumph before victory": not only in China but also in the whole of Europe it would be announced that the Jesuits had changed their opinion derived from their ancestors regarding the cult of the deceased. As a result, Filippucci decided to refrain from publishing the guideline on funerals until the bishop "was better informed on the practices and customs among the neophytes in China, by other theologians who had been in China for a longer time."[18]

The discussion about food and wine at funerals does not seem to concern the essence of the matter—whether these offerings are superstitious or not—but only whether a statement should be added or not. In his own commentary, however, Filippucci, who was very sensitive to any insinuation that the offerings were a sacrifice instead of simply expressions of a political cult,[19] makes it appear as if there is some dispute about the superstitious nature of those offerings.

That there was less difference of opinion on the interpretation of food as such appears from the "Pastoral norms established for the China mission [of the Spanish friars]" drawn up by de San Pascual, in which the author accepts food offerings while also requiring a statement of clarification (*protesta* in Spanish):

> 4. The ceremony to put or offer tables of food before the coffin or tablet—which important people usually perform when someone dies—cannot be argued to be an act of idolatry or superstition because this action is not by nature intrinsically bad (*intrinsece mala*). And though this ceremony is founded in gentile error, it seems to us that it can be allowed for Christians, with a statement of clarification (*protesta*) that they perform such ceremony in order to show the affection they displayed for the deceased and that they offer him the same things as if he were

alive, without believing that his soul comes or may come, or may eat these things. This statement of clarification modifies or makes explicit this offering as a political action and discards it from everything that the infidels conceive in it as error.[20]

8. [When the deceased is an infidel and the son a Christian,] . . . it happens that in this case a table of food is set out to provide satisfaction to the infidel family members. Though such action may be well considered, we find that it would be the best if the minister advises the neophyte to excuse himself from setting out such tables. But if according to prudent judgment [the neophyte] may find that they are unavoidable, then he can set out [a table with food]: with it a written statement of clarification (*protesta in scriptis*) evident to everybody, which declares that to set out these tables is a sign of affection and reverence displayed on behalf of the deceased father. With such an action the primary objective of such an offering is made explicit, which is to serve and revere the dead as if the dead were alive.[21]

Here the focus of analysis is not on the conflict between these two missionaries as such, but on what it reveals about rituals. These texts by de San Pascual show that he and Filippucci agree on the most fundamental aspect: the action of offering food is not by nature "intrinsically bad" and therefore cannot be considered "idolatry" or "superstition." For both writers, it is the meaning of a ritual that determines the ritual, and not primarily, as is often the case in China, the performance as such. In other words, orthodoxy defines praxis. If the ritual is an expression of filial piety, it is considered non-superstitious and can be tolerated. If, however, the ritual is performed because of a belief that the deceased will consume the food, then it is superstitious and the action should not be allowed. De San Pascual and Filippucci disagree on the use of a statement of clarification. To de San Pascual, there is a close link between the meaning and its expression: it is the *explicit explanation* of a ritual that gives it another dimension and allows it to be considered merely political. For Filippucci the link between meaning and expression is not necessary, so the explanation should remain implicit. This difference in concepts of rituality appears even more clearly in the discussion about the use of paper money.

Paper Money

The "Ritual Sequence" guideline rejects as superstitious the use of paper money, both when condoling (B14) and when visiting the tomb on the occasion of the *qingming* festival (B32). The guideline, however, adopts an attitude of accommodation with regard to gifts of paper money by non-Christian family members or relatives, "since it is emotionally difficult to refuse them," but instead of burning them, they should be destroyed by moistening them with water (B14). And at the visit of the tomb, "one can only use plain white paper and weigh it down with earth on top of the tomb, letting people know that someone is taking care of this tomb" (B32).[22]

The topic of paper money has risen in previous chapters. From the earliest times, missionaries had rejected this form of offering. It is also included among the prohibitions in Confucian-Christian morality books, such as *Book of the Warning Bell* (*Duoshu*), or in the discussion of rites by Li Jiugong. The reasons for such a rejection are linked to the Christian concept of body and soul. Aleni's discussion of the topic in his *Questions and Answers Regarding the West* (*Xifang dawen*) provides an example:

Question: Do you also burn paper money to help the ancestors to be affluent in the other world?

Answer: No. Man has a body and a soul. While the body is alive, it uses food, drink, and clothing to satisfy its hunger and ward off the cold. But after death the body becomes rotten flesh and decaying bones. How can it then feel heat or cold, hunger or satiety? Even if you offered it real food or clothes, it could not make use of them; how much more is this true of counterfeit things, such as false paper money? There is no sense in this. If you give counterfeit money to anybody in this life, you are liable to be tried by the laws of the country; and you want to offer it to the ancestors? To use counterfeit money is a crime; how much more so if you use false paper for gold and silver! Therefore, burning paper money is not only useless to the ancestors, but it is the height of blasphemy and deception. The substance of the soul is pure spirit and has no need of food, drink, or clothes. The good ascend to Heaven where happiness is complete and all wishes are fulfilled; why should they need false paper money? The wicked are thrown into Hell where their evil deeds are punished eternally, and they cannot be saved. But assuming that they could be saved, they might possibly be happy with real things. What use could they have for the ashes of silver ingots made of tin foil or coins cut out of coarse paper?

Someone might ask: It is clear now that paper money is a meaningless thing, not worth to be used to honour one's ancestors' memory. But how else is one to show respect if one does not use food, drink, or paper money?

To this I reply: Filial piety consists in imitating one's ancestors' virtues and in following their teaching. If you omit this and only honour them with wine and meat, which they cannot enjoy anyhow so that it returns to yourself in the end, can that be called filial piety? The ancients said: If a man does not treat his parents with filial piety while they are alive, it is useless to sacrifice to them after their death. How true that is! But food and similar things are at least real and not counterfeit; they can be distributed to the poor in the ancestors' name to spread their virtues and benevolence. The belief that false paper money and Buddhist services will help the dead in the other world is an absurd lie invented by the bonzes to deceive the people. In your country the *Family Rituals* of a famous Confucian scholar have clearly forbidden them. It is difficult to see why people believe in them, why they are sunk in superstition and will not awake from their folly.[23]

This explanation clearly shows that the idea of an exchange between living and dead in the Chinese tradition contrasts with the idea of a separation of body and soul in the Christian tradition. Rejecting the practice of burning money is argued on the basis of mainly rational elements, and in particular a discussion of efficacy. Aleni also uses emotive arguments: one is simply deceiving one's parents, especially since presenting them with paper imitations of gold and silver during their lifetime is already considered fraud. Similar arguments can be found in the *Diary of Oral Admonitions* (*Kouduo richao*). Yet facing a guest who is still not convinced by these arguments, Aleni appeals to history:

> The guest still had doubts and did not understand. The master [Aleni] again asked him: "Who are greater paragons of filial piety and respect towards their parents: the people of today or the sages of the ancient Three Dynasties?" He said: "The Ancients cannot be matched—how would I dare to belittle them?"
>
> The master said: "Before the Qin there was no paper, and in the sacrificial canons of the Three Dynasties the use of paper is not mentioned. If you, Sir, really do not intend to belittle them, why do you go on babbling like this?"
>
> The guest agreed and retired.[24]

This rejection of the use of paper money seems to have been commonly agreed upon among missionaries. The rules that arise from the Canton Conference, for instance, clearly prohibit the practice:

> 40. It is forbidden to Christians, as has been observed in praxis thus far, to make or sell paper money, which is dedicated to the cult of the idols and which is called *Kin in tim, chi cien, mà, cù*, etc.[25]

Despite this consensus, which seemed to have been shared by Chinese Christians, a new discussion arose in the 1680s.[26] Indeed, several missionaries initiated proposals to allow the use of paper money at funerals. A unique set of events and texts provides a broader cultural context for examining the issue of burning paper money in a chronological fashion.

In 1681, when the Kangxi Emperor ordered the entombment of the two Empresses who had died a few years earlier, Ferdinand Verbiest participated in the funeral procession. It is not known if his participation in this funeral procession prompted Verbiest to discuss funeral matters with the emperor, nor is it clear if that event encouraged him to compile his own explanation of the Catholic funerary rituals. What is known is that about one year later, Verbiest published *Questions and Answers Concerning Catholic Funeral Rituals* (*Tianzhujiao sangli wenda*), dated Kangxi 21/9/13, or 13 October 1682, a few days after the death of Lodovico Buglio on 7 October 1682.[27] Verbiest discusses the issue of burning paper money and objects at length.[28] The text was corrected for publication by his fellow Jesuits Claudio Filippo Grimaldi, SJ (1638–1712), and Tomé Pereira, SJ (1645–1708). In the same year the issue of burning money was certainly under discussion among the Jesuit missionaries. Francisco Gayoso, SJ (1647–1702), for example, reports on the matter to Verbiest in a letter dated 23 November 1683, and includes quotes from two letters by Verbiest, dated 19 August 1682 and 20 October 1682.[29]

But the emperor and his circle also talked about funeral rituals. Since the early days of the Manchu Empire, which began in 1644, Chinese officials had opposed the excessive burning of material goods during funerals. The emperor had agreed with its abolition and had promulgated a law to that end. In 1687, the Kangxi Emperor issued an edict directed primarily against wasteful funeral practices by Han bannermen. But Kangxi's attitude toward death rituals is best revealed in his observances for his beloved paternal grandmother, Xiaozhuang (1613–1688), when he decided to change the commonly accepted mourning rules. Xiaozhuang died in the final days of the 26th year of the reign of Kangxi (Kangxi 26/12/25, or 27 January 1688). Ferdinand Verbiest died one day later, on 28 January 1688. It seems quite possible that it was in 1689 that Kangxi read Verbiest's *Questions and Answers Concerning Catholic Funeral Rituals*; he added a few notes to the passages related to the burning of paper money. The copies in the Roman Archives of the Society of Jesus carry the name of Antoine Thomas (1644–1709), Jesuit Vice-Provincial in Beijing, who dates his signature 26 October 1701. He testifies that the copies were made from the original, with the emperor's notes included in red characters.[30]

This text by Verbiest serves as a starting point for an analysis of the discussion on burning paper:

> Why does one not burn paper money and other objects in Catholicism, or is therein some distinction between what is good and not good?

If human beings perform exterior acts, then one can probably not speak of good or bad regarding the acts themselves. Whether one calls them good or bad depends on the intention (*yi*) for which they will serve when the person is about to perform them. When they are performed with an appropriate intention, then they are called good, and when they are performed with an inappropriate intention they are called bad.

For instance, the burning of paper and other matters. If it expresses one's honest heart towards the deceased parents, relatives and friends, saying, What my heart wishes is precisely to use the large amount of money I have now in replacement of merits of penance, by using it to distribute it to the poor or to build orphanages and other works of charity, so as to save the parents, relatives, and friends and let them ascend to heaven and enjoy happiness, and therefore the money I burn now is not more than expressing the sincere intention (*chengyi*) of my honest heart; or saying, If I spent a large amount of money I can buy the resurrection of parents, relatives and friends, and my feeling is to give it away without being mean, then the money that is burnt before the tomb expresses only this intention; or saying, I would rather lose a large amount of money, treasures, houses, furniture, and other articles than bear the death of my parents, relatives, or friends, and therefore the money, treasures, houses, and other funerary objects that are now burnt before the tomb merely express this honest intention; then in all these cases, with such feelings and intentions, the burning of paper money and other things is not forbidden.[31]

In this paragraph Verbiest adopts a tolerant position with regard to burning paper money for the dead. In order to understand his position, it has to be seen in connection with the discussion that was taking place among some Jesuit missionaries, about which we are informed by the above mentioned letter by Gayoso, who was then missionary in Xi'an. In this letter, Gayoso argues in favor of an open consultation among the missionaries about the possibility of allowing Christians to burn paper under certain conditions. The reason for bringing up this discussion is the same as observed earlier: by not burning paper money, Christians are criticized for not honoring their ancestors.[32] In a very systematic and scholastic way Gayoso lists eight different arguments in favor of the acceptance of this practice and also addresses the objections made by his colleague in the Shanxi region, Christian Wolfgang Herdtrich, SJ (1625–1684). Gayoso is very much aware that this practice was prohibited by earlier missionaries and by their writings, such as *Refuting Stupidities* (*Piwang*), where it is mentioned as a "vain and futile rite" (*ritus vanus et futilis*).[33] A key element in his argument is whether the act is "intrinsically evil" (*malitia intrinseca*) or not. He is of the opinion that the possible evil is only "extrinsic" (*extrinseca*);

Verbiest holds the same opinion, as is evident in the above quotation from his *Questions and Answers Concerning Catholic Funeral Rituals*.[34] This means that the act of burning paper is not an evil act in itself—if it were that would imply that it is also a mortal sin to burn paper money—but that it depends on the "intention" (*intentio*) with which it is performed. If, for instance, one believes that the money is actually used by the dead, then it is a "wicked and superstitious intention" (*intentio prava et superstitiosa*) that has to be condemned. If, on the other hand, one does not believe that it will be used, but that one only performs it to signify one's piety and respect for the deceased (this is the so-called political or civil practice), it is considered a "correct and purified intention" (*recta et purificata intentio*).[35]

Gayoso compares the act of burning paper money with other practices accepted by the missionaries. The offering of food and incense is acceptable, under the condition that one does not believe that the dead eat the food or smell the incense. The use of a painting of the deceased is similarly permitted, as long as one does not believe that the spirit of the deceased is inside the painting. In Gayoso's thinking, the missionaries' rejection of the burning of paper on the one hand, and the acceptance of the offering of food and incense on the other, are probably inspired merely by the respective absence and presence of these practices in the European traditions. This so-called disparity is founded only on imagination, not on reasoning: if the superstitious aspect can be removed from the act of burning incense offerings, then the same could be done to the act of burning paper.[36] Herein Gayoso explicitly adopts the same position as the decree of the Congregation of Propaganda Fide in 1656, which ruled that "Chinese converts be allowed to use these ceremonies honouring their deceased, even with pagans, as long as they are not doing any thing superstitious (*sublatis tamen superstitiosis*)."[37] Moreover, Gayoso is of the opinion that Christians need not in all circumstances explicitly clarify, with some sort of "explanation" (*protestatio*), their intentions in the burning of paper.[38]

The examples of proper intention given by Verbiest can be classified under the same type of argumentation as Gayoso's. What is important for this analysis is not so much whether this argumentation is valid or not, but that by expounding the notions of extrinsic evil and intention, the missionaries are able to establish a split between the ritual act and its significance. To them, the meaning is extrinsic to the act itself, and depends on the intention of the people who engage in the act.

In *Questions and Answers Concerning Catholic Funeral Rituals*, after having presented the reasons why the burning of paper might be acceptable, Verbiest exposes what he sees as superstitious beliefs. The translation of his text below distinguishes the following elements: arguments copied from *Refuting Stupidities*

(*Piwang*) (in italics),[39] sentences the Kangxi Emperor had highlighted with circular dots (underlined), and the comments he added (in quotation marks within square brackets).

But the intentions by which the secular world burns paper at present are different from these previous intentions, and they contain many inappropriate aspects. Such is the one who wrongly thinks that the soul of the deceased needs money and other matters in hell to spend, and also needs clothing, food and servants, just like in the present world. Therefore they especially prepare money, houses, utensils, and human figures made of paper and use fire to burn them; and this means that they become real money, houses, utensils, and human beings, that have a real use; [Kangxi: "The words are well chosen and the reasoning is smooth" (*yan zheng li shun*).] these kind of things are very inappropriate.

Now the human being has a material body and an immaterial soul. During material life, one uses food and clothing to satisfy one's hunger and protect oneself from cold. When one dies, how would one's rotten body and spoilt bones know cold and heat or know hunger or satisfaction; then even if one offers them as real goods to be worn and eaten, they still cannot be used.[40]

As for the soul itself, it is purely spiritual and does not need food and clothes. The good people have already ascended to heaven, where they enjoy perfect happiness, so why should they need paper money; and the evil ones descend into hell and can never be saved. And even if one says they could be saved, then real things could also be fortuitous, but what about false things like paper money? *How could it be that humans see it as the ashes of paper, and the soul on the contrary would be the only one to consider it as real and true? Now, paper money and golden and silver paper ingots are nothing but paper before being burnt; how could they suddenly be transformed into real money and real gold and silver after being burnt?* [Kangxi: "This is put straightforwardly and thoroughly" (*shuo de shuangkuai touli*).][41]

The Kangxi Emperor shared Verbiest's position that the dead did not use paper money, but his agreement was not just a parroting of the Jesuits' ideas. What the emperor was agreeing with was also the core of one of the arguments his grandfather had put forward to oppose extravagant funerals. According to the Manchus, one of the pitfalls of Han ritual practice was wastefulness in mourning rituals. Emperor Huangtaiji was the first to suggest that mourning rituals should not waste precious resources. He criticized the popular practices of burning objects for the use of the dead and of burying objects with the dead. Even before the conquest of China, he issued an edict about this practice:

An edict to the officials in attendance. Mourning and funeral rites originally had set regulations. As to our country's customs of burying [things] with the dead, and transforming things for the use of the dead through burning, many adhere to these useless extravagances. Now if a man lives, then goods and clothes and food are what sustain him until he dies. If people have armour that they wish to bury with the dead, how can the dead make use of it? Hereafter whosoever would bury with the dead, or burn things for the use of the dead, must obey the regulations and not support such wastefulness.[42]

Like his grandfather, Kangxi had little patience for wastefulness in funeral practices. To him, such extravagances also revealed the wasteful and perhaps effete character of the Han Chinese. On 30 November 1687, for instance, he issued an edict directed primarily against wasteful funeral practices by Han bannermen.[43]

Missionaries were aware of this attitude of the early Qing emperors. In his letter, Gayoso offers another argument in which the burning of money might be allowed in light of imperial opinion. He mentions a memorial, approved by the emperor, in which the excessive burning of precious goods and furniture was opposed in favor of their replacement with paper money.[44] From this event Gayoso draws the following conclusion:

This superstition of burning paper money, which follows the distorted mind of the gentiles and bonzes, is removed by such a postulate of the Chinese emperors. If indeed the reason and cause they bring forward to use paper money is that very precious furniture, solid gold and silver, and precious stones should no longer be wasted uselessly, by which the superstitious disposition (*superstitiosa institutio*) of the bonzes is translated into a wise disposition (*prudens institutio*) following the authorization of the Chinese emperors, then, as a result the way is open to Chinese Catholic Christians to burn paper money in a licit way in honour of the deceased.[45]

Despite the common argument that the dead will not use the paper, the major concern of the emperor and the missionaries is different. The main preoccupation of the Qing emperors is that funerals should not be wasteful. The major concern of the missionaries is that they should not be superstitious. The reason for the Chinese emperor to allow the burning of paper money is that in such a way funerals would be less wasteful. The key argument for Gayoso to accept the burning of paper is that Christians should not be criticized for being perceived as not honoring their deceased. Since it is a "political" ritual, it should be allowed.

Verbiest, in the end, is not in favor of allowing the practice. After giving a further example of wrong belief, he returns to the topic of intention:

There is also the theory of "preparatory deposit." "Preparatory" refers to the fact that one prepares things in advance during life to be used after death. "Deposit" refers to the fact that one makes money, ingots, cloths, ornaments, goods, and other things out of paper or silk, and that one deposits them in hell. But hell is really like *a prison* where one suffers. *How, in the normal world, would people who have not yet committed any crime buy in advance with money [a place in] prison in which to live in the future?* [Kangxi: "This makes sense, this makes sense, but it may be offensive to some people" (*Youli youli dan kong dezui yu ren*).] *How, then, would people make a preparatory deposit and buy [a place in] hell for eternal calamities?* Because in the secular world one has this kind of inappropriate behaviour, therefore the Catholic teaching does not allow the burning of paper, in order to avoid giving people the wrong idea that we have recourse to the same absurdities as the secular world.

Moreover, secular practices are widely spread today. Suppose there were one or two famous scholars who want to burn paper with an appropriate intention fixed in their heart; it is still difficult to make people follow their intention. Because of what one or two persons privately do, one cannot change the widespread customs of the secular world as they have been practiced for a long time. For instance the word for "bad." Literati today use it to designate abominable things. But if one or two famous scholars want to use it to designate good things, then the mind of people will not follow it immediately, and this is because what has been fixed by private intention cannot change what is set by common intention.[46]

These final statements can be clarified by returning to the major ritual changes that occurred in China from the late Ming to the beginning of the Qing, especially during the Kangxi reign. In his study on mourning in late imperial China, Norman Kutcher identifies an important shift in ritual in the Ming period. He argues that the late Ming emphasis on emotion had specific ramifications for the world of ritual. The inherited texts on the performance of rituals—primarily Zhu Xi's *Family Rituals*—had presented an unvarying model for how the dead were to be mourned. Emotion was the product of rituals properly performed, and rituals were supposed to channel emotions. In the late Ming, however, the assumption was reversed: a preexisting emotion determined when and how, or even if, a ritual should be performed. Late Ming ideas on ritual also generally placed more emphasis on the individual as a source of authority. Emotion was to be the starting point for rituals, rather than the result of their proper observance.[47]

The Kangxi Emperor was the first Qing ruler to examine the system of mourning and formulate a consistent policy on it.[48] His thinking on mourning rituals coincided with many of the late Ming attitudes. Like many thinkers from that time, he believed that rituals should express, not regulate, the emotions. And he believed that rituals could and should be changed, even personalized, to make them better express emotions. As Kutcher points out, Kangxi's attitude toward death rituals is revealed in his observances for his beloved paternal grandmother Xiaozhuang.[49] This woman, who was given the title Grand Empress Dowager, had showered affection and guidance on the young Kangxi, whose mother had died in 1663. When she fell ill, Kangxi refused to move from her bedside for thirty-five days. After her death he grieved deeply. Much to the surprise of those at court, he declared that he would observe a full twenty-seven months' mourning period: that is, he would mourn her as one would mourn a parent. Members of the Grand Secretariat, princes, top officials, and even common people petitioned the emperor to observe a period of only twenty-seven days of mourning, one day for every month of the traditional mourning period for a parent. But Kangxi refused: "All the things that I do have sincerity (*cheng*) at their base. Observing three years of mourning is perfectly in accord with my intentions (*yi*). It is not because I wish to put on a false showing."[50] There are several conspicuous features in this and related decisions by the Kangxi Emperor.[51] The first concerns the private nature of his mourning. Kangxi issued few pronouncements on how mourning should be observed in Beijing or throughout the empire. Though he publicized his mourning observances, he did not act as though it were the responsibility of others to share his very private feelings of grief. His mourning was not only private, it was largely personalized. He made changes in the system of mourning because to him mourning was not a system. To him it was an expression of filial piety as pure emotion, of the loving obedience of a son to his parent.[52] Kangxi devised his mourning practices to show the extent of his devotion, though they violated all precedent. Finally, when Kangxi declared his intent to mourn for twenty-seven months, what was left unsaid was that his observation of the deepest mourning would in many ways be mourning in name only. He made clear that his practices would not interfere with the business of government. He meant only that he would wear mourning clothes while in his private apartments (not while holding court) and that he would refrain from attending auspicious functions. Mourning, he felt, should touch the emotions, but it should do so in a way that did not interfere with bureaucratic efficiency.

One of the key terms in these different texts is "sincere intention." The meaning of the term is understood differently by the Kangxi Emperor and by the missionaries. To the Kangxi Emperor, the correct intention concerns the right emotion, i.e., whether the ritual is a sincere expression of filial piety. To the missionaries, the correct intention of a ritual is linked to the theologically correct meaning, i.e., whether the meaning leads to a superstitious act or not. The Kangxi Emperor changes the ritual in order to express his emotion in a better way. The missionary is ready to accept a ritual as long as one knows that its meaning is different from the act itself, in other words that it is merely civil or political. The Kangxi Emperor privatizes the funeral rituals in order to give expression to his feelings. Verbiest, in the end, cannot allow that some scholars privatize the burning of paper, because to him, it is more important to avoid any public misunderstanding of an individual's correct intention.

This case leads to a cultural paradox. Christian tradition is often associated with orthodoxy, while Chinese tradition is associated with orthopraxy. Verbiest's stress on correct belief leads to a situation in which the correct praxis is ultimately more important. Kangxi, from his side, is so insistent on a correct expression of feeling that he ultimately disregards correct practice.

CONCLUSION

The tensions that may have arisen in the Chinese Christian communities and that are directly linked with ritual practices were to a large extent caused by the "imperative" of the missionaries, who wanted rituals to be brought into line with the orthodoxy of the Christian faith. Some rituals were considered civil and therefore could be allowed; others were considered superstitious and therefore forbidden. The tensions further illustrated the relationship between form and meaning in the acceptance and rejection of a specific ritual, and particularly the question of whether this meaning had to remain implicit or to be made explicit, as in the case of the "statement of clarification" (*protesta*). Besides the meaning there was also the intention. More than the correct meaning, the missionaries seem to have wanted to transmit the correct intention to their converts. In doing so, they had to dissociate the intention from the original rite. In other words, what was interior to the rite, the intention, had to be become external in order to be transmitted.

The ritual tensions had, without doubt, an influence on the life of the Christian communities in China. In fact, these tensions can help explain whether these communities were inclusive or exclusive. Death indeed not only unites a social group but can also divide it. As death highlights the exclusiveness of the family by demarcating its membership and setting it against outsiders, so it does in the Christian community.[53] As the Christian communities manifested themselves on the occasion of a funeral, they reveal inclusive as well as exclusive characteristics. They are inclusive because the Chinese Christian community fully participates in the elementary structure of the Chinese funeral rites and also participates in the most important ritual acts—bowing, kowtowing, weeping, etc.—in which people from outside the family take part. In terms of location the Christian community performs the rituals at the house of the deceased and does not isolate itself inside a church building. Even the prayers are inclusive to a certain extent. Anyone who regularly attends Chinese Christian funerals can in principle actively participate in the often repetitive prayers without having been baptized.

But the tensions exposed here show that the Christian community is also exclusive. Christian ritual exclusivity is often linked to sacraments, such as the Eucharist or confession, which are reserved for those who are baptized. Most of the sacraments are linked to the role of the priest who performs them. Funerals, however, are not a sacrament, and the priestly role that may induce exclusivity is reduced. Yet there are other ways in which exclusivity is expressed. At funerals, exclusivity is characterized not so much by the prohibitions against the participation of non-Christians at certain rituals, but rather by the restrictions on the participation of Christians in certain rituals, in certain circumstances, which therefore exclude them from the company of other communities such as a family or a group of relatives. But the separation is also manifested by the fact that Christians are not allowed to perform Christian rituals for non-Christians. For instance, articles B15 and B31 of the "Ritual Sequence" guidelines forbid the use, including at their tombs, of Christian prayers and other merit-making acts for non-Christians. These acts are not even allowed for the parents of Christians if the parents have not been baptized (B16). Christians are also not allowed to chant prayers in front of the ancestral tablet, even of a Christian (B13). As such, the tensions and conflicts that arose concerning "superstitious" rituals illustrate further the various ways the nascent Christian community related to its environment. It is not just the particularity of certain rituals that makes funerals in China "Christian;" the tension between inclusivity and exclusivity is also a large part of that identity.

7 / Imperial Sponsorship of Jesuit Funerals

Over the course of the seventeenth century, missionaries and Chinese Christians gradually paid more attention to the organization of their funerals. After the Jesuits' period of exile in Canton, from 1666 to 1671, these initiatives were, unexpectedly, also encouraged by imperial decisions. The imperial sponsorship in 1669 of the funeral of Johann Adam Schall von Bell—one of only four Jesuits who remained in Beijing during the exile—was one of the events that definitively marked the end of the Calendar Case controversy behind the exile. Moreover, in the post-exile period, three other funerals received imperial subsidies in the form of money, gifts, and recognition: that of Gabriel de Magalhães, who died 6 May 1677, Lodovico Buglio, who died 7 October 1682, and Ferdinand Verbiest, who died 28 January 1688. Both Chinese and Western documents produced by the missionaries extensively stress this imperial support, especially in the case of Verbiest's funeral.

FUNERAL SPONSORSHIP

Verbiest's death on 28 January 1688, in the final days of the twenty-sixth year of Kangxi's reign, followed just one day after the death of Kangxi's beloved paternal grandmother, Xiaozhuang. About one and a half months later, on 11 March 1688, Verbiest was buried with full imperial honors. Kangxi's sponsorship of his funeral must have impressed the missionaries deeply, as shown by the extensive reports on this imperial sponsorship.

One of the earliest reports, which formed the basis of later accounts, was written by Antoine Thomas, SJ (1644–1709), who had been involved in astronomical activities in Beijing since 1686.[1] A text that made the funeral widely known in Europe is the description included in *New Memoirs about the Present State of China, 1687–1692* (*Nouveaux mémoires sur l'état présent de la Chine 1687–1692*) by Louis Le Comte, SJ (1655–1728). Le Comte arrived in Beijing on 7 February 1688, too late to meet Verbiest, but in time to assist at his funeral on 11 March 1688. Le Comte describes these events in a letter to Marie, duchess de Nemours

(1625–1707).[2] In 1691, he returned to France as Procurator of the Jesuits, and there he included the report in a collection of letters in 1697 that was to play a role in the Rites Controversy on the European continent. Fifteen years after the fact, in 1703, Jean de Fontenay (1643–1710), another *mathématicien du Roi* (mathematician of the French King) who had arrived in Beijing together with Le Comte, still found it worthwhile to report about the funeral to François d'Aix de La Chaize, SJ (1624–1709), confessor of Louis XIV since 1675. This letter was published in *Edifying and Curious Letters* (*Lettres édifiantes et curieuses*), one of the most important sources of information about the Catholic missions in the eighteenth century, begun by the French Jesuit Charles Le Gobien (1671–1708) in 1702 and continued by Jean-Baptiste Du Halde (1674–1743) and others.[3] Le Comte's and Fontenay's reports were combined into one report in the famous work by Jean-Baptiste Du Halde, *Geographical, Historical, Chronological, Political, and Physical Description of the Chinese Empire and Chinese Tartary* (*Description geographique, historique, chronologique, politique et physique de l'empire de la Chine et de la Tartarie chinoise*), printed in Paris in 1735 and in the Hague in 1736.[4] Written more than forty-five years after Verbiest's death, this account begins as follows:

Such was this illustrious Missionary, who gained the Esteem and Favour of a deserving Prince, to that degree that he honoured him with an Encomium composed by himself, which he order'd two Noblemen to read before his Coffin, after having on his part performed all the Funeral Honours which are commonly rendered in China. The Encomium was as follows:

"I with myself seriously consider that P. Ferdinand Verbiest voluntarily quitted Europe to come into my Empire, where he pass'd a great part of his Life in my Service. And I ought to give him this Testimony, that during the time in which he presided over the Mathematics, his Predictions were never found false, but always agreeable to the Motions of the Heavens.

Besides, far from neglecting my Orders, he appeared in every Circumstance exact, diligent, faithful, and constant in every Undertaking till it was perfected, being always consistent with himself.

As soon as I heard of his Sickness, I sent my own Physician to his relief. But when I understood that the Sleep of Death had for ever separated us, my Heart was wounded with the most sensible Grief. I sent two hundred Ounces of Silver, and divers Pieces of Silk to contribute to his Obsequies; and I WILL, that this Edict be a publick Testimony of the sincere Affection I bear him."

The Grandees of the Court followed the Example of their Prince, and wrote the Encomiums of P. Verbiest on Pieces of Sattin, hung up in the Hall where his Corps was exposed.[5]

This report illustrates the essential interventions of the Kangxi Emperor and his entourage: the "encomium," the public reading of this encomium, the performing of "all the Funeral Honours which are commonly rendered in China" and the granting of a financial gift for the obsequies. These aspects all belong to the established system of funeral sponsorship.[6]

The technical term for funeral sponsorship is *xudian*. These honors, given by the state to a deceased member of the nobility or an official, were part of a ritual system that consisted of very specific rules and regulations. Many were decided on the basis of precedents. The specific rules for the funeral sponsorship are contained in *Supplementary Regulations and Precedents to the Institutes of the Great Qing Dynasty* (*Qinding daQing huidian zeli*, completed 1764, printed 1768) and *Regulations and Precedents of the Board of Rites* (*Qinding libu zeli*, 1794; second revision, 1841).[7] Though these works were compiled in the eighteenth century—much later than the 1680s—they include most of the regulations that were already being applied in the seventeenth century, as well as the changes that had occurred since that time.

In general, three different forms of funeral sponsorship can be distinguished. The first concerns the events that take place immediately after death. A request for funeral sponsorship was usually submitted by way of a memorial, and, if it was approved, officials would be sent to pay respects and perform a sacrifice (*zhiji*) at the home of the deceased. If a funerary ode (*jiwen*) was made, they would also read it aloud (*duwen*). The ritual of such a sacrificial visit, which had an allocated budget called "sacrifice money" (*(zhi)jiyin*), is prescribed in detail.[8] According to the deceased's rank in nobility or officialdom, the number of sacrifices, from one to three, varies as does the amount of the monetary contribution (forty *liang* for the highest rank of nobility, compared to twenty-five *liang* for an official of the highest rank), and a funerary eulogy may or may not be made.

The second form is a subsidy for the burial expenses, called "burial money" (*zangyin*).[9] This amount also varies according to the deceased's rank—six hundred and fifty *liang* for the highest nobility, compared to five hundred *liang* for an official of the highest rank. This burial money could help cover various costs involved in the burial, including the procession, but the prescriptions do not actually specify its use.

The third form of sponsorship is the granting of a posthumous title (*shi*). This favor was not automatic, not even if the sacrificial visit and funerary money were granted. When a posthumous title was granted, it was composed by the Inner Court (Grand Secretariat),[10] usually accompanied by the erection of a gravestone (*bei*) inscribed with a commemorative text (*beiwen*) composed by the Hanlin Academy. The Ministry of Works was in charge of granting the "stele money" (*libeigong jiayin*), again differentiated according to rank.

There are also regulations for the funerary sponsorship of foreigners. They treat the rules for imperial sponsorship of the funerals for kings of tribute countries who died in their native country. Moreover, specific regulations applied in the case of tribute delegates who died in Beijing or on their way to or from Beijing. In addition to specifications for sacrificial objects to be used and the funerary eulogy to be written, the regulations anticipate the return of the corpse to the native country, or the selection of a burial ground in China if the corpse is not returned home.[11]

RICCI'S BURIAL GROUND

Before analyzing the sponsorship of Verbiest's funeral in depth, it is necessary to refer to its precedents. Before Verbiest, some form of sponsorship had been granted for only four other Jesuits: Ricci, Schall, Magalhães, and Buglio.

Ricci's case is clearly different from that of early Qing Jesuits. At the time of Ricci's death on 11 May 1610, his companions and the officials he was acquainted with did not ask for funeral sponsorship in the form of a sacrifice or funeral money. There was no reason to do so, since Ricci did not occupy any official or honorary position in the Chinese bureaucracy. They did, however, request, and obtain, a burial ground. A detailed account of the acquisition of this ground, which is the first known example of how the burial of a missionary could become part of the Chinese system, appears in the last chapter of Trigault and Ricci's *The Christian Expedition into China*.[12]

Ricci's corpse was not carried to Macao, as had been the case with all missionaries who had died up to that time, but was kept in a sealed coffin in the mission house in Beijing. It was after his funeral Mass that a Chinese convert suggested that the Jesuits submit a petition requesting a burial plot. "This," the Jesuits believed, and Trigault wrote, "apart from being very honourable for the Father in the future, would also confirm our faith and the residence of our fathers in this empire."[13] Ricci's case thus became one of the earliest examples of a mission strategy evolving out of a burial place issue. De Pantoja and De Ursis composed a petition together with Chinese scholars, including the Christian Li Zhizao (1565–1630), and Wu Daonan (?–1623), acting Minister of Rites, wrote the supporting memorial. Their documents are written in the style characteristic of tribute petitions. Ricci and his companions, the petition argues, "have travelled the seas for three years because they were favourably inclined towards and admired the virtue and [cultural] transformations of the Heavenly dynasty;" "they offered local products as tribute"; and "they received government-supplied food for ten years." Since Ricci has no burial ground and since it is too difficult to carry his corpse home, the emperor is asked to offer a burial ground. "It is by the Holy Dynasty's virtue of benefiting those who have died and its benevolence of being gentle to those who have come from afar (*rouyuan zhi ren*), that it can strongly encourage the foreign barbarians and forever solidify their sincere inclination towards [our cultural] transformation."[14]

It is at this point that Trigault interrupts the first part of his narrative for a reflection to help his readers understand the reasons behind the petition's arguments:

> Before continuing our narrative, we must explain, in brief, a few points, which, if not clarified, might obscure the proper understanding of what is to follow. To begin with, one may, perhaps, entertain a doubt as to why it was written in the petition that the Fathers were prompted to come to China by the fame and the glory of the Chinese Empire, when their real motive for coming was to spread the Gospel. It must be understood that all foreigners are excluded from the Kingdom of China, save the three classes of people to whom the law grants an entrance. First, there are those who come annually, and of their own accord, from neighbouring kingdoms, to offer tribute to the King of China. This causes no worry or concern to the Chinese, because China is not bent upon conquest. Secondly, there are those who do not wish to be looked upon as paying tribute but, moved by the vast extent of the Chinese Kingdom, come to honour the King, as being the leader of all kings. . . . The third class is made up of those who are moved by the fame of the great empire, and come here to establish a permanent residence, attracted, as the Chinese think, by their reputation for virtue. Formerly there were many such, but now the Chinese are not as attractive as they imagine. The missionary Fathers have to work in China as belonging to this third class, so as to be within the law, and also because those belonging to the two former classes are inevitably sent back to their own countries. . . . It is under the third title, which is perhaps less real than assumed or appropriated, that the Fathers are permitted to remain in China and their brethren allowed to come in, and yet it is not to be thought that they conceal the purpose for which they came, namely, to preach the Gospel.[15]

Trigault further reflects on the Chinese system of administration, explaining its complex procedures of which he is well aware. While the ultimate decisions depend upon the fiat of the sovereign, decisions are only made after the submission of written documents. Moreover, they are not taken without the advice of the highest magistrates in the kingdom. The documents "are then returned for his approbation, and he seldom differs from their judgement. This system will be more clearly presented in the continuation of our narrative."[16] By further dwelling on this procedure and the complex relationships that the missionaries and their friends had to develop with officials in different ministries, Trigault makes clear that the favors granted to Ricci were not a personal decision of the emperor only, but that they depended on whether or not these fitted into the official system of protocols.

In fact, it appeared evident to them early on that "there was no Chinese law, nor any precedent, according to which a foreigner could acquire a place of burial."[17] The solution offered by the Jesuits' Chinese associates was to suggest an analogy between Ricci's case and that of a tribute delegate who had died on his way to the court.[18] They did this while acknowledging that in fact Matteo Ricci "had never been sent by his country [as a tribute delegate]."[19] In the memorial by Wu Daonan, reference is made to the stipulations in the *Institutions of the Ming* (*Ming huidian*),[20] on which the Qing stipulations for funeral sponsorship of foreign delegates were later based. These regulations appear under the rules for tribute delegations, not under the rules for funerals.[21] The request concerning Ricci was channelled through a complex procedure, and was eventually approved. His corpse was transferred to the Zhalan cemetery on 22 April 1611, and the solemn entombment took place on 1 November 1611.[22]

What emerges from Trigault's account is that the request for a burial place for Ricci was initiated for a very practical reason—the need or wish to have him buried in Beijing in order to avoid having to transport his corpse to Macao. At the suggestion of the Chinese Christian officials who were actively involved in his funeral, this problem was solved by fitting Ricci's case into the Chinese ritual system. The existing precedents suggested that he be treated as a foreigner. As Trigault acknowledges, the personal involvement of the emperor in this case was limited. The effect of this decision, however, was more important than appears at a first reading. Given the importance attached to burial grounds by the Chinese, Ricci's burial gave a certain stability to the Christian presence in Beijing.[23] From Trigault's description it is also clear that this stability was somehow in opposition to the usual practice of the foreigners residing in China on only a temporary basis. This dichotomy became manifest a few years later during the Nanjing persecution (1616–1617). Shen Que (1565–1624), the acting minister of the Nanjing Ministry of Rites, attempted to impeach the barbarians through a series of memorials. In one, he makes explicit reference to the problems linked to the designation of a burial place for Ricci and to how the Jesuits explained this designation. Shen Que takes the tomb of the King of Brunei, who died in 1408 in Nanjing, as a precedent for the emperor's intentions. In his third memorial stating his case, dated 7 January

1617, Shen Que remarks that, when the emperor had granted Ricci a burial place,

> This was simply a manifestation of the virtue which requires that distant people be treated with kindness (*rouyuan zhi ren*). It was similar to the action of Emperor Chengzu [1403–1425] granting a burial site to the King of Brunei. If the ministers and people of Brunei had used the generous granting of a burial site for their king as a pretext to stealthily enter China and scatter throughout the capitals and provinces, would Emperor Chengzu have tolerated that? Now these foreigners wish to use an isolated instance of imperial kindness towards distant people (*rouyuan zhi ren*) as a pretext for their despicable presence here. Their plotting and spying increase day by day. How can such activities be allowed to go unchallenged?[24]

Shen Que relies here on the ideology of "the benevolence of being gentle to those who have come from afar" (*rouyuan zhi ren*), an expression already utilized by Wu Daonan in his memorial on Ricci.[25] This classical expression refers to a policy of treating foreign guests graciously, so long as they are properly submissive. As Joseph Esherick has pointed out, the expression also contains a subjecting and controlling aspect.[26] Shen Que's memorial makes clear that even after the designation of a burial ground, the Jesuits could not escape the cultural imperative of China.

SCHALL'S REHABILITATION

After the granting of a place for Ricci's burial, other missionaries were subsequently buried at the same place, but for none of their funerals did the imperial court provide some form of sponsorship.[27] The first missionary to receive any funeral sponsorship was Johann Adam Schall von Bell, who in 1655 had received the emperor's permission to extend the Jesuit graveyard.[28] The circumstances of his funeral, however, were particular. Schall, who died on 15 August 1666 and was buried two weeks later on 29 August in the presence of five hundred Christians, was at first not awarded an imperial ceremony, because he had been disgraced as a result of the Calendar Case.[29] When he was posthumously rehabilitated in 1669, it was the granting of funeral sponsorship to him and several of his collaborators who had been condemned together with him that marked the full rehabilitation. On Kangxi 8/7/20, or 16 August 1669, Giyĕsu, the first Prince Kang (1645–1697), and others submitted a memorial to grant Schall a funeral sponsorship "according to his original rank,"[30] a request that was approved a month later: Schall was offered the "funeral money and the first rank sacrifice money; an official was sent to read the funeral ode and to pay respects and perform the sacrifice; the text of the funeral ode was to be compiled by the Inner Court."[31] Other sources mention that five hundred and twenty-five *liang* was offered,[32] which corresponds to the twenty-five *liang* sacrifice money and five hundred *liang* funeral money for an official of the highest rank. Schall's prestigious title "Grand Master for Splendid Happiness" (Guanglu dafu), originally granted in the first year of the Kangxi reign, was indeed a "1a" rank in the official hierarchy.[33]

In the following month, the ceremony took place before Schall's tomb, in the presence of Verbiest, de Magalhães, and Buglio.[34] The sacrificial ode, or *jiwen*, read out at that moment was later engraved on Schall's tombstone:

The Emperor ordered to make sacrifices to the soul (*ling*) of the deceased Johann Adam Schall von Bell, former Commissioner of the Office of Transmission [rank 3a], who was granted two additional classes [of rank] and later on one additional class, and Seal Holding Officer of the Directorate of Astronomy. [The imperial prayer] says:

To exert oneself to the utmost is the obligation of a subject, but to recompense his merits by granting [imperial] sponsorship at his death is the prescribed duty of the State. You, Johann Adam Schall von Bell, came from the Western Regions, and as you were proficient in astronomy you were entrusted with the task to supervise the calendar-calculation. Thereupon you were granted the title of "Teacher Who Comprehends the Mysterious." Suddenly you passed away and We were saddened by the news. We grant Our gracious sponsorship by sending officials to pay respects and perform a sacrifice. Alas! As you left Us your lasting merits, [We would wish] that you enjoy this insignificant recompense. If you should be aware [of Our feelings], mayest thou accept and enjoy [these offerings].

The 16th day of the 11th month of the 8th year of the Kangxi reign [8 December 1669].[35]

The text is a typical oration for use at worship in a condolence ritual. Such a sacrificial ode, usually partly biographical, had a more or less fixed structure. It was composed in prose or, more often, in verse and it was written for the purpose of addressing the deceased directly, in a rite in which it might be written on paper and burned.[36] Not only does the ode for Schall follow the classical order, but the whole phraseology is literally the same as other sacrificial odes written at that time.[37]

The Jesuits may not have been entirely comfortable with such a text. This appears from the Latin translation, which differs in two key passages from the original Chinese text. At the beginning of the Latin text, the emperor does not order the making of sacrifices for the "soul," as in the Chinese version (*Huangdi yu ji . . . Tang Ruowang zhi ling*) but rather the "granting of funeral honours to the pious hands of Johann Adam [Schall]" (*Imperator deferri iubens honores funebres pijs manibus Ioannis Adami*). And at the end, the calling of the soul to "accept and enjoy" the sacrifices (*shangke xinxiang*), is toned down to a more general statement, "you can certainly come and accept what we grant" (*potes utique venire, & quae deferimus, suscipere*).[38] This rephrasing shows that the Jesuits were aware of the potential problem of these two sentences. In other circumstances, the direct address to the soul and the request for the soul to consume offerings would clearly have been rejected by the Jesuits as constituting idolatry, as was the case in the "Ritual Sequence" of 1685.

Although the emperor is the subject of this sacrificial ode, it is clear from the negotiations leading to the granting of this sponsorship that the emperor himself did not write the text, but rather the Inner Court (Grand Secretariat) prepared it for him. The emperor's involvement in this sponsorship, therefore, was probably minimal. Once the decision was taken to rehabilitate Schall, the funeral sponsorship followed the routine of bureaucratic protocol. The Jesuits interpreted it as a rehabilitation of their whole mission, but by accepting these honors, they were also accepting sacrifices for which the soul of the deceased was explicitly invoked and of which the soul was invited to partake.

IMPERIAL FAVORS AT THE DEATHS OF MAGALHÃES AND BUGLIO

The next Jesuit who died in Beijing was de Magalhães, who passed away on 6 May 1677.[39] He and Buglio had briefly served at the court of Zhang Xianzhong (1601–1647), the anti-Ming rebel who established himself as king in Sichuan from 1644 to 1647. After their arrival in Beijing in early 1648, they were allowed to stay in the capital and resume their ministry, thanks to Schall's influence.[40] It took several years before they came to the attention of the emperor. When the Shunzhi Emperor offered them a house, revenue, and the permission to build a church, Magalhães made some curious and ingenious objects for the emperor to demonstrate his gratitude.[41] Buglio and Magalhães seem never to have occupied any official position, other than the official function that they had been forced to accept under Zhang Xianzhong, and they never refer to such positions in their writings.[42] Thus, the honors given to Magalhães seem to have resulted from the personal tie between Verbiest and the Kangxi Emperor, as emerges from Buglio's account of Magalhães' funeral. The day after Magalhães' death,

Verbiest, now Vice Provincial of this Mission, went betimes in the Morning to give notice to the King of the Death of the Father. The Prince bid him return home, whither he in a very short time would send him his own Orders what to do. Accordingly within half an hour, he sent three Persons the most considerable in his Court, with an Elogy in honour of the Father, two hundred *Taels*, or about fourscore pounds, and ten great pieces of Damask for his Shroud, with command to perform all the customary Ceremonies before the Corps of the Deceas'd, and to bewail him after the usual manner, which the two Messengers did, shedding a great number of Tears in the presence of the whole Assembly.[43]

Verbiest may or may not have submitted his request through the proper channels; he seems to have taken considerable liberties with administrative procedure, as he had done at other occasions.[44] According to Buglio's account, it seems that Verbiest went in person to the emperor and presented a private, oral petition to him. As a result, the favor offered, which seems to have been decided not by the regular bureaucracy—normally the Ministry of Rites—but by the Court exclusively, was therefore called a "special gift" (*teci*).[45] In the imperial edict granting the gift, Magalhães, who is named without any official title, is praised for the ingenious objects he had offered to the Shunzhi Emperor.[46]

For this occasion the Jesuits printed a "life" of Magalhães: *An xiansheng xingshu*.[47] The word *xingshu* in the title indicates that it falls within the genre of biographical notes or accounts of conduct that were compiled when important people died and that might actually be printed. Copies would go to authors of any epitaphs and to the official historiographers.[48] In the case of Magalhães, this text, together with the eulogy "was giv'n about to all the Princes, great Lords, Mandarins, to our friends and all that were Christians. Which was of great consequence and mainly contributory to the Credit and Reputation of our sacred Law, when the World should understand the high Esteem which the King had of the Preachers of the Gospel."[49]

This "life" (*An xiansheng xingshu*) is more an account of the funeral preparations than an account of Magalhães' life.[50] Several days after a first visit by three court officials, the three[51] returned to ask, in the name of the emperor, what day the funeral would take place and which rituals from the Catholic teaching they would use. In response, Buglio and Verbiest drew up a list of the objects they needed for the procession: an imperial baldaquin or canopy with the imperial edict inside; a baldaquin for the holy cross; one for the image of the holy mother of God; another for the image of the leader of all angels, Saint Michael; and finally one for the painting of Magalhães, made by imperial order. In addition, they gave details about banners, musical instruments, carriers of incense, candles, stove, and coffin, etc. When the three officials brought the list back to the emperor, he decreed that everything be prepared, and also asked whether the money provided earlier was enough, whereupon Buglio and Verbiest replied that it was "more than sufficient" (*youyu*). On the day of the funeral, the emperor sent the three officials to the burial place: "Following the imperial instructions they went in person to the tumulus and observed in detail the rituals that were performed by the Catholic teaching at the moment of entombment and how the faithful all together knelt and chanted prayers, and other rituals. And again they reported all that they had seen with their own eyes by writing in a memorial."[52]

The Western version gives a detailed description of the funeral procession and the entombment rituals:

Ten Souldiers march'd before with their Armes to clear the Streets; they were follow'd by ten Ushers of several Tribunals, that carry'd Tablets, wherein was written an Order of the Mandarins, to give way, under pain of punishment. Twenty four Trumpeters and Hoeboys, with several Sorts of other Instruments follow'd them, and preceded the King's Elogy that was written upon yellow Satin, and carry'd in a Litter, surrounded with four and twenty Pieces of Satin of various Colours. This Elogy was attended by several Christian Eunuchs, of which there were some that waited upon the King's Person. Afterwards appear'd three other Litters adorn'd with several Pieces of Silk. In the first was carry'd the Cross, in the second the Picture of the Holy Virgin, and in the third the Picture of St. Michael. These Litters observ'd a convenient distance one from the other, and in the spaces between there went a great number of Christians, of which some carry'd Lantherns, some Banners, and other Censors, others carry'd wax Tapers, sweet Odours and other things. After that in another Banner was carry'd the Portraiture of the Father surrounded with Pieces of Silk, which the King had order'd to be drawn to the Life three years before, together with the Pictures of all the rest of the Fathers, by a famous Painter of the Palace. This Picture was attended by a great Multitude of Christians, among which there were above threescore in Mourning. The Fathers came last, and just before the stately Coffin; which was put into an Herse varnish'd over with Gold and Vermillion, under a Canopy of a rich Piece of red Velvet, which was environ'd with certain Pieces of white and blew Damask, and was the King's gift. The Coffin was carry'd by seventy Men, who had every one a Mourning Bonnet upon their Heads, and the number of those that follow'd the Coffin was so great, that the Front was distant from the Rear above a Mile. When they came to the place of Enterrment, the Responses were Sung, with other usual Prayers and Ceremonies of the Christians. To which purpose eight Christian Mandarins in Surplices assisted the Father that perform'd the Office. The Christians also Sung with great Devotion, the Letanies of the Holy Virgin, and then the Body was put into a Sepulchre made of Brick. So soon as the Ceremony was over, you might hear the Lamentations and Moans of the whole Assembly accompany'd with Tears that shew'd the reality of their grief; the three Persons also sent from the Emperour perform'd their parts. And three days after they return'd by the King's Order, and pay'd the same Funeral respects as upon the burial day.

Never was seen in this Court a Funeral so Magnificent, whether you consider the Multitude of those that were at it, their Modesty, their Tears, and their sincere sorrow, or the Honours done to the Deceas'd by the King, and the Elogy which he gave him, contrary to the usual custom.[53]

This description clearly shows that not only were the missionaries reconciled to the idea of having a procession of pomp, but they also exploited it to their advantage. The whole structure of the procession is a typically Chinese and imperial framework: the emperor's edict is followed by the imperial gifts (the pieces of satin) and the portrait of the deceased, with the coffin and several imperial attributes, as the centerpiece, all preceded by noisy musical instruments at the beginning of the cortege. Moreover, the Christians carry not only the candles commonly used in Christian funerals, but also "banners, censors, . . . and other things." Onto this basic structure of the Chinese funeral procession are grafted Christian elements: the cross and pictures of the Holy Virgin and Saint Michael, as well as the presence of Christian participants, which includes eunuchs and officials. The author makes an effort to demonstrate the significance of the procession by underscoring that the rituals performed at the tomb in particular are a juxtaposition of both Christian and Chinese rituals. The Christian rituals include the recitation of the appropriate prayers, while the Chinese rituals include the weeping rituals, which are described as expressions of grief from all the people present.

According to the printed "life" of Magalhães, more than eight hundred people attended his funeral.[54] While the Western and Chinese texts are, on the whole, laudatory about the funeral, some sources suggest, however, that the imperial sponsorship had a limiting effect on the participation of the Christian community. In the eyes of Tomé Pereira, SJ (1645–1708), the processional cart with the lavishly decorated coffin was "according to the Chinese way (ao modo de China), which was difficult to contradict and the praxis of which was difficult to reduce, because this would go against the customs of the country that the emperor claimed." The regal pomp, however, prevented the local Christians from performing some of their customary funeral rituals: "The Christians gave up many things that we, with great effort, had prevented them from doing, but we were not able to stop them from other things without causing a great commotion." According to Pereira almost seven hundred church members joined the procession dressed in mourning white, the total number of people attending being one thousand.[55]

The subsidy given on the occasion of Magalhães' funeral shows that in addition to the regular subsidies, organized through the bureaucratic channels, the emperor also took the initiative for private subsidies. These non-statutory gestures of favor were largely personal ones from the emperor, made possible because they were founded on preexisting statutes and precedents. The emperor's personal sponsorship consisted of a contribution to the funeral expenses and the sending of imperial delegates to the funeral, though given the absence of details in the reports of Magalhães' funeral, these official representatives were not there necessarily to perform all rituals that were part of a regular funeral sponsorship.

The account of Magalhães' funeral is distinctive for another reason: it relates the ritual negotiations that took place between the Jesuits and the Court. While rituals were generally regarded as "fixed in heaven,"[56] the Manchu leaders were ready to adapt their funeral practices to accommodate the Jesuits. But the Jesuits too made considerable adaptations to their own standard practice. Whereas the Catholic rituals used were the usual ones and so could be readily explained to the Court delegates, and whereas the funeral procession was organized in the order that had become common among the Chinese Christians at that time, they also were agreeing to put these rituals in a new context. Indeed, the whole procession is fitted into an imperial framework, symbolized by the imperial edict at the beginning, a character that was in fact detrimental to the participation of local Christians. The Jesuits reinterpreted the emperor's personal favor, which was probably more a gesture of sympathy towards Verbiest than an honor paid to de Magalhães, transforming it into an expression of imperial protection for Christianity as a whole.

Lodovico Buglio, Magalhães' closest companion, died on 7 October 1682, after having spent more than forty years in China. The imperial subsidy and the funeral he received are very similar to those of Magalhães, but the reports about his case contain some additional information.[57] An imperial edict concerning the subsidy was sent and read to Buglio before he died. In this edict, the emperor, having heard about Buglio's illness through Zhao Chang, a member of the Imperial Bodyguard and a key intercessor with the emperor for the Jesuits in these years,[58] says that "it makes me feel sorry to see Lodovico Buglio bed-ridden in the capital without the help from relatives or acquaintances. Therefore I especially grant him two hundred taels of silver and ten pieces of silk, so as to express my benevolence for my servant who came from a distant place."[59] This passage indicates that the emperor, because he was aware that the missionaries did not have family to host funerals for them, through his sponsorship voluntarily assumed the role of hosting the funerals.[60] Just as in the case of Magalhães, the sponsorship of Buglio's funeral is a "special gift," which apparently emanated from the court alone. After Buglio had died, three people were sent from the palace, first to find out "which ceremonies of the Chinese they could perform before the dead Father," and next to honor the corpse with a sacrifice (*dian*) and a weeping ritual "following the custom of the Tartars"; they also shared the drinking of "Tartar tea and wine as was done in similar occasion for important persons."[61] This is the first mention of ceremonies that are clearly identified as Manchu.

The funeral procession was one of pomp, in accordance with the emperor's wishes, and did "not conform to the modesty of our Institute." At the front were carried the imperial edict, the painting of Buglio made by imperial order, the cross, the image of the Virgin Mary, and the image of Saint Michael, followed by incense carriers and musicians, and more than five hundred Christians. Three imperial delegates had been sent to the graveside. There the Christian ceremonies were first performed, "the mysteries of which were explained in a libretto with great benefit. Next, the usual civil ceremonies that the Gentiles performed for an important person followed."[62]

The case of Buglio's funeral seems to confirm that the subsidy and the rituals performed could be the initiative of the Court, adapted from statutory regulations, and in this case, based on precedents. Moreover, the funerals were once more negotiated. They combined Christian rituals and "civil ceremonies," including rituals that are identified as typically Manchu. The imperial sponsorship is again interpreted as a patronage of Christianity as a whole:

> God wanted the death of F. Buglio to be an instrument of his divine glory, as was his life, because he disposed the mind of the Emperor to make extraordinary manifestations of his esteem and affection for this Father, before and after his death; the manifestations resulted in the greatest good of the conversion, and of the honor of the Holy Law of God, be it either when his Majesty very often sent people to visit Buglio and inquire about the state of his illness, or much more concretely when he manifested his affection to the Father in the last days of life.[63]

COMPLETE SPONSORSHIP OF VERBIEST'S FUNERAL

In contrast to the select sponsorship of the funerals of Ricci, Schall, Magalhães, and Buglio, a complete sponsorship according to the bureaucratic channels was granted for the funeral of Ferdinand Verbiest, who died on Kangxi 26/12/26, or 27 January 1688, the day after Kangxi's grandmother, Xiaozhuang.[64]

One day before his death, Verbiest sent a memorial, composed with the help of a learned literatus, deploring the death of Xiaozhuang and explaining that he could not present his condolences in person because of his illness.[65] When the emperor read this memorial, Verbiest had already died. Thereupon the emperor decreed that a funeral sponsorship (*xudian*) would be bestowed on Verbiest "because of his many years of service in arranging the calendar, and for having constructed very effective military equipment at the time of war." The emperor asked the Ministry of Rites to check the precedents and to give the proper recommendations.[66] In its answer the Ministry of Rites states that, according to the fixed precedents,

> Vice Ministers with an added class up to the second rank who die of illness are granted according to their added class and rank the price of a complete funeral, and the sacrificial money for one sacrifice; officials will be sent to read the funeral eulogy and to pay respects and perform a sacrifice. Whether a posthumous title should be granted should be decided by imperial decree. For all officials who receive a posthumous title, the Ministry of Works grants the "stele money," the Ministry of Rites establishes the commemorative text (*beiwen*), and the funerary ode (*jiwen*) is made by the Grand Secretariat.[67]

The rules as stated in this memorial closely follow the regulations as mentioned in *Supplementary Regulations and Precedents to the Institutes of the Great Qing Dynasty* and *Regulations and Precedents of the Board of Rites* that were compiled in the next century.[68] On the basis of these regulations, the Ministry of Rites proposed granting to Verbiest the sponsorship that corresponded to his added class. The decision of giving a posthumous title was left to the emperor, who decreed that it should be granted.

This memorial indicates that in the case of Verbiest, in contrast to Magalhães and Buglio, the decision for sponsorship followed the normal and bureaucratic procedures. Not all aspects, however, are clear. The memorial of the Ministry of Rites does not mention how much money should be awarded. In the imperial decree, the subsidy, mentioned as a "special gift," is two hundred taels of silver and ten pieces of silk,[69] which is the same as the subsidy given to Magalhães and Buglio. The title that Verbiest used in his own memorial and that is used by the Ministry of Rites is the brevet rank of Vice Minister of the Right in the Ministry of Works with two added classes (*jia gongbu youshilang youjia erji*). He received this rank as a reward on Kangxi 21/4/10, or 16 May 1682, for casting one hundred and thirty-two regular cannon and two hundred and forty large cannon.[70] This honorific title was of a 3a rank in the early Qing (Verbiest did not formally hold an office), and with two added classes this became 2a.

According to this rank, however, Verbiest should have received four hundred taels (three hundred taels for rank 3). Moreover, the decree does not mention the sacrifice money, which should have been twenty taels for holding rank 2 (sixteen taels for rank 3). It seems, therefore, that as far as arriving at a monetary amount for the subsidy, the precedent of the funerals of Magalhães and Buglio was of greater importance than either Verbiest's own rank or the precedent of Schall's funeral, which possibly received a total subsidy of five hundred and twenty-five taels according to Schall's highest honorific title.[71]

The funeral sponsorship extended for Verbiest comprised several aspects. The passage quoted above describes the rituals performed in the name of the emperor in front of Verbiest's coffin in the Jesuit residence. Because of the mourning period for the Empress Xiaozhuang, they took place one month after her death, on Kangxi 27/1/27, or 28 February 1688, or later.[72] In Dunyn-Szpot these rituals are described as "Chinese and Tartar ceremonies and rites, of which [the emperor] knew very well in advance that they were permitted by the Christian Law."[73] Imperial delegates were also sent to assist at the burial ceremonies for Verbiest, which Jesuit sources describe as a major event for the Christian community in Beijing:[74]

> The eleventh of March, the Day fixed for his Funeral, the Emperor sent his Father-in-law, who was at the same time his Uncle,[75] with one of the first Lords of the Court,[76] a Gentleman of his Bed-Chamber, and five Officers of the Palace, to represent his Person. They arrived there about seven o'Clock in the Morning. The Corps of the Missionary was enclosed in a Coffin of three or four inches thick, varnished and gilded on the out-side after the Chinese manner, and so close shut that it was impenetrable almost to Air. The Coffin was then carryed thro' the Street upon a Bier, exposed under a kind of Pavilion supported by four Pillars, covered and ornamented by white Silk, which in China is the Colour of Mourning; from one Column to an other several Festoons of Silk of divers Colours hung. The Bier was fixed upon two Poles two Feet in Diameter, and proportionably long, to be carry'd on the Shoulders of sixty Men.
>
> The Father Superior, attended by all the Jesuits in Pe-king, placed himself on his Knees before the Corps, making three profound Reverences to the Ground, while the other Christians sent up Sighs that might have melted the most obdurate. Then every thing was ordered for the Procession, thro' two great Streets perfectly strait, in breadth a hundred Feet, and in length a League leading to the West Gate, which was about six hundred Paces distant from the Burying Place granted by the Emperor Van-lyê [Wanli] to P. Ricci.
>
> First appeared a Table, twenty-two Feet high, and four broad, on which was written upon a red Taffety Ground the Name and Dignity of P. Verbiest in Letters

of Gold. This Machine was supported by a great many Men, preceded by a Band of Musicians, and followed by another Company which carried Standards, Festoons and Streamers. Then followed a large Cross, adorn'd with little Flags, born betwixt two Rows of Christians in white, marching two and two with an exemplary Modesty, each holding in one Hand a lighted Taper, and in the other a Handkerchief to wipe off their Tears. At some distance, betwixt two other Rows of Tapers, followed the Images of the Holy Virgin, and the Infant Jesus, carrying in his Hand the Globe of the World, placed within a Frame set round with several Pieces of Silk, which form'd a kind of Cartouch. Next came a Picture of St. Michael with the like Ornaments.

And after it that of the Defunct, with the Eulogium composed by the Emperor, written on a large Piece of yellow Sattin, and surrounded by a great Croud of Christians and Missionaries in Mourning. At last came the Coffin, attended by the Deputies of the Court, and a great number of Noblemen on Horseback. Fifty Horsemen closed the Procession, which passed with a great deal of Order and Decency.

When they came to the place of Burial, the Missionaries in their Surplices repeated the Prayers of the Church; the Holy Water was sprinkled, and the usual Censings were perform'd, as directed by the Roman Ritual; the Corps was then let down into a deep Grave, built round with four Brick Walls, which were to be closed at top with an Arch.

When these Ceremonies were over, the Missionaries being upon their Knees, the Father-in-law of the Emperor on the Part of his Imperial Majesty made the following Speech.

"His Majesty, who is fully sensible of the Services P. Verbiest rendered to the State, has sent me to Day with these Lords, to make this publick Acknowledgment; to the end that all the World may know the singular Affection he always entertain'd for his Person, and the Grief he feels for his Death."

The Missionaries were at that time so overwhelmed with Sorrow, and so surprised with this Favour of the Emperor, that they were at a loss what to answer: When P. Pereyra, in the Name of the rest, made the following Reply to the Emperor's Father-in-law.

"Our Silence is more owing to the Emperor's Goodness than to our own Sorrows. Is it possible, Sir, that so great a Prince should treat Foreigners as if they had the Honour to be his natural Subjects? Not content to provide for our Health, our Reputation, and our Life, he honours even our Death by his Eulogies, by his Liberalities, by the Presence of the greatest Lords of his Court, and, what is more inestimable than all, by his Grief. How can we make a suitable Return for so many Favours? What we beg of You, Sir, is to tell him, that our Tears are this Day shed to testify the Greatness of our Affliction; but that we dare not speak, because Words would fall short of our grateful Sentiments."

When this Speech was reported to the Emperor, he was very well pleased. A few Days after the Tribunal of Rites petitioned the Emperor for permission to decree new Honours to P. Verbiest, which was granted. It appointed seven hundred Taëls of Silver[77] to erect a Monument to his Memory, the Imperial Eulogium to be engraved on a Marble Table, and a Deputation of Mandarins to perform the last Duties to him in the name of the Empire.[78]

This description of the procession and burial of Verbiest is similar to though much more detailed than the description of Magalhães' funeral. It confirms the preponderance of imperial symbols and rituals at the funeral, though Christian elements were still present. Moreover, as in earlier periods, missionaries interpreted the processions as a public manifestation, even a "triumph," of Christianity. Le Comte remarked, "It took up above a thousand paces, the streets all the way were lined by an infinite number of spectators, who with amazement beheld our Christian rites triumphing, even in their capital city, over pagan superstition."[79] Particular notice is given to ritual actions performed by the missionaries at the tomb, dressed "in their surplices."[80]

Both the dress and the rituals publicly manifested that the Jesuits in the end played two different roles that typologically belonged to two different spheres in the Chinese society: on the one hand the ideal of the Confucian scholar and official, and on the other hand the priest involved in ritual practices such as Mass, baptism, expulsion of devils, confessions of sins, funeral rites, etc., which resembled more the activities of a Daoist priest or Buddhist monk. With regard to these priestly functions, Roman Catholic Christianity as an ecclesiastical religion had no way to accommodate itself to Confucianism, since the priest has no Confucian counterpart. The Catholic priest's role of both scholar and priest was a combination of two roles that many Confucians experienced as incompatible, as Zürcher explains. Christianity could not confine itself to one of those two spheres as Confucianism and Buddhism did; true to its nature as a monopolistic religion, it had to encompass both. The two faces of early Chinese Christianity constituted an internal contradiction that was never resolved.[81]

The reference to both Chinese and Christian rituals indicates how those doing the reporting sought to reach a balance between representations of the two. On the one hand, they were eager to show how many honors the emperor had granted and how one benefited from the rituals that gave expression to these honors. On the other hand, the reports demonstrate that these rituals did not affect the correct performance of the Christian rituals. It is, however, the Chinese ceremonies, and not the Christian ones, that made these funerals a subject of extensive conversation and communication, unlike ordinary missionary funerals that merely followed the European liturgy. However, the noteworthy recognition and tolerance of Christianity lay not in the acceptance by the Chinese of Christian rituals; specific Christian rituals had long been accepted in China. Rather, it was the integration of Christian rituals into a broader framework of Chinese imperial rituals that confirmed the tolerance of, and, in the eyes of the missionaries, the support of the emperors for Christianity.

Verbiest was awarded the most complete funeral sponsorship of all Jesuits from the early Qing. A complete set of the funerary texts has been preserved. In addition to the encomium (or in fact, an imperial edict) quoted above, he was also granted a sacrificial ode, or *jiwen*, dated Kangxi 27/11/17, or 9 December 1688;[82] the posthumous title Qinmin, meaning diligent and adroit; and a commemorative text, or *beiwen*, dated Kangxi 28/4/1, or 19 May 1689.[83]

As is the case with other ritual texts, these texts too are probably the result of a process involving tensions and negotiations between the different actors participating in the funerals. In general, at least three different types of tensions can be identified in the writing of ritual biographical texts: a tension between literary style and ritual structure; between expression of emotion and mechanical composition; and, finally, between historical truth and moralistic eulogy.[84] To a certain extent, these three tensions correspond to the three different kinds of actors for whom the texts were written: texts for the deceased, introducing and locating the deceased in the spiritual world of ancestors; for the author himself, expressing the personal relationship between author and deceased and expressing the grief of the author; and for the living family and descendants, making the text into a family document meant to educate the children and to enhance the glory of the family descendants within their community.[85]

The text written for the deceased Verbiest, the sacrificial ode, corresponds closely to the structure of many other sacrificial odes used in worship, as did the one for Schall. First, the spirit (*ling*) of Verbiest is addressed; then his memories are briefly evoked; and finally, the text ends by imploring the spirit to accept the offering.[86] And also, as in the case of Schall, by accepting these honors, the Jesuits indirectly allowed sacrifices in which the spirit of Verbiest was invoked to partake in the sacrificial offering.

Yet funeral texts were not only written for the deceased, but also for the author. In general, the relationship between the writer and the dead inevitably had an impact on his writing. Since early times, the ability to honor and extol a loyal subject had been acknowledged as a sign of political acumen.[87] Thus, the writing of a funerary text does not only tell something about the deceased, but also about the moral and literary ability of the writer, in this case the emperor. It is difficult to fully assess to what extent the emperor personally intervened in the writing of Verbiest's funerary texts. While his *jiwen* has a formalized character, some effort was made to give it literary value.[88] As in the case of other imperial funeral texts, this text was almost certainly prepared by the office in charge, but the personal hand of the emperor cannot be completely excluded in this case. That there was some personal intervention is indicated by the fact that the decision of granting a posthumous title was left to the emperor, and that the characters chosen for Verbiest's title were already present in the edict that was written immediately after his death. More important than determining this personal involvement, however, is the power of concealment. In all these funerary ritual activities, the emperor was absent, but he was present through the ritual texts that were written in his name and that therefore enhanced his stature, as is clearly seen in the Jesuits' praise of his favors. This also reveals the tension between the personal favors granted to Verbiest by the emperor and the bureaucratic routine that decided upon the sponsorship, as well as the tension between the expression of the emperor's emotions toward Verbiest and the formalized language in which these texts needed to be written. The ambiguity resulting from these tensions and the ignorance among the intended readers with regard to imperial practices allowed the Jesuits to give a favorable interpretation to the text.

Chinese funerary texts, however, were also intended for the relatives and descendants of the deceased. Funerary writing has a tendency toward eulogizing. Because a funerary text was usually commissioned by surviving relatives upon the death of a senior family member, it was to a large extent written in praise of the deceased and of the bereaved family and intended not just for these descendants, but for the reading public as well, through its publication by local gazetteers. Nevertheless, an objective biographical record and unbiased evaluation at the time of death also held value. The tension between historical truth and moralistic eulogy also appears in the case of Verbiest, and affected the Jesuits and the wider Christian community. The Jesuits do not seem to have appreciated all the praise extended by the emperor. In the imperial edict granting the funeral subsidy, Verbiest is praised for his role both in the correction of the calendar as well as in the construction of cannon.[89] Yet the latter achievement is left out in the earliest translation by Thomas, and in all subsequent translations.[90] Verbiest's contribution to military equipment is included again both in the sacrificial and commemorative odes written in his honor.[91] It is not that this aspect was completely covered up by the Jesuits. Thomas's biography of Verbiest, later published by Le Comte, mentions that

Verbiest "gave directions for the casting of brass guns, which saved the states from ruin."[92] And Jesuit manuscript sources also acknowledge that mathematics and artillery were the two "human means that were the most effective in gaining a firm foothold in China."[93] But the prominent place they are given in the emperor's text has largely disappeared in the Jesuit texts.

The funerals in Beijing in the 1680s set the trend for the next century. Missionaries who served at the court received imperial sponsorship based on the rules of precedence, and public processions continued to be held. This does not mean that there were no conflicts. Apart from debates specifically related to the Rites Controversy,[94] other conflicts between ritual practices in Christian funerals expose just how much those rituals had already taken a Chinese shape. One example is the discussions concerning the funeral of Pietro Sigotti, a surgeon and member of the retinue of the papal legate Charles-Thomas Maillard de Tournon (1668–1710). Sigotti died on 12 December 1705, a few days after the arrival of the delegation in Beijing.[95] Thereupon, Maillard de Tournon asked for a detailed description of the funeral ceremonies usually practiced by the Jesuits during their obsequies in Beijing. To these, the legate immediately introduced some changes: no characters, not even the name of the deceased should appear in written form; the banquet should be abolished and instead the participants should be given some money to buy food themselves; and the priests should be dressed in a surplice from the beginning to the end of the ceremonies (including during the procession). In the report of the subsequent discussions about these changes, seen through the eyes of the Jesuit missionaries, it is striking that most of the argument is based on their defence of a tradition that had imperial blessing: "Because this new form of funeral could not remain secret as long as the emperor stayed in the city and would ask for the reasons why we had changed the old use which he had permitted till now."[96] The legate imposed his authority but in the end, at the tomb, not all ceremonies were performed because of the cold weather, "For the coldness was a sufficient reason for him that he could omit some of the holy ceremonies, because he felt the cold, but the reasons advanced by the Fathers not to go dressed with the surplice through the streets of Beijing were not sufficient because he did not feel them."[97]

CONCLUSION

For standard Chinese Christian funeral rites, the Christians, both missionaries and Chinese converts, played a leading role, but when imperial sponsorship was present, the missionaries were, so to speak, overtaken by Chinese rituals. The initiative was no longer in their hands and they were led into compromises that they had never allowed before. A change had occurred, therefore, in the evaluation of the funeral procession. At the beginning of the seventeenth century, missionaries such as Trigault considered Chinese funerals a "glorious Show." At the end of the century they took this show very seriously and gave it a specific meaning: the procession not only functioned as a public manifestation of Christianity, as the decisions of the Canton Conference made clear, but imperial sponsorship of the procession was considered the emperor's support of Christianity. The Chinese and the Jesuits interpreted the meaning of imperial sponsorship differently. While the emperor and his court sponsored the funerals of particular missionaries because they were members of the realm of officials, and not because they were members of the Society of Jesus, the Jesuits considered the sponsorship as an act of generosity towards themselves, which in subsequent years they would exploit to obtain further tolerance towards Christianity.[98] The Jesuits thus ascribed a meaning of their own straightforward interpretation to what the Chinese considered simply a system of protocol. The Jesuits had earlier objected to the pomp of the funeral procession for Ricci because "such display is more suited to a triumph than to a funeral" and "such pomp would have been out of keeping with our poverty and religious modesty"; now, in the 1680s, they saw that the imperial pomp that did not "conform to the modesty of our Institute" had "an infinite number of spectators" who could see "our Christian rites triumphing, even in their capital city, over pagan superstition." Such an imperial lead appears in changes to the whole structure of the procession. Over the course of much of the seventeenth century, the Christian funeral procession in China had acquired a more or less basic structure, with the consecutive, prominent display of different images such as the Savior, the Virgin Mary, and Saint Michael. Now, at processions with imperial sponsorship, this structure was reframed in a pattern in which the imperial symbols, such as the imperial edict at the beginning of the procession and the imperial eulogy, became the most important aspects. This also appears from the fact that these imperial texts were preserved on the tombstone. Moreover, during the procession, the imperial cover of the coffin linked the implied significance of the concealed body to the insignia that preceded it. In other words, to the observers watching the cortege pass through the streets of the capital city, the procession may well have looked like a typical imperially sponsored procession with some Christian elements, rather than a Christian procession with some Chinese paraphernalia. That the missionaries were overtaken by the Chinese rituals appears most clearly from the fact that they accepted the performance of certain Chinese and Manchu rituals that so obviously convey a specific religious belief, such as the prayer beseeching the deceased to come and take the offerings, which they would have rejected in other circumstances.

These conclusions cannot be generalized for the whole mission, since the imperial sponsorship of funerals remains a unique situation and so says little about the funerals of common Christians. Still, the texts written by missionaries in the beginning of the seventeenth century had tried to demonstrate that Christians in China were performing the funeral rites of the Catholic tradition, and performing them well. At the level of rhetoric, that aspect now disappears into the background. This does not mean that these specific Catholic rituals were not performed: the texts clearly mention the celebration of the Mass, the recitation of the Office of the Dead, the prayers and other rituals at the tomb. But in the whole discourse it is not the Christian elements but the Chinese form that is brought to the forefront.

8 / Conclusion

The Metaphor of Textile Weaving

If Christians in China were "buried according to the Chinese custom but with a Christian ritual," how can we evaluate the intermediary or "in-between status" of their funerals in the interaction between China and Europe in the seventeenth century? One way of understanding—and by no means the only one—is to approach this question from the perspective of contact between cultures.[1]

The funerals studied in this book offer a case of cultural interaction between China and Europe. There are different ways to study such interaction, each with its own methodology and outcome. Four analytical frameworks can be distinguished.[2]

The first may be termed the "transmission framework." Its main focus is the role of the transmitter, expressed by the main question, "How did the European missionaries transmit Christian funerary rites to China?" This approach was predominant until the 1960s and persists both implicitly and explicitly in recent research. The analysis in this book too makes use of this method. Some sections take the Western and Chinese texts by missionaries as a starting point and analyze how missionaries transmitted the European way of conducting funerals or how they reported their success or failure in doing so. Moreover, the transposition of European ritual funerary texts into Chinese language and culture has been verified through comparative analysis. This has necessarily involved an examination of the correspondence and congruity between the original European and the new Chinese culture. Christian prescriptive texts in Chinese have been compared to the originals produced elsewhere, such as João Fróis's *Rules for Helping to Obtain Merit towards a Good Death* (*Shanzhong zhugong guili*), and Lodovico Buglio's *Ritual for the Sacraments* (*Shengshi lidian*), both based on the *Manual for the Celebration of the Sacraments* (*Manuale ad sacramenta Ecclesiae ministranda*) that was produced in Japan in 1605. This textual analysis provided the basis by which the new funeral rites created by the Chinese Christians are compared with what had been transmitted. Such comparisons, guided by the ideal of perfect correspondence between what is transmitted and what is received, produce some interesting results, especially with regard to the reframing of European ritual into the encoffining and entombment phases of Chinese rituals.

However, this "transmission" approach has not been the main focus of research in this study because it has two major limitations. Both are linked to the fact that the question of transmission is most often directly related to the effectiveness of the transmission, i.e., was the missionary effective in transmitting the message to the Chinese? The emphasis of this framework is on effect, impact, contribution, and influence. The use of these terms is problematic because they are based on an ideal of a "pure" form of communication. In other words, in the most extreme manifestation of the framework, the transmission of a ritual is considered effective or successful if this ritual practiced by the receiver is exactly the same—as "pure"—as the ritual practiced by the transmitter. This is only possible if a distinction between subject and object is made, because such an ideal transfer would imply that Chinese Christians change in the process of accommodating to the imposed ritual requirements, while the ritual itself does not change. If the ritual is altered, and thus is no longer "pure," the transmission is considered a "failure." Implicit in this method of analysis is the assumption that the ritual can be transmitted independently of the person who transmits it, and that it can be received by a person who undergoes changes, without any alteration to the ritual itself. However, a ritual is always received in a context with which it interacts.

The second problem of this framework is the question of influence, i.e., what influence did the missionaries exercise? It is in relation to the change that the Chinese underwent that "influence" is evaluated as either a "success" or a "failure."[3] The major question here is what historians mean by influence. It appears from the history of the contact between China and Europe in the seventeenth century that historians often raise the question of influence and evaluate its success or failure, but rarely do they explicitly discuss how they determine this influence. The concept has been the object of research, mostly theoretical, in the social sciences, where it has been of primary importance for the analysis of, for instance, influences of modern means of communication, as in the influence of television on elections or on violence.[4] One definition of influence states that "the transmitter influences the receiver to the extent that the transmitter makes the receiver do certain things that the latter would not do otherwise."[5] Several examples of this explanation are found among the changes to funerals: without interaction with missionaries, the Chinese would not ask for a Mass to be celebrated on the occasion of the death of a family member and they would not chant specific Christian prayers, and without a funeral sponsorship missionaries would not accept a funerary eulogy for their fellow brothers. Still, it becomes much more difficult to determine overall influence. On what basis, for instance, can we determine the "success" of the funerals studied in this book: on the number of participants? On their increase? Or on their social level? Though the influence is usually defined as causing an explicit change of one sort or another, one effect of cultural contact can also be the absence of change—the confirmation of the status quo of existing values or practices, as was the case with several rules of the *Family Rituals* that continued to be observed. Distinctions should also be made between short-term and long-term effects, and among influences on individuals, groups, social institutions, or an entire culture. Moreover, there are cognitive (knowledge, opinions), affective (emotions, attitudes), and conative (behavior) influences, categories that are relevant even to funerals but that have been only lightly touched upon in this book.[6]

A second approach for studying funerals as cultural interaction is the "reception framework," which raises the question of whether the Chinese reacted positively or negatively to the introduction of European funeral rites. Here it is no longer the missionary as transmitter but the Chinese (with their Chinese texts) as receivers who are the center of research. The reception method, which arose in the 1960s and 1970s, is closely linked with the China-centered approach.[7] Research within the latter begins with Chinese problems set in a Chinese context, as a reaction against the paradigm of impact and response.

The research in this book also relied on the reception method. By looking at the texts written by Chinese authors it tried to understand how they reacted to the funerary rituals as transmitted by the missionaries. This required the use of a wide variety of texts, including diaries of community activities, manuscript guidelines, rules for associations, notes written by the emperor, funeral eulogies, etc. By comparing these texts with those of the transmitters it was possible to observe that funerals underwent significant changes upon reception. In the hands of the receiver they become something different from what they had been in the hands of the transmitter. Thus it became clear that the ritual itself underwent a process of change.

While this method has the clear advantage of being apt to reveal a wide variety of reactions to funerary rites, including negative ones, it also contains some limitations. In terms of communication, this framework is very much based on the same concepts as the transmission framework that presupposes a "pure communication" and a distinction between subject and object. In the case of reception, however, underlying assumptions appear in a different way. Though the focus of the scheme is the receiver, the focus of analysis is what is received—the funeral itself. In the transmission framework, the historian searches for the changes that occur in the receiver, while the funeral ritual itself is assumed to remain unchanged. In the extreme manifestation of the reception framework, the historian searches for the changes in the received ritual, while implicitly presuming that the Chinese do not or should not change. As a result the changes that occur in the ritual tend to be explained by historical, linguistic, or social contexts alone. For instance, the changes in the European funeral rites, such as the inclusion of expressions of filial piety, wailing, a shift in attitude to the corpse, etc., can be explained as arising from the nature of the Chinese world-view. Therefore this scheme may tend towards essentialism: Chinese are essentially different and will always remain so, and therefore will never be able to accept a "fully" Christian, European way of conducting a funeral.

Another problem with the "reception" framework lies in the concept of reception itself, which is basically conceived as passive. Though research within the framework of reception may be based on Chinese sources and may try to bring the Chinese actor to the forefront, this framework is still very much based on a scheme of "action and reaction."[8] The emphasis upon concepts of reception, response, or reaction assumes that European Christianity plays a truly *active* role, while China takes a much more *passive* or *reactive* one.[9] This book, too, is inevitably subject to an action-reaction scheme, partly because the first available sources are those written by the missionaries who travelled from Europe to China in order to transmit their message, and they often portray the missionaries as main actors. As a result, an analysis is easily subordinated to their interpretation. Yet, as has been pointed out on several occasions, what appeared to missionaries as a Christian funeral with some Chinese elements could just as well appear to Chinese as a Chinese funeral with some newly added European elements. This study has tried to show that in fact the Chinese, both Christians and non-Christians, were very often the primary agents in the process of change imposed on funerary rituals.

The third method, labeled "invention framework," is a rather recent development that originated in post-colonial and cultural studies.[10] Inspired by the theoretical approaches in line with Michel Foucault and by its application in Edward Said's *Orientalism*, it begins from a different premise: reality does not exist as such; it is invented, constructed, and created through expression in language and images. This is then applied to intercultural exchange: the transmitter, in approaching the receiver, constructs a symbolic reality (a discourse) of the receiver and of his or her culture; this symbolic reality in itself becomes a means to determine the receiver, to exercise power over him or her. Another important concept in this framework is the "locus of enunciation," which denotes the place not only of the transmitters but of the historians, i.e., the desires, the interests, the alliances, and, briefly, the politics of intellectual inquiry that are implied in their scholarly work.[11]

This book has benefited from this framework as well. By explicitly using travel writings, reports, translated texts, decisions of meetings, etc., written by European authors in European languages it has shown how the transmitters'—the missionaries'—vision of the other was based on their own European culture. Europeans used their own categories to interpret and reframe the Chinese notions of funerals: they classified them as "superstitious," "idolatrous," "non-superstitious," "civil," "political," etc. Imposing their categories on the native culture in this way helped them decide which rituals could be used and which should be rejected. Though the Chinese Rites Controversy, and the eighteenth-century Enlightenment in which its implications crystallized, have not been the object of this research, it is not difficult to show that the early categorization determined, to a large extent, European perceptions of China for a long time afterward.

The advantage of this framework is its focus on the subject. It reminds historians of how any use of language is an interpretation and how, by means of language and verbal constructions, power can be exercised over a culture perceived as other. It also reminds the author of this book that his own locus of enunciation inevitably affects observation, and so will the loci of enunciation of his readers.

Yet this framework has problems as well. The concept of communication is in fact, in its extreme manifestation, about the absence of communication. Placing the overall stress on the missionaries and on their act of construction risks denying the role or the place of the Chinese. The representation of Chinese funerals by the Europeans is thus thought to be constructed *independently* of any communication between the two. Much of their information on funerals, however, was acquired through interaction with Chinese informants. An insistence on discovering the "invention" of the missionaries risks underestimating the role of the native community in the process of constructing the other.[12]

Another problem with the invention framework is related to the very concepts of invention, construction, and deconstruction. They tend to lead to a static rather than a dynamic concept of contact between cultures. By focusing on the imposition of power exercised by Europeans rather than on the Chinese's resistance to it, and by ignoring the self-representation of the latter, a static framework of relations is promoted in which power and discourse seem to be possessed entirely by the missionary, leaving little or no room for negotiation or change.[13] As pointed out at the beginning of this book, what makes the China of the seventeenth century unique is that communication between Chinese and Europeans took place in the Chinese language, and not in a European one. In many regards, the Chinese occupied the dominant position. The risk of a stable interpretation pertains particularly to the locus of enunciation, which can be stressed to the point that the locus is stabilized even further: it then becomes difficult to accept that people—the participants or the historian—may be involved in different loci or that they may change their location, and thus their way of looking at things. After all, many of these missionaries spent more of their life in China than in any other part of the world. And many Chinese who entered into contact with Europeans were ready to change their vision of funerals. Thus, instead of thinking of the missionaries as having only what Walter Mignolo characterizes as a "monotopic" understanding, both missionaries and Chinese operated from a "pluritopic" understanding of the pluricultural world in which they lived.[14]

A fourth framework can be called "interaction and communication framework."[15] This framework is not a *radical* alternative to other frameworks, but rather it builds upon those previous frameworks. Like the transmission framework, it accepts that communication involves transmission, because people both aim to transmit messages or rituals to others and desire to be understood or to be engaged in shared rituals. The interaction framework differs from the transmission one, however, because, for example, it does not take the missionaries as its center: they are very often not the originators of a dialogue, but join a dialogue that is already in progress.[16]

The "interaction and communication" framework also involves reception, because reception is always a component of communication, although the framework incorporates the idea that reception, like transmission, is mutual. The interaction framework differs from the reception framework in that it does not merely seek to expose difference or non-correspondence. In analyzing ritual, this framework helps to reveal the internal coherence of rituals that are created anew as a result of the Chinese-European encounter. The starting question of the interaction framework is whether the Chinese, in the construction of the new ritual, have adopted the gestures and meanings offered by the Europeans, and vice versa. Instead of considering the new creation a misunderstanding, it explains the various ways of understanding by revealing their coherence. By "coherence" is meant that in the eyes of the authors, the new creation fits internally together, makes sense, and is considered effective, as was the case with different funerary rituals for local Christian communities. The interaction framework also helps maintain distance from any potentially essentialist tendencies of the reception framework, as in the idea that Chinese in the seventeenth century can only be or remain Chinese when they are

Confucian or Buddhist, and that they lose that identity by joining a new minority religion such as Christianity. By presupposing interaction, the framework allows for the human capacity to disengage from cultural determinism.[17] In any culture, as was clearly the case in seventeenth-century China, there are always people who open themselves up to others and who distance themselves from the dominant culture. The communication framework is interested in people who differ from those who conform to the mainstream culture.

Finally, the interaction framework builds upon ideas of the invention framework. The transmitter constructs a discourse about the other, and this discourse is linked to power, a process of invention that in this book is identified as the "imperative of the missionaries." But a relationship between power and invention exists within the discourse created by the Chinese as well, as illustrated by the "cultural imperative" of the Chinese. They also constructed and wielded power, engaging with the missionaries in ways that allowed them to carry out their own agendas. Although transmitter and receiver may ideally be considered equal partners, the invention framework shows they always engage one another within a context governed by mutual yet unequal power relationships: the missionary may occupy the role of teacher while giving a homily during Mass, but may be then subjected to the role of participant in a Chinese funeral orchestrated by a Chinese master of ceremonies. In contradistinction with the invention framework, however, the communication framework takes the group of Chinese participants more fully into account. It tries to avoid reducing the other to the role of a passive object, but considers the other an active subject. This other is not only an individual but also a ritual group with which the missionaries enter into contact, in which they participate, and of which they become a member. The invention scheme brings the constructive element to the forefront and stresses the subjective invention of the reality of the ritual. In the interaction and communication scheme, however, the stress is no longer on the subjective, individual, or personal construction of reality. The socio-cultural aspect is central: these ritual constructions are, to a certain extent, shared with others, both on the side of the transmitters and the receivers.[18]

As an attempt to understand the complexity of the history of contacts between cultures, the interaction and communication framework is ultimately founded on a specific theory of alterity, that is, on the specific view of the human being in relation to the other.[19] This view is primarily a conception of identity: the identity of the self is not only formed through an isolated effort of the self but also through the encounter with the other. In other words, who a person becomes is the result not only of that person's own activity but also the active or passive role of others. Human beings become persons through their encounters with other persons and the subsequent communication between them.

More fundamentally, human beings emerge as persons in a web of human (and other) relationships in which their inextricable connectedness to others is revealed. There is no self without the other.[20]

This is particularly true for identities that are formed as a result of cultural communication. The actors in this book did not have a fixed identity from early on in their life, but their identity came partly into being through the encounter and communication with persons from the other culture. To a certain extent, they occupied the role of the cultural "intermediaries," because they were functioning in-between two cultures, belonging at the same time to *both* of them and to *neither* of them.[21]

INTERWOVEN FUNERALS

The specific aims and related methods of the interaction and communication framework help to recast the material that has been analyzed in a new perspective. The primary focus of this framework is not the question of transmission, reception, or invention, but the result of interaction and communication. To what extent, then, did transmitters and receivers—roles played interchangeably by both Europeans and Chinese—create something new through their mutual exchange? To what extent did they construct a new rite using the ritual practices offered by the other? Can funerals be understood as a creative answer to the exchange between the missionaries and their Chinese partners?

Central to the communication framework is the concept of *space*—where interaction or communication takes place. The concomitant method starts from the presupposition that cultural creativity arises from the existence and creation of an interstitial space between transmitter and receiver, between object and subject, between self and other. This space can be physical, like the central hall of the house where the bier of the deceased is kept so that people can come and express condolence. It can even be a moving space, such as a funeral procession. But this space is often mediated by symbols: language, various forms of texts and images, material objects, or in this case, rituals. This ritual space both allows an encounter to take place, leading to interaction and communication, and also mediates the outcome of the encounter. In the example of the non-Christian Chinese who wanted to condole at the home of a deceased Jesuit or other Christian, his arrival created a space of interaction that led to the reframing of that space wherein traditional actions and ideas are reconceived. Thus the focus is neither on the transmitter nor on the receiver. The starting point is on the interstices, on what is "in between" them: the outcome of the exchange, which may be a text, an image, a ritual, or a social network that is considered the fruit of the interaction. Methodologically, therefore, there is a shift from the search for the other to the search for the space of interaction, a shift from the differences between the two worlds to what lies "in-between."[22] Since a funeral creates its own space in which a dialogue can take place, it offers a potent illustration of this method. For funeral rituals, the question is no longer whether they should be labelled "European" or "Chinese," but rather how they are the result of the interaction between the two cultural traditions.

The interaction framework allows for different and multiple perspectives on this encounter that have consequences for the way in which the texts studied here are perceived. The presupposition is that texts, like images, maps, social networks, communities, etc., are the result of communication. Whether it is a text by a missionary translating European ritual prescriptions into Chinese, a text by a Chinese Christian about funerary rituals, or a text reporting about Chinese funerals that is sent to Europe by a missionary, they all reflect a certain level of interaction. In this sense, all texts are to a large extent considered products of *coauthorship*. Therefore, the analysis of these texts as results of intercultural exchange cannot be limited to accepting the sole authorship of the person who signed the text. Very often other people are involved in the writing of the text. A text may be signed by a Western missionary or by a Chinese scholar but is usually produced through close interaction between the two. This is very clear for the texts that were studied in this book. The translations of the European prescriptive texts are not made without the help of Chinese collaborators. The *Diary of Oral Admonitions* (*Kouduo richao*) records the names of more than twenty-five members of the Fujian Christian community who participated in the recording and editing of the work. As for rituals in the "Ritual Sequence" guideline made in Guangzhou, Filippucci freely states that they were compiled by the catechist (Antonio) Li Andang. The four different versions of it also illustrate that the text, just like other texts, emerged from a process in which still others were involved: Leontio Li, the catechist of Bishop Luo Wenzao (Gregorio López), and the Franciscan friar Agustín de San Pascual. The same is true for texts that have been qualified as proto-ethnographic reports. They could not have been written without the intervention of local informants who undoubtedly left their traces in these texts. As long as such texts are ascribed solely to a missionary, questions about their European authorship inevitably arise. When they are considered as the result of the common interaction between European and Chinese experience, the analysis of these texts and the rituals they describe are less exclusively related to the European-Chinese divide. Thus any text is always an intertext, not only in the sense that other texts refer to it but also that the voice of the other can be heard within it.[23]

The communication framework accepts the existence of an objective reality but does not take it as its primary concern to verify whether that reality corresponds with what is being transmitted or received. Instead of searching only for correspondences between actions, searching for them as well as for the *coherence* that emanates from the space of interaction allows for the discovery of how something new emerges. In addition to analyzing ritual using the standard historical, critical methods, historians therefore try to discover the coherence of a ritual: how the different aspects of the new ritual fit together and are connected with each other.[24] The internal coherence of ritual is distinguishable from its external coherence, which is its *context*. The internal coherence of the Chinese Christian funeral ritual appears most clearly in the "Ritual Sequence" guideline, where the authors made the different aspects of the ritual fit within one framework that can be traced back to Zhu Xi's *Family Rituals*. The ritual guideline also illustrates how the authors experienced possible incoherence: for some, the ritual would be incoherent without a statement of clarification with regard to the offering of food, for example, while for others it would be incoherent with such a statement.

The external coherence is revealed as the larger context in which the Chinese Christian funerary ritual is connected and interacts, as in the case with the imperial sponsorship of funerals for missionaries whose status as officials or whose connection with the imperial house had an impact on how those rituals were conducted. But this case also shows how the evaluation of a funeral's coherence—how its parts fit and work together—by those directly involved largely depended on the context: at the beginning of the seventeenth century it was felt that sober and modest funerals were sensible, whereas at the end of the seventeenth century expensive and more ostentatious funerals were considered as fitting the context of that time.

The change of context also appears in the multiple reproductions of a single text describing a funeral. The story of Yang Tingyun's care for the funerals of his parents was reproduced in different contexts: European annual letters, a eulogistic biography by a Chinese scholar, and Chinese Christian morality books. A similar example is manifested by all the different versions describing Verbiest's funeral. The French and Dutch versions of Couplet's *Life of Madame Candida Xu* show that even the translation by the author himself can lead to significant variations. These stories were integrated within new contexts of reproduction of knowledge. The verification of the correctness of how these reports about the funeral are transmitted is here of less interest than how they are embedded within a new cultural context, whether it is how someone uses a particular story to prove the importance of the *Family Rituals* or how a report might be used to demonstrate the personal support of the emperor towards Christianity. The search is not for one objective reality of what happened at that ritual but for the connectedness of many different versions of reality that are presented through a variety of reports. This multiplicity does not lead to relativism or to the conclusion that reality does not exist. The main interest is the communicated cultural reality, and therefore, as the communication framework holds, ritual reality consists of the multiplicities in which people encounter each other.[25]

This multiplicity can be observed in at least four different domains: historical period, regional differences, social level, and type of rituals. Although certain generalizations cannot be completely avoided, these fields offer a method for *differentiation* and thus for unravelling variations in funerals. In other words, the practice of funerals in the beginning of the seventeenth century was not the same as in the 1680s; the funerary traditions in the Jiangnan region differed from those in Guangdong; there were some differences in the ways the poor or the elite buried their dead that were in turn different from the way an imperial funeral was conducted; and what happened to the funerals through cultural contact was not the same as what happened to the celebration of the Eucharist. In discussions about Christianity in China, these aspects are all too often brought together under the same denomination in which "China" is fixed and identified once and for all time.

Interaction is also characterized by *tensions* that are always present and that form the basis of its *process*: tension between the degrees of proximity from one actor to another; between the possibility and impossibility of understanding and being understood by the other; between willingness and reluctance to engage in a common ritual. The interaction therefore causes the partners to readjust, rethink, and reformulate ideas of self and other. The tension in the meeting of funeral rituals lies in whether the new ritual contradicts the transmitted ritual tradition, either Chinese or European. The texts reporting about a funeral capture the interaction at a certain moment, while the inner tension within funeral rituals over time, evident in looking at reports written over time, leads to a dynamism that can result in a ritual of another type. This process of change occurred in the attitude towards funerals during the initial years of the mission, as exhibited in the reports by Ricci and Trigault. It was also clear in the case of the "Ritual Sequence" guideline; having written at least four different editions of the guideline, each with its own characteristics, the authors clearly had no definitive fixed vision of the ritual.

Related to this tension, the communication framework also considers transmission as an exchange based on *negotiation*. People, through interaction, generally try to make choices that result in relatively sensible decisions, even if their choices are not always clear to the historian. Negotiations between groups about funeral rituals are evident in the experimentation by the Chinese Christians of the Fujian region, in the discussions that were held about funer-

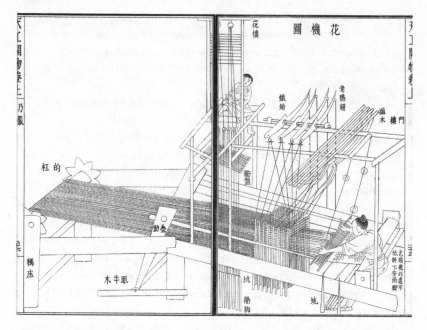

8.1. Textile weaving by a drawloom.

From Song Yingxing, *Tiangong kaiwu* (1637), *juan shang, naifu* 25b–26a. Courtesy of Princeton University, Gest Library.

als at the Canton Conference, in the different versions of the "Ritual Sequence" guideline, and in the exchanges between the Court and the missionaries that preceded the funerals receiving imperial sponsorship. Different strategies were used to render the new rituals acceptable. Chinese scholars, for instance, showed how the Christian funeral was congruent to the *Family Rituals* tradition, while missionaries used the classical notion of "civil" ritual to make Chinese rituals acceptable to their European counterparts.

The results of this negotiation can be categorized according to the levels of appropriation by visualizing a line between two extremes. On one end is the total absorption or appropriation of a ritual element in its pure form; on the other is total rejection. In the spectrum in between can be placed the variation of responses to foreign cultural elements by the native culture, i.e., ritual elements that are either accepted or rejected. Between the extremes of total acceptance or total rejection can also be set the agents of both cultures involved, from those who accept the other's ritual to those strongly opposed to it. While the cases of total appropriation or total rejection are rather exceptional, most types of temporary decisions can be classified between these two extremes, since in

8.2. Textile weaving by a drawloom, adapted from Song Yingxing.
From Jean-Baptiste Du Halde, *Description . . . de la Chine* (1735), vol. 2, between 222–223 (Hausard engraver) / (1736), vol. 2, between pages 246 and 247 / (1738–1741), vol. 1, between pages 352 and 353. Courtesy of Maurits Sabbe Library, Faculty of Theology, K. U. Leuven.

the end what is created inevitably contains elements of both cultures. In between, then, there is a wide variety of possibilities, such as adoption, integration, hybridity, etc.[26] These various possibilities have been explored in the conclusions of the different chapters in this book. This categorization between extremes of acceptance or rejection is not made to discern which ritual elements or texts belong entirely and exclusively to one culture or another. It rather aids in the observation of the variety of creations that emerge from the interaction between two cultures. Anthropologists and historians of religion use a wide range of terms to describe this result: mixture, *mélange*, syncretism, hybridization, *métissage* (mestizo), fusion, amalgamation, etc.[27] Several useful metaphors are also employed to denote this phenomenon: organ transplants, grafting, a mingling of chemical products, or a conflux of rivers.[28]

For this study, preference is given to the analogy of a textile in which the interaction between cultures is comparable to textile weaving; the product of the weaving, the cloth, is the cultural text (figs. 8.1, 8.2).[29] This metaphor is perhaps less organic than other metaphors, but the image of weaving has the advantage of insisting on the complexity of the diffusion. Cultural borrowing can be likened to the sort of interweaving that happens in creating textiles, where many different threads and fibers are drawn together in complicated ways. Such interweaving can also describe the interactions of social networks. Moreover, "text" is based on the same etymology as "texture," *texere*: to weave, join, fit together, fabricate, construct, build, etc., meanings that are also similar to that of the Chinese character *jing* that is used for both a classical writing and the warp of a textile. In the Chinese and European texts reporting about funerals, the strands of cultures join together like the strands of a textile.

The metaphor of the textile allows one to look at what happens to specific fibers or threads, at what happens to specific strands from different cultures that change rituals, but also to look at the use, function, form, and meaning of the fabric as a whole. Just as within one completed textile certain fibers have different functions, are of different color, and together contribute to a unique product, so too within the same person or the same geographical setting or the same social group, very different reactions are possible. One person accepts certain aspects of funerals, while rejecting or discarding some others. Some people oppose diffusion while others support it. These can all coexist within the same fabric. The textile thus represents a wide variety of cultural interactions. Using the analogy of weaving a textile, as outlined in Table 8.1, identifies a set of features that illustrate the many strands of the Chinese Christian funeral ritual. In some cases the identification concerns mainly elements of the existing Chinese funeral tradition, in other cases elements of the newly imported Christian tradition, though in most cases it affects both traditions. The result is a fresh way of seeing how these strands function and how they affect the evolution of that ritual.

This list of interweaving patterns is meant to underscore the possible complexity and variety of interactions between cultures. Moreover, the metaphor of interweaving illustrates that, despite the general notion that rituals are specific to a religious or cultural tradition, they can also undergo change and be interwoven with rituals of other traditions.[30]

Despite these advantages of the textile metaphor, it has some limits. The metaphor may give rise to the idea that the result of interaction is definitively constituted into a well-designed and seamless piece of fabric. Looking at the gradual embedding of Christian funerals over time has shown that the process constituted a long historical development with many different steps and choices. Thus many of the interactions were only temporary, and never the final, acceptable solutions. Another disadvantage of the weaving metaphor is that it suggests a harmonious interaction between cultures. But cultural interaction is often accompanied by tension, conflicts, and even violence. A fabric can be destroyed, the weaving interrupted, the threads broken. Though these

Table 8.1. Weaving Metaphors and Correspondences
with Chinese Christian Funeral Rituals

Weaving Metaphors	Chinese Christian Funeral Rituals
Reinforcement of existing thread	Reinforcement of respect for Confucian funerary practices (*Family Rituals*)
Removal (not replacement) of existing thread	Prohibition against burning mock money
Replacement of new thread by existing thread	Replacement of reusable coffin by airtight coffin
Retention of existing thread with change of meaning	Retention of genuflections as expressions of civil respect only
Replacement of one existing thread with another	Replacement of tomb offerings with natural, wool, or paper flowers
Redirection of existing thread	Redirection of food for consumption by officiants to food for the poor
Juxtaposition of existing and new threads	Juxtaposition of Chinese white mourning colors with European black ones
	Juxtaposition of virtues in Confucian and Christian stories in morality books
Addition of new thread without displacement of existing threads	Addition of crucifix to table of offerings and procession
Replacement of existing thread with new one with similar function and meaning	Replacement of Buddhist prayer beads with Christian rosary
	Replacement of Buddhist monks and Daoist priests with Catholic priests
Reconstitution of new thread into new meaning	Interpretation of the Christian funeral of Yang Tingyun's parents as a model of filial piety
Repositioning of new thread in existing fabric	Relocation of burial from church area to hill outside the village
Transformation of new threads into appealing product	Transformation of sober, simple funerals into more elaborate ones
Reframing of new fabric into shape of the existing fabric	Reframing of Christian funerals into Chinese structure with its key moments of encoffining, condolence, and entombment
Direction of weaving by social group	Care of funerals by associations
Removal of different layers returns new fabric to its original state	Removal (partial) of Christian funeral's clerical orientation (through lack of priests) returns funeral to a semblance of pre-tenth-century European funerals

conflicts are not the primary focus of this study, several controversies, such as the discussion about the burning of paper money, illustrate this aspect. The textile metaphor is also rather mechanical and thus less organic or dynamic than, for instance, the metaphor of the transplantation of organs that are alive and functioning, changing and sensitive to being changed by their environment. The image of a weaver who sits at the loom may convey the idea that cultural interaction is an intentionally planned operation according to a well-designed pattern. But there is no dominant "weaver" behind the whole of intercultural contacts; reactions towards contact can be as unpredictable and uncontrollable as those towards transplanted organs. The loom that draws upon threads for warp and weft illustrates still another limit: the image of interweaving may entail the suggestion that the result was an equally proportioned fusion between European and Chinese threads. However, this was not always the case, since in many instances the Christian elements were inserted into the Chinese funerary structure. Rather than a woven fabric, the result was often a patchwork, a textile made by sewing together pieces of fabric into a larger design and fastened onto the top of a quilt. In many respects the Christian funeral was "patched" onto the existing Chinese quilt. On several occasions in this book the metaphor of grafting has therefore been used as an explanatory analogy. It has the advantage of being more organic. It implies that the new element (the scion, here the European funeral ritual) was not merely patched on a pre-existing stable element (the stock, here the Chinese funeral), but that the interaction between the two also led to new fruits.

All these limits are reminders that the metaphor of interweaving, just like the other metaphors mentioned above, is intended only as a descriptive aid to understanding how cultural interaction may have happened, not as a prescriptive instruction of how cultural interaction should happen.

INTERWOVEN COMMUNITIES OF EFFECTIVE RITUALS

The metaphor of textile can also be used for the social networks that were created. Rituals such as funerals made it possible for people of different origin, status, and gender to interact when they normally would not have interacted. Although some lasting relationships could grow out of such an event, however, funerals were probably too occasional to establish relationships between people who otherwise would not have met. What they did do was to weave closely together the members of a more stable community, such as the Christian communities—the "communities of effective rituals." The Christian communities, and the rituals they performed, resembled those of other religions in China to such an extent that they can be considered a type representing a Chinese form of religiosity. Yet it is also reasonable to assume that this type of religiosity is characteristic of Christianity. In fact, a useful way to describe the purpose of the missionaries who went to China in the seventeenth century is to say they aimed at the installation of *christianitas* (Christendom), a term used by Europeans to refer to themselves and their civilization. *Christianitas* is defined by John Van Engen as "the rite and/or propriety by which people are called Christians."[31] This meaning also has an institutional manifestation, since, as confirmed by European sources of the mission in China, *christianitas* was the name used in the original sources to designate the concrete community in which rituals were put into practice. The whole process of christianization therefore required, in cultural terms, that the means had to be put in place for structuring Christian beliefs and practices, that is, the rituals and institutions that priests supervised. The spreading of Christianity in China seems to have been an effort at installing the same ritual life that was at the heart of Christian life in medieval and renaissance Europe. Thus the Christian communities of effective rituals in China, which resemble the European confraternities of laypeople, and which defined the life of the participants by ritual observances, are an indication of the gradual embedding of *christianitas* into China.

The communities of effective rituals therefore seem to be characteristic of both Chinese and Christian traditions. Yet there is an important question that is subject to further research: Did the Christian communities in China show the characteristics of an exclusive group that were clearly identified by the members themselves and that seem to be typical of the religions originating in the eastern Mediterranean area, also called abrahamic religions or the monotheistic religions of the Book, such as Judaism, Christianity, and Islam? The place of funerals will be essential in proposing a nuanced answer to this question.

The assumption on which this question is based has been deduced from the research conducted by Joël Thoraval on religious belonging in premodern Chinese society.[32] He analyzed the results of two surveys taken in Hong Kong in 1881 and 1911. The statistics produce some astonishing results: more than half of the population, in 1881, and three-quarters, in 1911, declared themselves "Confucian" (*rujiao*), while one third called themselves "laity" in 1881 (*sujia*, explained below) or "animist," in 1911. Even more significant is that while China is considered the country of the "three religions," the total number of Daoists and Buddhists at that time amounted to less than one percent of the total population. Finally, the Chinese Christians, who in the survey are clearly distinguished according to their denomination, exceed the number of Daoists and Buddhists. While this statistical analysis, based on a Western concept of religion, leads to minimal results in the analysis of the phenomenon of "religion" in premodern China, it still may reveal some aspects of how people identify their religious affiliation with regard to "Western" and "Chinese" religions.[33]

In this context, Thoraval's distinction between the status of the laity and the religious "professionals" is useful. In the modern West, people who claim to have a religious affiliation can be divided into communities or churches that can be relatively easily distinguished. Each of these communities has its own priests, its own place of worship, its own creed and rituals. They tend towards an exclusive belonging that unites both the believers *and* the religious special- ists (priests, rabbis, pastors, imams), who are *exclusively* at the service of the laity. There is no cross-membership. Likewise, except for special circumstances, a Methodist would not appeal to an Anglican priest, a Catholic would not pray in a Protestant church, a Baptist would not use a Catholic Bible, etc.

In premodern China the situation tended to be quite different, since a stronger distinction can be made between the "lay" community and religious specialists (Buddhist monk, Daoist master, or shaman) to whom one may appeal at one time or another. Thoraval states that it is important to understand that the lay community as a whole was, in principle, undivided, as opposed to the multiple and distinct worlds of the religious specialists. At the level of the latter, along with some very active, semiprofessional laypeople, exists an exclusive doc- trinal or ritual distinction and identification (the difference between a Buddhist monk and Daoist master), resembling the Western situation, though these differences are less marked than in the West. The community united in its cus- toms thus stands in contrast to the fragmented universe of the specialist who alone can be categorized by sect or school. (See Appendix, fig. A1.)

What is important for the subject of this study is that, though in the seven- teenth and eighteenth centuries there was mainly only one Christian denomina- tion in China, Catholicism at that time appears to have contained characteristics expressed in the analysis of the Hong Kong surveys. Indeed, when the in-origin eastern Mediterranean religions become established in China, they tend to reproduce their own exclusive community, which unites both laypeople and specialists around ritual and doctrine. Unlike Buddhist monks who would hardly intervene in the private life of the faithful, missionaries applied the European model, which implies an interference in and guidance of the private life of the converts. As a result, laypeople seem to have been much more dependent on priests than in Buddhism.[34] This also explains why Chinese belonging to a reli- gion originating in the eastern Mediterranean area easily distinguish themselves from other Chinese, no matter whether they are laity or specialists.

If this interpretation is confirmed, the communities of effective rituals exhibit characteristics in which European Christianity resembles premodern Chinese religion, as pointed out earlier. Yet, although these similarities should be understated, in China too Christianity tends to reproduce its exclusive institutional organization, as pointed out by Thoraval's model of interpretation.

The present research on rituals further clarifies the tension between an eastern Mediterranean and a Chinese type of religion, but the distinctions made between types of religions also help to give a deeper understanding of the role of funerals in the constitution of Christian communities in China. In the European Catholic communities, which were the background from which the missionaries originated, most of ritual life was organized around the seven sacraments: baptism, confirmation, Eucharist, confession, extreme unction, matrimony, and ordination to the priesthood. There are theological and historical reasons why only these seven rituals are defined as sacraments. The Council of Trent determined that these were efficacious, that is, by the materials used, the words spoken, and the gestures performed, an actual change or transition in the person occurs. The Council specifically states that a believer attains salvation by means of the sacraments.[35] There is a close link between the sacraments and those who perform or preside over them, i.e., the clergy. Though not necessary for all sacraments—baptism, for example, could in principle be performed by any layperson—in the late sixteenth and early seventeenth century priests and bishops were in fact the main agents of these rituals. Catholic ritual life was broader than these sacraments, since there were all kinds of ceremonies (also called sacramentals, which evoke or call to mind the presence of God), such as prayer sessions (vespers, matins, rosary, the Office of the Dead), blessings, incensing, sprinkling of holy water, processions, fasting, etc. In fact, at the heart of the Catholic liturgy stood the celebration of the Mass, but it was surrounded by these other ceremonies. And though the clergy was not necessary for all these ceremonies or practices, such as for praying the rosary and fasting, in fact the clergy was present at many of them. This is also true for funerals. Funerals are not considered a sacrament and, before the tenth century, were mostly a family ritual in the hands of laypeople. After a long process, however, they became gradually clericalized, and Mass became the essential part of the Catholic funeral ceremony in Europe. At the time missionaries went to China, rituals had contributed to the strong exclusive pillar structure of the religious denominations in Europe. Not only would Catholic laypeople not participate in rituals organized by other denominations, such as Protestant or Jewish, but almost all important liturgies were performed through the common presence of both clergy and laity, though each group had different ritual roles. Moreover, with the Council of Trent, the Catholic Church had started an intense process of standardization of its rituals. The Jesuits were exponents of this process, and from the beginning they emphasized the importance of a correct ritual and insisted on conformity of practice for specific ritual actions, particularly for the essential ritual of the Church—the celebration of Mass.[36] This was the European side (see Appendix, fig. A2).

To analyze the overall situation of rituals in China, the distinction between "institutional" and "diffused" brought forward by C. K. Yang may be helpful. Yang defined an "institutional" religion as having an independent theology or cosmic interpretation of the universe and human events, independent forms of worship consisting of symbols (such as gods, spirits, and their images) and rituals, and an independent organization to facilitate the interpretation of theological views or to pursue cultic worship. Yang therefore considers Buddhism and Daoism to be institutional religions. The research by Thoraval refines this analysis by pointing out that in Buddhism and Daoism this independency is in the first place true for religious professionals—Buddhist monks and Daoist priests, and also some lay specialists—while the majority of the laypeople belong to a larger community of undivided character. Diffused religion is a religion having its theology, cultus, and personnel so intimately diffused into one or more secular social institutions that they are part of the concepts, rituals, and structure of the latter, thus having no significant independent structure. The prescriptions in *Family Rituals*, often associated with what is called the Confucian tradition, belong to this category of diffused religion. The funeral rituals illustrate this quite well. In the funerals as prescribed by *Family Rituals*, the major actors, usually the eldest sons, are people who play the most important role in the family as a "secular" institution. Moreover, they perform ritual acts, such as bowing and kowtowing, that are performed on other occasions, such as New Year celebrations, and that do not require specialized apprenticeship. Finally, there is no independent theology about life after death, etc.

The situation of funerals in China at the end of the sixteenth and early seventeenth centuries shows only a partial overlapping of the diffused and institutional type of religious expression: most people performed rituals that corresponded to the elementary structure as also contained in *Family Rituals*, and funerals were themselves basically a family ritual. At the same time, in addition to their family rituals, most people would also call in some religious specialists, such as Buddhist monks or Daoist masters, to perform certain rituals. In other words the rituals of the institutionalized religion were grafted on those of the diffused religion. Specific for this period was the movement among certain members of the gentry to promote pure family rituals and thus to exclude the Buddhist and other rituals from funerals. This was the situation when the foreign missionaries arrived in China (see Appendix, fig. A3).

In the initial period of the mission, the overall picture of Christianity in China was very similar to the situation in Europe, at least in the way the missionaries report it. They stress how the small but rather exclusive community participated in the Christian rituals that were predominantly sacramental and clerical. This corresponded to the Jesuits' insistence that rituals should be administered in a proper and uniform way, all over the world.[37] The funerals, for missionaries and Chinese converts alike, were thus celebrated in a way that was very similar to Europe, with the Mass as the central rite, and the priest as main officiant. The evolution of the gradual embedding of the Christian funerals, however, demonstrates that over a period of about one hundred years, the situation became much more complex. The rituals that could be performed by laypeople, and not the sacramental or clerical rites, became the most important ones in the daily life of Chinese Christians. Thus there was a clearer differentiation among rituals: the sacramental rites, such as the Eucharist and confession, remained strictly clerical; baptism was practiced by the clergy and lay-catechists; prayer meetings and fasting, though also practiced by priests, became important ritual expressions by which Christian laypeople differentiated themselves from Chinese performing similar Buddhist or Daoist rituals; and funerals became primarily the ritual of the family and the Christian community, with only a marginal role reserved for the priest. The funeral ritual further differentiates family from community. The family rituals performed at the funerals of Christians overlapped with the prescriptions of *Family Rituals*, which are often interpreted as the diffused religion type: i.e., socially embedded with the bowing, kowtowing, and offering performed by the family members themselves. The rituals of the Chinese institutional religions, however, were excluded as much as possible. They required the presence of a ritual specialist who would be a competitor to the Catholic priest. The rituals of the Chinese institutional religions were substituted by some rituals performed by the missionaries, but mainly by rituals performed by the Christian community, such as prayers and the sprinkling of holy water. These required to a lesser extent the presence of ritual specialists, since they were performed by laypersons, though not necessarily members of the family (similar to sectarians). This differentiation corroborates the categorization used by the missionaries and Chinese Christians: the Catholic priest performed only the "rituals of the Holy Teaching"; the laypersons performed "rituals of the Holy Teaching," such as chanting Christian prayers, but also "non-superstitious rituals" such as bowing and kowtowing; the members of the family shared in the latter but also performed other "non-superstitious rituals" such as offering of food; rituals that were refused were those labelled "superstitious rituals," which could be certain rituals usually performed in the diffused religion, such as the burning of mock money, and all rituals directly related to the Chinese institutional religions, such as chanting Buddhist scriptures (see Appendix, fig. A4).

The categorizations of Thoraval can also be used to explain the role that funerals played in this transformation of Christianity. When Christianity was introduced into China it took the shape of an exclusive community, which is characteristic of all eastern Mediterranean religions. Rituals, such as baptism, Eucharist, and confession, were responsible for creating such exclusion, because they were intended for the "in" group. It is noteworthy that they underwent hardly any significant change after their arrival in China, compared with the same rituals in Europe.[38] Simultaneously, other rituals, such as funerals, made Christianity take another shape: that of a lay-oriented community that grafted or patched its rituals onto the existing family rituals. It was the Chinese cultural imperative, with its stress on orthopraxy, which caused this in-between situation. Certain rituals, destined for a transcendent being, within the purview of only practitioners who shared the same convictions and who performed rituals in their own specific way, occurred only in the margins of social life and in rather exclusive communities. But other rituals, destined for the secular realm, had to be performed the same way as in the ambient community. Thus the way Christian funerals were adapted in China provides valuable insight into the structure of Chinese religious life.

IDENTITY FORMATION AND FUNERALS

The interwoven character of these communities and their rituals raises the question of identity. In the present interaction framework, partners do not have a static and fixed identity but rather one that is constructed through an encounter with the other. Such a dynamic and dialogic conception considers identity as "the process by which a social actor recognizes itself and constructs meaning primarily on the basis of a given cultural attribute or set of attributes, that is/are given priority over other sources of meaning (or to the exclusion of a broader reference to other social structures)."[39] As many studies have shown, rituals can be an essential part of the construction of an identity.

Rituals in which different cultures are interwoven throw a specific light on this question of identity. The actors involved in funerary rituals could construct meaning on the basis of a wide variety of attributes: "Chinese," "Christian," "Confucian," "Jesuit," "Buddhist," etc. By participating in shared rituals, among other activities, the identity of the partners could also adopt a new shape. Due to the lack of explicit references, it is not always clear how they themselves claimed or proclaimed their identity. From a distance, however, their identity could be qualified as an identity of "intermediaries," who were earlier discussed. Like the rituals in which intermediaries were involved, such identity has the characteristics of "in-betweenness" (see Appendix, fig. A5). Moreover, vital features of a ritual, such as its liminal phase, can illuminate what this identity is like, to a certain extent. The notion of the liminal phase of the "rites of passage," as originally used by Arnold van Gennep, is further developed by Victor Turner. Van Gennep observes that all rites of passage or "transition" are marked by three phases: separation, margin (or *limen*, signifying "threshold" in Latin), and (re-)aggregation. The first phase of separation comprises symbolic behavior signifying the detachment of the individual or group either from an earlier fixed locus in the social structure, from a set of cultural conditions (a "state"), or from both. During the intervening "liminal" period, the characteristics of the ritual subjects (the "passenger") are ambiguous. They pass through a cultural realm that has few or none of the attributes of the past or coming state. In the third phase, the phase of reaggregation or reincorporation, the passage is consummated and the ritual subject, individual or corporate, is once more in a relatively stable state.[40] While this vocabulary was originally developed for specific rituals, Turner uses it for the genesis of religious movements and the process they go through.[41] Others have used similar discourse to describe three phases that occur in the dynamism of "transplantation of religions."[42]

The actors involved in funerary rituals may be said to have been in such a liminal, marginal, ambiguous, and in-between condition: between Europe and China, between Confucian and Christian. In fact, the funerary ritual, more than any other ritual, made them conscious of the tensions involved in a passage, but at the same time also made the passage possible. During the transition period, which this book spans, the actors of funeral rituals were in a process of constructing an identity. This construction implied in the first place a separation. After leaving Europe, missionaries were separated from the cultural realm that provided them the attributes of their identity. The Chinese Christians too, by engaging in these foreign practices, were in many ways detached from the original fixed locus in their culture. Separation was accompanied by a loss that was ritually expressed. Chinese Christians gave up certain rituals when they held funerals for their own family, such as Buddhist and Daoist ceremonies, and also did not participate in certain practices when they attended funerals of others, such as the burning of mock money. The losses were as large on the side of the missionaries. The Chinese cultural imperative ultimately dictated that the funeral as the most important ritual in Chinese culture remained out of their control. Contrary to the European practice in which the priest was the main actor at funerals, the organization and performance of funerary rites in China came into the hands of the lay-Christians who took charge of them from the beginning to the end.

Yet the participation in rituals not only caused a loss of identity but also the emanation of a new identity. Some rituals, usually those in which the other culture is hardly involved, seem to provide a rather clear and unambiguous identity: participating in Chinese New Year celebrations testifies to a Chinese identity, or attending Mass testifies to a Catholic identity. There seems to be a close link between the ritual expression of a cultural attribute and the priority one gives to it in constructing one's identity. It thus becomes almost impossible to prove one's Chinese identity while refusing to participate in Chinese New Year or one's Catholic identity while refusing to attend Mass.

This enquiry, which approached funerals from the point of view of contact between cultures, confirms that funerals are key events in identity formation in China. When improperly performed, damage is done not only to individuals but also to communities.[43] This was also the case for the funerals among Chinese Christians. When funerals were improperly performed, i.e., without proper rituals and pomp, the participants would be accused of lack of filial piety and thus of detaching themselves from what was considered the core of the ambient culture. Missionaries too gained another identity not only by taking care of the tombs of their deceased brothers, but also by accepting to be buried under imperial sponsorship. Formulated positively, Chinese Christians and missionaries could perform rituals such as Mass that they considered to be at the core of their identity, as long as they performed funerals in a proper way, thereby proving their acceptance of the imperative of Chinese identity. Funerals, however, are open rituals and thus will more easily submit to change. Most striking are the changes the Catholic funerals underwent under the influence of the Chinese cultural imperative. But funerals practiced by Christians were also subjected to the Christian imperative. Consequently, when improperly performed according the Christian imperative, they would no longer be considered "Christian."

This study has focused on funerals being "in-between" several traditions, just like the communities who performed them were "in-between." The funerals provided the ritual context in which a Chinese and Christian intermediary identity could be constituted and expressed. Probably the most important aspect of the Chinese Christian funeral ritual is that it not only identified the participants as Christians and consolidated their identity, but also allowed them to remain integrated within the wider Chinese community. Indeed, the funeral ritual facilitated nonexclusive integration, a phenomenon common in Chinese tradition itself.

Appendix

Schematic Representation of Communities

of Effective Rituals (see Conclusion)

Eastern Mediterranean communities   Premodern Chinese communities

1. Daoist master
2. Buddhist monk
3. Shaman
4. Fengshui master
5. Other

Professionals

Semiprofessional laity

Laity

A1. Comparison of eastern Mediterranean and premodern Chinese ritual communities (after Joël Thoraval).

Joël Thoraval distinguishes between the status of the laity (lower level of rectangles) and the religious "professionals" (top, shaded level). Ritual communities originating in eastern Mediterranean religions (left) tend toward a strong and exclusive pillar structure—an exclusive belonging, which unites the laity *and* religious professionals and in which there is no cross-membership between pillars (not only between different religions but also between Catholics, Presbyterians, Anglicans, and other Christian denominations). In premodern China (right) a stronger distinction can be made between the lay community and the religious specialists. The lay community was, in principle, undivided in its religion, as opposed to the multiple and distinct worlds of the religious specialists, who were, together with some very active semiprofessional laypeople, exclusive in their doctrines and rites.

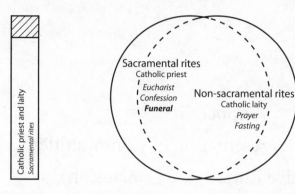

A2. Substantial overlap of Catholic professional and lay rites in Europe (after Robert Scribner).

The exclusive pillar structure had evolved in Europe into a situation in which the ritual practices (represented by circles) of professionals overlapped to a large extent with those of laity. Catholic priests were the main agents of sacraments, such as Eucharist and confession. Although the clergy was not necessary for non-sacramental rituals typically practiced by the laity, such as praying the rosary and fasting, in fact it was present at many of them. This was also true of funerals, which, although not considered a sacrament, had gradually become clericalized, with Mass presided over by a priest considered an essential part of the Catholic funerary ritual.

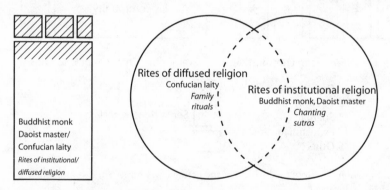

A3. Limited overlap of traditional Chinese professional and lay rites.

The distinction between the rites of diffused religion and of institutional religions in China, as proposed by C. K. Yang, corresponds with the distinction between the lay community and religious specialists as made by Thoraval. The laity upholding Confucian orthodoxy practiced rituals that were "diffused" in secular social institutions, such as those in the family, detailed in *Family Rituals*. In contrast, Buddhist monks and Daoist masters practiced rituals based on independent forms of worship, such as chanting sutras. At funerals these two circles overlapped only partially, with rituals of institutional religions grafted onto those of diffused religion. Some orthodox Confucians tried to exclude Buddhist and Daoist elements from family rituals.

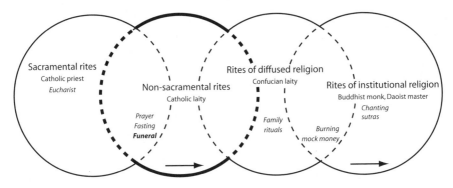

A4. Reorganization of Catholic rituals in seventeenth-century China.

The most significant change in Catholic rituality in China was that rituals that could be performed by laypeople, rather than sacramental rites performed by priests, became the most central ones in the life of Chinese Christians. In this move (indicated by the arrow on the left), there was less overlapping between the two types of rites than in Europe. Funerals, for instance, which had been a primarily clericalized ritual in Europe, became primarily rituals of the family and the Christian community in China, with only a marginal role reserved for the priest. The Christian rituals performed at a funeral overlapped partially with practices that were described in *Family Rituals* and were common to diffused religion. Thus, the Christian community occupied a position similar to that of institutional religions in relationship to diffused religion in premodern China. This was possible only with the exclusion of certain rituals (indicated by the arrow on the right), especially those of the other institutional religions.

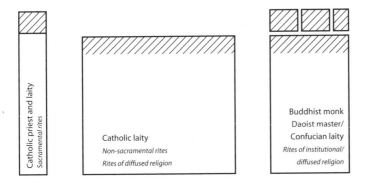

A5. The in-between situation of the Catholic community.

The in-between situation of the Christian community is evident in funeral practices in China. By practicing non-sacramental rituals and the rituals of diffused religion that were not considered superstitious, the Christian community constituted of lay persons was in-between a European structure stressing the rituals that united both believers and religious specialists, and a Chinese structure with a stronger distinction between the lay community and religious specialists.

Notes

INTRODUCTION

1. Verbiest's letter from Beijing, dated 15 September 1581, appears in Josson and Willaert (1938), 363, with a French translation in Bosmans (1912), 97; the letter is addressed to Charles de Noyelle, SJ (1615–1686), then Assistant General of the Society of Jesus. De Noyelle became vicar-general on 26 November 1681 and general on 5 July 1682.

Xiaocheng married the emperor in 1665 and died on Kangxi 13/5/3, or 6 June 1674, the day that she gave birth to Yinreng (1674–1725), the future proclaimed heir apparent; see *ECCP*, 924. Xiaozhao was the daughter of Ebilun, one of the four regents. First a concubine, she was elevated to empress in 1677, but died one year later on Kangxi 17/2/26, or 18 March 1678. The father of the Kangxi Emperor, the Shunzhi Emperor (1638–1661), had died when the Kangxi Emperor was only six years old, and his mother, Empress Xiaokang (1640–1663), passed away two years later.

Construction of Jingling, the mausoleum of the Kangxi Emperor, began after the death of his first empress in 1676 and was completed in 1681. Meanwhile, the coffins of the two empresses had been stored at Gonghua, located to the north of the capital city, on the banks of the Sha River. Tradition dictated that the body of a deceased emperor or empress, inside its coffin constructed of *nanmu*, a Chinese hardwood, should lie in state for two weeks. The coffin was then usually moved into temporary storage to permit workmen to cover it with forty-nine coats of lacquer and a final coat of gold lacquer. For more on the funerals of the two empresses and on imperial funerals generally, see Rawski (1988b), 228–53; Rawski (1998), 277–85, 292; and de Groot (1892–1897), vol. 3, esp. 1282–1290.

The transfer to the place of sepulture described in the passage quoted here took about one week. The bodies left the temporary place on Kangxi 20/2/19, or 7 April 1681, and arrived at the tomb on Kangxi 20/2/25, or 25 April 1681. The Chinese sources do not give the precise number of participants that is mentioned in the passage quoted here, listing only the large group of court members and officials who had to take part in the procession and in the rituals accompanying the transfer. See *Qing shilu* (1985), vol. 4, 1192–1194 (*Shengzu shilu*, j. 94, 19a-23a); *Kangxi qijuzhu* (1984), vol. 1,

668–70. See also the description in *DaQing huidian (Kangxichao)* (1696), 3525ff. (*juan* 68, *libu* 29, *sangli* 2, 18aff).

2. Van Engen (1986), 543. For the pronounced interest in ritual emerging in the work of several historians of early modern Europe published in the 1970s and 1980s, see Scribner (1997), 17.

3. Schipper (1996), 308.

4. On these shifts, see Standaert (1997).

5. Bell (1997). See also her earlier work (1992), which addresses more theoretical issues.

6. *HCC*, 300–308, 380–86.

7. See Zürcher (1994), 40–41.

8. Cohen (1984), 14.

9. On the study of funerals in the Chinese American cultural exchange, see Chung and Wegars (2005); on the study of Christian funerals in contemporary China, see Lozada (2001), 132–55.

1. CHINESE AND EUROPEAN FUNERALS

1. Watson (1988a), 12; for a critical discussion, see also Sutton (2007b), 128ff.

2. Ebrey (1991a), xiv.

3. This is a state-of-the-field chapter, based on the most recent research on the topic, mainly taken from secondary sources.

4. For general surveys of Chinese funerary rituals, see de Groot (1892–1897), Ebrey (1991a), Naquin (1988), Watson (1988a), and recent historical overviews: Chen Shuguo (2002), Wan (1998), Xu Jijun (1998), Zhang Jiefu (1995), Zheng (1995). These sources are based on numerous Chinese primary sources. For research overviews, see Tong (2004), 15ff, Oxfeld (2004), 965ff, Chung and Wegars (2005), 1ff.

5. The most important chapters on funerals in the *Liji* are: 31, *Bensang* (Rules on Hurrying to Mourning Rites); 32, *Wensang* (Questions about Mourning Rites); 33, *Fuwen* (Subjects for Questioning about the Mourning Dress); 34, *Jianzhuan* (Treatise on Subsidiary Points in Mourning Usages); 35, *Sannianwen* (Questions about the Mourning for Three Years); and 46, *Sangfu sizhi* (The Four Principles Governing the Dress of Mourning). In the *Yili*, they are: 11, *Sangfu* (Mourning Dress) and 12, *Shisangli* (Mourning Rites for the Common Officer).

6. Rawski (1988a), 30.

7. On the importance of the examination system in this regard, see Elman (2000); on printing, see Chow (2004).

8. The significance of these rites is confirmed by the space that is allotted them in other ritual handbooks or encyclopaedias; see also *Gujin tushu jicheng* (1726–1728) under *Liyidian*: *guanli* (capping) takes 5 *juan*, *hunli* (marriage) 17 juan, *sangzang*

(funerals) 68 *juan* and related chapters *shifa* (rules for posthumous names) 24 *juan*, *xudian* (funeral sponsorship) 2 *juan*, and *diaoku* (condoling) 4 *juan*.

9. Naquin (1988), 63.

10. Oxfeld (2004), 965.

11. This sequence is summarized primarily from Ebrey (1991a), 65ff, 194ff.; see also Naquin (1988), 38ff.; Watson (1988a), 12ff.; and *Jiali* (1341).

12. For a historical study of this system, see Ding (2000).

13. Kutcher (1999), 21.

14. The classic studies are the observations of Justus Doolittle ((1867), vol. 1, 168–235) on Fuzhou (1865); Henri Doré ((1911), vol. 1, 41–146) on the lower Yangzi (1911); and Jan Jacob M. de Groot (1892–1897) on Amoy. For an early overview of the variations according to the four regions of Yellow River, Yangzi River, Pearl River and Manchuria, see Chen Huaizhen (1934), 147. Fieldwork studies of the 1960s–1980s mainly concerned Taiwan, by such scholars as Arthur Wolf, Emily Martin Ahern, Xu Fuquan and others; and Hong Kong, by Maurice Freedman, James Watson, and others. More recent studies, especially by Chinese scholars, cover different regions in China mainland; see He Bin (1995) on Wenzhou, Zhejiang; Chen Gang (2000) on Changshou county, Chongqing Municipality; Adam Yuet Chau (2006) on Shaanbei, northern Shaanxi; Feng Jianzhi (2006) on Wuyuan county, Jiangxi; William Jankowiak (1993) on Inner Mongolia; Kenneth Dean (1988) on Fujian; Charlotte Ikels (2004) on Guangzhou; or places of the Chinese diaspora, as in Tong Chee-Kiong (2004) on Singapore. Especially noteworthy is the study of Chinese American death rituals by Chung and Wegars (2005). For a discussion of the tension between standardization and variation, see Sutton (2007b).

15. Naquin (1988), 58.

16. Naquin (1988), 52, 68.

17. For these different funeral specialists, see Watson (1988b).

18. Naquin (1988), 59.

19. Brook (1989), 492; Teiser (1994), 27.

20. Teiser (1994), 28.

21. This sequence is taken from Brook (1989), 481–82; see also Naquin (1988), 41; Teiser (1994), 23–27; and Welch (1967), 179–205, for recent descriptions of Buddhist rites for the dead.

22. Teiser (1994), 28–30. For a recent description of a Daoist funeral liturgy, see Lagerwey (1987), 168–237, Dean (1988); and several articles in Johnson (1989).

23. Ebrey (1991a), xx.

24. Ebrey (1991a), 79, 196.

25. *(Da)Ming jili* (1530), *juan* 36–38, *SKQS*, vol. 650, 128–87; see tables of contents in Ho (2000), 45–47.

26. Ho (2000), 49ff.; Chen Shuguo (2002), 303ff.

27. Ho (2000), 29ff.; Ebrey (1991b), 150ff.

28. Brook (1989), 476; Ebrey (1991b), 173ff.; Ho (2000), 160–61; Kojima (1996), 403–6; *Jiali yijie* (1518).

29. Ebrey (1991b), 188.

30. Ebrey (1991b), 157–58; Brook (1989), 466–68, 480–81.

31. Brokaw (1991), 4ff.; Ho (2000), 71, 90; Brook (1989), 470.

32. Xie (1959), 56, 120; Ad Dudink, "2.6.1. Sympathising Literati and Officials," in *HCC*, 477; Zhang Xianqing (2003), 53–54.

33. Xie (1959), 419.

34. On traditional arguments, see de Groot (1892–1897), vol. 2, 659ff.

35. Ho (2000), 60ff., 71, 88ff.; Zhang Shouan (1993), 70–73; Kutcher (1999), 23–24; Chen Jiang (2006), 95–97.

36. Ho (2000), 64, 97ff, 101ff.

37. Ho (2000), 67, 108ff. Cremation was condemned by article 200 of *The Great Ming Code* (2005), 119.

38. Ho (2000), 69–71, 85ff, 111ff, 116; Kutcher (1999), 22–23. See also article 200 of *The Great Ming Code* (2005), 119.

39. Ebrey (1991a), xxvi–xxvii; Brook (1989), 479; Ho (2000), 156; for an extensive list, see Ebrey (1991b), 231ff, and Ho (2000), 261ff.

40. *Jiali yijie* (1608); Standaert (1988), 46ff.

41. Lü Kun (1573) and (1614); Ebrey (1991b), 181.

42. Lü Weiqi (1624); Ebrey (1991b), 182.

43. Ebrey (1991b), 177–83; Ho (2000), 161ff.; Handlin (1983), 146.

44. Chow (1994), 130; Ho (2000), 165ff.; Zhang Shouan (1993), 74ff.; Ebrey (1991b), 189. Chow points out that in a similar way, Zhang Lüxiang's (1611–1674) *Sangji zashuo* (1640) criticized improper popular mourning and funerary customs.

45. Chen Que (1979), 433. Zhang Xianqing (2003), 54; for his praise of Western spectacles, see Chen Que (1979), 356, 668.

46. Chen Que (1979), 494–95; Ho (2000), 211.

47. Ho (2000), 178ff.

48. Brook (1989), 472–73; Ebrey (1991b), 158ff.

49. Brook (1989), 480.

50. Brook (1989), 486.

51. Brook (1989), 465–66.

52. Ho (2000), 9, 189ff.; Handlin (1983), 48.

53. Ho (2000), 11, 202ff.; Leung (1997), 218ff.; Handlin (1987).

54. Ebrey (1991b), 188–89; for a detailed analysis, see Chow (1994).

55. *Duli tongkao* (1696); Chow (1994), 51, 136. The work makes extensive use of writings on rituals by contemporary scholars, including Zhang Erqi (1612–1678), Wang Wan (1624–1690), Huang Zongxi (1610–1695), Lu Yuanfu (1617–1691), Ying Huiqian

(1615–1683), and those who helped Xu with its compilation. An important work in the eighteenth century, based on the model of *Duli tongkao*, is Qin Huitian's (1702–1764) well-known *Wuli tongkao* (Comprehensive Study of the Five Categories of Ritual, 260 *juan*, 1761). An official publication, which takes *(Da)Ming jili* as a model, is *DaQing tongli* (Comprehensive Study of the Great Qing Dynasty, 50 *juan*, 1736).

56. Chow (1994), 57, 131; Mao Qiling (Kangxi era) and (1697–1700).

57. Kutcher (1999), 87.

58. Kutcher (1999), 89 n. 56; Meng (1997), 57–59; Ta (1994), 49–51.

59. Meng (1997), 56–57; Kutcher (1999), 88.

60. Meng (1997), 57–58; Kutcher (1999), 88; Rawski (1998), 277; Elliott (2001), 263–64; Ta (1994), 48–49.

61. Kutcher (1999), 89; Ta (1994), 51–52.

62. Meng (1997), 58–59; Kutcher (1999), 90; Rawski (1998), 279; Ta (1994), 51.

63. Chow (1994), 44.

64. Brook (1989), 484–85; Ho (2000), 13–14.

65. Ebrey (1991b), 212–13.

66. Zhang Shouan (1993), 75.

67. Ho (2000), 72; Zhang Shouan (1993), 75.

68. Brook (1989), 493.

69. Jungmann (1961), 74–77. Jungmann's work provides one of the best surveys of the variations practiced within the Western liturgical tradition before the promulgation of the liturgical edicts from the Council of Trent. See also Maher (2002), 204.

70. Jungmann (1961), 105.

71. Since the missionaries were Catholics the focus will be on the Catholic funerary liturgy in use by the majority of Europeans at that time.

72. *Rituale Romanum* (1614): *Exsequiarum ordo* and *Officium Defunctorum*; for descriptions, see Gy (1955), passim; Philippeau (1956) and (1957), passim; Rowell (1977), 71–72; Rutherford (1970), 41, 69ff., 90ff.; Fortescue and O'Connell (1962), 392ff.; "Dodenliturgie," *Liturgisch Woordenboek* (1958–1962); and "Christian Burial," *Catholic Encyclopedia* (2003).

73. See Callewaert (1940); Ruland (1901), 189ff.; Binski (1996), 53–54; "Dodenofficie," *Liturgisch Woordenboek* (1958–1962); and "Office of the Dead," *Catholic Encyclopedia* (2003).

74. Wieck (1988), 124ff.; for a list of all the prayers of the Office, see 166–67; Wieck (1998), 117ff.

75. Very often together with the Little Office of the Blessed Virgin (*Officium Parvum Beatae Mariae Virginis*).

76. *Breviarium Romanum* (1568). "Brevier," *Liturgisch Woordenboek* (1958–1962). The Office of the Dead was read once a month, usually on a fixed date, and on some other special days in the year (e.g., 2 November).

77. *Missale Romanum* (1570).

78. *Manuale* (1605); López Gay (1970), 276–79; for a discussion: 272–95; Tsuchiya (1963), 221–32; Laures (1941); Laures (1957), 71–73; Kataoka (1997), 153ff. There are three copies in the Beitang library, including one that contains a partial Japanese translation in transliteration. See Verhaeren (1949), n. 1246–48; Laures (1941); for the other copies, see Laures (1957), 73; López Gay (1970), 272, n. 133; one more copy resides in the library of the University of Amsterdam (971 C 17) (information provided by A. Dudink). It was mainly based on the *Ritual of Toledo* (*Manual Toledano*, Salamanca, 1583); for a comparison of the table of contents of both works: López Gay (1970), 276–79, but partly on some other works among which the *Rituale Sacramentorum Romanum* (1584) by Antonio de Santorio (1532–1602) that was one of the main sources of the *Rituale Romanum* of 1614 (López Gay (1970), 273, 291ff). This explains the relatively high degree of similarity between the *Rituale Romanum* and the Japanese mission's *Manuale*.

79. Ariès (1977) and (1981); the findings of Ariès corroborate several earlier studies; see especially Gy (1955), Philippeau (1956) and (1957), Rowell (1977), Ruland (1901), and Rutherford (1970). Since the publication of the book by Ariès, several regional studies of death rituals in Europe were published, especially based on funeral instructions in wills, see, for example, Chiffoleau (1980) (on fifteenth-century Avignon), Eire (1995) (on sixteenth-century Spain), Lorenzo Pinar (1991) (on Spain of the sixteenth to eighteenth centuries), and Cohn (1988) (on Siena in the thirteenth to nineteenth centuries); see also Strocchia (1992) (on Florence of the fourteenth to sixteenth centuries).

80. Ariès (1977), 147–48 / (1981), 147–48.

81. Ariès (1977), 152–54 / (1981), 151–54; Ariès (1985), 160ff.

82. Rowell (1977), 70–72; Rutherford (1970), 58–62; Gy (1955), 74; Philippeau (1956), 203.

83. Ariès (1977), 154–56 / (1981), 154–56.

84. Ariès (1977), 161 / (1981), 161; Rutherford (1970), 54, 98.

85. Ariès (1977), 164–65 / (1981), 165; cf. Rowell (1977), 66; Gy (1955), 79–80; Ruland (1901), 189–99.

86. Ariès (1977), 165–66 / (1981), 165–66; Ariès (1985), 116–20; cf. Gy (1955), 72.

87. Ariès (1977), 146–47, 161 / (1981), 146, 161; cf. Rowell (1977), 61; Ruland (1901), 199–204. Later usage reserved the term *absolution* for the benediction of the living and the term *absoute* for the benediction of the dead, in order to distinguish clearly between the two.

88. Rutherford (1970), 55; Ariès (1985), 120–28.

89. Ariès (1977), 175 / (1981), 175–76; Rutherford (1970), 41.

90. Ariès (1977), 178 / (1981), 178; Rutherford (1970), 57; Rowell (1977), 70.

91. Ariès (1977), 168 / (1981), 168; Ariès (1985), 112–15.

92. Binski (1996), 55.

93. The existing rituals for the preservation of the body were not included in the *Rituale*, as discussed by Philippeau (1956), 204–6.

94. Ariès (1977), 172 / (1981), 172.

95. Eire (1995), 151, 180; Strocchia (1992), chapter 3; Cohn (1988), 182.

96. For an overview of anthropological studies of funerals, see Huntington and Metcalf (1979), 1–20; de Mahieu (1991); Tong (2004), 12ff.

97. See Ebrey (1991a), on sending gifts and condoling (99, 200); on the inscription stone (108–9, 201); on the tablet (123, 202); and on different offerings (129ff., 203ff.).

98. Watson (1988a), 8–9.

99. This book only discusses Catholic funerary traditions. Protestants rejected much of the Catholic eschatology, especially purgatory, denied the salvific value of ritual, and repudiated intercessory prayer. See Eire (1995), 119.

100. See Cole (1998) and Oxfeld (2004), 965.

101. Watson (1988a), 9–10.

102. See Berling (1987); Watson (1988a), 10; see also the discussions by Rawski (1988a), Oxfeld (2004) and especially Bell (1997), 191–97; see the special issue of *Modern China* devoted to a discussion of James Watson's ideas, especially Sutton (2007a) and the response in Watson (2007).

2. MISSIONARIES' KNOWLEDGE OF CHINESE FUNERALS

1. For an overview of the different types of sources, see Noël Golvers, "Western Primary Sources," in *HCC*, 162ff.

2. For a description of Bort's expedition and van Hoorn's embassy, see Lach and Van Kley (1993), vol. 3, book 1, 60–61; Wills (1984), chapters 1 and 2.

3. For a detailed study of the extensive sources Dapper used for his book on Africa, see Jones (1990).

4. Dapper (1670) / (1671). On this description, see Lach and Van Kley (1993), vol. 3, book 1, 490–91.

5. "Lijk-plicht of Lijk-staetsie, en rou over dooden," Dapper (1670), 407–30 / (1671), 373–92.

6. The original manuscript of Ricci's account, kept in ARSI Jap.Sin. 106a, was first edited by Pietro Tachi Venturi in 1911 (see *OS*), and later by Pasquale d'Elia (see *FR*).

7. Trigault and Ricci (1615) / (1978) / (1953); the modern English translations will be adopted from the 1953 edition. N. Golvers "Western Primary Sources," in *HCC*, 180–81.

8. Manuscript in British Library, mss. Sloane 1005.

9. Las Cortes (1991) / (2001). Dapper also used unpublished sources for other books of his. See Jones (1990), 185–86.

10. Semedo (1655) / (1996); Lach and Van Kley (1993), vol. 3, book 1, 349. Excerpts from it were published in contemporary French, Latin, and German compilations. Golvers, "Western Primary Sources," in *HCC*, 196. Semedo (1996) is only a slightly revised version of the French edition of 1645.

11. Martini (1981); Lach and Van Kley (1993), vol. 3, book 1, 381–82, 480–81.

12. Martini (1658); Lach and Van Kley (1993), vol. 3, book 1, 526–27.

13. Schall (1942); Lach and Van Kley (1993), vol. 3, book 1, 528.

14. For a short description on Ming funerals, and some other sources, see Lach and Van Kley (1993), vol. 3, book 4, 1625–1627 (late Ming); 1703–1704 (early Qing). See also the general description in Bartoli (1663), 38–43 (partly based on Trigault and Ricci). An important eighteenth-century description (also based on some seventeenth-century sources) is Jean-Baptiste Du Halde (1674–1743), *Description . . . de la Chine* (1735). On funerals, see "Des cérémonies qu'ils observent dans leurs devoirs de civilitez, dans leurs visites, & les présens qu'ils se font les uns les autres, dans les lettres qu'ils écrivent, dans leurs festins, leurs mariages, & leurs funérailles" (1735), vol. 2, 124–30 / (1736), vol. 2, 146–54 / (1738–1741), "Their Mourning and Funerals," vol. 1, 306–10.

15. On the idea of "proto-ethnographic" descriptions, see Odell (2001), 239; "ethnohistories" in Lach and von Kley (1993), vol. 3, book 4, 1566; and Rubiés (1993 and 1995).

16. On the changes to Ricci's text, see Shih (1978); Foss (1983); Fezzi (1999); and Gernet (2003).

17. Trigault and Ricci (1615), iii / (1978), 64 / (1953), xiv. Claims of truthfulness are common in introductions to travel book narratives of the sixteenth and seventeenth centuries. Not only do publishers praise the credibility of their own authors, but they also disparage the lack of accuracy in others. See also Odell (2001), 225.

18. Trigault and Ricci (1615), iv / (1978), 65 / (1953), xiv.

19. Trigault and Ricci (1615), iv / (1978), 65 / (1953), xv.

20. Trigault and Ricci's bestseller, *De Christiana expeditione apud Sinas* of 1615, had been preceded by Pantoja's booklet about China with the very similar title of *Relacion de la entrada de algunos Padres de la Compañia de Jesus en la China* (Seville, 1605), which was originally a letter written in Beijing in 1602. Pantoja, who had arrived in Beijing one year earlier, probably used the same sources (letters and personal notes of Ricci and others) that later became the basis for the first book in Trigault and Ricci's *De Christiana expeditione apud Sinas* (see Ricciardolo (2003), 35–38). This explains why there are several similarities between Trigault's and Pantoja's descriptions of funerals (see Pantoja (1605), 81r–86r / (1625), 367–68). A partial English translation of Trigault's treatise on funerals can also be found in Purchas (1625), III.ii, 393; it was shortened because the same volume contains a more extensive description of funerary customs by Pantoja (367–68). Purchas' collection mainly contains the ethnographic chapters of Trigault and Ricci. The description in Trigault's and

Ricci's *De Christiana expeditione apud Sinas* was later partly adopted by António de Gouvea, SJ (1592–1677); see de Gouvea (1995–2001), vol. 1, 105–6; 269–73.

21. Trigault and Ricci (1615), 63; *FR* I, 71. Trigault's and Ricci's title compares with the chapter title of the French version of 1616, "De quelques coutumes des Chinois" ([1978], 124). For "civilitie," see Purchas (1625), 391.

22. On superstition, see chapter 9 (*FR* I, 94); on the religious sects, chapter 10 (*FR* I, 108). Both Semedo and Schall use chapter titles directly related to funerals or the care of the dead: "Of the Funeralls and Sepultures of the Chinesses" (Semedo (1655), 73), and "De cura universim mortuorum apud Chinenses" (Schall (1942), 422).

23. Rubiés (1993), 170–71. These characteristics are developed in several other articles by the same author; see also Rubiés (1995).

24. Trigault and Ricci (1615), 79 / (1978), 138 / (1953), 72.

25. Dapper (1670), 407–8 / (1671), 373; cf. Trigault and Ricci (1615), 79–80 / (1978), 138 / (1953), 72. Compare this and the following sections with the original version of Ricci, *FR*, vol. 1, 83–85.

26. The reference to the Franciscan monks does not appear in the original Italian version by Ricci (*FR*, vol. 1, 83), though it does appear in Trigault and Ricci (1615), 79–80 / (1978), 138 / (1953), 72; but it appears first in Pantoja (1605), 81v / (1625), 368. The reference to "as in Europe" is added in the English version of Dapper ((1671), 373); in the Dutch version ((1670), 408) it is said: "gelijk ook hier te lande" (as also in this country). This comparison seems to apply to the variation of mourning periods rather than to the "three months"; in Trigault and Ricci the comparison does not appear.

27. Dapper (1670), 408–9 / (1671), 373–74; cf. Trigault and Ricci (1615), 80–81 / (1978), 138–39 / (1953), 72–73. *Cie* is probably *qi* (lacquer).

28. Dapper (1670), 409–10 / (1671), 374; cf. Trigault and Ricci (1615), 81–82 / (1978), 140 / (1953), 73–74. The phrase, "which is perform'd like the Romans Processioning," is added by Dapper; in the last sentence, the Latin version mentions "suburbanos."

29. For other descriptions of Chinese condoling practices, see Dapper (1670), 409 / (1671), 374; Trigault and Ricci (1615), 80–81 / (1978), 139 / (1953), 73 (compare *FR*, vol. 1, 84); Du Halde, (1735), vol. 2, 125 / (1736), vol. 2, 147 / (1738–1741), vol. 1, 307–8; see also Du Halde, (1735), vol. 3, 177 / (1736), vol. 3, 214 / (1738–1741), vol. 2, 63, based on an unidentified Chinese source, probably dating between 1680 and 1722 (Landry-Deron (2002), 232).

30. Semedo (1996) 112–13 / (1655), 75; compare Dapper (1670), 412 / (1671), 376–77 (where tea is transliterated as *Tee*).

31. Dapper (1670), 417 / (1671), 381; Schall (1942), 424.

32. Semedo (1996), 111–12 / (1655), 74–75; Dapper (1670), 412 / (1671), 376.

33. Semedo (1996), 111 / (1655), 73, 74; Dapper (1670), 410, 411 / (1671), 375, 376.

34. Semedo (1996), 111 / (1655), 73–74; Dapper (1670), 411 / (1671), 375.

35. Dapper (1670), 430 / (1671), 392 and Martini (1981), 155; Martini on page 153 also mentions explicitly that they do not use coffins as the Chinese do.

36. Dapper (1670), 416 / (1671), 380; Schall (1942), 422.

37. Dapper (1670), 416 / (1671), 381; Schall (1942), 425.

38. Dapper (1670), 419 / (1671), 382; Schall (1942), 428.

39. Naquin (1988), 42.

40. Dapper (1670), 420 / (1671), 383; Schall (1942), 430–31.

41. See Rubiés (1993), 160–62; (1995), 38.

42. For text and translation see Mish (1964).

43. Aleni (1637), *juan shang*, 24b–25a; trans. Mish (1964), 59.

44. Semedo (1996), 110 / (1655), 73; Dapper (1670), 410 / (1671), 375.

45. Dapper (1670), 416 / (1671), 380; Schall (1942), 422.

46. Aleni (1637), *juan shang*, 25a; trans. Mish (1964), 59–60; on the European location of graves, see also Aleni's discussion of siting and geomancy, Aleni (1637), addendum, 1aff.; trans. Mish (1964), 79ff.

47. For instance, burial places in sixteenth-century Madrid, discussed in Eire (1995), 91ff., or in Avignon, mentioned in Chiffoleau (1980), 154ff.

48. Semedo (1996), 111 / (1655), 74; Dapper (1670), 411 / (1671), 376.

49. Pantoja (1605), 84v / (1625), 368. For other descriptions of Chinese tombs, see Du Halde (1735), vol. 2, 125 / (1736), vol. 2, 147–48 / (1738–1741), vol. 1, 307.

50. Semedo (1996), 111 / (1655), 74; Dapper (1670), 411 / (1671), 376.

51. Dapper (1670), 416 / (1671), 380; Schall (1942), 423.

52. Las Cortes (1991), 188 / (2001), 463.

53. See Thompson (1988), 104, for an anthropological discussion.

54. *Mubei* is an epitaph on a tombstone (*bei*) or memorial stele (set up above ground). Its purpose is to provide facts about the identity of the deceased. In its simplest form, it always carries at least the family name of the occupant of the tomb, but a more extensive memorial stele might include the names of family members who erected the stone, the title or honors of the deceased, etc. Since the term *bei* signifies the instrument of composition, the nature of the medium is imputed to have influence over its content. Edwards (1948), 782, and Weinberg (2002), 6, 15ff.

55. *Muzhi*, also called *muzhiming* or *kuangming*, is a tomb epitaph, grave record, or funerary inscription. It is a brief laudatory biography inscribed on a stone tablet *buried* with or near the coffin. Its purpose (or one purpose) was to identify the remains should the grave be disturbed. At the end of the *muzhi*, and also of a *mubiao* (see below), a formal poem (*ming*) in praise of the deceased is often included, normally much shorter than the biography itself and adding no new facts about him. Edwards (1948), 781–82; Nivison (1962), 459; and de Groot (1892–1897), 1101ff.

56. Dapper (1670), 416–17 / (1671), 380; Schall (1942), 423–24.

57. *Recüeil de Tombeaux Chinois* (18th century). See also Cordier (1909), 222, "Sur

les plats armes de Bertin," and Gall (1990), 28, "Fonds Bertin" no. 7 (this was included in the Cabinet des estampes in 1793–1794; cf. 88–89). These illustrations belonged to the collection of Henri L. J.-B. Bertin (1719–1792), who as Secretary of State in France from 1762–1780 had maintained an intensive correspondence with the French Jesuits in Beijing.

58. Aleni (1637), *juan shang*, 25a–25b; trans. Mish (1964), 60.

59. Semedo (1996) 110 / (1655), 73; Dapper (1670), 410 / (1671), 375.

60. Watson (1988a), 14–15. In some places, such as Taiwan or Guangdong, the coffin is punctured prior to burial.

61. Pantoja (1605), 83v–84r / (1625), 368. For other descriptions of coffins, see Dapper (1670), 409, 416 / (1671), 374, 380; Trigault and Ricci (1615), 81 / (1978), 139 / (1953), 73 (compare *FR*, vol. 1, 84); Schall (1942), 422; Martini (1658), 156 (book 5); Du Halde (1735), vol. 2, 125 / (1736), vol. 2, 147 / (1738–1741), vol. 1, 306.

62. Aleni (1637), *juan shang*, 25b; trans. Mish (1964), 60.

63. Dapper (1670), 422 / (1671), 385; Martini (1658), 31 (book 1). For other descriptions of the mourning garments, see Dapper (1670), 407–8, 413–15 / (1671), 374, 377–79; Trigault and Ricci (1615), 79–80 / (1978), 138 / (1953), 73 (compare *FR*, vol. 1, 83); Semedo (1996), 113 / (1655), 74–75; and Du Halde (1735), vol. 2, 124 / (1736), vol. 2, 146 / (1738–1741), vol. 1, 306.

64. Dapper (1670), 420–21 / (1671), 383–84; Schall (1942), 431–32.

65. Las Cortes (1991), 189 / (2001), 156, 394–97.

66. Dapper (1670), 415 / (1671), 379.

67. So far attempts to identify the source, such as in collections of encyclopaedias for daily use (*riyong leishu*), have been unsuccessful; see, for example, the collection of late Ming encyclopaedias, *Chūgoku nichiyo ruisho shusei*.

68. *Sancai tuhui* (1607), vol. 4, 1551ff. (*yifu, juan* 3, 13ff.).

69. Dapper (1670), 414–15 / (1671), 378–79; Las Cortes (1991), 189–90 / (2001), 156, 404.

70. De Groot (1892–1897), vol. 2, 587–88; pl. xiv; fig. 26.

71. For an extensive description, see de Groot (1892–1897), vol. 1, 152–207.

72. Aleni (1637), *juan shang*, 26a–26b; trans. Mish (1964), 60–61.

73. See Eire (1995), 121–23, 134 and Chiffoleau (1980), 126ff, and also the description of the procession at the beginning of *Exsequiarum ordo* in *Rituale* (1614).

74. Semedo (1996), 113–14 / (1655), 76; Dapper (1670), 412–13 / (1671), 377.

75. On this difference, see also de Groot (1892–1897), vol. 1, 158.

76. Eire (1995), 122; Strocchia (1992), 7–8; both authors refer to Geertz (1977), where what Eire calls a "nearly universal pattern to funeral processions" is less explicit.

77. Dapper (1670), opposite 422–23 / (1671), opposite 388–89. It was adopted by the artist Bernard Picard (1673–1733) for another illustration; see *China on Paper* (2007), 152–53.

78. Du Halde (1735), vol. 2, between 126–27 (A. Humblot, designer, and A. Maisonneuve, engraver) / (1736), vol. 2, between 148–49 (J. C. Philip, engraver; of lesser quality) / (1738–1741), vol. 1, between 306–7.

79. For Chinese illustrations, see *Jiali yijie* (1608), juan 5, 52a–54b; *Sancai tuhui* (1607), vol. 5, 1952ff. (*yizhi, juan* 7, 12ff.); and illustration attached to chapter 65 of *Jinpingmei cihua* (1617), opposite 1808.

80. *DMB*, vol. 2, 856–59.

81. For a discussion of Herrera Maldonado, see Lach and Van Kley (1993), vol. 3, book 1, 335 and book 4, 1627.

82. Herrera Maldonado (1620), chapters 13–17, 90–121. It is not clear why he incorrectly dates the demise as 30 March 1617. Chapter 12 is a discussion of the funeral and burial rites.

83. Herrera Maldonado (1622) chapter 13–17, 314–408. The French version is in many regards more extensive than the Spanish version.

84. On his sources, see *Europe Informed* (1966), 20ff.

85. Herrera Maldonado (1622), 315–16. The first contained the ceremonies and sacrifices from the day of death until the burial; the second, the sacrifices to be performed at the place of the corpse and for the sepulture; and the third, the indulgences, graces, and privileges granted by the emperor to the nation.

86. Semedo (1996) 115 / (1655), 77–78.

87. See Herrera Maldonado (1622), 359–60, for Dias' participation.

88. Semedo (1996), 115–21 / (1655), 78–83 (chapter 17); Dapper (1670), 426–30 / (1671), 388–91. It is also adopted (from Semedo) by Antonio de Gouvea; see de Gouvea (1995–2001), vol. 1, 106–10; vol. 2, 353–58.

89. *Ming shilu* (1987), *Shenzong shilu, juan* 517–21, 9743–839. The sections that could correspond to these days in *Wanli qijuzhu* (1988) are missing.

90. Semedo (1996), 121–24 / (1655), 83–86 (at end of chapter 17); Dapper (1670), 430 / (1671), 391; *Ming shilu* (1987), *Shenzong shilu, juan* 596, 11448–450; for the regulations of his funeral, see *Ming shilu* (1987), *Guangzong shilu, juan* 2, 0023ff. See a more extensive account of the last days of the Wanli Emperor, the translation of his last will, and the description of some of the funerals, as well as the death of the Taichang Emperor, in *Histoire de ce qui s'est passe'es Royaumes de la Chine et du Japon . . .* (1625), 44 (from Trigault's report in *Littera Annua 1621*), 161ff. Compared to the description for the funeral of the mother of the Wanli Emperor, however, it is rather limited because, Trigault states, "he does not want to annoy the reader" ("Je ne dis rien icy du style de ces ceremonies, par ce que j'ennuyerois le Lecteyr") (ibid., 171).

91. Schall (1942), 434–49; Dapper (1670), 422–25 / (1671), 385–87. See also Väth (1991), 209–10.

92. *Qing shilu* (1985), vol. 4, 40ff.; see also *Qinding daQing huidian zeli* (1768), *juan* 85, 1–29; *SKQS*, vol. 622, 655–69.

93. Schall (1942), 428–29 (Dapper (1670), 425 / (1671), 387–88). Dongshi, also known as Dong'e fei (Imperial Secondary Consort of the Donggo clan) (1639–1660), was the favorite consort of the Shunzhi Emperor. She was posthumously made an empress and canonized as Xiaoxian huanghou. At her funeral, elaborate Buddhist ceremonies were conducted at enormous cost. Certain eunuchs and maids in the palace committed suicide hoping that their spirits might accompany her. This practice had long been abandoned by Chinese rulers, but was retained by the Manchus until this time. See *ECCP*, vol. 1, 301–2. Not copied by Dapper are the short references to funerals and processions for other members of the imperial family: Daisan, 1583–25 November 1648, second son of Nurhaci; Dorgon, 1612–31 December 1650; and the brother of Shunzhi emperor, probably eleventh son of Huangtaiji, who died at the age of 16 years, 22 August 1656. Schall (1942), 425–27; see also Du Halde (1735), vol. 2, 128–29 / (1736), vol. 2, 151–52 (which contains a short reference to the funeral of the emperor's mother) / (1738–1741), vol. 1, 309.

94. For later descriptions of funerals, such as the funeral of Empress Xiaosheng (1693–1777), mother of the Qianlong Emperor, see Amiot (1780) (Chinese text in BnF, Chinois 2322); see also Rawski (1988b), 245, and (1998), 279.

95. Rawski (1988b), 238–40; see also de Groot (1892–1897), vol. 2, 632ff.

96. Herrera Maldonado (1622), 322ff.

97. Semedo (1996), 119 / (1655), 82; Dapper (1670), 428 / (1671), 390. It is not entirely clear whether "eighth day" means the eighth day of the sixth month, or eight days preceding the funeral (as translated by Dapper); these details are not mentioned in *Ming shilu* (1987), *Shenzong shilu*, *juan* 521, 9729–31.

98. Rawski (1998), 279.

99. Dapper (1670), 424–25 / (1671), 387; Schall (1942), 446–47. Compare *Qinding daQing huidian zeli* (1768), *juan* 85, 10a–12a; *SKQS*, vol. 622, 660–61. See also the short description by Johann Grueber, SJ (1623–1680), who was at that moment in Beijing; Grueber (1985), 79–83.

100. *Qinding daQing huidian zeli* (1768), *juan* 85, 12a–b; *SKQS*, vol. 622, 661. Compared to the preceding (nineteenth of the second month, or 17 February) and subsequent (the seventh of the third month, or 7 March, seventh of the fourth month, or after one hundred days, or 5 April) sacrifices, the sacrifice on the twenty-seventh day was the most important one in terms of the objects burned (*Qinding daQing huidian zeli* (1768), *juan* 85, 9b, 13a, 18b; *SKQS*, vol. 622, 659, 661, 664).

101. Herrera Maldonado (1622), 332, 342, 372, 374, 393, 400.

102. Schall (1942), 406–7. Buddhist ceremonies are not mentioned in *Veritable Records*, but extensive sacrifices are; see *Qing shilu* (1985), vol. 3, 1076ff.

103. Semedo (1996), 115 / (1655), 77.

104. European funerals for kings were also major events; see, for example, the extensive discussion in Eire (1995), (book two), 255ff, of the funeral of King Philip II of Spain who died 13 September 1598.

105. Herrera Maldonado (1622), 314–15; compare (1620), 90v.

106. In the English version of Semedo, "ceremonies" always occurs in italics.

107. Herrera Maldonado (1622), 387–92.

108. *Qing shilu* (1985), vol. 4, 48; see also Rawski (1998), 282.

109. Dapper (1670), 423–24 / (1671), 386; Schall (1942), 442–45. The phrase in brackets at the beginning of the quote comes from Schall's own text (1942), 442–43; it does not appear in Dapper.

110. Compare for instance *Qinding daQing huidian zeli* (1768), *juan* 85, 10a–12a; *SKQS*, vol. 622, 660–61.

111. *Ming shilu* (1987), *Shenzong shilu*, *juan* 517, 9746–47.

112. Semedo (1996), 116–17 / (1655), 79–80; compare Dapper (1670), 427 / (1671), 389.

113. See Rawski (1988b), 253.

114. See Eire (1995), 360–61.

115. Dapper (1670), 409 / (1671), 374. These comparisons are on the whole quite limited and have little parallel with the distinction between Catholic and Protestant of the nineteenth century that was one of the most pervasive of the binary oppositions structuring Victorian Protestant perceptions of Chinese religions. Victorian Protestant missionaries so thoroughly embraced anti-Catholicism, especially in the rejection of Catholic ritual, that they projected their judgment of ritual onto their experience of Chinese ritual. See Reinders (2004), esp. 210–11.

116. See Ginzburg (1999), 77.

117. Todorov (1982b), 191 / (1984), 185.

118. Semedo uses the most emotive language in this regard. See also Dapper (1670), 416 / (1671), 380; Schall (1942), 422; and Martini (1658), book 1, 31. In Europe, funeral excesses were also criticized, but the criticism was of a slightly different nature. As Eire (1995), 151–53, has shown, even though funerals became increasingly complex throughout the sixteenth century, some restraint continued to be exercised in regard to mourning gestures. This may be due in part to the fact that certain ecclesiastical laws distinguished between those gestures that benefited the dead and those that affected only the survivors. Intercessory gestures, such as the participation of priests, friars, confraternities, and poor people were deemed not only acceptable but meritorious. Non-intercessory gestures, such as the wearing of mourning clothes or the lighting of a certain number of candles, had long been deemed tolerable but unessential—or even worse, un-Christian. The customs most excoriated were excesses in the wearing of mourning clothes, excesses in the use of candles, and uncontrolled "dolorous crying."

119. Rubiés (1995), 42–43.

120. In Dapper (1670), 422 / (1671), 375; Semedo (1996), 111 / (1655), 73.

121. Pantoja (1605), 81r / (1625), 367: "The thing wherein the Chinois are most observant, Ceremonious and Superstitious, is in their Burials, Funerals, and Mournings; for herein they shew their obedience and love to their Parents, whereof their bookes are full"; Martini (1658), 30 (book 1) (in Dapper (1670), 422 / (1671), 384): "It is very strange [*miram*: marvelous, extraordinary] to observe the Duty and Reverence which the Children shew to their Dead parents, wherein no other People may be compar'd to them."

122. Semedo (1996), 121 / (1655), 83.

3. THE GRADUAL EMBEDDING OF CHRISTIAN FUNERAL RITUALS IN CHINA

1. There is comparatively much more information on funerals of the first thirty years of the Christian mission in Japan: see Cieslik (1950), López Gay (1964) and (1970), 196–240; for Christian burial practices, see the discussion of findings from recent archaeological excavations of Christian tombs in Imano Haruki (2004).

2. Almeida died 17 October. *FR* I, 311–12; Bettray (1955), 303. Compare also with Trigault and Ricci (1615), 266 / (1978), 321 / (1953), 242.

3. *FR* I, 311–12; Bettray (1955), 303–4.

4. *FR* II, 334; Bettray (1955), 299. Compare with Trigault and Ricci (1615), 498–99 / (1978), 548 / (1953), 447.

5. *FR* II, 246; Bettray (1955), 300–1. Compare with Trigault and Ricci (1615), 469 / (1978), 516 / (1953), 427.

6. *FR* II, 247; Bettray (1955), 300–1.

7. Trigault and Ricci (1615), 469–70 / (1978), 516–17 / (1953), 427–28.

8. *FR* II, 249; Bettray (1955), 301; Trigault and Ricci (1615), 469 / (1978), 517–18 / (1953), 428–29.

9. *FR* II, 351 (*christianità*). Trigault and Ricci (1615), 517 (*ritu Christiano*) / (1978), 567 / (1953), 474.

10. *OS* II, 368.

11. *OS* II, 328 (letter to C. Aquaviva, 18 October 1607 quoting a report by M. Dias Sr.); Bettray (1955), 305.

12. *FR* II, 361; Bettray (1955), 310. Trigault and Ricci (1615), 521–22 / (1978), 571 / (1953), 477–78.

13. *FR* II, 516; Bettray (1955), 302 (this passage was written by Trigault). Trigault and Ricci (1615), 602–3 / (1978), 649 / (1953), 553.

14. *FR* II, 523 (in Portuguese: *estilo* and *cortezias*); Bettray (1955), 306. Compare with Trigault and Ricci (1615), 605 (*è ritu Sinensi . . . Ecclesiastico more*) / (1978), 652 / (1953), 556: the remark about past experiences is not mentioned.

15. See detailed discussion in chapter seven of this book.

16. *FR* II, 565–66; Trigault and Ricci (1615), 617 / (1978), 663 / (1953), 566–67 (slightly adapted).

17. *FR* II, 619–20; Trigault and Ricci (1615), 640 / (1978), 685 / (1953), 588 (slightly adapted); Bettray (1955), 309.

18. *FR* II, 628; Bettray (1955), 309. Trigault and Ricci (1615), 644 / (1978), 690 / (1953), 592.

19. Bettray (1955), 312.

20. This is a quote from the *Zhongyong* chapter in the *Liji* (see below).

21. *FR* I, 117–18; translation Rule (1986), 49 (slightly adapted). Rule (note 268) points out that this passage has been subjected to a great deal of critical examination. Compare with Trigault and Ricci (1615), 107–8 / (1978), 163–64 / (1953), 96.

22. For the history of the word "idolatry," see the study by Bernand and Gruzinski (1988); for "superstition," see Harmening (1979).

23. *Rito de' christiani, cerimonie ecclesiastiche* (*FR* II, 246); *è more Christiano, Ecclesiastico ritu* (Trigault and Ricci (1615), 469); *cerimonias da Igreja* (*FR* II, 516); *Ecclesiasticis ritibus* (Trigault and Ricci (1615), 602).

24. It is used in this sense in *FR* I, 311: *quando entrano in religione* (Ricci's answer to the Chinese who wondered why the Jesuits did not wear mourning garments), *Religiosos nostrates* (Trigault and Ricci (1615), 266).

25. For the history of the term *religio*, see the works by Smith (1963), Despland (1979), and Feil (1986) and (1997); the three authors came together in a conference to discuss their approaches and opinions: see Despland and Vallée (1992).

26. A good translation of *religio* in the seventeenth century seems to be "pratique cultuelle" ("pratique liée à une foi déterminée et à une certaine doctrine de la divinité"), see *Französisches etymologisches Wörterbuch* (1948–1957), vol. 10, 230–31; it had not so much the meaning of a "system" to be academically investigated; for this focus on ritual, see also Smith (1998), 270.

27. Bernand and Gruzinski (1988), 43–44, 234.

28. E. Feil, "From the Classical *Religio* to the Modern *Religion*: Elements of a Transformation between 1550 and 1650," in Despland and Vallée (1992), 32–56.

29. *FR* I, 108.

30. For an example of the use of these words, see *OS* II, 368.

31. *Riti gentilichi* (*FR* II, 249, 334), *cerimonia de' gentili* (*FR* II, 249), *cerimonie gentiliche* (*OS* II, 369), *Ethnicis ritibus* (Trigault and Ricci (1615), 498).

32. Trigault and Ricci (1615), 104 / (1978), 160: "Diverses sectes de fausse religion entre les chinois."

33. *Ex more (sinico)* (*FR* II, 565, 628; Trigault and Ricci (1615), 617, 644); *conforme ao custume da China* (*FR* II, 499); *è Sinensi consuetudine* (Trigault and Ricci (1615),

596). The term *more* is not exclusively used for China, it is also applied to Christianity: e.g., *è more Christiano, Eccelsiastico more* (Trigault and Ricci (1615), 469, 605).

34. *FR* I, 117: *come se fossero vivi*; Trigault and Ricci (1615), 107: *ac si essent superstites*. See also quote about Chinese rituals by Trigault in the previous chapter: *FR* I, 84: *come quando erano vivi*; Trigault and Ricci (1615), 81: *non secus ac si superessent*.

35. *Liji*: 32.13 (*Zhongyong* chapter, 19); also quoted in the chapter on rituals (*Lilun*) in *Xunzi* 19.

36. Plaks (2003), 37 (emphasis mine). Compare Legge (1991), vol. 1, 403: "Thus they served the dead as they would have served them alive; and served the departed as they would have served them had they been continued among them."

37. Ames and Hall (2001), 99: "Serving their dead as though they were living, and serving those who are long departed as though they were still here."

38. *Riti che non fossero conformi al rito de' christiani (FR* II, 246) *è more Christiano* (Trigault and Ricci (1615), 469); *non fare nessun rito contra le regole della christianità (FR* II, 361) *exclusa omni rituum superstitione* (Trigault and Ricci (1615), 522); *Riti che non erano contrarij alla religione christiana (OS* II, 369); see also, against the Christian creed (*profissão, Fede: FR* II, 500; Trigault and Ricci (1615), 596–97: *è Christianis legibus . . . praeceptorum legis Divinae custodiam*; mother of John Xu Leshan, grandfather-in-law of Candida Xu who died on 11 February 1611; (Dudink (2001), 107–8).

39. Augustine (1963), book VI, vol. 2, 313; see also O'Daly (1999), 101–9.

40. Or, *Litteratorum*. See, for example, Trigault and Ricci (1615), 104ff, and compare with Trigault and Ricci (1978), 160ff.

41. Lionel Jensen (1997) mistakenly attributes the manufacturing of the term "Confucianism" to the Jesuits of the seventeenth century; see book reviews by Willard J. Peterson in *Harvard Journal of Asiatic Studies* 59, no. 1 (1999): 276–83; Paul Rule in *Journal of Chinese Religions* 27 (1999): 105–11; and N. Standaert in *EASTM (East Asian Science, Technology, and Medicine)* 16 (1999): 115–32.

42. Trigault and Ricci (1615), 110, 112: *profanae Religionis*; compare with Trigault and Ricci (1978), 166, 170.

43. *Ministri degli idoli (FR* II, 246); *Bonzo o sacerdote degli idoli (OS* II, 369). From the writings of Ricci and his companions, it appears that the Jesuits used two main categories for describing the Chinese "religions." The first, *lex*, or "law," referred to the doctrinal side, including the juridical or prescriptive teaching, of what we today call religions. The term was also used for the three universal laws of *lex naturalis, lex Mosaica* and *lex evangelica*. The second category, *secta*, did not have the strong negative connotation that it has in Western languages today; it was a neutral term, derived from the verb *sequi* (to follow), and referring to, among other things, a following, a body of followers, or the adherence to a particular religious or philosophical teacher

or faith. As appears from the translations, in early seventeenth-century texts the terms *lex* and *secta* were often used interchangeably and therefore were apparently close in meaning. These terms correspond to a certain extent to the native terms *jiao* and *jia* as in the expression *rujiao* or *rujia*.

44. For the concept of "inflated difference," see Ruland (1994).

45. *Histoire de ce qui s'est passe'es Royaumes de la Chine et du Japon . . .* , 44 (*Littera Annua 1619* by M. Dias).

46. *Histoire de ce qui s'est passe'es Royaumes de la Chine et du Japon . . .* , 125–27 (*Littera Annua 1620* by W. P. Kirwitzer (Pantaleon)). The final paragraph makes reference to the anti-Christian movement led by Shen Que (1565–1624) that led to the expulsion of four Jesuits to Macao in 1617.

47. Bartoli (1663), 892.

48. "Wulin Yang mu Lü gongren zhuan," in Chen Jiru (ca. 1641), *juan* 45, 14a–16a; Chen Jiru also wrote a funeral ode for Yang Tingyun, "Ji Yang Qiyuan shiyu," in Chen Jiru (ca. 1641), *juan* 8, ff. 40a–41a.

49. Chen Jiru (ca. 1641), *juan* 45, 15a; Standaert (1988), 48.

50. Standaert (1988), 46–47.

51. *Yang Qiyuan xiansheng (chaoxing) shiji* (ca. 1630?), ff. 6a–7a; *CCT ZKW*, vol. 1, 224–25.

52. See Brokaw (1991), 4ff.; Handlin Smith (1987).

53. Cf. *HCC*, 422.

54. *Lixiu yijian* (ca. 1639–1645), 26b–27a; *WXSB*, vol. 1, 496–97; it is taken from *Yang Qiyuan xiansheng (chaoxing) shiji*.

55. For a short description of the funeral of Han's mother who died in 1626, see Margiotti (1958), 538.

56. Huang Yi-long (2004), 81; Huang Yi-long (2005), 274.

57. Zürcher (1993), 84–89.

58. *Duoshu* (ca. 1641), 6a–6b; *CCT ZKW*, vol. 2, 648–49.

59. See detailed discussion in chapter six of this book.

60. Zürcher (2005), 81, dates it from the 1670s. See also Chan (2002), 56–57, 59.

61. Li Jiugong (before 1681), *CCT ARSI*, vol. 9, 96–99; compare 63–65 (much shorter).

62. Li Jiugong (before 1681), *CCT ARSI*, vol. 9, 98; compare, 65. On these biographical genres, see Edwards (1948), 780, 782.

63. For a discussion of *zheng*, see Zürcher (1997), 615ff.; see also Liu Kwang-Ching (1990), 4ff.

64. Ebrey (1991a), 79, 196.

65. Li Jiugong (before 1681), *CCT ARSI*, vol. 9, 100–101; compare, 66–67.

66. Zhang Xiangcan (1680s?), *CCT ARSI*, vol. 11, 289. Date is unknown. The only indication is that it was presented to Vice-Provincial Giandomenico Gabiani

(1623–1694), who was vice-provincial from 1680 to 1683 and from 1689 to 1692; see Chan (2002), 59.

67. On these practices, see also Ebrey (1991a).

68. Zhang Xiangcan (1680s?), *CCT ARSI*, vol. 11, 290. The quote from *Jiali* comes from a section of the 1341 version reprinted in Ebrey (1991a), 98, 200.

69. Aleni (1637), vol. 1, 28a; Mish (1964), 63 (adapted).

70. Cf. Zürcher (1990a), 451.

71. For an annotated translation of the full text, see Zürcher (2007).

72. *Kouduo richao* (ca. 1630–1640), *juan 7*, 6b–7b, *CCT ARSI*, vol. 7, 468–70; trans. Zürcher (2007), n. VII.9. Zhang Geng's *Haoguai shi* is no longer extant.

73. Quoted in and translated by Menegon (2002), 102; Aleni in response to Juan Miao Shixiang's letter in Biblioteca Casanatense (Rome), ms 1073, 21v–22r; also collated with "Ritos Chinos," vol. 1, doc. 1, 214v–215r of Archivo de la Provincia del Santo Rosario, Manila and Avila (information provided by E. Menegon). For similar argumentation on the basis of the *Zhongyong* quote, see *Kouduo richao* (ca. 1630–1640), *juan 4*, 11b, *CCT ARSI*, vol. 7, 276; trans. Zürcher (2007), n. IV.10.

74. Aleni (1637), *juan shang*, 27a; trans. Mish (1964), 61.

75. Eire (1995), 141.

76. Li Jiugong (before 1681), *CCT ARSI*, vol. 9, 105; compare 70.

77. *Kouduo richao* (ca. 1630–1640), *juan 7*, 7b, *CCT ARSI*, vol. 7, 470; trans. Zürcher (2007), n. VII.9. Zürcher points out that an almost identical description is contained in Ricci: *FR* II, 481–82; Trigault and Ricci (1615), 589 / (1978), 635 / (1953), 541. *Zhao* and *mu* are ancient cultic terms indicating the hierarchical arrangement of positions, in an alternating sequence starting from the left side of the main personage.

78. Zürcher (2007), n. VII.9 and Zürcher (1990a), 452.

79. Zürcher (1990a), 452.

80. Reference to *Liji* (1992), chap. *Tangong xia*, 4.35.

81. The other version has *yi* (righteousness) instead of *dao*. Li Jiugong (before 1681), *CCT ARSI*, vol. 9, 69.

82. Reference to *Liji*, chap. *Sannianwen*, 39.1.

83. Li Jiugong (before 1681), *CCT ARSI*, vol. 9, 103–5; compare, 68–70.

84. Zürcher (1997), 634.

85. Welch (1967), 184ff.; Lagerwey (1987), 170ff.

86. See Brokaw (1991).

87. *Shengjing zhijie* (1636–1642), *juan 6*, 4b; *WXSB*, vol. 5, 2048.

88. Metzler (1980), 15–17. In 1629, André Palmeiro, SJ (1569–1635), the visitor of the mission, issued instructions summarising the conclusions of the Jiading (Zhejiang) conference where the Jesuits together with some well-known converts had discussed matters such as the name for God, the angels and the soul. The text of Palmeiro is

in many regards pastorally oriented but hardly discusses the funerals in detail. His major concern is the observance of the specific Christian rituals for the dead: the recitation of prayers, the Mass, and Office of the Dead at the commemoration service. Palmeiro, 25r–25v: nos. 16–18 (information provided by L. Brockey and E. Menegon); see also Brockey (2007), 84–85.

89. Menegon (2002), 100, 296. Those related to funerals will be discussed in chapter five of this book.

90. González (1955–1967), vol. 1, 393.

91. Lobo (1915), 384; see also Maas (1926), 103–4 and Biermann (1927), 48. Lobo had left the Society of Jesus and re-entered in 1635; he died in the Indies after having left the Society again (Dehergne (1973), 153).

92. See pontifical brief *Romanae Sedis Antistes* (27 June 1615): Bontinck (1962), 41–42. The use of the Chinese language was granted only to *Chinese* priests.

93. *Shanzhong zhugong guili* (before 1638); Chan (2002), 248: this is a reprint by the Yuedan tang in Jianwu (Jianchang, Jiangxi); the correctors were M. Dias, L. Cattaneo and Pedro Ribeiro (1570–1640); the imprimatur was given by Francisco Furtado (1589–1653); other copy ARSI Jap. Sin. I, 112 (Chan (2002), 161–62).

94. See the remark in Palmeiro (1629), 26r, no. 2 "[In baptism] we will use the ritual of Japan, and we will do the ceremonies that it orders since we do not have a copy of the Roman one."

95. *Manuale* (1605), 192–235; compare also Laures (1941), xviii. Fróis follows Cerqueira's *Manuale* relatively closely, but not always in the same detail, especially with regard to the instructions. As mentioned by Cerqueira (*Manuale* (1605), 198–200), the three considerations offered to the dying person (*CCT ARSI*, vol. 5, 352–55) are taken from Joannes Gerson's OP (1363–1429), *Opus tripartitum*; see Gerson (1966), 404–7: "332. La médecine de l'âme."

96. See "Ad R.P.N. Generalem. Judicium P. Ludovici Buglio circa promotionem Sinarum ad sacerdotium" (Beijing, 19 May 1678) (ARSI Jap. Sin., 124, ff. 129–33), repr. in Bontinck (1962), 462–72; for a discussion of this text, see *ibidem*, 180–86.

97. *Misa jingdian* (1670); Bernard (1945), no. 432; Pelliot (1924), 357, n. 2; Bontinck (1962), 155.

98. *Siduo kedian* (1674); Bernard (1945), no. 462; Pelliot (1924), 358, n. 3; Bontinck (1962), 157.

99. Buglio himself calls it "Rituale" in one of his letters, see Bontinck (1962), 466: letter of Beijing, 19 May 1678, 131.

100. *Shengshi lidian* (1675); Bernard (1945), no. 470; Pelliot (1924), 357, n. 4; Bontinck (1962), 157–58; Chan (2002), 211–12. The correctors were G. de Magalhães and F. de Rougemont; the imprimatur was given by F. Verbiest. According to one anonymous article (A. L. (1939), 242; cf. Bontinck (1962), 158, n. 26) the original manuscript of the translation of the *Rituale* and *Breviarium* were in the Beitang Library.

101. Some general differences: both Cerqueira's *Manuale* (1605) and *Shengshi lidian* (1675) start with a calendar; the *Rituale* does not include it. In the baptismal rites of both *Manuale* and *Shengshi lidian*, distinction is made between baptism of men and of women, but not in the *Rituale*. The short note on confirmation in both *Manuale* ((1605), 61) and *Shengshi lidian* ((1675), *CCT ARSI*, vol. 11, 429) is absent in the *Rituale*. In both *Manuale* and *Shengshi lidian*, the sacrament of marriage precedes the one of extreme unction; in the *Rituale* it follows after the section on the funerals.

102. *Shengshi lidian* (1675), *CCT ARSI*, vol. 11, 476–521. There are several detailed proofs that Buglio used *Manuale*, rather than *Rituale*. Just like *Manuale* ((1605), 200–201), *Shengshi lidian* (1675) includes the questioning of the sick person (476–77), which is not in *Rituale*. In the Litany of the Saints, Saint Joseph is left out in both *Manuale* and *Shengshi lidian*, though he is present in *Rituale* (after John the Baptist). Several of the specific instructions for the funerals in *Shengshi lidian* (491) can be found in *Manuale* (235), but not in *Rituale*. Both in *Manuale* (268–72) and *Shengshi lidian* (495–502), the verses of Psalm 50 are interrupted with an antiphon; in *Rituale* they are not. The psalms for the funerals of children are similar in *Manuale* (276–79) and *Shengshi lidian* (509–13) (Ps. 112, 148, 149, 150) but different from *Rituale* (Ps. 112. [118], 23, 148). The place and the order of the responsorial prayers is similar in *Manuale* (281–86) and *Shengshi lidian* (515–21); they do appear in *Rituale*, though in a different order and in a different place (under *Officium defunctorum*) and are also included in *Missale* (see sections *Missae defunctorum* and the different prayers for the dead (*Orationes diversae pro defunctis*)).

103. Compare *Shengshi lidian* (1675), *CCT ARSI*, vol. 11, 476–77, and 477ff. with *Shanzhong zhugong guili* (after 1638); *CCT ARSI*, vol. 5, 355–59 and 387f. Buglio shortened the text, leaving out the "Exhortationes" of Cerqueira's *Manuale* ((1605), 202–19) and keeping only the prayers.

104. This includes translations of Psalms 50, 112, 148, 149, 150.

105. Bontinck (1962), especially chapter 6 on Couplet.

106. *Shanzhong yiying lidian* (after 1675); Bernard (1945), no. 444; see also copy in ARSI Jap. Sin. I, 95; Chan (2002), 147–48. See also Brunner (1964), 111–13 (sometimes it is added as a supplement to another text). That *Shanzhong yiying lidian* (after 1675) is later than *Shengshi lidian* (1675) can be proven by the fact that every time there is a difference between the two, the *Shengshi lidian* is closer to the original version by Fróis. Compare, for example, differences between *Shanzhong zhugong guili* (before 1638), *CCT ARSI*, vol. 5, 490ff., *Shengshi lidian* (1675), *CCT ARSI*, vol. 11, 480, and *Shanzhong yiying lidian* (after 1675), 4aff.

107. Bernard (1945), no. 444 dates it ca. 1671, but it is certainly later than *Shengshi lidian* (1675). In comparison with the 1675 version of the *Shengshi lidian*, the vocabulary and phrasing of Buglio's *Shanzhong yiying lidian* have been occasionally altered.

108. *Yiwangzhe rikejing* (possibly after 1675); Bernard (1945), no. 443 (date: ca. 1670, but it is possibly later than 1675); see also copy in ARSI Jap. Sin. I, 96; Chan (2002), 96. It is possibly later than *Shengshi lidian* (1675), but it is not clear whether it was compiled before or after *Shanzhong yiying lidian* (after 1675). When one compares the prayers for the deceased in the three texts, in some cases *Shanzhong yiying lidian* is closer to *Shengshi lidian*, but in other cases *Yiwangzhe rikejing* is closer to *Shengshi lidian*. See *Manuale* (1605), 281ff.; *Shengshi lidian* (1675), *CCT ARSI*, vol. 11, 516ff.; *Shanzhong yiying lidian* (after 1675), 21aff.; *Yiwangzhe rikejing* (possibly after 1675), 5bff., 27aff.

109. See also, for example, instructions by Palmeiro (1629), 25r, n. 18: "If there is a sufficient number of Fathers, they will recite the entire *Office of the Dead*, according to the custom of the Society." The *Office* is included in the European *Breviarium* (1568), and similarly the Chinese translation of it, *Yiwangzhe rikejing* (possibly after 1675), is added at the end of some copies of *Siduo kedian* (1674), e.g., at the end of BnF, Chinois 7388.

110. Bontinck (1962), 412; Jennes (1946), 248 n. 42.

111. Brook (1989), 492.

112. Edwards (1948), 786–87.

113. Xu Jijun (1998), 2 and Watson (1988a), 14–15.

114. *Manuale* (1605), 235–301 (including the various prayers for the deceased that could be said at the ordinary Mass).

115. The subdivisions of *Manuale* (1605) are: 1) Funerals of clergy, religious persons or of lay people buried with solemnity; 2) Ordinary funerals of lay people; 3) Children.

116. *Shanzhong yiying lidian* (after 1675), 10a, 16a; compare with *Shengshi lidian* (1675), *CCT ARSI*, vol. 11, 492, *Anzang lijie* ("Funerary ritual"), and 506 small note.

117. On the clerical orientation of *Manuale* (1605), see also Rutherford (1970), 98 n. 41. The name of the prayers for encoffining is not given a separate section as it is in Fróis, though in *Shengshi lidian* (1675), *CCT ARSI*, vol. 11, on page 476, there is a small note, "See below the *rulianjing*."

118. The only explicit reference to someone liturgically responsible appears on 12a under the name *sidai* (the one replacing the priest).

119. The involvement of the Christian community is probably also an important reason why "the Jesuits could reconcile in their own corporate mind the fact that on one side of the Eurasian continent they insisted on strict adherence to [liturgical] rubrics while on the other side of it they accepted some very important variations" (Maher (2002), 217).

120. See also some of the prayers that are left out, such as the prayer for a deceased pope or priest (*Manuale* (1605), 284; *Shengshi lidian* (1675), *CCT ARSI*, vol. 11, 518;

Shanzhong yiying lidian (after 1675), 22b); only one prayer to be used at the anniversary of the commemoration of the death of a bishop is kept (*Yiwangzhe rikejing* (possibly after 1675), 6a; 27a).

121. Pfister (1932–1934), 240–41; Brunner (1964), 113 remarks that "The *Ritual for the Dead* of Buglio is very much liked by the Chinese Christians; children learn it by heart in the prayer schools. When a Christian dies in a village, it is very impressive to see the community united before the home of the deceased while chanting in choir like monks these prayers translated in a very beautiful style."

122. Gy (1955), 79–80.

123. *HCC*, 555; see also Menegon (2002), 112ff.

124. Wills (1994), 390, 394.

125. Ad Dudink, "2.6.1. Sympathising Literati and Officials," in *HCC*, 483.

126. *HCC*, 383–85.

127. *HCC*, 456ff. and Brockey (2007), chapters 9 and 10.

128. Handlin Smith (1987).

129. *FR* II, 482.

130. Standaert (1988), 65–66, 89–90; Wang Zheng (1634); Zürcher (1999), 278, 282. Margiotti (1958), 548–549.

131. The first six of these are listed in the biblical parable of the sheep and the goats (Matthew 25:31–46). They are the criteria by which Christ will judge people. As early as the third century the additional deed, burying the dead, was added. It was chosen for inclusion because it is highly praised in the book of Tobit (Tobit 1:17–19) (Kirschbaum (1968–1976), vol. 1, 246).

132. Zürcher (1990a), 441–42.

133. Handlin Smith (1987), 330–31.

134. Zürcher (1999), 281.

135. Black (1989), chapters 4 and 5; Maher (2002), 201.

136. Bürkler (1942), 13.

137. Dehergne (1956), 970; Margiotti (1961), 135; see also the list of congregations existing in Shanghai in 1683 in Pfister (1932–1934), 226–27.

138. See also Brockey (2007), chapters 9 and 10.

139. Black (1989), 104–7, 231–33; Eire (1995), 134ff.

140. For this date, see Chan (2002), 234.

141. *Shengmu huigui* (before 1673), *CCT ARSI*, vol. 12, 455. *Shanzhongjing* is possibly a reference to João Fróis' *Shanzhong zhugong guili* or to a section in a prayer book, i.e., Brunner (1964), 74, 265, 337–38.

142. "Renhui huigui" (n.d.), *CCT ARSI*, vol. 12, 475–76; see also the rules "Shengmu huigui" (n.d.), that refer to "Renhui huigui": "When a Christian is in agony of death, let his family notify the president, who will transmit to the neighbouring

Christians that they gather at his house to chant prayers. The rituals of funeral and burial should be performed as prescribed in the rules of the Association of Charity." *CCT ARSI*, vol. 12, 494 (cf. Chan (2002), 459).

143. Schall von Bell (1942), 328–31; Margiotti (1963), 57; see also the Congregation of the Good Death, canonically established in 1680 in Macao, and twenty years later in Beijing (54–57).

144. Schall von Bell (1942), 330–31.

145. Zhang Xianqing (2007a), "Conclusion"; see also Brook (1989) and Szonyi (2002).

146. On the Eucharist, see Dudink (2007); on confession see the various articles in *Forgive Us Our Sins* (2006).

147. For an analysis of the creation of new rituals within a lineage, see Szonyi (2002), 143ff.

148. For variation in Confucian rituals, see Ebrey (1991b), 209.

4. FUNERALS AS PUBLIC MANIFESTATION

1. The child was born Shunzhi 14/10/7, or 12 November 1657, and died Shunzhi 15/1/24, or 25 February 1658, before having received a name. Contrary to practice, the child was posthumously made a prince of the first class. He was buried Shunzhi 15/8/27 (24 September 1658).

2. For Magalhães' European evaluation at that time of Schall's role in this Bureau, see Romano (2004).

3. On this controversy, see Ad Dudink, "2.6.3. Opponents." In: *HCC*, 513–15; Huang Yi-long (1991).

4. Twenty-one Jesuits, three Dominicans and one Franciscan; four Dominicans in Fujian were "overlooked."

5. Metzler (1980), 23ff.; Cummins (1993), 150.

6. German partial translation and summary are in Metzler (1980), 24–28; for the original sources, see Metzler (1980), 28 n. 11, and the printed version in *Acta Cantonensia Authentica* (1700); a Latin version is also included in Dunyn-Szpot (1700–1710), Tomus II, Pars I, Cap. VI, n. 2 (1668), 195r–197v.

7. Dunyn-Szpot (1700–1710), Tomus II, Pars I, Cap. VI, n. 2 (1668), 197v (for translation and discussion, see in part 4 of this article); Metzler (1980), 28.

8. *Acta Cantonensia Authentica* (1700), 30; Dunyn-Szpot (1700–1710), Tomus II, Pars I, Cap. VI, n. 2 (1668), 197r–v; Metzler, 27. *Acta Cantonensia Authentica* has "cum funereo apparatu" (absent in Dunyn-Szpot) and "committitur" ("relinquitur" in Dunyn-Szpot).

9. Dunyn-Szpot (1700–1710).

10. "Funerum et Exequiarum Christianarum Ratio à Patribus Exulibus Cantone

instituta, et ad Praxim reducta": this title can be found in the index at the end of the second volume. It is not clear whether this section, like the preceding one, originates from Adrien Grelon, SJ (1618–1696), *Dissertatione de Sinis Ieiunantibus* as mentioned in the margin of Dunyn-Szpot (1700–1710), Tomus II, Pars III, Cap. IV, n. 8 (1677–1678), 285v.

11. Dunyn-Szpot (1700–1710), Tomus II, Pars III, Cap. IV, n. 8 (1677–1678), 286v.

12. The link between this accusation and the decisions of the Canton Conference is made explicit by the fact that the first sentence of article 34 of the Canton Conference is quoted literally by Dunyn-Szpot (1700–1710), Tomus II, Pars III, Cap. IV, n. 8 (1677–1678), 286r.

13. Suffragia are interventions by the living faithful (Mass, prayers, alms, works of piety) for other faithful, especially for the consolation and the liberation of the souls in purgatory. See "Suffragium" in *Liturgisch Woordenboek* (1958–1962) and Héris (1955).

14. Dunyn-Szpot (1700–1710), Tomus II, Pars III, Cap. IV, n. 8 (1677–1678), 287r–v.

15. Ibid.

16. First printed in French in 1688 with the title, *Histoire d'une dame chrétienne de la Chine, ou par occasion les usages de ces Peuples, l'établissement de la Religion, les manières des Missionnaires, & les Exercices de Pieté des nouveaux Chrétiens sont expliquez*, with Spanish (1691), Dutch (1694), and Italian translations. The Dutch version, titled *Historie van eene groote, christene mevrouwe van China met naeme mevrouw Candida Hiu*, is more extensive and sometimes more detailed than the French. Therefore the notes will refer first to the Dutch and then to the French version.

17. *Shengjiao guicheng* concerns a manuscript that belonged to the Beitang library. The Chinese text and French translation were published in Verhaeren (1939–1940). For dating and authorship, see Verhaeren (1939–1940), 451–53. The reason to attribute it to Pacheco (Chinese name: Cheng Jili) or Couplet (Chinese name: Bo Yingli) is that the text is signed by someone for whom the final character of his name was *li*. Pacheco was as vice-provincial of China one of the persons responsible for the Canton Conference. There are also similarities between several rules and descriptions in this text and in Couplet's *Life of Madame Candida Xu* (including the funeral cross).

18. Couplet (1694), 91–92 / (1688), 86–87; similar passage (1694), 144 / (1688), 136. Since Couplet left Macao on 5 December 1681, most of the information included in this book dates from before that date. One may notice that in 1671 Couplet himself brought the remains of Brancati, who had died in Canton 25 April 1671, to his former mission in Shanghai to be buried there (Chan (1990), 69).

19. Couplet (1694), 92–94 / (1688), 87–88. See also Dunyn-Szpot (1700–1710), Tomus II, Pars III, Cap. I, n. 2 (1672), 253r–v. Chinese text: *Xichao ding'an* (version 3), 61a–64b; *XC*, 116–7.

20. For Christian cemeteries in seventeenth- and eighteenth-century China, see Ad Dudink, "3.3. Church Buildings, Cemeteries and Tombstones," in *HCC*, 586–91; concerning the use of consecrated cemeteries in the 1660s, see also the reference in Brockey (2007), 118.

21. Couplet (1694), 141 / (1688), 133.

22. Chan (1990), 70–71.

23. Couplet (1694), 142 / (1688), 134.

24. Couplet (1694), 93–94 / (1688), 88–89. At this occasion it was discovered that the body of M. Martini, buried for eighteen years, had been fully preserved.

25. Golvers (1999), 316, 336; see also "Account book," 150, 165, 166, 216.

26. *Shengjiao guicheng* (n.d.), 472–73; French translation in Verhaeren (1939–1940), 460–61.

27. Couplet (1694), 150–51 (reference to four thousand families) / (1688), 141–42.

28. Du Halde (1735), vol. 2, between 78–79 / (1736), vol. 2, between 120–21 / (1738–1741), vol. 2, between 12–13. See also "Figure de la Croix avec laquelle les chrestiens de la Chine ont accoustumé de se faire ensevelir" (engraved by F. De Louvement). ARSI Jap. Sin. III, 22.5 (Chan (2002), 496).

29. See Henschenius and Papebrochius (1685–1688), in the section *Danielis Papebrochii e Soc(ietatis) Jesu paralipomena addendorum, mutandorum aut corrigendorum in conatu chronico-historico ad catalogum Romanorum Pontificum* (1688) (one folio after 141). The Bollandist Daniël Papebrochius, SJ (1628–1714), was an active supporter of Philippe Couplet during his stay in Europe (1683–1692). See Golvers (1998).

30. This question had already been raised in Ricci's time; see Bettray (1955), 310–11.

31. *Shengjiao guicheng* (n.d.), 472–74; French translation in Verhaeren (1939–1940), 460–61.

32. "Against the Catholics" is added in the Dutch version.

33. Couplet (1694), 144 / (1688), 136–37.

34. Watson (1988a), 14.

35. Couplet (1694), 145 / (1688), 137. The final remark only appears in the Dutch version.

36. The Dutch version reads "three times."

37. Couplet (1694), 152 / (1688), 143.

38. Instead of "a eulogy, or," the Dutch version reads "a tomb inscription, and."

39. Couplet (1694), 152–53 / (1688), 143–44.

40. See especially the preliminary laying out and the final laying out, described in Ebrey (1991a), 81ff. and Naquin (1988), 39–41; see also the family condolence sequence in an early twentieth-century description (originally 1917), *Qingbai leichao* (1996), (*sangjilei*), vol. 8, 3544; on funerary portraits in China see Ebrey (1991a), 78 (Zhu Xi questioned the use of such portraits); and Xu Jijun (1998), 487–88.

41. Many details appear in *The Golden Lotus* (1988), especially in chapter 62 (The Death of the Sixth Lady) and chapter 63 (The Sixth Lady's Funeral) in vol. 3, 142ff. For example, table with incense (143, 154), curtain (146, 152), portrait (146, 151, 153, 158, 161), women behind a curtain (161), printed obituary notice (155), funeral dress (155), and panegyric (159). As pointed out in chapter two, above, these details are also present in the contemporary European descriptions. For more on women behind curtains, see Dapper (1670), 412 / (1671), 373–74; and Semedo (1996), 112 / (1655), 75. See also illustrations attached to chapter 63 of *Jinpingmei cihua* (1617): selection of the portrait (opposite 1764), and women behind the curtain (opposite 1765).

42. The practice of using effigies of the deceased is mentioned in several other contemporary European sources: Dapper (1670), 409, 412, 419–20 / (1671), 374, 376, 383; Trigault and Ricci (1615), 80 / (1978), 139 / (1953), 73 (compare *FR*, vol. 1, 84); Semedo (1996), 112 / (1655), 75; Schall (1942), 430–31. Portraits of Jesuits in China include those of Matteo Ricci (1610) by Manuel Pereira (Trigault and Ricci (1615), 614 / (1978), 660 / (1953), 564 (compare *FR*, vol. 2, 543)); Niccolò Longobardo (1654), by order of the Emperor (Schall (1942), 308–9); and Gabriel de Magalhães (1677) and Lodovico Buglio (1682), also by order of the Emperor (Couplet (1694), 143 / (1688), 135). Xu Guangqi, wanting to imitate the example of Ricci, refused to have a portrait made during his lifetime (*FR*, vol. 2, 543 n. 3). For an example of the use of a portrait for a common Christian, see *Kouduo richao* (ca. 1630–1640), juan 7, 7b, *CCT ARSI*, vol. 7, 470.

43. Aleni (1637), *juan shang*, 27a; translation in Mish (1964), 61. On the realistic representation of a person recently deceased as a new theme in portrait painting since the beginning of the sixteenth century, see Ariès (1985), 199ff. The works are few in number and do not include many men or members of the laity—the custom appears to have been mainly reserved for nuns.

44. Stuart and Rawski (2001), 52, 56.

45. Couplet (1691), opposite 1 (with Latin explanation); compare with Couplet (1688) (with French explanation) / (1694) (with Dutch explanation). In Du Halde (Humblot designer, Foubonnen engraver) the funeral portrait is transformed into a standing figure. Du Halde (1735), vol. 2, between 78–79 / (1736), vol. 2, between 120–21 / (1738–1741), vol. 3, between 16–17.

46. Couplet (1694), 120–21 / (1688), 114–15. For the title of *shuren*, see Hucker (1985), n. 5438. This title corresponds to the third rank of honorary title. Franke (1942), 52.

47. Stuart and Rawski (2001), 58. Compare the portrait of Candida Xu with that of Lady Guan (circa mid-seventeenth to early eighteenth century; inscription dated 1716) who is depicted with Buddhist prayer beads. Stuart and Rawski (2001), 53, fig. 2.1.

48. Couplet (1694), 153–54 / (1688), 144–45.

49. Cf. *Jiali* (1341): Ebrey (1991a), 98–100; Naquin (1988), 41–42; Zheng (1995), 266ff.; Xu Jijun (1998), 490; *The Golden Lotus* (1988), vol. 3, 158–59.

50. Couplet (1694), 154 / (1688), 145–46.

51. Couplet (1694), 154–55 / not in French version.

52. Cf. Naquin (1988), 43; for descriptions of pompous funerary processions, see also *The Golden Lotus* (1988), chapter 65 (The Burial of the Lady of the Vase), vol. 3, 180ff., and *A Dream of Red Mansions* (1978), chapter 14 (Lin Ruhai Dies in Yangzhou), vol. 1, 195ff. See also illustration attached to chapter 65 of *Jinpingmei cihua* (1617), opposite 1808.

53. Schall (1942), 442–43. Though it is not always said clearly, they seem to have attended all public ceremonies and sacrifices that accompanied these funerals. An earlier example is Manuel Dias, superior of the Jesuits, who presented in 1614 his condolences to the emperor himself upon the death of his mother. Herrera Maldonado (1622), 359–60.

54. Josson and Willaert (1938), 363. French translation in Bosmans (1912), 97. See introduction of this book.

55. Yang (1961), 37–38. For a detailed account of two funeral processions, including the expenses, written in 1924 by Gu Jiegang (1893–1980), see Gu (1928–1929) / (1981).

56. Couplet (1694), 91 / (1688), 85–86; similar passage in (1694), 144 / (1688), 136. Since Couplet left Macao on 5 December 1681, most of the information included in this book dates to before his departure.

57. "Descriptio Processionis non visae in Europa": Funeral of Xu Guangqi (died 1633; transfer of coffin to Shanghai 1634; burial 1641), in Dunyn-Szpot (1700–1710), Tomus I, Pars I (1641), 6r–7r. See also the funeral of G. Rho, who died 26 April 1638 and was buried 5 May 1638, in Väth (1991), 129–30. For the funeral procession of the Dominican Friar Domingo Coronado (1614–1665), who died and was buried in Beijing after being summoned there due to the Calendar Case, see Gabiani (1673), 349–50.

58. In the eighteenth century there are also several descriptions of elaborate Christian funeral processions. For a detailed description of the funeral procession of Bernardino della Chiesa, OFM (1644–1721; died 20 December 1721; buried 7 April 1722), bishop of Beijing diocese, see "Relatio de Illmi D. Bernardinus della Chiesa Exsequiarum celebratione a P. Carolo de Castorano Illmo D. Ioh. Fr. Nicolai Data, Lintsing 10 Septembris 1722," in *SF* V, 798–803.

One important case was the controversy that arose from the (excessive) funeral of Girolamo Franchi, SJ (1667–1718; died 13 February 1718; buried 10 April 1718), celebrated by Miguel Fernández Oliver, OFM (1665–1726); see "Relatio examinis circa exsequias Patris Hieronymi Franchi a P. Fernández Oliver celebratas, Tsinan-fu 23 Maii 1719," in *SF* VIII, 2, 970–78, and also several other documents in *SF* V and *SF* VIII (see also Mungello [2001], 91–103). Oliver was criticized for having organized an extravagant funeral service and procession. To this criticism he answered: "Why with so much and exaggerated pomp? . . . With such pomp I wanted to counter the claim I have heard for many years, that [the members of] our sacred law bury their own [dead] as if they are dogs, and that they do not give them those final honors that even the enemy usually gives to the enemy, qualifying us as non-pious, even toward the fathers who brought us here, the masters who taught us, and the friends who loved us" (*SF* VIII, 2, 974).

Another example is the case of Dominique Parrenin (1665–1741; died 29 September 1741; buried 15 November 1741); see Gaubil (1970) (letter of 21 November 1741 to Du Halde), "Le 15 novembre fixé pour l'enterrement, fut un jour de *triomphe* pour la religion," 547–50; see also Naquin (2000), 579.

59. The images of "elephants, camels and tigers" are mentioned by several European sources, but it is not clear how widespread this practice was.

60. Johann Adam Schall von Bell died in 1666, but received funerary honors only after his rehabilitation in 1669. The next one to receive such honors was Thomas Pereira in 1708. A detailed discussion appears in chapter seven of this book.

61. Zürcher (1994), 40–41.

62. Chow (1994), 12–14; these two modes of transmission can be compared to Yan Yuan's (1635–1704) argumentation that moral order was sustained not through writing and words but through concrete ritual practice. Shang Wei (2003), 39ff.

63. Turner (1969), 96ff.

5. FUNERALS AS COMMUNITY PRACTICE

1. This is the only guideline found for the seventeenth century so far; for the eighteenth century, see, for example, the funeral instructions and guidelines for the condolence sequence for the Yunnan–Sichuan region compiled by Joachim de Martiliat, MEP (1706–1755), in 1744. Launay (1920), vol. 2, 7–11.

2. "Linsang chubin yishi" (earlier version), ARSI Jap. Sin. II, 169.4; *CCT ARSI*, vol. 5, 439–46.

3. "Linsang chubin yishi" (later version), ARSI Jap. Sin. I, 153; *CCT ARSI*, vol. 5, 447–65.

4. "Sangzang yishi" (earlier version), ARSI Jap. Sin. I, 164; *CCT ARSI*, vol. 5, 467–79.

5. "Sangzang yishi" (later version), ARSI Jap. Sin. I, 164a; *CCT ARSI*, vol. 5, 481–91.

6. Though text A may very well be the original version on which text B was based, there are major differences between them. Text A is much shorter, nineteen articles in total, versus thirty-two articles in text B. Three have been split into two articles of text B and one into three articles of text B; thus, text A1 corresponds to B2 plus

B3; A5 corresponds to B9 plus B10 plus B11; A6 corresponds to B24 plus B25; and A12 corresponds to B28 plus B29. Two articles of text A become one in text B, namely, A17 combines with A19 to make B30. The corresponding number of articles is also limited: eight of the nineteen articles of text A (8, 9, 10, 13, 14, 15, 16, 18) have not been retained in text B or the subsequent texts. The articles unique to text A mainly concern instructions for prayer. Text B is the longest text. It is very similar to texts C and D, but it has two articles more: article 23 (formula of the necrology) and article 25 (invitation of community leader to burial service). Besides some minor differences in vocabulary or phrasing, the other major differences consist in the content of article 11 (see below). Texts C and D are identical, except for one sentence in article 11.

7. There are no notes on text A.

8. "Linsang chubin yishi" (later version), *CCT ARSI*, vol. 5, 448; trans. Chan (2002), 205.

9. "Sangzang yishi" (earlier version), *CCT ARSI*, vol. 5, 470; trans. Chan (2002), 214 (slightly adapted here).

10. For a biography, see *SF* III, 333–51 and *SF* VII, 123–32. Unfortunately, his correspondence does not make reference to the apparent conflict that required the various revisions of "Ritual Sequence" guideline. On his Chinese treatises, see Bernard (1945), nos. 461, 502, 503, and 520; on the pastoral norms, see "Normae pastorales pro seraphica missione statutae, Cantone exeunte a. 1683," *SF* VII, 187–95.

11. Giovanni Francesco Nicolai da Leonissa (1656–1737), *SF* IV, 463–77; *SF* VI, 3–18.

12. "Sangzang yishi" (later version), *CCT ARSI*, vol. 5, 482; trans. Chan (2002), 215. This document is signed 15 May 1685 (in fact one day earlier than text C). The phrase, "solemn declaration of protest" of "Sangzang yishi" (earlier version) has changed into "statement of clarification." The detailed discussion of the reasons for this withdrawal follows in the next chapter.

13. Dunyn-Szpot (1700–1710) also remarks that he is not sure whether it was ever printed. See next note.

14. Filippucci was of the opinion that it was difficult to condemn on the basis of one protest a practice that for many years had taken a stable form for Jesuits and that was put into practice by neophytes without stigma of error in faith. See the section, based on a letter by Filippucci (Canton, 23 February 1686), "Controversia inter Basilicanum and Philippucium ob ritum quondam Sinensium à morte vita functorum fieri solitum" in Dunyn-Szpot (1700–1710), Tomus II, Pars IV, Cap. VII, n. 2 (1685), 73r–v.

15. "Linsang chubin yishi" (later version), *CCT ARSI*, vol. 5, 447–65. Subtitles have been added in this translation, within square brackets, in order to illustrate that the guideline closely follows the sequence of the *Jiali* laid out in chapter 1. The numbering of the statutes is original.

16. No mention is made here of the washing or dressing of the body, a step that *Jiali* includes at this point of the preparations.

17. The phrase appears in article 19 where *bendi zhi li* of text B has been replaced by *yuezhong zhi li* of texts C and D. That the reference is to customs within Guangdong is additionally confirmed by the fact that the title page of text B bears the three large characters for Dayuantang as place of production ("Linsang chubin yishi" [later version], *CCT ARSI*, vol. 5, 448). This is the Jesuit church then existing in Canton.

18. For an overview of this structure, see Watson (1988a), 12–15 and Ebrey (1991a), 65–70. In the translation the elementary structure has been added between square brackets.

19. Ebrey (1991a), 81 and 84; Naquin (1988), 39–40. This reference is left out in the other versions.

20. Yan Mo (ca. 1694).

21. These three are also called *daqi*; see Zheng (1995), 263 and Chen Huaizhen (1934), 140; compare also Naquin (1988), 41.

22. Watson (1988a), 7, 12, 18; Watson (1988b), 133.

23. Watson (1988b), 118–19.

24. Watson (1988b), 118.

25. Watson (1988b), 122.

26. See DuBois (2005), 53, 179, 183, 191. It is partly because the sectarians are cheaper than monks. How far back this practice goes is unclear, however.

27. These are instructions for a day watch—morning, midday, and evening— and not for the night watch, as mentioned in A7 (B26), with evening, midnight, and morning prayers.

28. For these prayers, see also Brunner (1964), 275ff. The number of repetitions for the Our Father and Hail Mary prayers is the same as in "Renhui huigui" (n.d.), *CCT ARSI*, vol. 12, 476.

29. Fróis, *Shanzhong zhugong guili* (before 1638), *CCT ARSI*, vol. 5, 428 (*rulian qiannian*), 431 (*rulian hounian*), 433 (*anzang qiannian*), 434 (*anzang hounian*); Buglio, *Shanzhong yiying lidian* (after 1675), 9a (*zhonghou daowen*); compare with *Shengshi lidian* (1675), *CCT ARSI*, vol. 11, 489.

30. For *lianbujing* (A3), see *shenglian bujing* in Brunner (1964), 111.

31. Making four genuflections, instead of the more customary three, was quite common in China. It is mentioned in *Jiali* (1341) (Ebrey (1991a), 29, 189), and also in numerous contemporary writings, such as Xu Qianxue's *Duli tongkao* (1696), *SKQS*, vols. 112–14.

32. See also Lozada (2001), 150. Lozada gives an anthropological description of Christian funerals in "Little Rome," a village in the province of Guangdong in the 1990s. The funeral ritual as he observed it and the ritual process as stipulated in the "Ritual Sequence" guideline from the seventeenth century, from the same prov-

ince, are surprisingly similar. Compare also with Kang Zhijie (2006), 305–33, which includes a description of the Catholic funeral liturgy in Mopanshan (northwest Hubei) and a comparison with "Linsang chubin yishi" (later version).

33. Compare with the role of the funeral associations for the spreading of Confucian ideas, in Ho Shu-yi (2000), 209.

34. Brunner (1964), 184, 278; see also *Misa jingdian* (1670) (end of final volume *zhusheng guiyi*), 59a.

35. According to Chen Gang (2000), 80, *xiaozi* is a general term for filial descendant that refers to the deceased's sons and daughters, sons- and daughters-in-law, grandchildren, nieces and nephews, and their spouses and children.

36. Watson (1988b), 115.

37. This conflict will be analyzed in the next chapter.

38. Watson (1988a), 4; Thompson (1988), 73. For Arnold Van Gennep's analysis of rites of passage, see Huntington and Metcalf (1979), 8 ff.; Bell (1997), 94ff.; and Tong (2004), 147.

39. Watson (1988a), 10. An exceptional text on the correct interpretation and belief with regard to funeral rites is Ferdinand Verbiest's *Tianzhujiao sangli wenda* (1682) (see especially the next chapter of this book).

40. Thompson (1988), 73; Granet (1922), 105.

41. See the use of the same quotations by Ricci and Aleni in chapter three.

42. On this notion, see "Communion des saints," in *Dictionnaire de théologie catholique* (1903–1972), vol. 3, 429–79.

43. For an explanation of the prayer at funerals and especially prayers of intercession for those who are in purgatory, see Verbiest (1682), 1a–2aff.; *CCT ARSI*, vol. 5, 495–97; this text on Christian funerals is sometimes printed with Verbiest's treatise on the related theme of remuneration of the good and the bad: *Shan'ebao lüeshuo* (1670), *CCT ARSI*, vol. 5, 509–30 (Chan [2002], 36).

44. Ariès (1985), 139–47.

45. *Shengshen xiangtonggong* concerns the exchange of merit between the faithful and from the saints to the faithful. *Jiaoyao jielüe* (1615), *CCT ARSI*, vol. 1, 203–4; Brunner (1964), 275. For other references to *tonggong*, see also: *Shengmu huigui* (before 1673), *CCT ARSI*, vol. 12, 456; Li Jiugong (before 1681), *CCT ARSI*, vol. 11, 104–5. On *tonggongdan*, see also Zhang Xianqing (2007b). See, for example, the *tonggongdan* (printed in 1740) in BnF. Chinois 7441, with the names of Clara and Anna. See also the different *tonggongdan* of Peter Huang (died 10 June 1783 at the age of eighty-five years) and Monique Zhao (died 9 July 1783 at the age of eighty-one years; the pamphlet was attached to a memorial by the Governor of Huguang reporting about Christian activities, 31 October 1784). See *Qingzhongqianqi xiyang tianzhujiao zaihua huodong dang'an shiliao* (2004), 421, no. 197.

46. *Shengjiao guicheng* (n.d.), 472; French translation by Verhaeren (1939–1940), 460. The work of mercy of burying the dead was one of the core tasks of many associations: see *Shengmu huigui* (before 1673), *CCT ARSI*, vol. 12, 455; "Renhui huigui" (n.d.), *CCT ARSI*, vol. 12, 475. Some associations were especially established with the purpose of helping the dying and organizing funerals; for example, a congregation established by J. A. Schall von Bell in Beijing (to counter the criticism that Christians neglect funerals), in Schall von Bell (1942), 328–31 (Margiotti [1963], 57–59); see also the association of the "good death" established in Macao in 1680 and later introduced in the mainland (Margiotti [1963], 54–57).

47. Cf. Lozada (2001), 12.

48. Chen Gang (2000), 181; Granet (1922), 105–6; Lozada (2001), 12, 150.

49. Yang (1961), 35–38.

50. Yang (1961), 35; see also Granet (1922), 107–10; Johnson (1988); Huntington and Metcalf (1979), 23ff.; Ebersole (2000), 238.

51. Dapper (1670), 409, 412, 417, 418, 419 / (1670), 374 ("crying and lamenting; cry without ceasing"), 377 ("cry"), 381 ("formal Lamentations," "continual doleful noise"), 382 ("they make a hideous noise, more like howling than weeping," "crying a second or third time"); Trigault and Ricci (1615), 81 / (1978), 139 / (1953), 73 (compare *FR* I, 84); Las Cortes (1991), 190 / (2001), 156; Semedo (1996), 112 / (1655), 75; Schall von Bell (1942), 425, 426, 429.

52. Le Comte (1990), 83–84 / (1737), 50, concerning the funeral procession for F. Verbiest, writes, "Christians hold in one hand a lighted taper and in the other a handkerchief to wipe off their tears. The Gentiles are accustomed at such solemnities to shed feigned tears; but the Christians' loss made them [the Christians] shed real ones." See also the remark in Du Halde (1735), vol. 2, 127 / (1736), vol. 2, 150 / (1738–1741), vol. 1, 308: "Nothing can be more surprising than the Tears which the Chinese shed, and the Cries they make at these Funerals; but the Manner, in which they express their Sorrow, seems too regular and affected to excite in a European the same Sentiments of Grief that [one] is the Spectator of." The English translator added the following note: "The Irish still put forth as many doleful Cries over the Dead as the Chinese, and perhaps shed so many Tears: whether as unfeignedly I will not say, because the Irish Mourners are for the most part hired." For a discussion of tears expressing "real" emotions, see Ebersole (2000), 213ff.

53. The expression in A2 is not adopted in the corresponding articles of B, C, and D; the expression in B7 is not adopted in the corresponding articles of C and D (idem in B20).

54. Yang (1961), 37.

55. Chau (2006), 133ff. Ritual banquets were also the culmination of burial ceremonies throughout early modern Spain; see Eire (1995), 148.

6. CHRISTIAN VERSUS SUPERSTITIOUS RITUALS

1. *HCC*, 680–88.

2. Thus the time frame chosen for this book ends when the sharpest discussions of the Rites Controversy begin.

3. Dunyn–Szpot (1700–1710), Tomus II, Pars III, Cap. IV, n. 8 (1677–1678), 287r.

4. The word *xie* has been translated as "superstitious" when it is related to ritual (the neologism "heteroprax" might also be used), and as "heterodox" when related to doctrine, as in the prohibition of entering heterodox words in eulogies (B22).

5. Texts C and D, the versions adopted by Bishop Luo Wenzao, OP, and Agustín de San Pascual, OFM, seem less restrictive because they leave out the prohibition and the adjective "non-superstitious" (*wuxie*) (see also article B16): "The rituals of the Holy Teaching and the local rituals are different. Therefore it is appropriate that followers of the Teaching first perform the rituals of the Holy Teaching and next the local rituals." A similar difference appears at the beginning of article 13, where texts A and B read, "Before the funerary tablet of the deceased, it is not appropriate to chant prayers, but only to perform the local rituals." Texts C and D leave out the prohibition of chanting prayers, so that the sentence reads, "Before the funerary tablet of the deceased, one only performs the local rituals." These are minor changes, but they indicate that the way in which a prohibition is explicitly or implicitly mentioned reflects a difference in attitude towards the other tradition.

6. For a discussion in the early period, see Bettray (1955), 296ff.

7. Original text: *CPF* (1893), no. 1698; *CPF* (1907), no. 114; translation: *100RD*, no. 1.

8. "The Congregation of the Holy Office, March 23, 1656 to China missionaries," original text: *CPF* (1893), no. 1699; *CPF* (1907), no. 126; translation: *100RD*, no. 2 (slightly adapted).

9. "Normae pastorales pro seraphica missione statutae, Cantone exeunte a. 1683," *SF* VII, 187–95.

10. This part of the sentence is unclear in the original text.

11. "Normae pastorales pro seraphica missione statutae, Cantone exeunte a. 1683," *SF* VII, 189.

12. The four ritual guidelines contain little explicit description of "superstitious rituals." What is considered superstitious can only be deduced from the different prohibitions the text makes—what is "not allowed."

13. *Shengjiao guicheng* (n.d.), 472; French trans. Verhaeren (1939–1940), 460.

14. *Liji* (1992), 4.27; Legge (1885), 177.

15. "Sangzang yishi" (earlier version), *CCT ARSI*, vol. 5, 473–74.

16. "Sangzang yishi" (later version), *CCT ARSI*, vol. 5, 485–86.

17. "Sangzang yishi" (earlier version), *CCT ARSI*, vol. 5, 470; "Sangzang yishi"

(later version), *CCT ARSI*, vol. 5, 482; Chan (2002), 214–15; Chan, 214 translates: "to add a solemn declaration of protest to number eleven." The same term also appears twice in the above quoted "The Congregation of the Holy Office, March 23, 1656 to China missionaries."

18. See the section "Controversia inter Basilicanum & Philippucium ob ritum quondam Sinensium à morte vita functorum fieri solitum," based on a letter by Filippucci (Canton, 23 Febr. 1686), in Dunyn-Szpot (1700–1710), Tomus II, Pars IV, Cap. VII, n. 2 (1685), 73r–v. At this point Dunyn-Szpot himself mentions that Filippucci was not ignorant of the Instruction from Propaganda Fide to the three new Vicars Apostolic in Tonkin and Cochin China (1659): "Do not try to persuade these peoples to change their rites, their customs, their ways, as long as they are not openly opposed to religion and good morals. What would be sillier than to import France, Spain, Italy, or any other country of Europe into China? Do not import these, but the faith. The faith does not reject or crush the rites and customs of any race, as long as these are not evil. Rather, it wants to preserve them." Dunyn-Szpot gives the reference to "Philippus Couplet in sua Relatione." Original text: *CPF* (1907), no. 135; translation: *100RD*, no. 3.

19. In 1682, a few years earlier than the "Ritual Sequence" guideline, Filippucci had written an extensive rejection of the seventeen questions Morales had raised to the Propaganda Fide. In this rejection Filippucci contests the "false assumption" (*falsa suppositio*) that offerings for the dead are sacrifices. This document was written in Macao in 1682 (Filippucci (1700), 155: 25 November 1682; manuscript version is dated 23 March 1683) and published in Paris in 1700. See Filippucci (1700), 21–28 (nos. 24–29), 45ff.

20. "Normae pastorales pro seraphica missione statutae, Cantone exeunte a. 1683," *SF* VII, 189.

21. "Normae pastorales pro seraphica missione statutae, Cantone exeunte a. 1683," *SF* VII, 190; see another reference in article 17, *SF* VII, 194.

22. On the origin of this practice, see de Groot (1892–1897), vol. 2, 711ff.; Doré (1911), vol. 1, 114. For descriptions of the burning of paper money and objects in contemporary European sources, see Dapper (1670), 409, 413, 418, 419 / (1671), 374, 377, 381, 382; Trigault and Ricci (1615), 82 / (1978), 140 / (1953), 74 (compare *FR*, vol. 1, 84); Semedo (1996), 113 / (1655), 76; Schall von Bell (1942), 428.

23. Aleni (1637), *juan shang*, 27a–28a; trans. Mish (1964), 62–63; slightly adapted. Compare with the discussion about "real" and "false," in M. Dias' *Shengjing zhijie* (1636–1642), *juan* 6, 4b–5a; *WXSB*, vol. 5, 2048–49 (see chapter three of this book).

24. *Kouduo richao* (ca. 1630–1640), *juan* 4, 11b–12a, *CCT ARSI*, vol. 7, 276–277; trans. Zürcher (2007), n. IX.10.

25. *Acta Cantonensia Authentica* (1700), 32; Dunyn-Szpot (1700–1710), Tomus II, Pars I, Cap. VI, n. 2 (1668), 197v; Metzler (1980), 28. *Kin in tim* is *jinyinding. Chi cien*

is probably *zhiqian*, though Dunyn-Szpot has a comma between *chi* and *cien*. The characters for the final word(s) are not yet identified: *cù* can be *gu/ku* or *zu/cu*. According to Margiotti (1958), 463, n. 54 it should be *ma-tsu* (*mazu*). *Ma* could also refer to *zhima*, paper on which were printed the horse-head guardians of the underworld (see Doré (1911), vol. 1, 62–63).

26. Several Chinese Christians reject the use of paper money explicitly in their writings; see Li Jiugong (before 1681), *CCT ARSI*, vol. 11, 94, 96, 100; Zhang Xiangcan (ca. 1680s?), *CCT ARSI*, vol. 11, 290 (on the basis of the fact that it is not mentioned in *Jiali*); "Sangli ailun" (n.d.), *CCT ARSI*, vol. 11, 272–73 (similar argument as previous text). On Zhu Xi's opinion about the use of paper money, see Ebrey (1991a), 98 n. 91; de Groot (1892–1897), vol. 2, 716.

27. On the occasion of Buglio's death, Verbiest received an imperial edict granting a subsidy for funeral costs (see discussion in next chapter). ARSI Jap.Sin. II, 165.2; Chinese text and translation in Chan (2002), 452. See detailed discussion in the next chapter.

28. Verbiest (1682); Chan (2002), 35–36. The date is added at the end of the text (f. 7b) in a different script from the rest of the text; see also the other copy in ARSI Jap.Sin. I, [38/42] 38/2.1.

29. Gayoso was a Spanish Jesuit who came to China from the Philippines in 1678. He is rather unknown, partly because he returned to the Philippines in 1685 or 1686. See Reil (1970). Gayoso's letter appears in Gayoso (1683), with references to Verbiest's letters on 3v–4r. Information provided by Noël Golvers. A critical edition and summary are to be published by Golvers in *Supplement to F. Verbiest's Correspondence*.

30. See Chan (2002), 35–38. At earlier occasions officials sent by the Kangxi Emperor had asked questions on funeral rituals; at the death of G. de Magalhães (6 May 1677), they asked "What [funerary] rituals does Catholicism use?" (*An xiansheng xingshu* (ca. 1677) *CCT ARSI*, vol. 12, 328); at the death of Buglio (7 October 1682), they asked "What ceremonies of the Chinese could [they] perform before the deceased?" (Grimaldi (1927), 326).

31. Verbiest (1682), 5a–6a; *CCT ARSI*, vol. 5, 503–5.

32. Gayoso (1683), 1v (7a ratio), 2r (8a ratio), and 4r, the discussion of Verbiest's letters.

33. Gayoso (1683), 3v, writes, "in illo libello, a nostris scripto, qui titulo praenotatur *Pie vam*." This reference was identified by Ad Dudink (Dudink (2001), 122) as *Piwang* (1615?) and is an important argument in his conclusion that *Piwang* is probably falsely attributed to Xu Guangqi. Both the fourth (*WXXB*, vol. 2, 629–34; *CCT ZKW*, vol. 1, 46–51) and the ninth section (*CCT ZKW*, vol. 1, 68–70) of *Piwang* (1615?) contain a condemnation of the burning of paper.

34. On the question of intrinsic evil, see the similar argument in the pastoral rules for the Franciscans, n. 4, in "Normae pastorales pro seraphica missione statutae,

Cantone exeunte a. 1683," *SF* VII, 189. On extrinsic evil, see esp. Gayoso (1683), 1v (4a–5a ratio); see also 2v, 3v, 4r (discussion with Herdtrich).

35. "Political" is mentioned in Gayoso (1683), 1v, "*rationem polyticam*"; "*parte Sinarum polyticâ*"; and 4v, "*cultum polyticum*"; he refers to purified intentions in a discussion with Herdtrich on 2v, and also on 2r (8a ratio).

36. Gayoso (1683), 1v (5a ratio); see also 4r–v.

37. Gayoso (1683), 3v. See the above-mentioned text of "The Congregation of the Holy Office, March 23, 1656 to China missionaries," original in *CPF* (1893), no. 1699; *CPF* (1907), no. 126; translation: *100RD*, no. 2.

38. Gayoso (1683), 4r.

39. Verbiest (1682), 6a9; *CCT ARSI*, vol. 5, 506 = *Piwang* (1615?), 6b5 (*WXXB*, vol. 2, 630); Verbiest (1682), 7a1–2; *CCT ARSI*, vol. 5, 507 = *Piwang* (1615?), 7a4–5 (*WXXB*, vol. 2, 631); Verbiest (1682), 7a2–7; *CCT ARSI*, vol. 5, 507 = *Piwang* (1615?), 8a1–8 (*WXXB*, vol. 2, 633) (identification provided by Ad Dudink).

40. For this sentence the Kangxi Emperor did not use circle dots but commas.

41. Verbiest (1682), 6a–7a; *CCT ARSI*, vol. 5, 505–7. A similar argument appears in "Sangli ailun" (n.d.), *CCT ARSI*, vol. 11, 273.

42. Trans. Kutcher (1999), 91; *DaQing shichao shengxun* (1965), *juan* 6, 3a (Huangtaiji 2/1/5, or 9 February 1628); on Huangtaiji's funeral policy, see also Zhang Jiefu (1995), 264ff.

43. Kutcher (1999), 91–92; on the basis of *Kangxi qijuzhu* (1984), vol. 2, 1676–77.

44. The same event is mentioned in Schall von Bell (1942), 428 (see also Dapper (1670), 419 / (1671), 382).

45. Gayoso (1683), 2v (discussion with Herdtrich). The expression for "Chinese Catholic Christians" is "*Christiani Sinenses Catholici.*"

46. Verbiest (1682), 7a–b; *CCT ARSI*, vol. 5, 507–8. One will find the same argument with regard to the prostrations in front of the funeral tablet in Doré (1911), vol. 1, 108.

47. Kutcher (1999), 48, 50.

48. Kutcher (1999), 92–93.

49. Kutcher (1999), 92ff.

50. *Qing shilu* (1985), vol. 5, 434 (*Shengzu shilu, juan* 133, 3a); trans. Kutcher (1999), 93.

51. Kutcher (1999), 96.

52. The attention paid by Kangxi to the notion of filial piety (*xiao*) also appears in the *Xiaojing yanyi* (100 *juan*), an exposition and amplification of the *Classic of Filial Piety*. This work was commissioned in 1656, completed in 1682, and printed in 1690. The preface (*Xiaojing yanyi xu*), written by Kangxi in 1690, was translated into French (probably by Joachim Bouvet, SJ [1656–1730]) as "Système abrégé des rites de la pieté filiale des Chinois par l'Empereur Camhi" (ARSI Jap.Sin. IV 28), dated

Kangxi 29/14/11, or 14 December 1690, while the *SKQS* version of the original Chinese preface is dated Kangxi 29/4/24, or 1 June 1690.

53. Tong (2004), 147–48.

7. IMPERIAL SPONSORSHIP OF JESUIT FUNERALS

1. Thomas wrote about Verbiest in "Mors, Funus, & Compendium vitae seu Elogium P. Ferdinandi Verbiest," which is based primarily on reports by Thomas (1688) in Beijing, in Dunyn-Szpot (1700–1710), Tomus II, Pars IV, Cap. XII, nn. 1–5 (1688); Thomas, "Carta acerca de la muerte del Padre Fernando Verbiest, Flamenco, de la Compania de Jesus, que sucedió à 28. de Enero del ano de 1688, en PeKim, Corte de la China," in Couplet (1691), 216–46, and the funeral specifically on 239–42; Thomas (1726) "Von Dem Apostolischen Leben und Seeligen Todt R.P. Ferdinandi Werbiest," in *Der Neue Welt-Bott* vol. 1, Theil 2, no. 38, 8–13; and in a short reference in his letter dated 8 September 1688, in Thomas (1688), 188–93. See also Bosmans (1914).

2. Le Comte (1990), 82–86 / (1737), 43–53.

3. The letter is dated Zhoushan, 15 February 1703. For the passage on the funeral, see Fontenay (1707), 129–39 / (1979), 117–20. Part of this letter is also included in *Der Neue Welt-Bott* (1726), vol. 1, Theil 5, no. 97 (a map of the arrangement of the tombs is included).

4. Du Halde (1735), vol. 3, 98–100 / (1736), vol. 3, 118–22 (in section "De l'etablissement & du progrès de la Religion Chrétienne dans l'Empire de la Chine") / (1738–1741), vol. 2, 20–21.

5. Du Halde (1738–1741), vol. 2, 20.

6. Other occasional honors will not be discussed here. For instance, at the death of Christian Herdtrich, SJ (1625–1684), the Kangxi Emperor, at the request of Verbiest, wrote the calligraphic text *Haiyu zhi xiu* (Outstanding person from an overseas region) that was brought by Grimaldi to Jiangzhou to be installed as a horizontal tablet at Herdtrich's tomb. See Couplet (1694), 142–43 / (1688), 134–35; Margiotti (1958), 154–56; letter of Verbiest to Nicolas Avancini, SJ (1612–1686), in Josson and Willaert (1938), 473–82; and Dudink (2006), 41 (n. 19.927).

7. *Qinding daQing huidian zeli* (1768), *juan* 91, 29–39; *SKQS*, vol. 622, 874–79; *Qinding libu zeli* (1844), vol. 2, 1010–17 (*juan* 167). See also *Gujin tushu jicheng* (1726–1728) under *Liyidian: xudian* (funeral sponsorship), *juan* 130–31. For the Ming regulations, see *DaMing huidian* (1587), *juan* 101, 1555ff.; see also *Libu zhigao* (1620), *juan* 34, 1a–14a (*SKQS*, vol. 597, 624–31).

8. *Qinding libu zeli* (1844), vol. 2, 1012 (*juan* 167, 4b).

9. *Qinding daQing huidian zeli* (1768), *juan* 91, 30a; *SKQS*, vol. 622, 875 mentions also the "money for the construction of the tomb" *zaofengong jiayin* (amount for an official of the highest rank three hundred *liang*).

10. The Inner Court (*neiyuan* or *neichao*) refers to the palace halls and, by extension, those who served in them: the Grand Secretariat (*neige*). It was the most distinguished and influential body in the central government, staffed with Grand Secretaries of the Hanlin Academy dispatched to establish offices within the imperial palace to handle the Emperor's paperwork, recommend decisions in response to memorials received from the officialdom, and draft and issue imperial pronouncements. The Manchus had originally structured the central government with Three Palace Academies (*neisanyuan*), of which the *Nei* (*Hanlin*) *mishuyuan* was in charge of, among other matters, funeral texts such as *jiwen*. In 1658 they were organized into a Hanlin Academy and a Grand Secretariat of the Ming sort, and several other reorganizations followed. See Hucker (1985), n. 4193.

11. *Qinding libu zeli* (1844), vol. 2, 1017–19 (*juan* 168).

12. *FR* II, chapter 22. This chapter, written in Latin, is an extract from the annual letter of 1611 that was compiled by Trigault (see *FR* II, 564, n. 1); a short description also appears in chapter 10 of De Ursis' account of Ricci; see De Ursis (2000), 87–92 (Italian translation), 155–60 (Portuguese). Trigault's text served as a basis of the account in Bartoli (1663), 535–38, entitled "Esequie, sepoltura, e titoli d'onore al P. Matteo Ricci." An abbreviated English translation of Trigault's description can be found in Purchas (1625), III.ii, 407.

13. *FR* II, 566–67; Trigault and Ricci (1615), 617 / (1978), 663 / (1953), 567 (adapted).

14. See critical edition of Wu Daonan's memorial (14 June 1610), including the petition by D. de Pantoja and S. De Ursis in *FR* III, 3–8; the translation of the petition is also included in *FR* II, 568–72 and Trigault and Ricci (1615), 618–20 / (1978), 664–66 / (1953), 568–69.

15. *FR* II, 572–75; Trigault and Ricci (1615), 620–21 / (1978), 666–67 / (1953), 569–70 (slightly adapted).

16. *FR* II, 576; Trigault and Ricci (1615), 621 / (1978), 667 / (1953), 570.

17. *FR* II, 578; Trigault and Ricci (1615), 622 / (1978), 668 / (1953), 571 (adapted).

18. The term "funeral sponsorship" (*xu*) is not mentioned in de Pantoja's or in Wu Daonan's text. Yet, a few years later, in the inscription for the imperial gift of a place of burial and a residence (29 March 1615) written by Wang Yinglin (1545–1620), at that time Metropolitan Governor of Beijing, de Pantoja's petition is called a request for funeral sponsorship (*xu*). Cf. *FR* III, 15, 16.

19. Memorial by Wu Daonan, *FR* III, 7.

20. *FR* III, 6.

21. These are the protocols of the Bureau of Receptions (*zhuke qinglisi*): *DaMing huidian* (1587), 1624 (*juan* 108, 28a: *chaogong tongli*); *Qinding daQing huidian zeli* (1768), *juan* 94, 27bff.; *SKQS*, vol. 622, 941ff.; *Qinding libu zeli* (1844), vol. 2, 1017ff. (*juan* 168, 1aff).

22. *FR* II, 619ff., 626ff.

NOTES TO CHAPTER 7

23. Even if the burial grounds were confiscated on several occasions, i.e., during the Calendar Case and the Cultural Revolution. The place, however, retains its stability even today.

24. *Poxie ji* (1640), *juan* 1, 16a; trans. by Kelly (1971), 288; see Dudink (2000), 150–51.

25. Wang Yinglin repeats the expression in his inscription (*FR* III, 16). See also Dudink (2000), 151.

26. Esherick (1998), 143–44.

27. Johann Schreck Terrenz (1630), Giacomo Rho (1638), Br. Christopher (Xu Fuyuan, 1640), Br. Pascoal Mendes (Qiu Lianghou, 1640), Niccolò Longobardo (1654), and the Dominican Domingo Coronado (1665) were all buried there; see Malatesta and Gao (1995), 35–38.

28. Malatesta and Gao (1995), 35–36; Stary (1998), 156–59.

29. Väth (1991), 320.

30. *Xichao ding'an* (version 1), *WX*, 115–27; *XC*, 77–80. A similar request was made for Li Zubai and others "according to their original office" (*WX*, 122; *XC*, 79).

31. *Xichao ding'an* (version 1), *WX*, 129–30; *XC*, 83. The exact day of the ninth month on which the request was granted has been wiped out. For Western sources on Schall's rehabilitation through funeral sponsorship, see letters by Giovanni Filippo De Marini, SJ (1608–1682) to Balthasar Moretus in Antwerp, 20 Oct. 1670 and 8 Dec. 1670, in *Der Neue Welt-Bott* (1726), vol. 1, Theil 1, no. 14, 46–47; the original letters are kept in ARSI, see Väth (1991), 331, n. 28.

32. Väth (1991), 331, mentions the 525 *liang* but the source of his information is not clear; the letter by De Marini in *Der Neue Welt-Bott* does not mention the amount, and no references could be found in the letters Väth refers to on 331, n. 28 (checked by N. Golvers); see also *Zhengjiao fengbao* (1894), 62a: 524 *liang*; and Huang Yi-long (1992), 164.

33. Huang Yi-long (1992), 164.

34. *Xichao ding'an* (version 1), *WX*, 131–32; *XC*, 83 (the exact day of the tenth month has been wiped out).

35. Malatesta and Gao (1995), 133 (translation by Ad Dudink); dated Kangxi 8/11/16, or 8 December 1669 (slightly adapted); *Xichao ding'an* (version 1), *WX*, 131–32 (dated Kangxi 8/10/-); *XC*, 83; the Chinese text and a Latin translation are also found in A. de Gouvea's *Innocentia Victrix* (1671), 27r–29v; another modern English translation is in *CCS* 6 (1933), 32, and a German translation in Väth (1991), 331–32; see also "Grabschrifft" translated in De Marini's letter, dated 8 December 1670, in *Der Neue Welt-Bott* (1726), vol. 1, Theil 1, no. 14, 46–47. It is not clear whether this is a translation of the same text or of an unknown *beiwen* (commemorative text). Schall could also retain his original honorific title Tongwei jiaoshi (see also imperial edict in *Xichao ding'an* [version 1], *WX*, 133–34; *XC*, 84).

36. Edwards (1948), 786; Nivison (1962), 459; de Groot (1892–1897), vol. 3, 1127ff.; Honey (1981), 76ff.; Weinberg (2002), 6, 30ff.

37. See the sacrificial odes, or *jiwen*, that are included in the *juan shou* of *Huguang tongzhi* (Yongzheng 11, or 1733), f. 4a (Kangxi 1, or 1662), 5b–6a (three texts; Kangxi 17, or 1678), 31b (Yongzheng 4, or 1726), *SKQS*, vol. 531, 20–21, 33 (discovered by searching the Siku quanshu electronic database).

38. Malatesta and Gao (1995), 133; Gouvea (1671), 29r–29v; Väth (1991), 332 n. 29.

39. The most important sources for Magalhães' funeral are: the short biography *An xiansheng xingshu* by Lodovico Buglio and Ferdinand Verbiest (ca. 1677); and the description in the life and death by L. Buglio, see [Buglio] (1688), 380–85 / (1689), 348–52.

40. Zürcher (2002), 363.

41. [Buglio] (1688), 378 / (1689), 346; Pfister (1932–1934), 253; Pih (1979), 131–32.

42. In fact Magalhães strongly criticized the official positions occupied by Schall and Verbiest; see Pfister (1932–1934), 254; Pih (1979), chap. 3; Zürcher (2002), 372.

43. [Buglio] (1688), 380 (converts the two hundred taels into "approximately eight hundred francs") / (1689), 348 (the French version does not specify the final "two" messengers).

44. Vande Walle (1994), 511. Verbiest had done so when, in 1673, he asked the emperor that G. Gabiani be allowed to transport the body of the deceased G. F. De Ferrariis to Xi'an. *Xichao ding'an* (version 3), 61a–64b; *XC*, 116–7.

45. Compare with the "special edict" (*tezhi*), referring to the appointments made by the emperor without recourse to normal selection and appointment procedures, which were often resented by the officialdom (Hucker [1985], n. 6333); the possibility for this course of action was foreseen in the rules for the funeral sponsorship (see *Qinding libu zeli* [1844], *juan* 167, 2b; vol. 2, 1011).

46. "Imperial edict of Kangxi 16/IV/6, or 7 May 1677, given on the death of G. de Magalhães," ARSI Jap. Sin. II, 165.4, text and English translation in Chan (2002), 453; another copy (printed in red) can be found in the British Library, Chinese collection 15303.d.7; the text also appears in *Xichao ding'an* (version 4), 1a, after 199; *XC*, 127; *Zhengjiao fengbao* (1894), 76a–b; and *An xiansheng xingshu* (ca. 1677), *CCT ARSI*, vol. 12, 327–28; *XC*, 408; the Chinese text is carved on the tombstone, as mentioned in Malatesta and Gao (1995), 145; the French translation is in [Buglio] (1688), 383 / (1689), 349; and appears in Portuguese in Pereira (1677), 566r; another modern English translation is in *CCS* 6 (1933), 32–33.

47. *An xiansheng xingshu* (ca. 1677), *CCT ARSI*, vol. 12, 323–34; *XC*, 408; part of the text is also in *Xichao ding'an* (version 4), 2a–2b, after 199; *XC*, 128.

48. Edwards (1948), 780–81; Nivison (1962), 460; de Groot (1892–1897), vol. 3, 1109ff.; Weinberg (2002), 6, 37ff.

49. [Buglio] (1688), 382 / (1689), 349–50.

50. *An xiansheng xingshu* (ca. 1677), 328–32; *XC*, 408–9; compare also with the account of the funeral in [Buglio] (1688), 382–85 / (1689), 350–52.

51. Huang Bolu, in *Zhengjiao fengbao* (1894), 76b, gives the name of one of the three as Imperial Guard (*shiwei*) Xi Sa.

52. *An xiansheng xingshu* (ca. 1677), 331; *XC*, 408–9.

53. [Buglio] (1688), 384–85 / (1689), 350–52. In the final paragraph one word is unclear in the English version.

54. *An xiansheng xingshu* (ca. 1677), 332; *XC*, 409.

55. Pereira (1677), 568r/v (information provided by L. Brockey). The Jesuits attempted to make up for this public slight to their Christians by holding a private prayer ceremony in memory of Magalhães after the burial. Brockey (2005), 64–65.

56. This expression comes from Esherick (1998), 149, who was inspired by a quotation of Dai Zhen (1724–1777) in Chow (1994), 189: "Rituals are the rules and the laws of heaven and earth; they are the perfect rules, only those who understand heaven will know them."

57. Concerning Buglio's death and funeral, there is a short report by Filippo Grimaldi, written on 4 October 1682: Grimaldi (1927), 325–28. See also the short references in Du Halde (1735), vol. 2, 128 / (1736), vol. 2, 150 / (1738–1741), vol. 1, 308: "Particularités de celles [funerals] du P. Broglio [Buglio]." See also the short biography *Li xiansheng xingshu* by Ferdinand Verbiest, Claudio Filippo Grimaldi and Tomé Pereira (ca. 1682).

58. See Witek (1982), 43 and Wills (1984), 161.

59. "Imperial edict of Kangxi 21/11/7 (7 October 1682) given to Ferdinand Verbiest and others," ARSI Jap.Sin. II, 165.2: text and translation in Chan (2002), 452; text also in *Xichao ding'an* (version 4), 1b, after 199 (where it is wrongly dated by one year, namely Kangxi 22/11/7, or 26 October 1683); *XC*, 127–28; *Zhengjiao fengbao* (1894), 82b–83a; the Chinese text is carved on the tombstone (see Malatesta and Gao [1995], 149); another modern English translation is in *CCS* 6 (1933), 33.

60. On the importance of hosting, see Chau (2006), 126.

61. See remark after the imperial edict *Xichao ding'an* (version 4), 1b, after 199; *XC*, 128; Grimaldi (1927), 326. According to *Li xiansheng xingshu* (ca. 1682), *CCT ARSI*, vol. 12, 339; *XC*, 410 and *Zhengjiao fengbao* (1894), 83a, Zhao (Chang) and Xi (Sa) were among the court delegates.

62. Grimaldi (1927), 327.

63. Grimaldi (1927), 325.

64. According to Thomas (1688), it was Xiaozhuang who made the formal gesture of tearing into pieces the order from the four regents for Schall von Bell's death sentence. Dunyn-Szpot (1700–1710), Tomus II, Pars IV, Cap. XII, n. 1 (1688).

65. *CCT ARSI*, vol. 12, 389–92; *Xichao ding'an* (version 2), *WXXB*, vol. 3, 1729–31;

XC, 167. The help of the literatus is mentioned in Dunyn-Szpot (1700–1710), Tomus II, Pars IV, Cap. XII, n. 1 (1688). In order to spread this memorial more widely, it was later examined by the Astronomical Bureau, which added four characters to improve the style. Some opponents in the Catholic camp believed that a superstitious meaning had been added.

66. *CCT ARSI*, vol. 12, 391; *Xichao ding'an* (version 2), *WXXB*, vol. 3, 1731; *XC*, 167. This answer of the emperor is mentioned in *Kangxi qijuzhu* under the date of Kangxi 27/2/7, or 8 March 1688.

67. *CCT ARSI*, vol. 12, 393–95; *Xichao ding'an* (version 2), *WXXB*, vol. 3, 1735–37; *XC*, 167.

68. *Qinding daQing huidian zeli* (1768), *juan* 91, 29–39; *SKQS*, vol. 622, 874–79; *Qinding libu zeli* (1844), *juan* 167, 1–14; vol. 2, 1010–17.

69. *CCT ARSI*, vol. 12, 381–83; *Xichao ding'an* (version 2), *WXXB*, vol. 3, 1733–34; *XC*, 168; the edict is dated Kangxi 27/1/27, or 28 February 1688, one month after Verbiest's death; the delay was due to the funeral activities for Xiaozhuang. See also *Zhengjiao fengbao* (1894), 87aff.

70. *Xichao ding'an* (version 4), 183a–84b; *XC*, 147; (cf. Vande Walle [1994], 513, adapted). Verbiest received one added class at this time; it is not clear when he was granted a second added class.

71. This rule of precedence lasted well into the eighteenth century. At the death of José Soarez (1736), missionaries still referred to the precedent of Magalhães and Buglio. Two years later, at the death of Jean-Baptiste Régis (1738), they referred to the precedent of Tomé Pereira (1708) and Antoine Thomas (1709) (see *Ruijian lu* (1735–1737), Qianlong 1, 6b; Qianlong 3, 4b). Missionaries who received sponsorship in the eighteenth century quite consistently received two hundred *liang*; besides those previously mentioned, they include Franz Stadlin (1740), Dominique Parrenin (1741), Ehrenbert Xaver Fridelli (1743), André Pereira Jackson (1743), Ignatius Koegler (1746), Teodorico Pedrini (1746), Giovanni (da) Costa (1747), Valentin Chalier (1747), Joseph Marie Anne de Mailla de Moyriac (1748), Anton Gogeisl (1771), August von Hallestein (1774), Michel Benoist (1774), Ignaz Sichelbarth (1780), Félix da Rocha (1781), Jean Matthieu Ventavon Tournu (1787), and José d'Espinha (1788). Exceptions were those who received 100 *liang*: Noël d'Incarville Le Chéron (1757), Léonard de Brossard (1758), Etienne Rousset (1758), and Gilles Thébault (1766). The reasons for these exceptions are not entirely clear. The single other major exception was Giuseppe Castiglione (1766), the only missionary who received three hundred *liang*. In the early nineteenth century the subsidy changed: one hundred and fifty *liang* for José Bernardo de Almeida (1805) and Alexandre de Gouvea (1808), and one hundred *liang* for Domingos-Joachim Ferreira (1824). All these missionaries were Jesuits or had been Jesuits (the Society of Jesus having been suppressed in China in 1775), except for Pedrini and Ferreira who were Lazarists, and de Gouvea who was a

member of the Regular Third Order of St. Francis. For these data, see the text on their tombstones given in Malatesta and Gao (1995) and Chen Dongfeng (1999).

72. Thomas (1688), 188v.

73. Dunyn-Szpot (1700–1710), Tomus II, Pars IV, Cap. XII, n. 1 (1688).

74. For a description of the Christian community of Beijing (with ca. ten thousand Christians) at the eve of Verbiest's death, see Witek (1995).

75. Dunyn-Szpot (1700–1710), Tomus II, Pars IV, Cap. XII, n. 1 (1688): "Tumquechamus" (normally transcription similar to Tong Guozhang); see also *Zhengjiao fengbao*, 89b. This is probably Tong Guowei (d. 1719), uncle of the Kangxi Emperor and father of an imperial consort who was raised to the rank of Empress in 1689 (with the posthumous name Xiaoyi Renhuanghou); see *ECCP*, 795–96. Tong Guowei's brother Tong Guogang (d. 1690) was also addressed by Kangxi as "uncle" (*jiujiu*). He was one of the signers of the Treaty of Nerchinsk in 1689; see *ECCP*, 794–95.

76. Dunyn-Szpot (1700–1710), Tomus II, Pars IV, Cap. XII, n. 1 (1688) mentions "Chao laoye," most probably the aforementioned Zhao Chang; see also *Zhengjiao fengbao* (1894), 89b.

77. Le Comte (1990), 85, mentions "sept cents écus d'or" / (1737), 52: "seven hundred golden crowns"; Thomas speaks of "trecenti & quinquageni [350] aurei nummi Sinici" (Dunyn-Szpot [1700–1710], Tomus II, Pars IV, Cap. XI, n. 4 (1688)); the latter corresponds to the stele money of an official of the first rank. See *Qinding libu zeli*, *juan* 167, 1b; vol. 2, 1010; *Qinding daQing huidian zeli* (1768), *juan* 91, 30a; *SKQS*, vol. 622, 875.

78. Du Halde (1738–1741), vol. 2, 20–21. Compare with Du Halde (1735), vol. 3, 98–100; (1736), vol. 3, 118–22.

79. Le Comte (1990), 84 / (1737), 50.

80. A surplice is a ritual dress, a large-sleeved half-length tunic made of fine linen or cotton, shorter than an alb. It is the choir dress worn by the clergy and also the vestment for processions or the administration of certain rituals, and is also worn by assistants.

81. Zürcher (1997), 630–32, 650.

82. *Xichao ding'an* (version 2), *WXXB*, vol. 3, 1747–48; *XC*, 171.

83. *Xichao ding'an* (version 2), *WXXB*, vol. 3, 1781–82; *XC*, 178–9; Malatesta and Gao (1995), 139; another modern English translation is in *CCS* 6 (1933), 33–35.

84. Cf. Honey (1981), 85ff.

85. Based on Weinberg (2002), 72, 145–46, 193.

86. Honey (1981), 85.

87. According to Liu Xie's *Wenxin diaolong*, "those who can write an elegy (*lei*) on the occasion of a death are capable of becoming ministers. . . . It was not the prac-

tice for a person inferior in social status to write an elegy for his superior, or for a younger man to write an elegy for an older one. In case of the ruler, heaven was invoked to write his elegy. To read an elegy before the dead and to confer upon him a posthumous title is a ceremony of very great importance." Liu Xie (Liu Hsieh) (1959), 64 / (1998), 109.

88. The phraseology of Schall's *jiwen* can be found almost in its entirety in other *jiwen*; this is not the case for Verbiest's *jiwen*, nor for his *beiwen* (conclusion based on searching the *Siku quanshu* electronic database).

89. *CCT ARSI*, vol. 12, 381; *Xichao ding'an* (version 2), *WXXB*, vol. 3, 1733; *XC*, 168.

90. "Mors, Funus, & Compendium vitae seu Elogium P. Ferdinandi Verbiest," based on report of A. Thomas, Beijing, 1688. In Dunyn-Szpot, Tomus II, Pars IV, Cap. XII, n. 1 (1688).

91. *Xichao ding'an* (version 2), *WXXB*, vol. 3, 1747, 1781; *XC*, 171, 179; Malatesta and Gao (1995), 139.

92. Le Comte (1737), 44 / (1990), 75: "Il fit des canons qui furent le salut de l'État"; see also "Compendium vitae" by A. Thomas, in Dunyn-Szpot (1700–1710), Tomus II, Pars IV, Cap. XII, n. 4 (1688): "military machines, cast after a European model and introduced amidst the armed battle-array."

93. In a letter most probably written by Grimaldi, SJ (Oct. 1681), ARSI Jap.Sin. 163, 108r (information provided by N. Golvers).

94. One example is the conflicts that occurred between the Jesuits and Matteo Ripa (1682–1746) and other missionaries sent by the Propaganda Fide when they attended the funeral services for the Kangxi Emperor (died Kangxi 61/11/13, or 20 December 1722) and for the mother of the Yongzheng Emperor (died Yongzheng 1/5/23, or 25 June 1723). See Ripa (1939), 119–20; 126–27. The original (more complete) documents will be published by Michele Fatica in the forthcoming volumes of Matteo Ripa, *Giornale (1705–1724)*. For some later examples, see Laamann (2006), 33–34.

95. The events are related in "Acta Pekinensia" (Beijing Journal, or Historical Diary of the Things that Happened since 4 December 1705, the First Arrival of his Excellency Charles-Thomas Maillard de Tournon, Patriarch of Antioch, Apostolic Visitor, with the Power of a Legate a latere) compiled by Kilian Stumpf, SJ (1655–1720), which is currently being translated into English. [Stumpf] (1705–1712), 16ff.; von Collani (2004), 23ff. (information provided by C. von Collani).

96. [Stumpf] (1705–1712), 21.

97. [Stumpf] (1705–1712), 26.

98. See, for example, the reference to the funerary honors in the memorial by Pereira and Thomas (Kangxi 31/11/16, or 2 February 1692) in *Xichao ding'an* (version 2), *WXXB*, vol. 3, 1786–87; *XC*, 183.

8. CONCLUSION: THE METAPHOR
OF TEXTILE WEAVING

1. It is hoped that the readers of this book, on the basis of the material presented, will bring forward other interpretations.

2. For a detailed engagement with the philosophical background on cultural interaction and its methods of study, which is here applied to ritual, see Standaert (2002).

3. For a good discussion of the different reasons for the apparent "failure" of the Jesuit mission in China, see Zürcher (1990b).

4. For an overview of the state of the field in social sciences, see Chazel (1990).

5. As proposed by Robert Dahl in Chazel (1990), 299.

6. Van den Bulck (1996), 34–35, 46.

7. Cohen (1984).

8. See also the subtitle of Jacques Gernet (1982), *Chine et christianisme: Action et réaction*; the title of the English version (1985) turns the book into an "impact model": *China and the Christian Impact: A Conflict of Cultures*.

9. Cohen (1984), 9, 53.

10. For an overview of this approach, see Loomba (1998), esp. 43ff.

11. See, for example, Mignolo (1995), 324. Mignolo applies this method to "Ricci's world map."

12. For more, see Pratt (1992), 6, and Schwartz (1994), 7.

13. Loomba (1998), 49.

14. Mignolo (1995), 18.

15. For the term "interaction" and its related notion of "interactive emergence" applied to the study of the history of maritime Asia, see Wills (1993); Pratt (1992), 6, prefers the term "contact." For similar approaches in the field of anthropology, see especially the writings by Tedlock (1979) on "dialogical anthropology" and Tedlock and Mannheim (1995) on the "dialogic emergence of culture"; in the history of art, see Bailey (1999) and his notion of "global partnership," especially chapter 2.

16. Tedlock and Tedlock (1985), 142.

17. Todorov (1989), 428.

18. Van den Bulck (1996), 93.

19. For the place of the "other" in history, see de Certeau (1969) and especially de Certeau (1973), chapter 4, "L'autre du texte" and the conclusion, "Altérations."

20. For a discussion of this theory of alterity, see Standaert (2002), 28ff., and also Todorov (1979) and (1982a).

21. On this topic see the article by Curto (2005), partly inspired by the collective volume edited by Michel Vovelle (1981).

22. For more on this, see Tedlock (1979), 388; Waldenfels (1995), 43.

23. Tedlock and Tedlock (1985), 122; Clifford (1988), 41, 43, 46–47 (both based on Bakhtin).

24. The underlying assumption from which the search for coherence begins is that any text or ritual is coherent (in the sense defined here), even if certain elements may appear incoherent, illogical, or unrelated to the experience of the twenty-first-century reader. Thomas Kuhn (1977), xii, makes the following suggestion, which can be applied to the text of any culture: "When reading the works of an important thinker, look first for the apparent absurdities in the text and ask yourself how a sensible person could have written them. When you find an answer . . . when those passages make sense, then you may find that more central passages, ones you previously thought you understood, have changed their meaning."

25. Van den Bulck (1996), 23, 98–100.

26. For a general topology of such interaction, see Standaert (2001). The works by Luzbetak (1963) and (1988) have been the inspiration for much of the clarification of these categories.

27. For these words, see Gruzinski (1999), 34–36, 40–42, 56.

28. An overview of these analogies and their application to the cultural exchange between China and Europe in the seventeenth and eighteenth centuries is provided in Standaert (2001), 103ff.

29. For a seventeenth-century representation of a drawloom (*huaji*), see Song Yingxing (1637), *juan shang, nai fu* 25b–26a; for a translation, see Song Yingxing (Sung Ying-hsing) (1966), 55–56. In the European version the male weaver becomes female: Du Halde (1735), vol. 2, between 222–223 (Hausard engraver) / (1736), vol. 2, between 246–247 / (1738–1741), vol. 1, between 352–353.

30. Ivan Marcus (1996) similarly demonstrates how easily medieval Jews could borrow elements of rituals, stories as well as gestures, from the dominant Christian culture.

31. Van Engen (1986), 540–41.

32. See Thoraval (1992).

33. See the appendix for diagrams that help to visualize these characteristics and those that follow. The diagrams are inspired by Scribner, "Ritual and Popular Belief in Catholic Germany at the Time of the Reformation," in Scribner (1987), 45.

34. See also Zürcher (1990b), 33, and Zürcher (1997), 630–32.

35. Herein Catholics differ from Protestants, since for Protestants the very idea that mere human words and gestures could force the Divine Will to act was nothing less than blasphemy and heresy. Catholics claimed that the ritual *presented* God's action, while the Protestant community on the other hand held that ritual at best *represented* or pointed to God's action. See Maher (2002), 196–97.

36. Maher (2002), 204.

37. Maher (2002), 216–17.

38. See Dudink (2007) and *Forgive Us Our Sins* (2006).
39. Castells (1996), 22 and (1997), 6.
40. Turner (1969), 94–95.
41. Turner (1969), 131ff.
42. Pye (1969), 237, describes "contact—ambiguity—recoupment."
43. Lozada (2001), 153.

Chinese Glossary

Authors' names and titles of books mentioned in the bibliography are not repeated in this list.

airen 愛人
anzang houjing 安葬後經
anzang hounian 安葬後念
Anzang lijie 安葬禮節
anzang qianjing 安葬前經
anzang qiannian 安葬前念
anzanghou 安葬後
anzangqian 安葬前
bei 碑
beiwen 碑文
bendi zhi li 本地之禮
Bensang 奔喪
biji 筆記
Bo Yingli 柏應理
buzuo foshi 不做佛事
cha 茶
Changshou 長壽
Changshu 常熟
chaogong tongli 朝貢通例
Cheng Jili 成際理
cheng 誠
chengyi 誠意
chengzhu 成主
chusang 除喪
chuxing gongfu 初行工夫
Cisheng 慈聖
citang 祠堂
dagong 大功

Dai Zhen 戴震
Daisan 代善
dalian 大歛 or 大殮
dao 道
Daoxue 道學
daqi 大七
Dayuantang 大原堂
dian 奠
dianjiu 奠酒
diaoku 弔哭
ding 訂
Dong shi 董氏
Dong'e fei 董鄂妃
Dorgon 多爾袞
Duan 段
duanqizhai 斷七齋
duode 鐸德
duwen 讀文
fangshenghui 放生會
fangxiang 方相
fengshui 風水
foshi 佛事
fufu 俯伏
Fuqing 福清
Fuwen 服問
Giyěsu 傑淑
gong 功
gongguoge 功過格

283

Gonghua 鞏華

gongyang 供養

Gu Yanwu 顧炎武

Guanglu dafu 光祿大夫

Guanglusi 光祿寺

guanli 冠禮

gui 歸

Haiyu zhi xiu 海隅之秀

Han 韓

Hanlin 翰林

Haoguai shi 好怪事

he 合

Hongloumeng 紅樓夢

huaji 花機

Huangdi yu ji . . . Tang Ruowang zhi
    ling 皇帝諭祭 . . . 湯若望之靈

Huangtaiji 皇太極

Huang Zongxi 黃宗羲

Huating 華亭

Huguang tongzhi 湖廣通志

hui 會

huiyue 會約

huizhang 會長

hunli 婚禮

ji 祭

"Ji Yang Qiyuan shiyu" 祭楊淇園
    侍御

jia gongbu youshilang youjia erji 加工
    部右侍郎又加二級

jia 家

Jiading 嘉定

jiali 家禮

jian 儉

Jianchang 建昌

Jiang Dejing 蔣德璟

Jiangfu yinshi jing 降福飲食經

Jianwu 建武

Jianzhuan 開傳

jiao 教

jiaoyou 教友

jiaozhong zhongyou 教中眾友

jiaxun 家訓

jiazhongren 家中人

jin 近

jing 經

Jingling 景陵

Jingshan 景山

jinshi 進士

jinyinding 金銀錠

jiujiu 舅舅

jiwen 祭文

ju'ai 舉哀

ju'ai zhi li 舉哀之禮

jue 覺

juren 舉人

Kang 康

Kangxi 康熙

koutou 叩頭

kuangming 壙銘

lei 誄

Li 李

li 理 (last character of a personal
    name)

li 禮 (ritual)

Li Zhizao 李之藻

Li Zicheng 李自成

Li Zubai 李祖白

lian 殮

lianbujing 殮布經

liang 兩

lianhoujing 殮後經

lianqianjing 殮前經

libeigong jiayin 立碑工價銀

libu 禮部

Lilun 禮論

ling 靈

Linsang yishi 臨喪儀式

Lishi 李氏

Liyidian 禮儀典

Loukeke 漏刻科

Lu Yuanfu 陸元輔

Lü 呂

Luo Wenzao 羅文藻

makui 麻盔

mazu 媽祖

meigui shiwuduan 玫瑰十五端

Miao 繆

Miao Shixiang 繆士向

Mindong 閩東

ming 銘

mingqi 明器

mu 穆

mubei 墓碑

mubiao 墓表

muzhi 墓誌

muzhiming 墓誌銘

naifu 乃服

nanmu 楠木

Nei (Hanlin) mishuyuan 內翰林密書院

neichao 內朝

neige 內閣

neiyuan 內院

nianfohui 念佛會

Nurhaci 努爾哈赤

qi 漆

Qin 秦

Qinmin 勤敏

qinqi 親戚

Qintianjian 欽天監

Qiu Lianghou 邱良厚

qu 去

Renhui yue 仁會約

renhui 仁會

rike 日課

riyong leishu 日用類書

Rong 榮

rouyuan zhi ren 柔遠之仁

rujia 儒家

rujiao 儒教

rulian hounian 入殮後念

Rulian lijie 入殮禮節

rulian qiannian 入殮前念

rulianhou 入殮後

rulianjing 入殮經

rulianqian 入殮前

sang 喪

Sangfu sizhi 喪服四制

Sangfu 喪服

Sangji zashuo 喪祭雜說

sangjilei 喪祭類

sangli 喪禮

Sangli yishi 喪禮儀式

sangzang 喪葬

Sannianwen 三年問

Sashengshuijing 洒聖水經

Sha 沙

Shaanbei 陝北

shangdi 上帝

shangke xinxiang 尚克歆享

shangxiang 上香

shanshu 善書

Shanzhonghui 善終會

Shanzhongjing 善終經

Shaozhou 韶州

Shen Que 沈榷

shen 深 (deep)

shen 神 (spirit)

Shenerfu 申爾福

shenfu 神父

Shenglian bujing 聖殮布經

Shengmu daowen 聖母禱文

Shengmujing 聖母經

Shengren liepin daowen 聖人列品禱文

shengshen (or: *zhusheng*) *xiangtonggong* 聖神(諸聖)相通功

shengyu 聖諭

shi 事 (to serve)

shi 實 (solid)

shi 時 (timely)

shi 諡 or 謚 (posthumous title)

shifa 諡法

shiqin 事親

Shisangli 士喪禮

shisi ru sheng, shiwang ru cun 事死如生, 事亡如存

shiwei 侍衛

shixue 實學

Shouhuangdian 壽皇殿

Shunzhi 順治

shuo de shuangkuai touli 說得爽快透理

Shuren 淑人

sibai 四拜

sidai 司代

sima 緦麻

sujia 俗家

Taiguan rumu anzang 抬棺入墓安葬

"Tangong" 檀弓

Tangong xia 檀弓下

teci 特賜

tezhi 特旨

tian 天

tianzhu 天主

Tianzhujing 天主經

tie 帖

Tong Guogang 佟國綱

Tong Guowei 佟國維

tonggong 通功

tonggongdan 通功單

tongshanhui 同善會

Tongwei jiaoshi 通微教師

Wan Sitong 萬斯同

Wang Wan 汪琬

Wang Yangming 王陽明

Wang Yinglin 王應麟

wei 位

Wensang 問喪

Wenzhou 溫州

Wu Daonan 吳道南

"Wulin Yang mu Lü gongren zhuan" 武林楊母呂恭人傳

wuxie 無邪

Xi Sa 襲薩

xianggong 相公

xiangyue 鄉約

xiao 孝

Xiaocheng 孝誠

Xiaocilu 孝慈錄

xiaogong 小功

Xiaojing yanyi 孝經衍義

Xiaojing yanyi xu 孝經衍義序

Xiaokang 孝康

xiaolian 小斂 or 小殮

Xiaosheng 孝聖

xiaoshun fumu 孝順父母

Xiaoxian huanghou 孝獻皇后

Xiaoyi Renhuanghou 孝懿仁皇后

Xiaozhao 孝昭

Xiaozhuang 孝莊

xiaozi 孝子

xie 邪

Xingli daquan 性理大全

xingshu 行述

Xinjing 信經

Xintiansi 新添司

xiucai 秀才

Xu (Hiu) 許

Xu Fuyuan 徐復元

Xu Guangqi 徐光啟

Xu Leshan 許樂善

Xu Qianxue 徐乾學

Xu Yongchang 徐永昌

Xu Zuanzeng 許纘曾

xu 卹 (sponsorship)

xu 虛 (void)

xudian 呬典

Yan Ruoju 嚴若璩

Yan Yuan 顏元

Yan Zanhua 嚴贊化

yan zheng li shun 言整理順

Yang Guangxian 楊光先

Yang Tingyun 楊廷筠

yi 意 (intention)

yi 義 (righteousness)

yifu 衣服

Yili 儀禮

Ying Huiqian 應撝謙

Yinreng 胤礽

yiwan gongfu 已完工夫

yizhi 儀制

youli youli dan kong dezui yu ren 有理
  有理但恐得罪於人

youyu 有餘

yue 閱

Yuedan tang 曰旦堂

yuezhong zhi li 粵中之禮

zang 葬

Zangshu 葬書

zangyin 銀葬

zaofengong jiayin 造墳工價銀

Zhalan 柵欄

zhancui 斬衰

Zhang 張

Zhang Erqi 張爾歧

Zhang Geng 張賡

Zhang Lüxiang 張履祥

Zhang Xianzhong 張獻忠

zhao 昭

Zhao Chang 趙昌

zheng 正

(zhi)jiyin （致）祭銀

zhiji 致祭

zhima 紙馬

zhiming 誌銘

zhiqian 紙錢

zhong 終

zhong(ren) 眾（人）

zhonghou daowen 終後禱文

Zhongyong 中庸

zhongyou 眾友

Zhoushan 舟山

Zhu Xi 朱熹

Zhu Yizun 朱彝尊

zhu 主

zhuanzhuang 傳狀

zhubao shengren 主保聖人

zhuke qinglisi 主客清吏司

zhusheng guiyi 祝聖規儀

zhuwen 祝文

zicui 齊衰

Ziyang jiafa 紫陽家法

zu 卒

zuku 卒哭

zuogongde 做功德

zuoqi 做七

zuoshenggong 做聖功

zuoyi 作揖

Abbreviations

100RD: 100 Roman Documents Concerning the Chinese Rites Controversy (1645–1941). 1992. Trans. Donald F. St. Sure. Ed. Ray R. Noll. San Francisco: Ricci Institute.

ARSI Jap.Sin.: Archivum Romanum Societatis Iesu, Japonica-Sinica Collection, Rome.

BAV: Bibliotheca Apostolica Vaticana, Rome.

BnF: Bibliothèque nationale de France, Paris. See also Maurice Courant. 1902–1912. *Catalogue des livres chinois, coréens, japonais, etc.* 8 vols. Paris: Ernest Leroux.

CCS: Collectanea Commissionis Synodalis (in Sinis). 1928–1947. Beijing.

CCT ARSI: Yesuhui Luoma dang'anguan MingQing tianzhujiao wenxian 耶穌會羅馬檔案館明清天主教文獻 *(Chinese Christian Texts from the Roman Archives of the Society of Jesus).* 2002. 12 vols. Ed. Nicolas Standaert (鐘鳴旦) and Ad Dudink (杜鼎克). Taibei: Ricci Institute.

CCT ZKW: Xujiahui zangshulou MingQing tianzhujiao wenxian 徐家匯藏書樓明清天主教文獻 *(Chinese Christian Texts from the Zikawei Library).* 1996. 5 vols. Ed. Nicolas Standaert (鐘鳴旦), Ad Dudink (杜鼎克), Huang Yi-long (黃一農) and Chu Ping-Yi (祝平一). Taibei: Fu Jen Catholic University Press.

CMCS: Siku quanshu cunmu congshu 四庫全書存目叢書. 1997. Jinan: Qi Lu shushe chubanshe.

CPF (1893): *Collectana S. Congregationis de Propaganda Fide seu decreta, instructiones, rescripta pro apostolicis missionibus ex tabulario eiusdem Sacrae Congregationis deprompta.* 1893. Rome: Typographia Polyglotta.

CPF (1907): *Collectana S. Congregationis de Propaganda Fide seu decreta, instructiones, rescripta pro apostolicis missionibus.* Vol. 1: *Ann. 1622–1866.* 1907. Rome: Typographia Polyglotta.

DMB: Dictionary of Ming Biography. 1976. 2 vols. Ed. L. Carrington Goodrich and Chao-ying Fang. New York and London: Columbia University Press.

ECCP: Eminent Chinese of the Ch'ing Period (1644–1912). 1943–1944. 2 vols. Ed. Arthur W. Hummel. Washington, D.C.: Government Printing Office.

FR: Matteo Ricci. *Fonti Ricciane.* 1942–1949. 3 vols. Ed. Pasquale d'Elia. Rome: La Libreria dello Stato.

HCC: Handbook of Christianity in China: Volume One (635–1800). 2001. Ed. Nicolas Standaert. Leiden: Brill.

OS: *Opere Storiche del P. Matteo Ricci S.I.* Vol. 1: *Commentari della Cina*, 1911. Vol. 2: *Le Lettere dalla Cina (1580–1610), con appendice di documenti inediti*, 1913. Ed. Pietro Tacchi Venturi. Macerata: Filippo Giorgetti.

SF: *Sinica Franciscana*

    III. Anastasius van den Wyngaert, ed. 1936. *Relationes et Epistolas Fratrum Minorum Saeculi XVII*. Quaracchi [Florence].

    IV. Anastasius van den Wyngaert, ed. 1942. *Relationes et Epistolas Fratrum Minorum Saeculi XVII et XVIII*. Quaracchi-Florence.

    V. Anastasius van den Wyngaert and Georges Mensaert, ed. 1954. *Relationes et Epistolas Illmi D. Fr. Bernardini della Chiesa O.F.M*. Rome.

    VI. Georges Mensaert, ed. 1961. *Relationes et Epistolas Primorum Fratrum Minorum Italorum (Saeculi XVII et XVIII)*. Rome.

    VII. Georges Mensaert, Fortunato Margiotti, and Antonio Sisto Rosso, ed. 1965. *Relationes et Epistolas Fratrum Minorum Hispanorum in Sinis qui a. 1672–1681 Missionem Ingressi Sunt*. Rome.

    VIII. Georges Mensaert, ed. 1975. *Relationes et Epistolas Fratrum Minorum Hispanorum in Sinis qui a. 1684–1692 Missionem Ingressi Sunt*. Rome.

SKQS: *(Wenyuange) Siku quanshu* (文淵閣) 四庫全書. 1983–1986. Taibei: Commercial Press.

WX: *Tianzhujiao dongchuan wenxian* 天主教東傳文獻. 1965. Ed. Wu Xiangxiang 吳相湘. (Zhongguo shixue congshu 中國史學叢書 24) Taibei: Xuesheng shuju.

WXSB: *Tianzhujiao dongchuan wenxian sanbian* 天主教東傳文獻三編. 1972. 6 vols. Ed. Wu Xiangxiang 吳相湘. (Zhongguo shixue congshu xubian 中國史學叢書續編 21) Taibei: Xuesheng shuju.

WXXB: *Tianzhujiao dongchuan wenxian xubian* 天主教東傳文獻緒編. 1966. 3 vols. Ed. Wu Xiangxiang 吳相湘. (Zhongguo shixue congshu 中國史學叢書 40) Taibei: Xuesheng shuju.

XC: *Xichao chongzhengji-Xichao ding'an (waisanzhong)* 熙朝崇正集-熙朝定案 (外三种). 2006. Ed. Han Qi 韩琦 and Wu Min 吴旻. Beijing: Zhonghua shuju.

Bibliography

A. L. 1939. "La classificazione e catalogazione dell'antica biblioteca del Pe-t'ang." *Il Pensiero missionario* 11: 242–43.

Acta Cantonensia Authentica in quibus praxis Missionariorum Sinensium Societatis Jesu circa ritus Sinenses approbata est communi consensu Patrum Dominicanorum, & Jesuitarum, qui erant in China; atque illorum subscriptione firmata. 1700. s.l.

Ahern, Emily Martin. 1973. *The Cult of the Dead in a Chinese Village.* Stanford: Stanford University Press.

Aleni, Giulio 艾儒略. 1637. *Xifang dawen* 西方答問. 2 *juan.* BAV, Borgia Cinese 324.17. Repr. in John L. Mish, "Creating an Image of Europe for China: Aleni's *Hsi-fang ta-wen.*" *Monumenta Serica* 23 (1964): 4–30.

Ames, Roger T., and David L. Hall. 2001. *Focusing the Familiar: A Translation and Philosophical Interpretation of the Zhongyong.* Honolulu: University of Hawai'i Press.

Amiot, Joseph Marie. 1780. "Mort et funérailles de l'Impératrice Mère (1777)." In *Mémoires concernant l'histoire, les sciences, les arts, les mœurs, les usages des Chinois,* vol. 6, 346–73. Paris: Nyon.

An xiansheng xingshu 安先生行述 (also entitled *Yuanxi Jingming An xiansheng xingshu* 遠西景明安先生行述). Ca. 1677. Ed. Lodovico Buglio 利類思 & Ferdinand Verbiest 南懷仁. ARSI Jap.Sin. III, 23.5; II, 165.3. In *CCT ARSI,* vol. 12, 323–34. See also modern punctuated version in *XC,* 407–9.

Ariès, Philippe. 1977. *L'homme devant la mort.* Paris: Seuil.

———. 1981. *The Hour of Our Death.* Trans. H. Weaver. Harmondsworth, U.K.: Penguin.

———. 1985. *Images of Man and Death.* Trans. J. Lloyd. Cambridge, MA: Harvard University Press.

Augustine. 1963. *The City of God Against the Pagans.* 7 vols. Trans. William M. Green. Cambridge: Harvard University Press.

Bailey, Gauvin Alexander. 1999. *Art on the Jesuit Missions in Asia and Latin America, 1542–1773.* Toronto: University of Toronto Press.

Bartoli, Daniello. 1663. *Dell'historia della compagnia di Giesu: La Cina terza parte dell'Asia.* Rome: Varesei.

Bell, Catherine. 1992. *Ritual Theory, Ritual Practice.* Oxford: Oxford University Press.

———. 1997. *Ritual: Perspectives and Dimensions*. Oxford: Oxford University Press.

Berling, Judith A. 1987. "Orthopraxy." In *The Encyclopedia of Religion*, ed. Mircea Eliade, vol. 11, 129–32. New York: Macmillan.

Bernand, Carmen, and Serge Gruzinski. 1988. *De l'idolâtrie: Une archéologie des sciences religieuses*. Paris: Seuil.

Bernard, Henri. 1945. "Les adaptations d'ouvrages européens: bibliographie chronologique depuis la venue des portugais à Canton jusqu'à la Mission française de Pékin, 1514–1688." *Monumenta Serica* 10: 1–57, 309–88.

Bettray, Johannes. 1955. *Die Akkommodationsmethode des P. Matteo Ricci S.J. in China*. Rome: Univ. Pont. Gregoriana.

Biermann, Benno. 1927. *Die Anfänge der neueren Dominikanermission in China*. Münster: Aschendorff.

Binski, Paul. 1996. *Medieval Death: Ritual and Representation*. London: The British Museum Press.

Black, Christopher. 1989. *Italian Confraternities in the Sixteenth Century*. Cambridge: Cambridge University Press.

Bontinck, François. 1962. *La lutte autour de la liturgie chinoise aux 17e et 18e siècles*. Leuven: Nauwelaerts.

Bosmans, Henri. 1912. *Ferdinand Verbiest: Directeur de l'observatoire de Peking (1623–1688)*. Leuven: Cueterick.

———. 1914. "La notice nécrologique de Ferdinand Verbiest." *Annales de la société d'émulation de Bruges* 64: 102–33.

Breviarium Romanum (ex Decreto Sacrosancti Concilii Tridentini restitutum). 1568. Repr., Antwerpiae: Ex officina Plantiniana, 1617.

Brockey, Liam Matthew. 2005. "Flowers of Faith in an Emporium of Vices: The 'Portuguese' Jesuit Church in Seventeenth Century Peking." *Monumenta Serica* 53: 45–71.

———. 2007. *Journey to the East: The Jesuit Mission to China, 1579–1724*. Cambridge, MA: Harvard University Press.

Brokaw, Cynthia J. 1991. *Ledgers of Merit and Demerit: Social Change and Moral Order in Late Imperial China*. Princeton: Princeton University Press.

Brook, Timothy. 1989. "Funerary Ritual and the Building of Lineages in Late Imperial China." *Harvard Journal of Asiatic Studies* 49 (2): 465–99.

Brunner, Paul. 1964. *L'Euchologe de la mission de Chine: Editio princeps et développements jusqu'à nos jours (Contribution à l'histoire des livres des prières)*. Münster (i.W.): Aschendorffsche Verlagsbuchhandlung.

[Buglio, Lodovico]. 1688. "Abrégé de la vie et de la mort du R. Père Gabriel de Magaillans, de la Compagnie de Jesus, Missionnaire de la Chine: Fait par le R. Père Loüis Buglio, son Compagnon inséparable durant trente-six ans; & envoyé de Pe Kim l'an 1677." In *Nouvelle relation de la Chine, contenant la description des particularitez les plus considerables de ce grand empire*, by Gabriel de Magalhães, 371–85. Paris: Claude Barbin.

———. 1689. "An Abridgment of the Life and Death of F. Gabriel Magaillans, of the Society of Jesus, Missionary into China, written by F. Lewis Buglio, his inseparable Companion for six and thirty Years; and sent from Pe Kim in the Year 1677." In *A New History of the Empire of China, Containing a Description of the Politick Government, Towns, Manners and Customs of the People, &c.*, by Gabriel de Magalhães, 340–52. London: Samuel Holford.

Bürkler, Xaver. 1942. *Die Sonn- und Festtagsfeier in der katholischen Chinamission: Eine geschichtlich-pastorale Untersuchung*. Rome: Herder.

Callewaert, Camillus. 1940. "De officio defunctorum." In *Sacris Erudiri*, by Camillus Callewaert, 169–77. Steenbrugge: Abbatia S. Petri de Aldenburgo.

Castells, Manuel. 1996. *The Rise of the Network Society*. Oxford: Blackwell.

———. 1997. *The Power of Identity*. Oxford: Blackwell.

Catholic Encyclopedia, Online Edition. 2003.

Certeau, Michel de. 1969. *L'étranger ou l'union dans la différence*. Paris: DDB.

———. 1973. *L'absent de l'histoire*. Paris: Maison Mame.

Chan, Albert. 1990. "Towards a Chinese Church: The Contribution of Philippe Couplet S.J. (1622–1693)." In *Philippe Couplet, S.J. (1623–1693), The Man Who Brought China to Europe*, ed. J. Heyndrickx, 55–86. Nettetal: Steyler Verlag.

———. 2002. *Chinese Books and Documents in the Jesuit Archives in Rome: A Descriptive Catalogue: Japonica-Sinica I–IV*. New York: M. E. Sharpe.

Chau, Adam Yuet. 2006. *Miraculous Response: Doing Popular Religion in Contemporary China*. Stanford: Stanford University Press.

Chazel, François. 1990. "Influence." In *Encyclopaedia Universalis*, vol. 12, 299–301. Paris: Encyclopaedia Universalis.

Chen Dongfeng 陈东风. 1999. *Yesu huishi mubei renwu zhi kao* 耶稣会士墓碑人物志考. Beijing: Zhongguo wenlian chubanshe.

Chen, Gang. 2000. "Death Rituals in a Chinese Village: An Old Tradition in Contemporary Social Context." Ph.D. diss., Ohio State University.

Chen Huaizhen 陳懷楨. 1934. "Zhongguo hunsang fengsu zhi fenxi" 中國婚喪風俗之分析. *Shehui xuejie* 社會學界 8 (June): 117–53.

Chen Jiang 陈江. 2006. "Mingdai zhongwanqi de liyi zhi bian jiqi shehui neihan: Yi Jiangnan diqu wei kaocha zhongxin" 明代中晚期的礼仪之变及其社会内涵: 以江南地區为考察中心. *Shilin* 史林 (1): 92–102.

Chen Jiru 陳繼儒. Ca. 1641. *Chen Meigong xiansheng quanji* 陳眉公先生全集. 60 *juan*.

Chen Que 陳確. 1979. *Chen Que ji* 陳確集. 2 vols. Beijing: Zhonghua shuju.

Chen Shuguo 陈戍国. 2002. *Zhongguo lizhishi: Yuan Ming Qing juan* 中国礼制史: 元明清卷. Changsha: Hunan jiaoyu chubanshe.

Chiffoleau, Jacques. 1980. *La comptabilité de l'au-delà: Les hommes, la mort et la religion dans la région d'Avignon à la fin du moyen age*. Rome: Ecole française de Rome.

China on Paper: European and Chinese Works from the Late Sixteenth to the Early

Nineteenth Century. 2007. Edited by Marcia Reed and Paola Demattè. Los Angeles: Getty Research Institute.

Chow, Kai-wing. 1994. *The Rise of Confucian Ritualism in Late Imperial China: Ethics, Classics, and Lineage Discourse.* Stanford: Stanford University Press.

———. 2004. *Publishing, Culture, and Power in Early Modern China.* Stanford: Stanford University Press.

Chūgoku nichiyo ruisho shusei 中國日用類書集成. 1999–. Tokyo: Kyuko shoin.

Chung, Sue Fawn, and Priscilla Wegars. 2005. *Chinese American Death Rituals: Respecting the Ancestors.* Lanham, MD: AltaMira Press.

Cieslik, Hubert. 1950. "Begräbnisritten in der alten Japan-Mission." *Zeitschrift für Missions- und Religionswissenschaft* 34: 241–57. Repr. in Hubert Cieslik, *Publikationen über das Christentum in Japan: Veröffentlichungen in europäischen Sprachen,* ed. Margret Dietrich and Arcadio Schwade, 325–37. Frankfurt am Main: Peter Lang, 2004.

Clifford, James. 1988. *The Predicament of Culture: Twentieth-Century Ethnography, Literature, and Art.* Cambridge, MA: Harvard University Press.

Cohen, Paul A. 1984. *Discovering History in China: American Historical Writing on the Recent Chinese Past.* New York: Columbia University Press.

Cohn, Samuel K. 1988. *Death and Property in Siena, 1205–1800.* Baltimore: Johns Hopkins University Press.

Cole, Alan. 1998. *Mothers and Sons in Chinese Buddhism.* Stanford: Stanford University Press.

Collani, Claudia von. 2004. "The Events of Beijing: Ritual Problems from China as Described in the 'Acta Pekinensia' by Kilian Stumpf SJ." Paper presented at the workshop "Chinese and Christian Rituality in Late Imperial China," K. U. Leuven, 17–19 June 2004.

Cordier, Henri. 1909. *Catalogue des albums chinois et ouvrages relatifs à la Chine, conservés au Cabinet des estampes de la bibliothèque nationale.* Paris: Imprimerie Nationale. Same version in *Journal asiatique,* September–October, 1909, 209–62.

Couplet, Philippe. 1688. *Histoire d'une dame chrétienne de la Chine, ou par occasion les usages de ces Peuples, l'établissement de la Religion, les manières des Missionnaires, & les Exercices de Pieté des nouveaux Chrétiens sont expliquez.* Paris: Esteinne Michallet.

———. 1691. *Historia de una gran Señora christiana de la China, llamada Dona Candida Hiu.* Madrid: Antonio Roman.

———. 1694. *Historie van eene groote, christene mevrouwe van China met naeme mevrouw Candida Hiu.* Antwerp: Knobbaert by Franciscus Muller.

Cummins, James Sylvester. 1993. *A Question of Rites: Friar Domingo Navarrete and the Jesuits in China.* Aldershot: Scolar Press.

Curto, Diogo Ramada. 2005. "The Jesuits and Cultural Intermediacy in the Early Modern World." *Archivum Historicum Societatis Iesu* 74: 3–22.

DaMing huidian (Wanli) 大明會典 (萬曆). 1587. Repr., Taibei: Xinwenfeng, 1976.

(Da)Ming jili (大) 明集禮. 1530. 53 *juan*. Ed. Xu Yikui 徐一夔. Beijing: Neifu. In *SKQS*, vols. 649–50.

Dapper, Olfert. 1670. *Gedenkwaerdig bedryf der Nederlandsche Oost-Indische Maetschappye, op de kuste en in het keizerrijk van Taising of Sina: behelzende het tweede gezandschap . . . en het derde gezandschap aen Konchy, Tartarsche keizer van Sina en Oost-Tartarye: onder beleit van zijne Ed. Pieter van Hoorn. Beneffens een beschryving van geheel Sina . . . geschreven door Dr. O. Dapper.* Amsterdam: Jacob van Meurs.

———. 1671. [erroneously attributed to Arnoldus Montanus] *Atlas Chinensis: Being a Second Part of A Relation of Remarkable Passages in Two Embassies from the East-India Company of the United Provinces to the Vice-Roy Singlamong and General Taising Lipovi and to Konchi, Emperor of China and East-Tartary. . . .* London: J. Ogilby.

DaQing huidian (Kangxichao) 大清會典 (康熙朝). 1696. 162 *juan*. Repr., Taibei: Wenhai chubanshe, 1992.

DaQing shichao shengxun 大清十朝聖訓. 1965. Taibei: Wenhai chubanshe.

DaQing tongli 大清通禮. 1736. 50 *juan*. In *SKQS*, vol. 655.

Dean, Kenneth. 1988. "Funerals in Fujian." *Cahiers d'Extrême Asie* 4: 19–78.

Dehergne, Joseph. 1956. "Les congrégations dans l'empire de Chine aux XVIIe et XVIIIe siècles." In *Maria: Études sur la Sainte Vierge*, ed. Hubert du Manoir, vol. 4, 967–80. Paris: Beauchesne.

———. 1973. *Répertoire des jésuites de Chine de 1552 à 1800.* Rome: Institutum Historicum S.I.

Der Neue Welt-Bott: Allerhand so Lehr- als Geistreiche Letter, Schrifften und Reis-Beschreibungen, Welche von denen Missionariis der Gesellschafft Jesu Aus Beyden Indien, und andern Über Meer gelegenen Ländern Seit An. 1642. biß auf das Jahr 1726 in Europa angelanget seynd (Tomus 1). 1726. Ed. Joseph Stöcklein. Augspurg: Veith.

Despland, Michel. 1979. *La religion en Occident: Évolution des idées et du vécu.* Montréal and Paris: Fides and Cerf.

Despland, Michel, and Gérard Vallée. 1992. *Religion in History: The Word, the Idea, the Reality.* Waterloo, ON: Wilfrid Laurier University Press.

De Ursis, Sabatino. 2000. "P. Matheus Ricci S.I. Relação escripta pelo seu companheiro, P. Sabatino De Ursis S.I." ARSI Jap.Sin. 113. Modern edition, *Relazione della morte del P. Matteo Ricci: Uno dei primi Padri della Compagnia di Gesù che entrarono nel regno della Cina con alcune cose riguardanti la sua vita*, ed. and trans. Gaetano Ricciardolo. Rome: private edition.

Dictionnaire de théologie catholique. 1903–1972. 15 vols. Paris: Letouzey.

Ding Linghua 丁凌华. 2000. *Zhongguo sangfu zhidu shi* 中国丧服制度史. Shanghai: Renmin chubanshe.

Doolittle, Justus. 1867. *Social Life of the Chinese: With Some Account of their Religious, Governmental, Educational, and Business Customs and Opinions.* 2 vols. New York: Harper.

Doré, Henri. 1911. *Recherches sur les superstitions en Chine*. Vol. 1, *Les pratiques supersti-tieuses*. Shanghai: Impr. de la Mission catholique.

A Dream of Red Mansions (*Hong lou meng* 紅樓夢). 1978. 3 vols. Trans. Yang Hsien-yi and Gladys Yang. Beijing: Foreign Languages Press.

DuBois, Thomas D. 2005. *The Sacred Village: Social Change and Religious Life in Rural North China*. Honolulu: University of Hawai'i Press.

Dudink, Ad. 2000. "*Nangong shudu* (1620), *Poxie ji* (1640), and Western Reports on the Nanjing Persecution (1616/1617)." *Monumenta Serica* 48: 133–265.

———. 2001. "The Image of Xu Guangqi as Author of Christian Texts (A Bibliographical Appraisal)." In *Statecraft and Intellectual Renewal in Late Ming China: The Cross-Cultural Synthesis of Xu Guangqi (1562–1633)*, ed. Catherine Jami, Peter Engelfriet, and Gregory Blue, 99–152. Leiden: Brill.

———. 2006. *Chinese Books and Documents (pre-1900) in the Royal Library of Belgium at Brussels*. Brussels: Koninklijke Bibliotheek van België.

———. 2007. "The Holy Mass in Seventeenth and Eighteenth Century China." In *A Lifelong Dedication to the China Mission: Essays Presented in Honor of Father Jeroom Heyndrickx, CICM*, ed. Noël Golvers and Sara Lievens, 207–326. Leuven: Ferdinand Verbiest Institute.

Du Halde, Jean-Baptiste. 1735. *Description geographique, historique, chronologique, poli-tique et physique de l'empire de la Chine et de la Tartarie chinoise*. 4 vols. Paris: P.-G. Le Mercier.

———. 1736. *Description geographique, historique, chronologique, politique et physique de l'empire de la Chine et de la Tartarie chinoise*. 4 vols. La Haye: H. Scheuleer.

———. 1738–1741. *A Description of the Empire of China and Chinese-Tartary, Together with the Kingdoms of Korea and Tibet: Containing the Geography and History (Natural as well as Civil) of those Countries*. 2 vols. London: T. Gardner.

Duli tongkao 讀禮通考. 1696. 120 *juan*. Ed. Xu Qianxue 徐乾學. In *SKQS*, vols. 112–14.

Dunyn-Szpot, Thomas-Ignatius. 1700–1710. "Collectanea Historiae Sinensis ab anno 1641 ad annum 1700 ex variis documentis in Archivo Societatis existentibus excerpta, duobus tomis distincta." ARSI Jap.Sin. 104–5, I–II.

Duoshu 鐸書. Ca. 1641. Ed. Han Lin 韓霖. In *CCT ZKW*, vol. 2, 599–862.

Ebersole, Gary L. 2000. "The Function of Ritual Weeping Revisited: Affective Expression and Moral Discourse." *History of Religions* 39 (3): 211–46.

Ebrey, Patricia Buckley, trans. 1991a. *Chu Hsi's Family Rituals: A Twelfth-Century Chinese Manual for the Performance of Cappings, Weddings, Funerals, and Ancestral Rites*. Princeton: Princeton University Press.

———. 1991b. *Confucianism and Family Rituals in Imperial China: A Social History in Writing about Rites*. Princeton: Princeton University Press.

Edwards, E. D. 1948. "A Classified Guide to the Thirteen Classes of Chinese Prose." *Bulletin of the School of Oriental and African Studies* 12: 770–88.

Eire, Carlos M. N. 1995. *From Madrid to Purgatory: The Art and Craft of Dying in Sixteenth-Century Spain*. Cambridge: Cambridge University Press.

Elliott, Mark C. 2001. *The Manchu Way: The Eight Banner and Ethnic Identity in Late Imperial China*. Stanford: Stanford University Press.

Elman, Bejamin A. 2000. *A Cultural History of Civil Examinations in Late Imperial China*. Berkeley: University of California Press.

Esherick, Joseph W. 1998. "Cherishing Sources from Afar." *Modern China* 24 (2): 135–61.

Europe Informed: An Exhibition of Early Books Which Acquainted Europe With the East. 1966. Cambridge and New York: Harvard College Library et al.

Feil, Ernst. 1986. *Religion: Die Geschichte eines neuzeitlichen Grundbegriffs von Frühchristentum bis zum Reformation*. Göttingen: Vandenhoeck & Ruprecht.

———. 1997. *Die Geschichte eines neuzeitlichen Grundbegriffs zwischen Reformation und Rationalismus (ca. 1540–1620)*. Göttingen: Vandenhoeck & Ruprecht.

Feng Jianzhi 冯建至. 2006. "Wuyuanxian Xitouxiang Xiachengcun sangzang yishi kaocha baogao" 婺源县溪头乡下呈村丧葬仪式考察报告. *Zhongguo yinyuexue* 中国音乐学 1: 101–4.

Fezzi, Luca. 1999. "Osservazioni sul *De Christiana Expeditione apud Sinas suscepta ab Societate Iesu* di Nicolas Trigault." *Rivista di Storia e Letteratura Religiosa* 35 (3): 541–66.

Filippucci, Francesco Saverio. 1700. *De Sinensium ritibus politicis acta, seu R. P. Francisci Xaverii Philipucci Missionarii Sinensis è Societate Jesu, Praeludium ad plenum disquisitionem, an bonâ vel malâ fide impugnentur opiniones et praxes Missionariorum Societatis Jesu in regno Sinarum ad cultum Confucii et defunctorum pertinentes*. Paris: Nicolaum Pie. Ms. version in Biblioteca Nazionale Centrale Vittorio Emanuele II, Rome Ges. 1249/7.

Fontaney, Jean de. 1707. "Lettre du Pere de Fontaney, missionnaire de la Compagnie de Jésus à la Chine, au R. P. de La Chaize, de la mesme Compagnie, Confesseur du Roy. A Tcheou-chan, port de la Chine dans la province de Tche-Kian a 18 lieues de Nimpo, le 15 fevrier 1703." In *Lettres édifiantes et curieuses, écrites des Missions Étrangères par quelques Missionnaires de la Compagnie de Jésus: VII. Recueil*, 61–366. Paris: Nicolas Le Clerc.

———. 1979. "Les débuts de la mission française de Pékin." In *Lettres édifiantes et curieuses de Chine par les missionnaires jésuites 1702–1776*, ed. Isabelle and Jean-Louis Vissière, 116–43. Paris: Garnier-Flammarion.

Forgive Us Our Sins: Confession in Late Ming and Early Qing China. 2006. Ed. Nicolas Standaert and Ad Dudink. Monumenta Serica Monograph Series 55. Sankt Augustin/Nettetal: Steyler Verlag.

Fortescue, Adrian, and J. B. O'Connell. 1962. *The Ceremonies of the Roman Rite Described*. London: Burns & Oates. Originally published 1917.

Foss, Theodore N. 1983. "Nicholas Trigault, S.J.—Amanuensis or Propagandist? The

Rôle of the Editor of *Della entrata della Compagnia di Giesù e Christianità nella Cina.*" Addendum to *International Symposium on Chinese-Western Cultural Interchange in Commemoration of the 400th Anniversary of the Arrival of Matteo Ricci, S.J. in China.* Taipei: Fujen.

Franke, Herbert. 1942. "Patents for Hereditary Ranks and Honorary Titles during the Ch'ing Dynasty." *Monumenta Serica* 7: 38–67.

Französisches etymologisches Wörterbuch. 1948–1957. 14 vols. Edited by Walther von Wartburg. Tübingen: Mohr Siebeck.

Freedman, Maurice. 1974. "On the Sociological Study of Chinese Religion." In Arthur P. Wolf, ed., *Religion and Ritual in Chinese Society,* 19–42.

Gabiani, Giandomenico. 1673. *Incrementa Sinicae Ecclesiae Tartaris Oppugnatae.* Vienna: L. Voigt.

Gall, Anne. 1990. "Inventaire avec indication de provenance des collections d'albums d'estampes et de peintures chinoises au departement des estampes." s.l. Photocopied list. Cabinet des estampes, Bibliothèque nationale de France.

Gaubil, Antoine. 1970. *Correspondance de Pékin, 1722–1759,* ed. R. Simon. Geneva: Droz.

Gayoso, Francisco. 1683. "Letter to Ferdinand Verbiest," 23 November. Latin Autograph in Madrid, Archivo Histórico Nacional, Jesuitas, Leg. 270, nr. 161. Copy in Bibliotheca da Ajuda, Lisbon, Jesuítas na Ásia 49–V-19: nr. 111, 408r–415r.

Geertz, Clifford. 1977. "Centers, Kings, and Charisma: Reflections on the Symbolics of Power." In *Culture and Its Creators: Essays in Honor of Edward Shils,* ed. Joseph Ben-David and Terry Nichols Clark, 150–71. Chicago: University of Chicago Press.

Gernet, Jacques. 1982. *Chine et christianisme: Action et réaction.* Paris: Gallimard.

———. 1985. *China and the Christian Impact: A Conflict of Cultures.* Cambridge: Cambridge University Press.

———. 2003. "*Della entrata della Compagnia di Giesù e Christianità nella Cina* de Matteo Ricci (1609) et les remaniements de sa traduction latine (1615)." In *Académie des Inscriptions & Belles-Lettres: Comptes rendus des séances de l'année 2003 (janvier–mars).* Paris: Boccard.

Gerson, Jean. 1966. *Oeuvres complètes.* Vol. 7, *L'oeuvre française.* Paris: Desclée.

Ginzburg, Carlo. 1999. "Alien Voices: The Dialogic Element in Early Modern Jesuit Historiography." In *History, Rhetoric, and Proof,* 71–91. Hanover, NH: University Press of New England.

The Golden Lotus (Jin ping mei 金瓶梅). 1939/1988. Trans. C. Egerton. 4 vols. Singapore: Graham Brash.

Golvers, Noël. 1998. "D. Papebrochius, S.J. (1628–1714), Ph. Couplet (1623–1693) en de Vlaamse jezuïetenmissie in China." *De zeventiende eeuw* 14 (1): 39–50.

———. 1999. *François de Rougemont, S.J., Missionary in Ch'ang-shu (Chiang-nan): A Study of the Account Book (1674–1676) and the Elogium.* Leuven: Leuven University Press.

González, Jose Maria. 1955–1967. *Historia de las misiones dominicanas de China.* 5 vols. Madrid: Imprenta Juan Bravo.

Gouvea, António de. 1671. *Innocentia Victrix sive Sententia Comitiorum Imperij Si[nici] pro Innocenti[a] Christianae Religionis.* Trans. François de Rougemont. Canton.

———. 1995–2001. *Asia extrema.* 2 vols. Edited by Horácio P. Araújo. Lisbon: Fundação Oriente.

Granet, Marcel. 1922. "Le langage de la douleur d'après le rituel funéraire de la Chine classique." *Journal de psychologie*, 15 February, 97–118.

The Great Ming Code / Da Ming lü (1397). 2005. Trans. Jiang Yonglin. Seattle: University of Washington Press.

Grimaldi, Filippo. 1927. "Breve relazione della vita e morte del P. Ludovico Buglio Missionario della Cina, scritta dal P. Filippo Grimaldi nella Corte Imperiale di Pekim alli 4 ottobre 1682." Mss. Archivio Segreto Vaticano, Miscellanea, Armadio VIII, t. 58. Repr., "Onoranze della Corte Imperiale di Pekino: In morte di un missionario, nel secolo XVII," [by M. Barbera]. *La Civiltà Cattolica* 78, no. 2 (1927): 322–30.

Groot, Jan Jacob M. de. 1892–1897. *The Religious System of China. Book I. Disposal of the Dead.* 3 vols. Leiden: Brill.

Grueber, Johannes. 1985. *Als Kundschafter des Papstes nach China: 1656–1664: Die erste Durchquerung Tibets.* Edited by Franz Braumann. Stuttgart: Erdmann.

Gruzinski, Serge. 1999. *La pensée métisse.* Paris: Fayard.

Gu Jiegang 顧頡剛. 1928–1929. "Liangge chubin de daozizhang" 兩個出殯的道子賬. In Gu Jiegang 顧頡剛. Repr., *Su yue de hunsang* 蘇粵的婚喪, 30–41. Taibei: Fulu tushu gongsi, 1969.

——— (Ku Chieh-kang). 1981. "Funeral Processions." Trans. Nancy Gibbs. In *Chinese Civilization and Society: A Sourcebook*, ed. Patricia Buckley Ebrey, 289–93. New York: The Free Press.

Gujin tushu jicheng 古今圖書集成. 1726–1728. Ed. Chen Menglei 陳夢雷 et al. Beijing: Neifu. Repr., Shanghai: Zhonghua shuju, 1934.

Gy, Pierre-Marie. 1955. "Les funérailles d'après le rituel de 1614." *La Maison-Dieu* 44 (September): 70–82.

Handlin, Joanna F. 1983. *Action in Late Ming Thought: The Reorientation of Lü K'un and Other Scholar-Officials.* Berkeley: University of California Press.

Handlin Smith, Joanna F. 1987. "Benevolent Societies: The Reshaping of Charity during the Late Ming and Early Ch'ing." *The Journal of Asian Studies* 46: 309–37.

Harmening, Dieter. 1979. *Superstitio: Überlieferungs- und theoriegeschichtliche Untersuchungen zur kirchlich-theologischen Aberglaubensliteratur des Mittelalters.* Berlin: Schmidt.

He Bin 何彬. 1995. *JiangZhe Hanzu sangzang wenhua* 江浙汉族丧葬文化. Beijing: Zhongyang minzu daxue chubanshe.

Henschenius, Godefridus, and Daniël Papebrochius. 1685–1688. *Acta sanctorum quotquot toto orbe coluntur, vel a catholicis scriptoribus celebrantur: Propylaeum ad 7 Tomos Mensis Maii.* Antwerp: J. B. Verdussen. Repr., Paris and Rome: Victor Palme, 1868.

Héris, Ch.-V. 1955. "Théologie des suffrages pour les morts." *La Maison Dieu* 44 (September): 58–67.

Herrera Maldonado, Francisco de. 1620. *Epitome historial del Reyno de la China, muerta de su Reyna, madre de Este Rey que oy viue, que sucedio a treinta de Março del Año de mil y seiscientos y diez y siete. Sacrificios y Ceremonias de su Entierro. Con la Description de aquel Imperio. Y la Introduccion en el de nuestra Santa Fe Catolica.* Madrid: Andreas de Parra.

———. 1622. *Nouuelle histoire de la Chine, ou la mort de la Reyne Mere du Roy qui regne auiourd'huy en la Chine, les Ceremonies & les Sacrifices qui se firent à ses Funerailles sont fidellement racontez, Avec le commencement & le progrez que les P.P. de la Compagnie de Iesus ont fait faire à la Religion Chrestienne en ce Royaume là.* Trans. I. I. Bellefleur Percheron. Paris: Charles Chastellain.

Histoire de ce qui s'est passe'es Royaumes de la Chine et du Japon, Tirées des lettres escrites és années 1619, 1620 & 1621, Adressées au R. P. Mutio Vitelleschi, General de la Compagnie de Jesus. 1625. Paris: Sébastien Cramoisy.

Honey, David B. 1981. "Liturgy or Literature? Three Approaches to *Ji wen* in the *Wen xuan.*" *Journal of Asian Culture* 5: 76–106.

Ho Shu-yi [He Shuyi] 何淑宜. 2000. *Mingdai shishen yu tongsu wenhua: Yi sangzang lisu wei li de kaocha* 明代士紳與通俗文化: 以喪葬禮俗為例的考察 (*Elites and Popular Culture: A Study on Death Rituals in Ming Times*) Taibei: Institute of History of the National Taiwan Normal University.

Huang Yi-long 黃一農. 1991. "Zeri zhi zheng yu 'Kangxi liyu'" 擇日之爭與康熙曆獄. *Qinghua xuebao* 清華學報 21 (2): 1–34. Translated as "Court Divination and Christianity in the K'ang-hsi Era." *Chinese Science* 10 (1991): 1–20.

———. 1992. "Yesuhuishi Tang Ruowang zai hua enrong kao" 耶穌會士湯若望在華恩榮考. *Zhongguo wenhua* 中國文化 7: 160–70.

———. 2004. "Cong Han Lin *Duoshu* shitan Mingmo tianzhujiao zai shanxi de fazhan" 從韓霖《鐸書》試探明末天主教在山西的發展. *Qinghua xuebao* 清華學報 34 (1): 67–102.

———. 2005. "*Duoshu*: Guoshang guanfang cecai de tianzhujiao xiangyue"《鐸書》: 裏上官方色彩的天主教鄉約. In *Liang tou she: Mingmo Qingchu de di yi dai tianzhujiaotu* 兩頭蛇: 明末清初的第一代天主教徒, by Huang Yi-long 黃一農, 253–85. Taibei: Guoli qinghua daxue chubanshe.

Hucker, Charles. 1985. *A Dictionary of Official Titles in Imperial China.* Stanford: Stanford University Press.

Huguang tongzhi 湖廣通志. 1733. 120 *juan.* Ed. Mai Gui 邁桂. In SKQS, vols. 531–34.

Huntington, Richard, and Peter Metcalf. 1979. *Celebrations of Death: The Anthropology of Mortuary Ritual.* Cambridge: Cambridge University Press.

Ikels, Charlotte. 2004. "Serving the Ancestors, Serving the State: Filial Piety and Death Ritual in Contemporary Guangzhou." In *Filial Piety: Practice and Discourse in Contemporary East Asia*, ed. Charlotte Ikels, 88–105. Stanford: Stanford University Press.

Imano Haruki 今野春. 2004. "Kirishitan no sōsei: Kōkogaku teki kenchi kara no kenshō" キリシタンの葬制: 考古学的見地からの検証. *Kirishitan bunka kenkyū kaihō* キリシタン文化研究会会報 123: 1–52.

Jankowiak, William R. 1993. *Sex, Death, and Hierarchy in a Chinese City: An Anthropological Account*. New York: Columbia University Press.

Jennes, Joseph. 1946. "A propos de la liturgie chinoise: Le Bref Romanae Sedis Antistes de Paul V (1615)." *Neue Zeitschrift für Missionswissenschaft* 2: 241–54.

Jensen, Lionel. 1997. *Manufacturing Confucianism: Chinese Traditions and Universal Civilization*. Durham: Duke University Press.

Jiali 家禮. 1341. Comp. Zhu Xi 朱熹. *Zhu zi cheng shu* 朱子成書 edition. Repr. in Patricia Buckley Ebrey, *Chu Hsi's Family Rituals: A Twelfth-Century Chinese Manual for the Performance of Cappings, Weddings, Funerals, and Ancestral Rites*, 183–212. Princeton: Princeton University Press, 1991.

Jiali yijie 家禮儀節 (also entitled *Wengong Jiali yijie* 文公家禮儀節). 1474, ed. 1518. 8 *juan*. Comp. Qiu Jun 丘濬. In *CMCS, jingbu* 經部 114, 430–636.

Jiali yijie 家禮儀節 (also entitled *Wengong Jiali yijie* 文公家禮儀節). 1608. 8 *juan*. Comp. Qiu Jun 丘濬. Repr. ed. Yang Tingyun 楊廷筠. Tokyo: Naikaku bunko.

Jiaoyao jielüe 教要解略. 1615. Ed. Alfonso Vagnone 王豐肅. ARSI Jap.Sin. I, 57. In *CCT ARSI*, vol. 1, 117–306.

Jinpingmei cihua 金瓶梅詞話. Pref. 1617. Ed. Xiaoxiaosheng 笑笑生. Repr., *Quanben Jinpingmei cihua* 全本金瓶梅詞話. Hong Kong: Taiping shuju, 1993.

Johnson, David. 1989. *Ritual Opera, Operatic Ritual: "Mu-lien Rescues his Mother" in Chinese Popular Culture*. Berkeley: IEAS Publications.

Johnson, Elizabeth L. 1988. "Grieving for the Dead, Grieving for the Living: Funeral Laments of Hakka Women." In *Death Ritual in Late Imperial and Modern China*, ed. Watson and Rawski, 135–163.

Jones, Adam. 1990. "Decompiling Dapper: A Preliminary Search for Evidence." *History in Africa* 17: 171–209.

Josson, Henri, and Léopold Willaert. 1938. *Correspondance de Ferdinand Verbiest de la Compagnie de Jésus (1623–1688)*. Brussels: Palais des Académies.

Jungmann, Joseph. 1961. *The Mass of the Roman Rite: Its Origins and Development (Missarum Sollemnia)*. 4th ed. Trans. F. Brunner. London: Burns & Oates.

Kang Zhijie 康志傑. 2006. *Shangzhu de putaoyuan: Exibei Mopanshan tianzhujiao shequ yanjiu (1636–2005)* 上主的葡萄園—鄂西北磨盤山天主教社區研究 (1634–2005). Xinzhuang (Taibei): Furen daxue chubanshe.

Kangxi qijuzhu 康熙起居注. 1984. Beijing: Zhonghua shuju.

Kataoka, Inácia Rumiko. 1997. *A vida e a acção pastoral de D. Luís Cerqueira S.J., bispo do Japão (1598–1614)*. Macau: Instituto Cultural.

Kelly, Edward T. 1971. "The Anti-Christian Persecution of 1616–1617 in Nanjing." Ph.D. diss., Columbia University.

Kirschbaum, Engelbert et al. 1968–1976. *Lexikon der christlichen Ikonographie*, 8 vols. Rome: Herder.

Kojima Tsuyoshi 小島毅. 1996. "Mingdai lixue de tedian" 明代禮學的特點. Trans. Zhang Wenchao 張文朝. In *Mingdai jingxue guoji yantaohui lunwenji* 明代經學國際研討會論文集, ed. Lin Qingzhang 林慶彰 and Jiang Qiuhua 蔣秋華, 393–409. Taibei: Zhong-yanyuan wenzhesuo.

Kouduo richao 口鐸日抄. Ca. 1630–1640. 8 *juan*. Ed. Li Jiubiao 李九標 et al. ARSI Jap.Sin. I, 81. In *CCT ARSI*, vol. 7, 1–594.

Kuhn, Thomas S. 1977. *The Essential Tension: Selected Studies in Scientific Tradition and Change*. Chicago: University of Chicago Press.

Kutcher, Norman. 1999. *Mourning in Late Imperial China: Filial Piety and the State*. Cambridge: Cambridge University Press.

Laamann, Lars Peter. 2006. *Christian Heretics in Late Imperial China: Christian Inculturation and State Control, 1720–1850*. London: Routledge.

Lach, Donald F., and Edwin J. Van Kley. 1993. *Asia in the Making of Europe*. Vol. 3: *A Century of Advance*, bk. 1, *Trade, Missions, Literature* and bk. 4, *East Asia*. Chicago: University of Chicago Press.

Lagerwey, John. 1987. *Taoist Ritual in Chinese Society and History*. New York: Macmillan.

Landry-Deron, Isabelle. 2002. *La Preuve par la Chine. La "Description" de J.-B. Du Halde, jésuite, 1735*. Paris: Editions de l'EHESS.

Las Cortes, Adriano de. 1991. "Relación del viage, naufragio y captiverio que, con otras personas, padeció en Chaucao, reino de la gran China. . . ." In *P. Adriano de las Cortes (S.I.), Viaje de la China*, ed. Beatriz Moncó. Madrid: Alianza. Ms. in mss. Sloane 1005, British Library, London.

———. 2001. *Le voyage en Chine d'Adriano de las Cortes s.j. (1625)*. Trans. Pascale Girard and Juliette Monbeig. Introd. by Pascale Girard. Paris: Editions Chandeigne.

Launay, Adrien. 1920. *Histoire des missions de Chine: Missions du Se-tchoan*. Paris: Téqui.

Laures, Johannes. 1941. *Japanische Ansprachen und Gebete aus einem alten Rituale gedruckt zu Nagasaki 1605: Text und deutsche Übersetzung*. Tokyo: Sophia Universität.

———. 1957. *Kirishitan Bunko: A Manual of Books and Documents on the Early Christian Mission in Japan*. Tokyo: Sophia University.

Le Comte [Lecomte], Louis. 1990. *Un jésuite à Pékin: Nouveaux mémoires sur l'état présent de la Chine 1687–1692*. Ed. Frédérique Touboul-Bouyeure. Paris: Phébus. Originally published as *Nouveaux mémoires sur l'état présent de la Chine*. Paris: Jean Annison, 1697.

———. [Lewis Le Comte]. 1737. *Memoirs and Remarks . . . Made in above Ten Years Travels through the Empire of China*. London: J. Hughs.

Legge, James. 1885. *The Li Ki.* F. Max Müller, *The Sacred Books of the East*, vol. 27. Oxford: Oxford University Press.

———, trans. 1991. *The Chinese Classics.* 5 vols. Repr. Taibei: SMC Publishing.

Leung Ki Che [Liang Qizi] 梁其姿. 1997. *Shishan yu jiaohua: MingQing de cishan zuzhi* 施善與教化: 明清的慈善組織. Taibei: Lianjing.

Libu zhigao 禮部志稿. 1620. Ed. Yu Ruji 俞汝楫. In *SKQS*, vols. 597–98.

Liji 禮記. 1992. Ed. *Liji zhuzi suoyin* 禮記逐字索引. The ICS Ancient Chinese Text Concordance Series. Hong Kong: The Commercial Press.

Li Jiugong 李九功. n.d. [before 1681]. "Zhengli chuyi" 證禮蒭議. ARSI Jap.Sin. I, 38/42, 42/2c, and 40/8. In *CCT ARSI*, vol. 9, 63–90, 91–118.

Liturgisch Woordenboek. 1958–1962. 2 vols. Roermond: Romen.

"Linsang chubin yishi" 臨喪出殯儀式. "earlier version" [text "A"]. Anon. ARSI Jap.Sin. II, 169.4. In *CCT ARSI*, vol. 5, 439–46.

"Linsang chubin yishi" 臨喪出殯儀式. "later version" [text "B"]. Ed. Antonius Li 李安當 and Francesco Saverio Filippucci 方濟各. ARSI Jap.Sin. I, 153. In *CCT ARSI*, vol. 5, 447–65.

Liu, Kwang-Ching. 1990. "Introduction: Orthodoxy in Chinese Society." In *Orthodoxy in Late Imperial China*, ed. Kwang-Ching Liu. Berkeley: University of California Press.

[Liu Xie 劉勰] Liu Hsieh. 1959. *The Literary Mind and the Carving of Dragons*, trans. Vincent Yu-chung Shih. New York: Columbia University Press.

———. 1998. *Wenxin diaolong jinyi* 文心雕龍今譯, ed. Zhou Zhenfu 周振甫. Beijing: Zhonghua shuju.

Li xiansheng xingshu 利先生行述. Ca. 1682. Ed. Ferdinand Verbiest 南懷仁, Claudio Filippo Grimaldi 閔明我 and Tomé Pereira 徐日昇. ARSI Jap.Sin. II, 165.1. In *CCT ARSI*, vol. 12, 335–40. See also modern punctuated version in *XC*, 409–10.

Li Xiaoti 李孝悌. 1993. "Shiqi shiji yilai de shidafu yu minzhong—yanjiu huigu" 十七世紀以來的士大夫與民眾—研究回顧. *Xinshixue* 新史學 4 (4): 97–139.

Lixiu yijian 勵修一鑑. Ca. 1639–1645. Ed. Li Jiugong 李九功. In *WXSB*, vol. 1, 411–529.

Lobo, Inácio. 1915. "Carta del P. Ignacio Lobo S.J. al Antonio de Santa María O.F.M.—Fo-Cheu-Fu: 19 de Septiembre de 1635." In *Archivum Franciscanum Historicum*, vol. 8, 584–85. Quaracchi-Florence: Collegium S. Bonaventurae.

Loomba, Ania. 1998. *Colonialism/Postcolonialism.* London/New York: Routledge.

López Gay, Jesús. 1964. "La 'liturgia de los difuntos' en la misión del Japón del siglo XVI." *Missionalia Hispanica* 21: 5–23.

———. 1970. *La liturgia en la misión del Japón del siglo XVI.* Rome: Univ. Gregoriana.

Lorenzo Pinar, Francisco Javier. 1991. *Muerte y ritual en la edad moderna.* Salamanca: Ediciones Universidad de Salamanca.

Lozada, Eriberto P. 2001. *God Aboveground: Catholic Church, Postsocialist State, and Transnational Processes in a Chinese Village.* Stanford: Stanford University Press.

Luzbetak, Louis J. 1963. *The Church and Cultures: An Applied Anthropology for the Religious Worker.* Techny, IL: Divine Word Publishing.

———. 1988. *The Church and Cultures: New Perspectives in Missiological Anthropology.* Maryknoll, NY: Orbis Books.

Lü Kun 呂坤. Pref. 1573. *Sili yi* 四禮翼. 8 *juan*. In *CMCS, jingbu* 經部 115, 80–111.

———. Pref. 1614. *Sili yi* 四禮疑. 6 *juan*. In *CMCS, jingbu* 經部 115, 36–79.

Lü Weiqi 呂維祺. Pref. 1624. *Sili yueyan* 四禮約言. 4 *juan*. In *CMCS, jingbu* 經部 115, 112–22.

Maas, Otto. 1926. *Die Wiedereröffnung der Franziskanermission in China in der Neuzeit.* Münster: Aschendorff.

Maher, Michael W. 2002. "Jesuits and Ritual in Early Modern Europe." In *Medieval and Early Modern Ritual: Formalized Behavior in Europe, China and Japan*, ed. Joëlle Rollo-Koster, 193–218. Leiden: Brill.

Mahieu, Wauthier de. 1991. "Begrafenisrituelen toegelicht vanuit de antropologie." *Tijdschrift voor Liturgie* 75: 226–37.

Malatesta, Edward, and Gao Zhiyu, ed. 1995. *Departed, Yet Present: Zhalan, The Oldest Christian Cemetery in Beijing.* Macau: Instituto Cultural.

Manuale ad sacramenta Ecclesiae ministranda. D. Ludouici Cerqueira Japonensis Episcopi opera ad usum sui cleri ordinatum. 1605. Ed. Luís Cerqueira. Nangasaquij: In Collegio Japonico Societatis Iesu.

Mao Qiling 毛奇齡. Kangxi era. *Sangli wushuo* 喪禮吾說. 10 *juan*. In *CMCS, jingbu* 經部 87, 646–735.

———. 1697–1700. *Sannian fuzhi kao* 三年服制考. In *Congshu jicheng xubian* 叢書集成 續編, vol. 9 (*jingbu* 經部), 61–69. Shanghai: Shanghai shudian, 1994.

Marcus, Ivan G. 1996. *Rituals of Childhood: Jewish Acculturation in Medieval Europe.* New Haven, CT: Yale University Press.

Margiotti, Fortunato. 1958. *Il Cattolicismo nello Shansi dalle origini al 1738.* Rome: Edizioni 'Sinica Franciscana.'

———. 1961. "Congregazioni mariane della antica missione cinese." In *Das Laienapostolat in den Missionen*, ed. J. Specher and P. W. Bühlmann, 131–51. Festschrift J. Beckmann, NZM Supplement 10. Schöneck-Beckenried: NZM.

———. 1962–1963. "Congregazioni laiche gesuitiche della antica missione cinese." *Neue Zeitschrift für Missionswissenschaft* 18 (1962): 255–74; 19 (1963): 50–65.

Martini, Martino. 1658. *Sinicae historiae decas prima, res à gentis origine ad Christum natum in extrema Asia, sive Magno Sinarum Imperio gestas complexa.* Munich: J. Wagner.

———. 1981. *Novus Atlas Sinensis.* Trento: Museo Tridentino di Scienze Naturali. Reprint of first edition. Amsterdam: Blaeu, 1655.

Menegon, Eugenio. 2002. "Ancestors, Virgins and Friars: The Localization of Christianity in Late Imperial Mindong (Fujian, China), 1632–1863." Ph.D. diss., University of California, Berkeley.

Meng Lin 蒙林. 1997. "Manzu ji qi xianshi sangzang xisu zhi liubian" 满族及其先世丧葬习俗之流变. *Neimenggu shehui kexue* 内蒙古社会科学 4: 54–60.

Metzler, Josef. 1980. *Die Synoden in China, Japan und Korea 1570–1931.* Paderborn: Schöningh Verlag.

Mignolo, Walter D. 1995. *The Darker Side of the Renaissance: Literacy, Territoriality, and Colonization.* Ann Arbor: University of Michigan Press.

Ming shilu 明實錄. 1987. Repr. Beijing: Zhonghua shuju.

Misa jingdian 彌撒經典 (*Missale Romanum, auctoritate Pauli V Pont. M., Sinice redditum*). 1670. Ed. Lodovico Buglio 利類思 Beijing. BAV, Borgia Cinese 352.1–5.

Mish, John L. 1964. "Creating an Image of Europe in China: Aleni's *Hsi-fang ta-wen.*" *Monumenta Serica* 23: 1–87.

Missale Romanum (ex Decreto Sacrosancti Concilii Tridentini restitutum). 1570. Repr. 1574. Antwerp: Ex officina Christophori Plantini.

Mungello, David E. 2001. *The Spirit and the Flesh in Shandong, 1650–1785.* Lanham, MD: Rowman & Littlefield.

Naquin, Susan. 1988. "Funerals in North China: Uniformity and Variation." In *Death Ritual in Late Imperial and Modern China,* ed. Watson and Rawski, 37–70.

———. 2000. *Peking: Temples and City Life, 1400–1900.* Berkeley: University of California Press.

Nivison, David S. 1962. "Aspects of Traditional Chinese Biography." *Journal of Asian Studies* 21: 457–63.

O'Daly, Gerard. 1999. *Augustine's City of God: A Reader's Guide.* Oxford: Clarendon Press.

Odell, Dawn. 2001. "The Soul of Transactions: Illustration and Johan Nieuhof's Travels in China." *De zeventiende eeuw* 17 (3): 225–42.

Oxfeld, Ellen. 2004. "'When You Drink Water, Think of Its Source': Morality, Status, and Reinvention in Rural Chinese Funerals." *The Journal of Asian Studies* 63 (4): 960–90.

Palmeiro, André. 1629. "Ordens que o Padre Andre Palmeiro Visitador de Japão e Chine deixou a Viceprovincia da China vizitandoa no anno de 1629 aos 15 de Agosto." ARSI Jap.Sin. 100: 20r–39v.

Pantoja, Diego de. 1605. *Relacion de la entrada de algunos Padres de la Compañia de Jesus en la China, particulares sucessos que tuvieron, y de cosas muy notables que vieron en el mismo Regno. . . . Carta del Padre Diego de Pantoja, Religioso de la Compañia de Jesus, para el Padre Luys de Guzman Provincial en la Provincia de Toledo, su fecha en Paquin, corte del Rey de la China, a nueve de Março de mil y seiscientos y dos años.* Seville: Alonso Rodriguez Gamarra.

———. 1625. "A Letter of Father Diego de Panoia, one of the Company of Iesus, to Father Luys de Guzman, Provinciall in the Province of Toledo; written in Paquin, which is the Court of the King of China, the ninth of March, the yeere 1602." In

Hakluytus Posthumous or Purchas His Pilgrimes, by Samuel Purchas, vol. 3, bk. 2, 350–79. London: Fetherstone.

Pelliot, Paul. 1924. "La Brevis Relatio." *T'oung Pao* 23: 355–72.

Pereira, Tomé. "Relação Breve da Morte e Emterramento do Padre Gabriel de Magalhães em Pekim." Peking, 25 June 1677. Bibliotheca da Ajuda, Lisbon: Jesuítas na Ásia 49–V-17: 565r–569v.

Pfister, Louis. 1932–1934. *Notices biographiques et bibliographiques sur les Jésuites de l'ancienne mission de Chine, 1552–1773*. 2 vols. Shanghai: Imprimerie de la Mission.

Philippeau, H. R. 1956. "Origines et évolution des rites funéraires." In *Le mystère de la mort et sa célébration*, 186–206. Lex orandi 12. Paris: Cerf.

———. 1957. "Pour un souhaitable ressourcement et complément du rituel de l'agonie et des funérailles." *Ephemerides liturgicae* 71: 369–407.

Pih, Irene. 1979. *Le Père Gabriel de Magalhães: Un Jésuite portugais en Chine au XVIIe siècle*. Paris: Fundação Caluste Gulbenkian.

Piwang 闢妄 (also *Pi Shishi zhuwang* 闢釋氏諸妄). 1615? In *WXXB*, vol. 2, 621–51. In *CCT ZKW*, vol. 1, 37–70.

Plaks, Andrew, trans. 2003. *Ta Hsüeh and Chung Yung (The Highest Order of Cultivation and On the Practice of the Mean)*. London: Penguin Books.

Poxie ji 破邪集. 1640. 8 *juan*. Ed. Xu Changzhi 徐昌治. Repr., Japan, 1855.

Pratt, Mary Louise. 1992. *Imperial Eyes: Travel Writing and Transculturation*. London/New York: Routledge.

Purchas, Samuel. 1625. *Hakluytus Posthumus or Purchas his Pilgrimes, Contayning a History of the World, in Sea Voyages, & Lande Travells, by Englishmen & Others*. London: Fetherstone.

Pye, E. M. 1969. "The Transplantation of Religions." *Numen* 16: 234–39.

Qinding daQing huidian zeli 欽定大清會典則例. 1768. 180 *juan*. In *SKQS*, vols. 620–25.

Qinding libu zeli 欽定禮部則例. 1844. Repr., Taibei: Chengwen, 1966.

Qingbai leichao 清稗類鈔. 1996. 9 vols. Ed. Xu Ke 徐珂. Beijing: Zhonghua shuju.

Qing shilu 清實錄. 1985. Beijing: Zhonghua shuju.

Qingzhongqianqi xiyang tianzhujiao zaihua huodong dang'an shiliao 清中前期西洋天主教在華活動檔案史料. 2004. 4 vols. Ed. Zhongguo diyi lishi dang'anguan 中國第一歷史檔案館. Beijing: Zhonghua shuju.

Qin Huitian 秦蕙田 1761. *Wuli tongkao* 五禮通考. 260 *juan*. In *SKQS*, vols. 135–42.

Rawski, Evelyn S. 1988a. "A Historian's Approach to Chinese Death Ritual." In *Death Ritual in Late Imperial and Modern China*, ed. Watson and Rawski, 20–34.

———. 1988b. "The Imperial Way of Death: Ming and Ch'ing Emperors and Death Ritual." In *Death Ritual in Late Imperial and Modern China*, ed. Watson and Rawski, 228–53.

———. 1998. *The Last Emperors: A Social History of Qing Imperial Institutions*. Berkeley: University of California Press.

Recüeil de Tombeaux Chinois. 18th century. BnF, Cabinet des estampes, Oe 27.

Reil, Sebald. 1970. "Neues zur Missionsgeschichte Shensis: Ein unbekannter Brief des P. Francisco Gayosso SJ." *Zeitschrift für Missionswissenschaft und Religionswissenschaft* 54: 1–13.

Reinders, Eric. 2004. *Borrowed Gods and Foreign Bodies: Christian Missionaries Imagine Chinese Religion.* Berkeley: University of California Press.

"Renhui huigui" 仁會會規. n.d. anon. ARSI Jap.Sin. II, 169.1. In *CCT ARSI*, vol. 12, 473–78.

Ricciardolo, Gaetano. 2003. *Oriente e Occidente negli scritti di Matteo Ricci.* Napoli: Chirico.

Ripa, Matteo. 1939. *Memoirs of Father Ripa, During Thirteen Years' Residence at the Court of Peking in the Service of the Emperor of China.* Selected and trans. Fortunato Prandi. London: John Murray, 1855. Repr. Beijing.

Rituale Romanum (Pauli V. Pont. Max. Jussu Editum). 1614. Repr. 1617. Antwerp: Ex officina Plantiniana.

Romano, Antonella. 2004. "Observer, vénérer, servir: Une polémique jésuite autour du Tribunal des mathématiques de Pékin." *Annales: Histoire, Sciences Sociales* 59 (4): 729–56.

Rowell, Geoffrey. 1977. *The Liturgy of the Christian Burial: An Introductory Survey of the Historical Development of Christian Burial Rites* (Alcuin Club Collections 59). London: S.P.C.K.

Rubiés, Joan Pau. 1993. "New Worlds and Renaissance Ethnology." *History and Anthropology* 6 (2–3): 157–97.

———. 1995. "Christianity and Civilization in Sixteenth-Century Ethnological Discourse." In *Shifting Cultures: Interaction and Discourse in the Expansion of Europe*, ed. Henriette Bugge and Joan Pau Rubiés, 35–60. Münster: Lit Verlag.

Ruijianlu 睿鑒錄. 1735–1737. Ed. Ignatius Koegler 戴進賢. Rome: Biblioteca Casanatense, Ms. 2104.

Ruland, Ludwig. 1901. *Die Geschichte der kirchlichen Leichenfeier.* Regensburg: G. J. Manz.

Ruland, Vernon. 1994. "The Inflated Catholic Difference." *America,* June 4, 20–22.

Rule, Paul. 1986. *K'ung-tzu or Confucius? The Jesuit Interpretation of Confucianism.* Sydney: Allen & Unwin.

Rutherford, Richard. 1970. *The Death of a Christian: The Rite of Funerals.* New York: Pueblo Publishing Company.

Sancai tuhui 三才圖會. 1607. 106 *juan.* Ed. Wang Qi 王圻. Repr., 6 vols. Taibei: Chengwen, 1970.

"Sangli ailun" 喪禮哀論. n.d. anon. ARSI Jap.Sin. I, [38/42] 40/9c. In *CCT ARSI*, vol. 11, 269–78.

"Sangzang yishi" 喪葬儀式. "earlier version" [text "C"]. Ed. Antonius Li 李安當 and Francesco Saverio Filippucci 方濟各. ARSI Jap.Sin. I, 164. In *CCT ARSI*, vol. 5, 467–79.

"Sangzang yishi" 喪葬儀式. "later version" [text "D"]. Ed. Antonius Li 李安當 and Francesco Saverio Filippucci 方濟各. ARSI Jap.Sin. I, 164a. In *CCT ARSI*, vol. 5, 481–91.

Schall [von Bell], Johann Adam. 1942. Ed. and trans. Paul Bornet and Henri Bernard. *Lettres et mémoires d'Adam Schall S.J.: Relation historique. Texte latin avec traduction française.* Tianjin: Hautes Etudes. Originally published as *Historica Narratio de Initio et Progressu Missionis Societatis Jesu apud Chinenses, Praesertim in Regia Pequinensi.* Vienna: M. Cosmerovi, 1665.

Schipper, Kristofer. 1996. "Some Naive Questions about the Rites Controversy: A Project for Future Research." In *Western Humanistic Culture Presented to China by Jesuit Missionaries (XVII–XVIII centuries): Proceedings of the Conference held in Rome, October 25–27, 1993,* ed. Federico Masini, 293–308. Rome: Institutum Historicum S.I.

Schwartz, Stuart B. 1994. "Introduction." In *Implicit Understandings: Observing, Reporting, and Reflecting on the Encounters between Europeans and Other Peoples in the Early Modern Era,* ed. Stuart B. Schwartz. Cambridge: Cambridge University Press.

Scribner, Robert W. 1987. *Popular Culture and Popular Movements in Reformation Germany.* London: The Hambledon Press.

———. (Bob) . 1997. "Historical Anthropology of Early Modern Europe." In *Problems in the Historical Anthropology of Early Modern Europe,* ed. R. Po-Chia Hsia and R. W. Scribner, 11–34. Wiesbaden: Harrassowitz.

Semedo, Álvaro. 1655. *The History of the Great and Renowned Monarchy of China: Wherein all the Particular Provinces are Accurately Described: As Also the Dispositions, Manners, Learning, Lawes, Militia, Government, and Religion of the People, Together with the Traffick and Commodities of the Countrey.* London: E. Tylor.

———. 1996. *Histoire Universelle du Grand Royaume de la Chine.* Trans. and introd. Jean-Pierre Duteil. Paris: Kimé. Originally published as *Histoire universelle de la Chine.* Paris: Sébastien Cramoisy, 1645.

Shang, Wei. 2003. *Rulin waishi and Cultural Transformation in Late Imperial China.* Cambridge: Harvard University Asia Center.

Shanzhong yiying lidian 善終痤瑩禮典. After 1675. Ed. Lodovico Buglio 利類思. BAV, Borgia Cinese 324 (9).

Shanzhong zhugong guili 善終助功規例. Before 1638. João Fróis 伏若望. ARSI Jap.Sin. I, 186. In *CCT ARSI*, vol. 5, 333–438.

Shengjiao guicheng 聖教規程. n.d. anon. Ms in Beitang Library. Repr. in Hubert Verhaeren, "Ordonnances de la Sainte Église." *Monumenta Serica* 4 (1939–1940): 469–77.

Shengjing zhijie 聖經直解. 1636–1642. 14 *juan.* Manuel Dias 陽瑪諾. In *WXSB*, vols. 4–6, 1553–3106.

Shengmu huigui 聖母會規. Before 1673. Ed. Humbert Augery 洪度貞. ARSI Jap. Sin. I, 173.2a. In *CCT ARSI*, vol. 12, 439–62.

"Shengmu huigui" 聖母會規. n.d. anon. ARSI Jap.Sin. II, 169.3. In *CCT ARSI*, vol. 12, 489–94.

Shengshi lidian 聖事禮典 (*Manuale ad Sacramenta ministranda iuxta ritum S. Rom. Ecc. Sinice redditum*). 1675. Ed. Lodovico Buglio 利類思. Beijing. ARSI Jap.Sin. I, 161 and 161a. In *CCT ARSI*, vol. 11, 205–598.

Shih, Joseph. 1978. "Introduction." In Ricci and Trigault, *Histoire de l'expédition chrétienne au royaume de la Chine (1582–1610)*, 11–59.

Siduo kedian 司鐸課典 (*Breviarium Romanum Sinice redditum*). 1674. Ed. Lodovico Buglio 利類思. Beijing. BnF, Chinois 7388–7389.

Smith, Jonathan Z. 1998. "Religion, Religions, Religious." In *Critical Terms for Religious Studies*, ed. Mark C. Taylor, Chicago: University of Chicago Press.

Smith, Wilfred Cantwell. 1963. *The Meaning and End of Religion*. New York: Macmillan.

Song Yingxing 宋應星. 1637. *Tiangong kaiwu* 天工開物. 3 *juan*. Repr., Wujin: Sheyuan Taoshi, 1929.

———. (Sung Ying-hsing). 1966. *Chinese Technology in the Seventeenth Century: T'ien-kung k'ai-wu*. Trans. E-tu Zen Sun and Shiou-chuan Sun. University Park: The Pennsylvania State University Press. Repr., Mineola: Dover, 1997.

Standaert, Nicolas. 1988. *Yang Tingyun, Confucian and Christian in Late Ming China: His Life and Thought*. Sinica Leidensia 19, Leiden: Brill.

———. 1997. "New Trends in the Historiography of Christianity in China." *Catholic Historical Review* 83 (4): 573–613.

———. 2001. "Christianity in Late Ming and Early Qing China as a Case of Cultural Transmission." In *China and Christianity: Burdened Past, Hopeful Future*, ed. Stephen Uhally, Jr. and Xiaoxin Wu, 81–116. London and New York: M. E. Sharpe.

———. 2002. *Methodology in View of Contact Between Cultures: The China Case in the 17th Century*. CSRCS Occasional Paper no. 11. Hong Kong: Centre for the Study of Religion and Chinese Society, Chung Chi College, The Chinese University of Hong Kong.

Stary, Giovanni. 1998. "Mandschurische Inschriften und Zeugnisse zu Johann Adam Schall von Bell." In *Western Learning and Christianity in China: The Contribution and Impact of Johann Adam Schall von Bell, S.J. (1592–1666)*, ed. Roman Malek, 155–89. Monumenta Serica Monograph Series 35 (1). Nettetal: Steyler Verlag.

Strocchia, Sharon T. 1992. *Death and Ritual in Renaissance Florence*. Baltimore: The Johns Hopkins University Press.

Stuart, Jan, and Evelyn S. Rawski. 2001. *Worshiping the Ancestors: Chinese Commemorative Portraits*. Washington, D.C.: Smithsonian Institution; Stanford: Stanford University Press.

[Stumpf, Kilian], 1705–1712. "Acta Pekinensia seu Ephemerides Historiales eorum, quæ Pekini acciderunt à 4.â Decembris Anni 1705 1.â adventûs III.mi et Exc.mi Dni. D.

Caroli Thomæ Maillard de Tournon Pariarchæ Antiocheni Visitatoris Apostolici, cum potestate Legati de latere &c." ARSI Jap.Sin. 138.

Sutton, Donald S. 2007a. "Ritual, Cultural Standardization, and Orthopraxy in China: Reconsidering James L. Watson's Ideas." *Modern China* 33: 3–21.

———. 2007b. "Death Rites and Chinese Culture: Standardization and Variation in Ming and Qing Times." *Modern China* 33: 125–53.

Szonyi, Michael. 2002. *Practicing Kinship: Lineage and Descent in Late Imperial China.* Stanford: Stanford University Press.

Ta Na 塔娜. 1994. "Manzu chuantong sangzang xisu" 满族传统丧葬习俗. *Manzu yanjiu* 满族研究 1: 48–52.

Tedlock, Barbara, and Dennis Tedlock. 1985. "Text and Textile: Language and Technology in the Arts of the Quiché Maya." *Journal of Anthropological Research* 41 (2): 121–46.

Tedlock, Dennis. 1979. "The Analogical Tradition and the Emergence of a Dialogical Anthropology." *Journal of Anthropological Research* 35 (4): 387–400.

Tedlock, Dennis, and Bruce Mannheim. 1995. *The Dialogic Emergence of Culture.* Urbana and Chicago: University of Illinois Press.

Teiser, Stephen F. 1994. *The Scripture on the Ten Kings and the Making of Purgatory in Medieval Chinese Buddhism.* Honolulu: Kuroda Institute/ University of Hawai'i Press.

Thomas, Antoine. 1688. "Lettre du Pere Antoine Thomas, ecrite de Pekin, le huit Sept. 1688." BnF, 7485 n.a.F.: 188–93.

Thompson, Stuart E. 1988. "Death, Food, and Fertility." In *Death Ritual in Late Imperial and Modern China*, ed. Watson and Rawski, 71–108.

Thoraval, Joël. 1992. "Pourquoi les 'religions chinoises' ne peuvent-elles apparaître dans les statistiques occidentales?" *Perspectives chinoises* 1: 37–44. Translated as "The Western Misconception of Chinese Religion: A Hong Kong Example." *China Perspectives* 3 (1996): 58–65.

Todorov, Tzvetan. 1979. "Bakhtine et l'altérité." *Poétique* 40 (November): 502–13. Also published in *Mikhaïl Bakhtine, le principe dialogique*, by Tzvetan Todorov, 145–71. Paris: Seuil, 1981. Translated by Wlad Godzich as "Philosophical Anthropology," in *Mikhail Bakhtin: The Dialogical Principle*, by Tzvetan Todorov, 94–112. Minneapolis: University of Minnesota Press.

———. 1982a. "Comprendre une culture: Du dehors / du dedans." *Extrême-Orient Extrême-Occident* 1: 9–15.

———. 1982b. *La conquête de l'Amérique: La question de l'autre.* Paris: Seuil.

———. 1984. *Conquest of America: The Question of the Other.* Trans. Richard Howard. New York: Harper & Row.

———. 1989. *Nous et les autres: La réflexion française sur la diversité humaine.* Paris: Seuil. Translated by Catherine Porter as *On Human Diversity: Nationalism, Racism and Exoticism in French Thought.* Cambridge, MA: Harvard University Press, 1993.

Tong, Chee-Kiong. 2004. *Chinese Death Rituals in Singapore*. London: RoutledgeCurzon.

Trigault, Nicolas, and Matteo Ricci. 1615. *De Christiana expeditione apud Sinas. Suscepta ab Societate Iesu. Ex P. Matthaei Ricij eiusdem Societatis commentarijs*. Augsburg: Christoph Mangium.

———. 1953. *China in the Sixteenth Century: The Journals of Matthew Ricci, 1583–1610*. Trans. Louis J. Gallagher. New York: Random House.

———. 1978. *Histoire de l'expédition chrétienne au royaume de la Chine (1582–1610)*. Paris: DDB/Bellarmin. Originally published as *Histoire de l'expedition chrestienne au royaume de la Chine entreprise par les PP. de la Compagnie de Iesus*. Trans. David de Riquebourg-Trigault. Lyon: Horace Cardon, 1616.

Tsuchiya, Franz-Xaver. 1963. "Das älteste bekannte Missions-Rituale: Nagasaki 1605." *Trierer Theologische Zeitschrift* 72: 221–32.

Turner, Victor W. 1969. *The Ritual Process: Structure and Anti-Structure*. London: Routledge & Kegan Paul.

Van den Bulck, Jan. 1996. *Kijkbuiskennis: De rol van televisie in de sociale en cognitieve constructie van de realiteit*. Leuven: Acco.

Vande Walle, Willy. 1994. "Ferdinand Verbiest and the Chinese Bureaucracy." In *Ferdinand Verbiest (1623–1688), Jesuit Missionary, Scientist, Engineer and Diplomat*, ed. John Witek, 495–515.

Van Engen, John. 1986. "The Christian Middle Ages as a Historiographical Problem." *American Historical Review* 91 (3): 519–52.

Van Hée, Louis. 1931. "Les Jésuites Mandarins." *Revue d'Histoire des Missions* 8: 28–45.

Väth, Alfons. 1991. Repr. *Johann Adam Schall von Bell S.J.: Missionar in China, kaiserlicher Astronom und Ratgeber am Hofe von Peking, 1592–1666: Ein Lebens- und Zeitbild*. Monumenta Serica Monograph Series 25. Nettetal: Steyler Verlag.

Verbiest, Ferdinand 南懷仁. 1670. *Shan'ebao lüeshuo* 善惡報略說. ARSI Jap.Sin. I, [38/42] 38/1.2. In *CCT ARSI*, vol. 5, 509–30.

———. 1682. *Tianzhujiao sangli wenda* 天主教喪禮問答. ARSI Jap.Sin. I, [38/42] 38/1.1. In *CCT ARSI*, vol. 5, 495–508.

Verhaeren, Hubert. 1939–1940. "Ordonnances de la Sainte Église 聖教規程." *Monumenta Serica* 4: 451–77.

———. 1949. *Catalogue de la Bibliothèque du Pé-T'ang*. Beijing: Imprimerie des Lazaristes; repr. 1969. Paris: Les Belles Lettres.

Vovelle, Michel. 1981. *Les intermédiaires culturels: Actes du Colloque du Centre Meridional d'Histoire Sociale, des Mentalités et des Cultures, 1978*. Aix-en-Provence: Université de Provence.

Waldenfels, Bernhard. 1995. "Response to the Others." In *Encountering the Other(s): Studies in Literature, History, and Culture*, ed. G. Brinker-Gabler, 35–44. Albany, NY: SUNY.

Wan Jianzhong 万建中. 1998. *Zhongguo lidai zangli* 中国历代葬礼. Beijing: Beijing tushuguan chubanshe.

Wanli qijuzhu 萬曆起居注. 1988. Beijing: Beijing daxue.

Wang Zheng 王徵. 1634. *Renhui yue* 仁會約. BnF, Chinois 7348.

Watson, James L. 1988a. "The Structure of Chinese Funerary Rites: Elementary Forms, Ritual Sequence, and the Primacy of Performance." In *Death Ritual in Late Imperial and Modern China*, ed. Watson and Rawski, 3–19.

———. 1988b. "Funeral Specialists in Cantonese Society: Pollution, Performance, and Social Hierarchy." In *Death Ritual in Late Imperial and Modern China*, ed. Watson and Rawski, 109–34.

———. 2007. "Orthopraxy Revisited." *Modern China* 33: 154–58.

———. and Evelyn S. Rawski, eds. 1988. *Death Ritual in Late Imperial and Modern China.* Berkeley: University of California Press.

Weinberg, Neil L. 2002. "Muzhi: The Transformation of a Ritual Genre." Ph.D. diss., Harvard University.

Welch, Homes. 1967. *The Practice of Chinese Buddhism 1900–1950.* Cambridge, MA: Harvard University Press.

Wieck, Roger S. 1988. Repr. 2001. *Time Sanctified: The Book of Hours in Medieval Art and Life.* New York: George Braziller.

———. 1998. *Painted Prayers: The Book of Hours in Medieval and Renaissance Art.* New York: George Braziller.

Wills, John. E. 1984. *Embassies and Illusions: Dutch and Portuguese Envoys to K'ang-hsi, 1666–1687.* Cambridge, MA: Harvard University Press.

———. 1993. "Maritime Asia, 1500–1800: The Interactive Emergence of European Domination." *American Historical Review* 98 (1): 83–105.

———. 1994. "Brief Intersection: Changing Contexts and Prospects of the Chinese-Christian Encounter from Matteo Ricci to Ferdinand Verbiest." In *Ferdinand Verbiest (1623–1688), Jesuit Missionary, Scientist, Engineer and Diplomat*, ed. John Witek, 383–94.

Witek, John W. 1982. *Controversial Ideas in China and in Europe: A Biography of Jean-François Foucquet, S. J. (1665–1741).* Rome: Institutum Historicum S.I.

———, ed. 1994. *Ferdinand Verbiest (1623–1688), Jesuit Missionary, Scientist, Engineer and Diplomat.* Monumenta Serica Monograph Series 30. Nettetal: Steyler Verlag.

———. 1995. "Reporting to Rome: Some Major Events in the Christian Community in Peking, 1686–1687." In *Actes du VIIe colloque international de sinologie, Chantilly 1992: Échanges culturels et religieux entre la Chine et l'Occident*, 301–18. Variétés Sinologiques 83. Taibei: Ricci Institute.

Wolf, Arthur P., ed. 1974. *Religion and Ritual in Chinese Society.* Stanford: Stanford University Press.

Wuli tongkao 讀禮通考. 1761. 260 *juan*. Ed. Qin Huitian 秦蕙田. In *SKQS*, vols. 135–42.

Xichao ding'an 熙朝定案 (version 1). In *WX*, 71–224.

Xichao ding'an 熙朝定案 (version 2). In *WXXB*, vol. 3, 1701–1804.

Xichao ding'an 熙朝定案 (version 3). BnF, Chinois 1329ii.

Xichao ding'an 熙朝定案 (version 4). BnF, Chinois 1330ii.

Xie Zhaozhe 謝肇淛. 1959. *Wuzazu* 五雜俎. 2 vols. Beijing: Zhonghua shuju.

Xu Fuquan 徐福全. 1984. "Taiwan minjian chuantong sangzang yijie yanjiu." 臺灣民間傳統喪葬儀節研究. Ph.D. diss., Taiwan shifan daxue.

Xu Jijun 徐吉军. 1998. *Zhongguo sangzang shi* 中国丧葬史. Nanchang: Jiangxi gaoxiao chubanshe.

Xunzi 旬子. 1996. Ed. *Xun zi zhu zi suo yin* 旬子逐字索引. The ICS Ancient Chinese Text Concordance Series. Hong Kong: The Commercial Press.

Yang, C. K. [Qingkun]. 1961. *Religion in Chinese Society: A Study of Contemporary Social Functions of Religion and Some of Their Historical Factors*. Berkeley: University of California Press.

Yang Qiyuan xiansheng (chaoxing) shiji 楊淇園先生(超性)事蹟. n.d. [ca. 1630?]. Ed. Ding Zhilin 丁志麟 and Giulio Aleni 艾儒略. In *CCT ZKW*, vol. 1, 217–37.

Yan Mo 嚴謨. Ca. 1694. "Lishi tiaowen" 李師條問. ARSI Jap.Sin.I [38/42] 40/2. In *CCT ARSI*, vol. 11, 115–216.

Yili 儀禮. 1992. Ed. *Yili zhuzi suoyin* 儀禮逐字索引. The ICS Ancient Chinese Text Concordance Series. Hong Kong: The Commercial Press.

Yiwangzhe rikejing 已亡者日課經. Possibly after 1675. Ed. Lodovico Buglio 利類思. Beijing. BnF, Chinois 7397.

Zhang Jiefu 張捷夫. 1995. *Zhongguo sangzang shi* 中國喪葬史. Taibei: Wenjin.

Zhang Shouan 張壽安. 1993. "Shiqi shiji Zhongguo ruxue sixiang yu dazhong wenhuajian de chongtu: Yi sangzang lisu wei li de tantao" 十七世紀中國儒學思想與大眾文化閒的衝突—以喪葬禮俗為例的探討. *Hanxue yanjiu* 漢學研究 11 (2): 69–80.

Zhang Xiangcan 張象燦. n.d. [ca. 1680s?] "Jiali hejiao lu" 家禮合教錄. ARSI Jap.Sin. I, (38/42) 40/9d. In *CCT ARSI*, vol. 11, 279–304.

Zhang, Xianqing. 2003. "An Examination of Giulio Aleni's Attitude to Fujian Folk Beliefs and his Influences." Translated by Esther Tyldesley. *China Study Journal* 18 (1–2): 41–58.

———. 張先清. 2007a. *Guanfu, zongzu, yu tianzhujiao: 17–19 shiji Fu'an xiangcun jiaohui* 官府, 宗族與天主教:17–19 世紀福安鄉村教會. Hong Kong: The Chinese University Press.

———. 2007b. "Qingdai jinjiaoqi tianzhujiao jingjuan zai minjian de liuchuan" 清代禁教期天主教经卷在民间社会的流传. In *Shiliao yu shijie: Zhongwen wenxian yu zhongguo jidujiao shi yanjiu* 史料与视界: 中文文献与中国基督教史研究, ed. Zhang Xianqing 张先清, 84–142. Shanghai: Renmin chubanshe.

Zhengjiao fengbao 正教奉褒. 1894. Ed. Huang Bolu 黃伯祿. Shanghai: Cimutang.

Zheng Xiaojiang 郑小江. 1995. *Zhongguo siwang wenhua daguan* 中国死亡文化大观. Nanchang: Baihuazhou wenyi chubanshe.

Zürcher, Erik. 1990a. "The Jesuit Mission in Fujian in Late Ming Times: Levels of Response." In *Development and Decline of Fukien Province in the 17th and 18th Centuries*, ed. Edward B. Vermeer, 417–57. Leiden: Brill.

———. 1990b. "Bouddhisme et christianisme." In *Bouddhisme, christianisme et société chinoise*, 11–42. Paris: Conférences, essais et leçons du Collège de France. Translated as "The Spread of Buddhism and Christianity in Imperial China: Spontaneous Diffusion Versus Guided Propagation." In *China and the West (Proceedings of the International Colloqium held in the Koninklijke Academie voor Wetenschappen, Letteren en Schone Kunsten van België, Brussels, November 23–25, 1987)*, 9–18. Brussels: Paleis der Academiën, 1993.

———. 1993. "A Complement to Confucianism: Christianity and Orthodoxy in Late Imperial China." In *Norms and the State in China*, ed. Chun-Chieh Huang and Erik Zürcher, 71–92. Leiden: Brill.

———. 1994. "Jesuit Accommodation and the Chinese Cultural Imperative." In *The Chinese Rites Controversy: Its History and Meaning*, ed. David E. Mungello, 31–64. Monumenta Serica Monograph Series 33. Nettetal: Steyler Verlag.

———. 1997. "Confucian and Christian Religiosity in Late Ming China." *The Catholic Historical Review* 83 (4): 614–53.

———. 1999. "Christian Social Action in Late Ming Times: Wang Zheng and his 'Humanitarian Society.'" In *Linked Faiths: Essays on Chinese Religions and Traditional Culture in Honour of Kristofer Schipper*, ed. Jan A. M. De Meyer and Peter M. Engelfriet, 269–86. Sinica Leidensia 46. Leiden: Brill.

———. 2002. "In the Yellow Tiger's Den: Buglio and Magalhaes at the Court of Zhang Xianzhong, 1644–1646." *Monumenta Serica* 50: 355–74.

———. 2005. "Li Jiugong and his *Meditations (Shensi lu)*." In *Encounters and Dialogues: Changing Perspectives on Chinese-Western Exchanges from the Sixteenth to Eighteenth Centuries*, ed. Wu Xiaoxin, 71–92. Monumenta Serica Monograph Series 55. Sankt Augustin / Nettetal: Steyler Verlag.

———, trans. 2007. *Kouduo richao: Li Jiubiao's Diary of Oral Admonitions, A Late Ming Christian Journal*. Monumenta Serica Monograph Series 61. 2 vols. Sankt Augustin / Nettetal: Steyler Verlag.

Index